Marcus Tullius Cicero

TEN SPEECHES

Marcus Tullius Cicero

TEN SPEECHES

Translated, with Notes and Introduction, by
James E. G. Zetzel

Hackett Publishing Company, Inc.
Indianapolis/Cambridge

14 13 12 11 10 09   1 2 3 4 5 6 7

For further information, please address:

Hackett Publishing Company, Inc.
P.O. Box 44937
Indianapolis, Indiana 46244-0937

www.hackettpublishing.com

Cover design by Listenberger Design Associates
Text design by Meera Dash
Composition by William Hartman
Maps by William Nelson
Printed at Victor Graphics, Inc.

Library of Congress Cataloging-in-Publication Data
    Cicero, Marcus Tullius.
        [Speeches. English. Selections]
        Ten speeches / Marcus Tullius Cicero ; translated, with
    notes and introduction, by James E. G. Zetzel.
            p. cm.
        Includes bibliographical references (p.   ) and index.
        ISBN 978-0-87220-989-3 (pbk.) —
        ISBN 978-0-87220-990-9 (cloth)
        1. Cicero, Marcus Tullius—Translations into English.
    2. Speeches, addresses, etc., Latin—Translations into
    English.   I. Zetzel, James E. G.   II. Title.
    PA6307.A4Z48 2009
    875'.01—dc22

                                        2009020994

Contents

Preface

A new translation of some of Cicero's speeches needs no excuse. Some of the speeches included here are not available in English in a convenient and relatively inexpensive form. The selection of speeches given here, unlike most available translations, stretches over Cicero's entire career and all the major contexts for his oratory, before the senate, the people, and the courts. The speeches illustrate (or are a part of) the major political crises of Cicero's time; many of them are also relevant to the cultural and literary debates of the late Republic. In making my selection, I have had the valuable advice of three anonymous scholars consulted by the publisher; I have also relied on my own experience in teaching Cicero to undergraduates for many years.

A full list of acknowledgments could extend for some pages, as far back as my friend and teacher David Coffin, who first led me through the speech on the Manilian law and the Catilinarians in 1961, and as recent as the students in my class on ancient law in 2009, on whom I have inflicted several of the speeches included here. In studying the speeches and drafting my translation, I have learned a great deal about Ciceronian language and Roman history from Robert Kaster's recent edition of *Pro Sestio* and D. H. Berry's lucid translations of several of the speeches I too have translated here. In my choice of style and tone, I have felt liberated by Douglass Parker's grand version of Seneca's *Apocolocyntosis* and by Amy Richlin's *Plautus and the Mysterious Orient*. And in addition to such brilliant work, which I can admire but not emulate, I have constantly had in mind the memorable Homeric adaptations of the late Professor Stephen Leacock.

I have more specific debts as well. Robert Morstein-Marx, Sarah Nooter, and Gareth Williams have all read portions of this volume and have made valuable suggestions; Bruce Frier has, as often, patiently answered ignorant questions about Roman law. Jane Crawford, who read the manuscript for the publisher with scrupulous care, has improved this book immensely and has saved me from more mistakes, of Latin, English, and fact, than I am willing to admit having made. Susanna Zetzel rightly sent me to John Quincy Adams' lectures on rhetoric and tactfully reined in some of my less felicitous excursions into the vernacular. I am grateful to the Stanwood Cockey Lodge Fund of Columbia University for a grant defraying the cost of the maps. That I am deeply indebted to Deborah Wilkes for editorial advice, assistance, and patience goes almost without saying.

James Zetzel
Elizabethtown, NY
July 14, 2009

Introduction

1. Cicero in Public Life[1]

A fragment of a lost speech by Publius Cornelius Scipio Aemilianus Africanus, one of Cicero's most-admired political and intellectual figures of the second century BCE, states succinctly the values of the aristocratic and competitive culture in which Cicero moved: "The child of blamelessness is worthiness; of worthiness, public office; of public office, military power; of military power, freedom."[2] The crucial element in this sentence is the last: only someone who had power was truly free, and that power came through holding high office with *imperium*, the power of military command. Two features above all characterized the ruling class of Republican Rome: the importance of heredity and family and the ruthless competition for the glory and freedom that came with military command and conquest. Cicero's lifetime was marked by civil wars, coups and attempted coups, the assassination of the dictator Caesar, and bloody and vengeful proscriptions, the first by Sulla when Cicero was in his twenties, the last by the triumvirs Antony, Lepidus, and Octavian in 43 BCE, which resulted in Cicero's own death. It was also marked by extended and equally brutal military conquests and adventures; Caesar's conquest of Gaul in the 50s is the most famous, but the long campaigns against

---

1. It should be clear that what follows is a very brief and superficial sketch of a well-documented life in a complex historical context; bibliographical references are few and general. More detail is given in the introductions to particular speeches. The two best biographies of Cicero in English are those of Rawson (1975) and Mitchell (1979, 1991). For broad historical background, the relevant chapters of Crook et al. (1994) are recent, magisterial, and lucid; among the many other studies of the age, Syme (1939) is fundamental; see also Gruen (1974) and the essays in Wiseman (1985b). On Roman expansion and its development in this period, I rely heavily on Morstein-Marx (1995).

2. Fr. 32 Malcovati (1976): "Ex innocentia nascitur dignitas, ex dignitate honor, ex honore imperium, ex imperio libertas." The fragment is only known through quotation by Isidore of Seville in the seventh century CE; we cannot be sure that Cicero knew it. On Scipio Aemilianus, see particularly Astin (1967); for Cicero's references to him, see the Biographical Index. On Roman nomenclature, see Roman Institutions and Offices.

Mithridates VI of Pontus in northern Asia Minor were the most influential, culminating in Pompey's conquest and reorganization of the East in the 60s, from the Black Sea to Syria and Palestine.

This somewhat lurid summary of some of the events of the first century BCE provides a background to Cicero's career, important precisely because it is only background. Cicero does not fit the patterns of public (mis)behavior normal in his time. Marcus Tullius Cicero (106–43 BCE) was neither an aristocrat nor a general. Coming from a family of local magnates in Arpinum (sixty miles from Rome),[3] he rose to the consulate, the highest office in Rome, not through heredity, military success, political connections, bribery, or violence, but through the sheer power of his voice.[4] His swift rise reflects the increasing importance in Roman government and society of the elite of rural Italy. It is also emblematic of the increasingly complex nature of Roman public life: Cicero was the first (indeed, the only) person to achieve such high office on the basis of his words alone. His chosen arena for the acquisition of distinction and power was the courts and, once he had achieved office and position, the senate and the forum.

The basic facts of Cicero's public career are straightforward. He began as a courtroom orator in 81 BCE; by the time he first stood for public office in 76, he was well known and successful. As quaestor in 75, he was sent to Sicily, where he administered the finances of his province with honesty and fairness to the provincials. As a result, the people of Sicily asked him to represent them in their extortion suit against Gaius Verres in 70; his prosecution was so effective that Verres went into exile before the trial was concluded. During that case, moreover, Cicero was elected plebeian aedile for 69, followed by being chosen praetor for 66, and finally consul for 63—the first "new man" for a very long time to reach the highest office in the earliest year he was eligible, at the age of forty-two.

In politics, ability is neither a necessary nor a sufficient explanation for success. In Rome, oratorical ability was distinctly less valued than military glory, while from the point of view of the urban aristocracy,

---

3. The other family from Arpinum that made a strong impression on Rome was that of Marius, who took a very different route to glory. Arpinum had received Roman citizenship in 188 and, unlike areas enfranchised only in the first century, was thoroughly Romanized in Cicero's day.

4. On Roman offices and governmental institutions, see Roman Institutions and Offices.

Cicero was a foreign upstart.[5] And while legal or oratorical skill
was enough to launch a public career, the final step to the consulate
required somewhat more.[6] In this case, one suspects, what elevated
Cicero was what he was not, rather than what he was. Unlike his main
electoral opponent, Catiline, Cicero provided no cause for alarm. He
was not only eloquent but also reliable, intelligent, and conservative;
he was a safe choice, even if he was an outsider. But to appreciate the
political context of Cicero's success, some sense of the political (and
military) background is essential.

   Between Cicero's arrival in Rome to begin training for public life, sometime before he was fifteen, and his first actual court
appearance some ten years later,[7] a set of upheavals, political, social,
and military, began a major reshaping of Roman life that was to
end only in 30 BCE, when Gaius Julius Caesar Octavianus (soon
to become Augustus) became sole ruler of the Roman world.[8] This
is not the place for a full account of the complex events of the 80s,
but three must be mentioned because of their lasting effect on
Cicero's own career: the war between Rome and its Italian allies
(known as the Social War) that broke out in the fall of 91 BCE;
the attack on Roman rule in Asia Minor and Greece in 89 led by
Mithridates VI Eupator, king of Pontus;[9] and the dictatorship of
Lucius Cornelius Sulla in 82–80. The Social War created lasting unrest in Italy and political disputes in Rome over how much
power to allow the Italians, while Rome's preoccupation with the
war gave Mithridates an opportunity to attack Roman influence in
Asia. The desire to command the Roman army against Mithridates
led to civil war in Rome and Sulla's first coup; Sulla's inconclusive
defeat of Mithridates—including a brutal and destructive siege of

---

5. According to Sallust (*Conspiracy of Catiline* 31.7), Catiline called Cicero
an *inquilinus civis*, probably meaning "a temporary citizen" or "resident alien
citizen," reflecting Cicero's non-Roman origins.

6. See *In Defense of Lucius Murena* for Cicero's condescension (motivated by
the case) toward the great jurist Sulpicius Rufus.

7. Cicero's first speech was *In Defense of Quinctius*, a civil suit argued in 81
while Sulla was still dictator.

8. Indeed, not even then. The social and governmental structure of the
principate took shape only gradually.

9. On Mithridates and the Mithridatic Wars, see *In Support of Manilius'
Law*.

Athens—was followed immediately by his second march on Rome, his dictatorship, the proscription of his enemies, and his reactionary reconstruction of Roman government in the interests of the senate. It was followed, for a much longer period, by further wars against Mithridates and the great commands of first Lucullus and then Pompey, resulting by 62 in Roman annexation of the entire eastern Mediterranean basin except for Egypt, a vast expansion of direct rule by Rome—before Mithridates, Rome had very little direct interest in the eastern Mediterranean—and an equally vast expansion of Roman revenue. It also resulted in huge power and influence accruing to a single man, Pompey. That in turn led to the Second Civil War, between Pompey and Caesar, in 49.

The chain of causation sketched in the previous paragraph is obviously an oversimplification: there is no one thread linking all these events without including other, often more important, elements. On the other hand, from the point of view of a Roman living in the period, it would have been hard not to trace the violence and unrest of the period, even the rise of Octavian/Augustus, to the single figure of Sulla: Sulla using his army from the Social War to attack Rome; Sulla violently reclaiming the command against Mithridates; Sulla wreaking brutal havoc in Rome among the ruling class; and Sulla attempting to destroy any signs of popular resistance to senatorial control.[10] The decade after Sulla, when Cicero was first elected to public office, was marked by the revolt of Marcus Aemilius Lepidus against the Sullan constitution, continued by the revolt of the ex-Marian Sertorius in Spain and the slave revolt of Spartacus in Italy. It was consequently also marked by the need for extended commands and the constant violation of Sulla's tidy administrative organization—which had been meant to keep anyone else from repeating what Sulla had done.

In many ways, it was Cicero's success in dealing tactfully and cautiously with the aftermath of Sulla that led to his political success. His early court cases (notably the defense of Roscius of Ameria in 80 and the lost defense of a woman from Arretium) required opposing some of the effects of Sulla's rule, but he managed to do so without

---

10. My approach to Sulla owes a great deal to Badian's study "Waiting for Sulla" in Badian (1964) 206–32. See also Badian (1970) and Keaveney (1982).

attacking Sulla himself.[11] The greatest case of his early career was his prosecution of Verres in 70, in which he again managed to criticize the effects of Sulla's laws while still presenting himself as a supporter of senatorial government. Cicero portrayed himself, not unfairly, as eminently reasonable, and even if he was not an aristocrat, he claimed to represent the values that had made earlier aristocrats (and Rome) great. Cicero is always the advocate of reform, never of sudden or violent change. The year of the prosecution of Verres also saw the end of the Sullan restrictions on the tribunate, under the leadership of the consuls Pompey and Crassus. Cicero made the case of Verres a touchstone for the integrity of the courts, and he made himself a representative of good government rather than of any particular policy.

When Pompey became consul in 70, he had held none of the prior offices required under Sullan (and earlier) laws, but he had held a series of extraordinary commands, some of them self-awarded (beginning with his raising of a private army to help Sulla in 82); by the end of the 70s, he was too powerful and too popular to resist.[12] Thus, when he was offered even more extensive commands—against the pirates in 67 and against the ever-resourceful Mithridates in 66—Cicero was a supporter, both speaking in favor of the Manilian law giving Pompey the command against Mithridates (below, *In Support of Manilius' Law*) and defending in court the power of the tribunate to represent popular wishes even against the law and against senatorial desires.[13] At the same time, however, he presented both Pompey and the tribunes as being constitutional in a higher sense, representing the sovereignty of the Roman people against the lingering remnants of Sullan oligarchy. Cicero's careful self-presentation, always supporting the constitution (whatever it was) against unwise or rash change, always representing good government against corruption, led to his election as praetor in 66—when his first speech was in support of the Manilian law—and three years later to his being accepted as a constitutionalist and thus a bulwark against the corrupt ex-Sullan Catiline.

---

11. Some scholars have suggested that Cicero's year of study in the East that followed these speeches was politically expedient rather than (as Cicero says) to improve his speaking ability.

12. For Cicero's account of Pompey's career, see *In Support of Manilius' Law*.

13. In the very fragmentary speech *In Defense of Cornelius*, a tribune being prosecuted on a charge of treason.

In certain respects—and certainly in his own opinion—Cicero's foiling of Catiline's conspiracy in 63 was the high point of his career and of his service to Rome; in terms of his year of office, it was the last of several conservative gestures—against radical land reform, against populist attacks on senatorial government, against the continuing unrest in the countryside of Italy that was a legacy of Sulla.[14] Catiline was a patrician—his family traced its ancestry back to one of Aeneas' Trojan companions—who had supported and profited from Sulla's rule, had been prosecuted for extortion in his governorship of Africa (and thus forced to delay his candidacy for the consulate), and was in desperate need of office in order to recoup his fortunes. He was perhaps no more corrupt than many provincial governors; Cicero in fact thought seriously of defending him in 65. In the elections in 64, Cicero defeated Catiline; when Catiline failed again in the elections in 63, he turned to less constitutional methods, planning a coup and an attack on Rome using the disaffected and dispossessed Sullan veterans in rural Italy. Cicero discovered the plan, moved against it, forced Catiline to leave Rome and declare himself, captured several of the conspirators who remained in Rome, and, on December 5 of 63, had them put to death without trial on the basis of a senatorial resolution.[15] Cicero was cheered and honored, escorted home by throngs of citizens, and a thanksgiving was decreed in his honor; but only four weeks later, at the end of his term of office, the tribune Metellus Nepos blocked him from making the customary farewell speech, accusing him of putting citizens to death without trial. And

---

14. See the introduction to *Second Speech against Catiline*.

15. Formally, Cicero's right to execute the conspirators rested on the so-called *senatus consultum ultimum* ("final decree of the senate") "that the consuls should make sure that the commonwealth suffer no harm." That decree had been invented for use against the Gracchi and was then used several times to quell popular (or populist) agitation; Cicero's speech in 63 defending the elderly Rabirius on a charge of treason for having taken part in the killing of the tribune Saturninus thirty-seven years earlier was in fact a defense of the *senatus consultum ultimum*. The decree formally had no legal standing—the senate could not legislate or act as a court—and could not override the long-standing laws forbidding the execution of Roman citizens without trial or the right of appeal to the people. Its validity depended on the strength of the senate, not on the law. Catiline himself was killed in battle early in 62.

it was that description of his actions against the conspirators that led directly to his exile in 58.

Cicero was not always self-aware, and he overestimated both his own importance and the extent to which either aristocrats or generals valued his contributions. As the first nonsoldier to be awarded a thanksgiving and as the civilian victor who had defeated armed conspirators, he trumpeted his glory: "let arms give way to the toga, let the victor's laurel yield to civic praise," went a much-criticized verse of his much-criticized epic on his own achievements. And just as much as the aristocrats resented the self-aggrandizement of the new man, so did Pompey dislike having Cicero's achievements equated with his own.[16] Cicero claimed to have created "agreement of all good men" and "harmony of the orders" in his suppression of Catiline, but that harmony rapidly dissolved in the pursuit of less altruistic goals. In 61 Cicero made the mistake of testifying against the young and disruptive aristocrat Publius Clodius when he was accused of profaning the rites of the Good Goddess; Clodius had supported Cicero against Catiline in 63 but now became his bitter enemy. And when Cicero in 60 opposed the pact between Crassus, Pompey, and Julius Caesar (conventionally known as the First Triumvirate), they did not mind using Clodius' hatred of Cicero to demonstrate their own power to control their opponents. Caesar, as consul in 59, permitted Clodius' fictitious adoption by a plebeian, making him eligible to become a tribune of the plebs. Clodius, elected tribune for 58, lost no time in proposing a law exiling anyone who had put citizens to death without trial. The new consuls, Piso and Gabinius, refused to stand in Clodius' way. Cicero found he had much less support or goodwill than he had hoped or expected, and he fled into exile before Clodius' bill could be passed. It was a long eighteen months before the next consuls could orchestrate his recall. In the meantime, his family had been harassed, he had written innumerable self-pitying letters to his family and friends, his house on the Palatine had been sacked, and Clodius had dedicated a "shrine of Liberty" in its place.

According to Cicero himself, his return to Rome in 57 was triumphal: he was greeted by crowds in every town along his route,

---

16. "Cedant arma togae, concedat gloria laudi" parodied as ". . . gloria linguae" (to the tongue). Cicero hotly defends his poem and the line in *Pis.* 72–81; in the same passage he replies to Piso's suggestion that Pompey was angry at Cicero's self-aggrandizement at his (Pompey's) expense.

the senate voted to restore his house at public expense, he delivered speeches of thanks to both senate and people, and he proceeded to vilify his enemies (Clodius, Piso, and Gabinius) on every possible occasion—without, of course, expressing anger at the more powerful men, Caesar and Pompey, who had permitted his catastrophe. In 56 he planned to question the renewal of Caesar's command in Gaul—until the triumvirs warned him in no uncertain terms to restrain himself. And for the next few years, while he had an active forensic career, he sequestered himself from political life and instead wrote his two greatest nonforensic works, the Platonic dialogues *On the Orator* and *On the Commonwealth*.[17] But even Cicero recognized that his public influence had diminished. Forced by new legislation to govern the province of Cilicia in 51, he was absent for much of the maneuvering that led in 49 to the outbreak of the Civil War between Pompey (and the senate) and Caesar. Cicero reluctantly followed Pompey, but as soon as possible after the defeat at Pharsalus he returned to Italy, where he was forced to remain in Brundisium until Caesar permitted him to return to Rome in 47.

For the voice of moderation and constitutionalism, life under Caesar's dictatorship was not easy or happy. To have had to be granted pardon was awkward; to have left the Pompeian side so rapidly was equally awkward. Caesar was friendly, but Cicero was uncomfortable taking part in public life under a dictatorship, and he devoted most of his time (from his return in 47 to Caesar's assassination in 44) to writing. Most of his philosophical works were composed during this period, as were *Brutus* and *Orator* on the history and technique of oratory. He did not speak in the senate at first; it was only on the occasion of Caesar's reluctant grant of clemency to Marcus Claudius Marcellus in 46 that Cicero addressed Caesar, advocating a return to constitutionalism. But between the dictatorship and the sudden death of his daughter in early 45, Cicero found life very difficult.

After the Ides of March, even though Cicero was not himself involved in the assassination, things changed drastically. Cicero returned to senatorial debate, working hard in the interests of Brutus, Cassius, and the Republic, but amid the confusion and violence of the months after Caesar's death, he made the tragically wrong choice of

---

17. He also began (but did not finish) a third Platonic dialogue, *On the Laws*.

supporting Caesar's heir, the young Octavian, expecting gratitude and the opportunity to guide him.[18] Supporting Octavian and the Liberators simultaneously was not a realistic possibility; thinking Antony the greatest enemy of the Republic was a terrible blunder, and the fourteen Philippics, though magnificently virulent, did not do much for either the Republic or Cicero himself. When Antony and Octavian came to terms late in 43 and instituted proscriptions, Cicero was among their first victims. His head and hands were cut off and placed on the speaking platform in Rome.

2. Cicero's Speeches[19]

Cicero's career as a speaker lasted thirty-eight years, from 81 BCE, when he was twenty-five, until his death in 43. His speeches were, with a few exceptions, given in one of three contexts:[20] the courts, the senate, and public assemblies in the forum. Speaking in the senate was formal: Cicero's senatorial speeches in fact often use a more complex style and syntax than parallel speeches delivered to the public at large. A public speech (*contio*) was delivered either by a magistrate or by someone invited by a magistrate. These public meetings took place in the forum; they were intended to present issues or individuals of some importance, but no voting (either legislative or electoral) ever took place there. A *contio* was not a placid or orderly affair; it could be a raucous and even violent gathering of many people, and the orator needed vigor, speed, wit, and volume

---

18. His ill-chosen witticism, "we must praise the boy, we must honor him, we must remove him" (*ad Fam.* 11.20.1—Decimus Brutus reporting to Cicero on Octavian's reaction), will not have appealed to Octavian, already, in Syme's famous phrase, "a chill and mature terrorist" (Syme [1939] 191).

19. A good, brief introduction to the speeches is Nisbet (1964), but a great deal has been written about them since then. Two useful collections of essays are May (2002)—including the superb analytical bibliography of Craig (2002)—and Powell and Patterson (2004). Among broader studies in English (many cited in the introductions to individual speeches), of particular value are Craig (1993), May (1988), Morstein-Marx (2004), Riggsby (1999), Steel (2001), and Vasaly (1993).

20. Exceptions: *On His Own House*, before the college of priests; *In Defense of Ligarius* and *In Defense of King Deiotarus* before Caesar as sole judge.

to keep the audience's attention. A weak, ineffective, or unpopular speaker would be shouted down, if not worse.[21]

The third venue—from which a plurality of the extant speeches derives—was the courts, and it requires slightly more attention. Despite some unfortunate recent attempts to turn Cicero into a British barrister,[22] the actual performance of justice (and it was a performance) had very different manners from a modern courtroom.[23] Roman trials took place in the open, in the forum. The jury was large (up to seventy-five members), and a popular speaker (as Cicero was) could attract a large crowd; like a *contio* but probably smaller, it was raucous and active, and the advocate had to play to the crowd as much as to the jury. Cicero describes the scene in *Brutus* (290):

> This is what should happen for a real orator: when people hear he's going to speak, the benches are filled, the court is packed, the clerks take money to give up their seat to someone else, the crowd is thick, the judges are all ears. When the speaker gets up, the crowd calls for silence; that's followed by frequent sounds of agreement and admiration. When he wants it, there's laughter; when he wants it, there's weeping.

Cicero himself studied with the great actor Roscius and uses him as a point of comparison for the orator in this passage. The Roman court was much more theatrical than most modern trials, and while there were no encores, there were cheers, hisses, and not a little influence on the jury from the crowd. What is more, trials, at least in the major permanent tribunals, were highly political. Defendants were of the senatorial or equestrian orders, and the jury was composed entirely of men of wealth and standing. Most of Cicero's cases involve politically active and ambitious defendants; the crimes with which

---

21. For a fine discussion of the *contio* and for comparison of parallel senatorial and popular speeches, see Morstein-Marx (2004), esp. 34–42 on the conventions of public meetings. Note that *contio* can refer either to the gathering or to the speech given to it.

22. In particular, see the introduction to Powell and Patterson (2004).

23. On Roman legal procedure, the standard work remains Greenidge (1901); for a brief account, see Lintott (2004).

they are charged are frequently also political.[24] The rules of evidence were almost nonexistent, arguments did not have to be germane, and character assassination (or eulogy) was part of normal forensic strategy. Cicero attacks his opponents, at times viciously; he flatters individual jurors by name; he says whatever will help win the case. At times it was all too obvious that the defendant was guilty (few Roman elections in the first century took place without bribery, and few provinces were governed without some extortion); the question was whether it was useful to society, as represented by the jury, for the defendant to get off. Guilt and innocence mattered in the verdict, but then, as now, the job of the defense is to win acquittal, whether the defendant is innocent or not. But modern analogies are dangerous and misleading. Roman justice did not play by the same rules as a modern court, British or American—and modern courts themselves sometimes seem scarcely to respect the theoretical rule of law.

Cicero gave many more speeches than are now extant, many more than he chose to make public.[25] This volume contains a representative sample of his oratory: four courtroom speeches (of which one, the fourth book of the Second Verrine, was never delivered) ranging in date from 70 to 46; three before the senate, from 63 to 43; and three before a *contio*, from 66 (his first) to 44. Some of them deal with narrow issues (whether or not the poet Archias was a citizen) or involve personal vendetta (the attack on Piso in the senate), while others concern the great affairs of state: Pompey's command, the conspiracy of Catiline, the political and military maneuvers following Caesar's death. But what is striking about even relatively minor cases, including many not included here, is how Cicero elevates his gaze from the particular to the general, from criminal behavior to public morals. In so doing Cicero is not unique, but he is extraordinarily successful in making his audience believe in the importance of the issue, linking it to the well-being of Rome and indeed of the world at large. John Quincy Adams described this aspect of Cicero's oratory as "the logician uniting with the moralist" and viewed it as

---

24. From 82 to 70 BCE, the juries consisted of senators alone; after 70, one-third of the jurors were senators, one-third knights, and one-third "treasury tribunes" (*tribuni aerarii*), another group of wealthy men. On the flexible and political nature of criminal trials, see Riggsby (1999), esp. 151–71.

25. For the lost speeches, see Crawford (1984); for the fragmentary speeches, see Crawford (1994) and my review, Zetzel (1994).

the most important quality of the speeches for the modern student of rhetoric:[26]

> I have dwelt with peculiar emphasis on this topic . . . from my sense of its extreme importance. It is this very faculty of pointing the general principles of moral and political science to the specific object in debate, and of extracting from the subject in discussion new scintillations of light to illumine the paths of civilized life, that constitutes the permanent powers and glory of the public speaker. As mere historical facts, of what consequence is it to you or me, whether Verres was or was not a robber? . . . Whether Archias was or was not a Roman citizen? These are points as immaterial to the peace and happiness of mankind, as . . . the achievements of Arthur and his round table knights. But by this art of rhetorical ratiocination the orator acquires a new and a more venerable character. He is no longer pleading the cause of an individual, but that of human improvement. It is no longer Cicero, the advocate of his friends, or the prosecutor of a thief. It is Cicero, the instructer of ages, the legislator of human kind.

Not every case lent itself to such grandeur, and some speeches are tailored more narrowly to a particular occasion. The speeches in this volume, however, and others that might have been included, do just what Adams says: even though the citizenship of Archias is a trivial question, Cicero makes the speech concern the value of education and literary culture; Verres the thief becomes the vehicle for broad thoughts on ethical government and Roman tradition; Catiline and Antony become emblems of evil itself.

The loftiness of Cicero's approach to some of his cases raises an obvious question: did it work in a setting as raucous and undisciplined

---

26. Adams (1962) 2:56–57. I cite Adams not merely because his comments are apposite, but because he is one of the few rhetorical theorists who (like Cicero) was also an experienced politician and one of the great orators of his time. When he wrote the *Lectures on Rhetoric and Oratory* (between 1806 and 1808), he was the first holder of the first chair of rhetoric in the United States and simultaneously U.S. senator from Massachusetts; he resigned the chair in 1808 to become ambassador to Russia.

as a Roman court? There are two possibilities: either the Roman audience had very high standards in language and rhetoric, or the written text is not quite the same as what Cicero said in court.[27] What were the conventions governing the presentation and the reading of the text of a Roman speech? Before Cicero's time, few orators circulated many speeches, and a striking number of the extant quotations are either from funeral orations or from defenses of the speaker's own actions and career. That suggests that they were preserved by the speaker's descendants and only later became available to antiquarians and archaists. The innovator in making speeches more generally available as texts was Cato the Censor; Cicero says that 150 of his speeches still existed a century after his death, and Cato went so far as to include some of them in his history of Rome, the *Origines*. But aside from Cato and, to a lesser extent, Gaius Gracchus and Cicero's own teacher Lucius Crassus, very little oratory was widely circulated. Cicero seems to have proceeded differently; where Cato seems to have been unselective (we have fragments of too many speeches for him to have made many choices) and Gracchus and Crassus are known to have circulated only speeches of political importance, Cicero chose a middle path, selecting from a broad range of speeches. From his first speech in 81, the circulated texts buttressed his reputation as a speaker and advocate; some of them were meant to draw attention to his extraordinary skill as a speaker, many to enhance or support his political position and fame. For a nonsoldier, the circulated speeches were a sort of substitute for military victories and martial glory. The pen was not so mighty as the sword, but it was still sharp and effective.[28]

On the most literal level, however, it is obvious that these texts are not speeches; they are written, not oral. While they are probably fair representations of the order and arguments of the speeches as delivered, no written text is ever identical to the spoken word; it lacks gesture and intonation and emphasis, and we should not by any means

---

27. There is far less reason to believe that senatorial, or even assembly, speeches pose the same problem, and what is said here applies largely to the forensic speeches.

28. There is now general agreement that not all the speeches were made public for the same reason; in the past it has been argued that they were all intended for educational use or that they were all political. Neither absolute is true.

assume that the texts are verbatim transcripts of what Cicero said.[29] Speeches were not written in advance; they were not delivered from a text, and the circulated text, even if the author aimed at accuracy, was based on the speaker's memory, not on a script. The written texts of ancient speeches were recollected and presumably embellished as a result of the oral performance—they are representations rather than records of what was said, and they represent, presumably with a high degree of plausibility, the formal characteristics of delivered speeches, whether forensic, senatorial, or in a *contio*.

As representations, of course, these texts must accurately reflect the experience provided by a genuine speech. Some of them, at least, were circulated as models for other aspiring orators, and false representations would not be useful to the budding speaker. But that does not mean that they reproduce a particular speech verbatim. These texts are not speeches but "speeches"; they are literary representations of speech, and in many ways they are no more to be thought of as accurate records of a specific performance than are the speeches of ancient historians or the speeches in Platonic dialogues. That does not reduce their value as evidence of what Ciceronian oratory was like and for the historical events they describe and of which they were elements, but they must also be seen to have another, and more complex, dimension—as literature, not as historical record.

That one should approach these texts not simply as historical documents is clear from the outset. The Second Speech against Verres (Second Verrine), of which a portion is translated here, was never delivered, and indeed is so long that even Cicero could not have held the jury's attention for a speech that runs to more than four hundred pages in the standard edition.[30] As a representation of a speech, it includes imaginary interjections by the audience and addresses to

---

29. The debate over the relationship between oral and written has been long and heated; the modern consensus that the written speeches were close to, but not identical to, the oral versions (see Riggsby [1999] 178–84; Powell and Patterson [2004] 52–57) has recently been challenged, at least for forensic speeches, by Lintott (2008) 19–32. His arguments, that the speeches have been heavily revised, are largely convincing; a new and full study of the problem is needed.

30. It is sometimes suggested that the extant Second Verrine (divided into five books) actually is the speech that Cicero would have delivered, and that it was made public in the form in which it was (not) delivered. That seems

the defendant (who was long gone); so, too, some of Cicero's other major "speeches," notably *In Defense of Milo* and *Second Philippic*, were never delivered. Nor was Cicero the only person to circulate fictitious speeches as political pamphlets: according to Quintilian (10.1.22), Hortensius' defense of Verres was available for study, as was the prosecution speech of Tubero to which Cicero's *In Defense of Ligarius* was a reply. If these were genuine—and in fact they may have been school exercises that fooled Quintilian—then they were pamphlets written after the fact; we know, for instance, that in the trial of Verres, Hortensius had very little to say.

That written speeches became a literary form in the first century BCE is not surprising. In the Greek literary world of the third and second centuries BCE, it was normal practice to elevate the status of lower genres such as mime and epigram; indeed, epigram became one of the dominant forms of literary production, and some Romans were imitating Greek epigrams by the middle of the second century. Cicero himself, probably before he was twenty, translated the third-century *Phaenomena* of Aratus, a Stoic poem on the cosmos of inexplicable popularity in antiquity. His translation is not the work of an inspired poet, but it shows someone completely aware of the formal requirements of Greek and Latin verse; it is learned and technically very advanced. So too with rhetoric. Cicero had studied the highly elaborate theories developed in the Greek world in the third and second centuries; his earliest extant work is his treatise on "invention" (how to identify and create useful arguments for a given situation), the first of the five divisions of formal rhetoric. A few years later, when he left Rome for a year after Sulla's death, he visited Athens and studied both philosophy and rhetoric with experts (Posidonius and Molon) on Rhodes. Perhaps more than anyone else of his generation, Cicero was widely read in Greek poetry, philosophy, and rhetoric. To turn speeches into "speeches" was, if not an obvious choice, a very reasonable one for someone of Cicero's ambitions, both political and literary. In many cases, there would be little difference between the oral and written versions. Public speeches such as *In Support of Manilius' Law* or most of the Philippics were delivered as political statements and rapidly made public as political pamphlets. But even in the political sphere that is not always true: the four speeches

---

implausible: the present text is constructed as a written argument, not an oral one.

against Catiline were not collected and circulated as a group until three years after the fact, in a collection of ten "consular" speeches designed collectively to reinforce Cicero's political position.[31] Some of them may be close to the oral version, but others, notably the Fourth Catilinarian, were circulated in a form much more appropriate to 60 BCE than to the original moment of delivery.[32]

Apart from speeches with an immediate political goal, however, things are more complicated. For much of Cicero's life, being literary or being attuned to Greek culture was not unproblematic. "Greek" was a term of opprobrium in upper-class Rome; Roman magistrates were supposed to be courageous and honorable men, but having an interest in culture was not considered a virtue. Even those who, like Cicero, actually enjoyed reading Plato or Demosthenes or Euripides in Greek, or who were interested in the finer points of Greek sculpture and painting, were expected in public to conceal or even to ridicule such tastes as un-Roman and affected. When Cicero pretends ignorance of Greek artists' names or incomprehension of the value Greeks place on Greek art in the Verrines, he is clearly being disingenuous; so too in the defense of Archias, when he equates reading poetry with playing ball or gambling. At the same time, however, he flatters his juries, claiming that they will be perfectly at home with his discussions of philosophy or poetry, and he makes philosophical, legal, and literary jokes (sometimes playing off Roman culture, sometimes Greek).[33]

What would the original audience have made of some of this? We have no real idea, but it is important to be aware of the problem. It is clear, for instance, that the sentences and the ideas are simpler in the texts of *contio* speeches than they are in senatorial speeches, and to that extent it may be that the texts do reflect reality: the most ironic and ambiguous of the speeches in this respect—*Against Verres, In Defense of Lucius Murena, In Defense of Marcus Caelius,* and *Against Lucius Calpurnius Piso*—are aimed at senatorial (or at least upper-class) audiences, and hence the greater complexity of presentation may reflect social realities. But the circulated texts are literary works

---

31. On the consular speeches, see Cape (2002) and the introduction to *Second Speech against Catiline.*

32. See Lintott (2008) 17–18.

33. On Cicero's ambivalent Hellenism, see Zetzel (2003). For the intellectual milieu of the first century, see Rawson (1985) and Griffin (1994).

independent of the original context of delivery, and on the whole they offer a portrait of the orator as artist, a Cicero who is totally in control of tone, style, and humor and who challenges his reader to appreciate what he is up to.

3. On This Translation

The double nature of these texts—as records of performance and as literary works in their own right—is one of the qualities that make them difficult to translate into English. One problem in fixing a style for translating Cicero's speeches is that there is no formal equivalent for them in the twenty-first century. The high political rhetoric of recent decades—and there still is high rhetoric in occasional use—I have heard rather than read. Rarely in person, but on television, on politicians' Web sites, on YouTube or podcast. To *read* a speech is relatively rare, and the texts I have seen are generally verbatim transcripts with every grammatical infelicity faithfully reproduced— unless they are texts written and circulated in advance of delivery. All that is very different from how one encountered speeches before the twentieth century; for the majority of people, they were read and not heard, and they existed solely as examples of formal, rhetorical prose. Oral (or visual) experience of a speech is completely different from encountering it only in writing, in collected and dusty volumes of "Great American Orations."

Most translations of Cicero's speeches aim at the formal style of nineteenth-century written oratory rather than the more relaxed and colloquial idiom of spoken language. But formal translation loses a great deal of the effect of the original speech. In fact, it is hard to imagine most formal translations actually keeping their hearers awake, much less entertaining them. Unlike most other forms of artful writing, however, the paramount goal of a speech is immediate comprehensibility for a listening audience, and keeping its attention and interest: you can't convince or move or even entertain someone who falls asleep.

Formality inevitably loses a great deal of the variety, wit, and energy of Cicero's style. According to Plutarch, when Cicero made fun of Cato's Stoicism in the defense of Murena, Cato was heard to say, "We have a stand-up comic as consul."[34] Cicero's wit seems far

---

34. *Comparison of Demosthenes and Cicero* 1.5.

away in some modern versions, or at least it sounds much too professorial. The real Cicero was renowned for his humor (collections of his jokes circulated), his capacity for savage repartee and parody, and his ability to leap from one style to another at a moment's notice. He was capable of astonishing eloquence—the kind of power that moves the hearer to tears or leaves her open-mouthed at the sheer force of the words and images. But although he was criticized toward the end of his life for his taste for excessive display and verbiage in his speeches, he was completely aware that high rhetoric cannot successfully be sustained for long. Some of his sentences are long and complex; others are one or two words. Some of his language is artificial, formal, and stylized, but he is eminently capable of using slang, sexual innuendo, and vulgarity. The speeches in this volume vary in tone both from speech to speech and within themselves: wit, vitriol, and parody abound in the defenses of Murena and Caelius, the prosecution of Verres, and the invective against Piso; formality and stylized artifice dominate the speech on Pompey's command; and every speech contains some passages of simple narrative and others of emotional appeal, of everyday language and of elevated diction. Cicero is a great speaker because he is the master of all styles, not just of the stately periodic prose we think of as "Ciceronian."

My hope here is to provide a version that, however inadequate a representation of the original, at least preserves some of Cicero's energy and wit. To that end, I have paid less attention to the complex word order in long and involved sentences, something possible only with the resources of a highly inflected language, than to the rhetorical goals of a speech. Similarly, I have tried to avoid flattening Cicero's choice of words to the propriety and dullness of dictionary definitions. Nor have I tried to maintain a kind of universal English idiom: this is a translation in American English. And although I have tried to avoid blatant or unnecessary anachronisms, I have had no qualms about using modern expressions that I believe an orator speaking in the twenty-first century would use in contexts similar to Cicero's. I am well aware that Cicero did not say "yellow brick road" or "friendship with benefits," but such expressions match the tone of what he did say better than using more decorous translations.[35]

---

35. In the language of translation theory, this is a "domesticating" rather than a "foreignizing" translation. In thinking about the problems of translating Cicero, I have learned a great deal from Roberts (2007).

Although I am sure I have not achieved my goal entirely, the goal itself is meaningful. Cicero is now only texts, but the texts represent a real, funny, vigorous, effective speaker. If the language I use is sometimes jarring and unlike what I, too, was educated to think "Cicero" sounded like, then at least it will keep him, at least some of the time, from sounding like an ancient bore.

Roman Institutions and Offices

1. Names

The Romans viewed the "three names" (*tria nomina*) as a distinctive feature of Roman citizenship. The minimal form of name for a male citizen was simply a *praenomen* (first name) and a *nomen* (family name), such as **Marcus Antonius.** But by the late Republic, most men, certainly most men of the upper classes, had the full three names, adding a *cognomen* to the first two. This cognomen might be hereditary, indicating a branch of a large family, such as **Marcus Licinius Crassus** or **Publius Cornelius Scipio.** It might be a personal honorific title, such as those either given or assumed after a military victory, such as **Quintus Caecilius Metellus Numidicus,** so named after his success in the Numidian war against Jugurtha. As in this instance, it is possible to have more than one cognomen. The other common sources for *cognomina* are adoption and the acquisition of citizenship. The younger Scipio Africanus was the biological son of Lucius Aemilius Paullus and was adopted by Publius Cornelius Scipio; he became **Publius Cornelius Scipio Aemilianus** (and had a third cognomen, **Africanus,** which he both inherited from his adoptive grandfather, the victor in the Second Punic War, and earned for himself, as conqueror of Carthage in the Third Punic War). When an individual (such as the poet Archias) was awarded citizenship, he generally took the nomen of his patron and his original name became his cognomen: **Aulus Licinius Archias** (the source of **Aulus** is mysterious; his patron was Lucius Licinius Lucullus).

Women in the first century BCE generally had only one name, the feminine form of the family name. Thus the sisters of Publius Clodius Pulcher are all named **Clodia,** and two of them are generally identified by the names of their husbands: the Clodia of *In Defense of Marcus Caelius* is **Clodia Metelli,** as the wife of **Quintus Caecilius Metellus Celer.** The inconvenience and ambiguity of this system led to the increased use of *cognomina* among women.

In this translation, I have generally used familiar forms of names if they exist: thus **Mark Antony, Catiline,** and **Pompey** rather than **Marcus Antonius, Lucius Sergius Catilina,** and **Gnaeus Pompeius Magnus.**

2. Public Offices

The system of magistracies developed over centuries; its form in the late Republic was regularized by Sulla.[36] The highest office (which was collegial, like all Roman magistracies) was the **consulate,** held by two men simultaneously. It was the culmination of what the Romans called the *cursus honorum* (literally, the road or race of offices): to hold the consulate (minimum age 42), it was necessary to have held the **praetorship** (minimum age 39; there were eight praetors each year); to hold the praetorship it was necessary to have held the **quaestorship** (minimum age 30; there were twenty each year). Optionally (but good for one's career), it was possible to be **aedile** or **tribune of the plebs** between quaestorship and praetorship. All offices were for one year, beginning on January 1 (except tribunes of the plebs, who entered office on December 10).

In ascending order, the functions of these offices were:

quaestor   One quaestor was assigned to each praetor and consul and to each proconsul governing a province; their responsibilities were largely financial. Election to the quaestorship carried automatic membership in the senate.

aedile   Two pairs, the curule aediles and the plebeian aediles (Cicero was one of the latter in 69). They were in charge of urban affairs, including markets, civil order, and some games and festivals.

tribune of the plebs   Formally not a magistracy of the Roman people, but a magistracy of the Roman plebs. The tribunate (ten annually) could only be held by a plebeian (hence Clodius had himself adopted into a plebeian family in 59 before standing for election as a tribune). The original function of the tribunes was purely negative, to veto official actions or intercede on behalf of plebeians, and hence their persons were sacrosanct. Their effective role in the first century was broad: most legislation was introduced by tribunes and passed by the plebeian assembly (*concilium plebis*) over which they presided. By tradition they remained advocates of the people and were often the source or leaders of popular action in the city. Sulla drastically reduced their powers and influence, but their position was gradually restored in the decade after his death.

---

36. For a succinct account of the Roman constitution, see Lintott (1999).

praetor   The eight praetors had, after Sulla, primarily legal responsibilities. Six of them presided over specific *quaestiones* (standing courts dealing with extortion, electoral corruption, and other major crimes); the peregrine praetor (*praetor inter peregrinos*) was responsible for the administration of justice in Rome between citizen and noncitizen; the urban praetor was the primary administrator of civil law in Rome. After their year of office, praetors were expected to serve for a year (as propraetor or proconsul) governing a province, although they often (e.g., Cicero himself) did not do so.

consul   The two consuls were the chief magistrates of Rome; they might remain in the city administering public affairs, or they could be put in charge of a major military campaign. After their year of office, they generally served as proconsul in a major province for a year or more. The praetors and consuls were elected by the more oligarchic centuriate assembly, and they alone (as well as proconsuls) had *imperium*, the power to command; it was limited in the city by the right of appeal, but unlimited in the provinces. As long as a magistrate had *imperium* he was attended by lictors (six for a praetor, twelve for a consul) carrying the *fasces* (bundles of rods) as a symbol of power; the *fasces* contained an axe outside the city, indicating the power of life and death.

censor   Not a regular magistracy, but often the summit of a public career. Two censors were supposed to be chosen to serve for eighteen months every five years; they supervised the roll of citizens and of the senate and knights, often expelling people on moral grounds; they were also responsible for the administration of public works and contracts. The election of censors was very irregular in the late Republic.

3. Political Institutions and Groupings

The Roman citizen body (*populus*) could be divided in several different ways. Earliest, and in classical times least important, is the distinction between patrician and plebeian. Certain priesthoods were still reserved for patricians, but for the most part patricians were excluded from functions rather than controlling them: there could be no more than one patrician consul in a given year, and a patrician could not become tribune of the plebs. But by Cicero's day there were very few patrician families left, and while individual members of the families mattered, the distinction between patrician and plebeian was relatively unimportant.

Much more important than the patrician/plebeian dichotomy is that between "nobles" and everyone else. Nobility was a self-defined class rather than one recognized in law: nobles were men who had an ancestor who had held the consulate. Cicero was ennobled by being elected to the consulate; most of those with whom he was in political contention had been noble for generations.

For the purposes of election and the passage of laws, the people were divided into two quite different assemblies, the assembly by centuries (*comitia centuriata*) and the assembly by tribes (*comitia tributa*). The former was oligarchic: a "century" was not a hundred men but an arbitrary division of one of the five property classes; the first (wealthiest) property class had the largest number of centuries but the smallest number of members and thus dominated the elections for consul and praetor. It was rarely called for other purposes, although it did pass the law summoning Cicero back from exile.

The assembly by tribes, while scarcely democratic, was at least geographic in origin rather than being based on wealth. Four of the thirty-five tribes were urban and tended to have a disproportionate number of voters and of the poor, although the distribution of newly enfranchised citizens was itself a matter of contention. The tribes voted (as did the centuries) as units, both for elections and for the passage of laws; in its structure the *comitia tributa* was identical to the *concilium plebis*—except that patricians were not allowed to take part in the latter.

The most significant smaller groupings of citizens are the two "orders" of the senate and the knights (*equites*). The senate, in Cicero's day, had roughly six hundred members; election to the quaestorship automatically conferred membership, which was permanent (except for expulsion by the censors). The senate had *auctoritas* (authority) rather than formal legislative powers, but by tradition it was responsible for foreign affairs and the assignment of provinces to magistrates and for passing resolutions (*senatus consultum*) and decrees that often served as the basis for laws or for consular actions. Senators were not allowed to engage in trade or other degrading activities and were distinguished by their dress in public.

The knights were originally the cavalry of the Roman army, and a ceremonial portion of them retained the title of "knights with a public horse" (*equites equo publico*) and were reviewed by the censors.

But by the late Republic the knights were simply the nonpolitical portion of the ruling (senatorial) class: men who were wealthy and often noble but chose not to seek office (or were not elected) and instead often engaged in commerce. A significant number of them were *publicani*, members of the companies that contracted to collect provincial taxes, and Cicero generally assumes that the interests of the knights and the interests of the tax-farmers were identical.

Chronological Table

Speeches in this volume are in *boldface italic* type. Cicero's correspondence is not included.

YEAR	EVENTS	CICERO'S EXTANT WRITINGS
106	Cicero's birth (January 3)	
91	Beginning of Social War	
90–89	Italians given citizenship	
88	Outbreak of First Mithridatic War Sulla's first march on Rome	
86	Death of Marius	*On Invention* (approximate date)
85	Treaty of Dardanus (end of First Mithridatic War)	Translation of Aratus (approximate date)
82	Sulla's second march on Rome Proscriptions instituted	
81	Sulla dictator	***In Defense of Quinctius***
80	Sulla's second consulship	***In Defense of Roscius of Ameria***
79–78	Cicero's eastern trip; study on Rhodes	
77		***In Defense of Roscius the Actor*** (approximate date)
75	Cicero quaestor in Sicily	
73–71	Verres' governorship of Sicily Slave revolt of Spartacus	

YEAR	EVENTS	CICERO'S EXTANT WRITINGS
70	First consulship of Crassus and Pompey End of senatorial monopoly of juries	*Against Verres* (three speeches in seven books)
69	Cicero plebeian aedile	*In Defense of Fonteius*
67	Pompey given command against pirates	
66	Cicero praetor Pompey given command against Mithridates	*In Support of Manilius' Law* *In Defense of Cluentius*
63	Cicero consul Conspiracy of Catiline	*On the Agrarian Law* (three speeches) *In Defense of Rabirius on a Charge of Treason* *Against Catiline* (four speeches) *In Defense of Lucius Murena*
62	Clodius at the rites of Bona Dea	*In Defense of Sulla* *In Defense of the Poet Archias*
61	Trial and acquittal of Clodius for sacrilege	*In Defense of Flaccus*
60	Formation of so-called First Triumvirate (Caesar, Crassus, Pompey)	
58	Cicero exiled	
57	Cicero's return from exile (September)	*Speech of Thanks to the Senate* *Speech of Thanks to the People* *On His Own House*

YEAR	EVENTS	CICERO'S EXTANT WRITINGS
56	Renewal of First Triumvirate; Cicero warned to behave	*Defense of Sestius* *Interrogation of Vatinius* **In Defense of Marcus Caelius** *On the Answer of the Haruspices* *On the Consular Provinces* *In Defense of Balbus*
55	Second consulship of Crassus and Pompey	**Against Lucius Calpurnius Piso** *On the Orator*
54		*In Defense of Plancius* *In Defense of Scaurus* *On the Commonwealth* begun
53	Death of Crassus at Carrhae	*In Defense of Rabirius Postumus*
52	Killing of Clodius by Milo Sole consulship of Pompey	*In Defense of Milo*
51	Cicero governor of Cilicia (51–50)	*On the Commonwealth* completed *On Laws* (unfinished)
49	Cicero's return from Cilicia (January) Outbreak of Civil War between Caesar and Pompey Cicero joins Pompey (June)	
48	Defeat of Pompey at Pharsalus (August) Murder of Pompey in Egypt (September) Cicero returns to Brundisium	
47	Cicero returns to Rome (July) Caesar returns to Rome (September)	

YEAR	EVENTS	CICERO'S EXTANT WRITINGS
46	Defeat of republicans at Thapsus; suicide of Cato (April)	*Brutus* *Orator* *Stoic Paradoxes* **On Behalf of Marcus Marcellus** *In Defense of Ligarius*
45	Death of Cicero's daughter Tullia (February) Final defeat of republicans at Munda (March)	*In Defense of King Deiotarus* *Academica* *On Moral Ends* *Tusculan Disputations* *On the Nature of the Gods*
44	Caesar named permanent dictator Assassination of Caesar (March 15) Antony consul Cicero away from Rome July–August	*On Old Age* *On Divination* *On Fate* *Topics* *On Friendship* **Philippic Orations 1–4** *On Duties*
43	Battle of Mutina; death of consuls Hirtius and Pansa (April) Second Triumvirate formed (Antony, Lepidus, Octavian) Cicero killed (December 7)	**Philippic Orations 5–14**

Note on Texts

The translations in this volume are based on the following editions:

Against Verres: Peterson (1917), with consultation of Baldo (2004)

In Support of Manilius' Law: Clark (1905)

Second Speech against Catiline: Maslowski (2003)

In Defense of Lucius Murena: Clark (1905), with consultation of Adamietz (1989)

In Defense of the Poet Archias: Clark (1911)

In Defense of Marcus Caelius: Austin (1960)

Against Lucius Calpurnius Piso: Nisbet (1961)

On Behalf of Marcus Marcellus: Clark (1918)

Fourth and Ninth Philippics: Manuwald (2007)

Where applicable, I have also made use of the commentaries in these editions in my own annotations.

The titles of the most commonly cited works of Cicero are abbreviated as follows:

Speeches in This Volume

Arch.	*Pro Archia Poeta*	*In Defense of the Poet Archias*
Cael.	*Pro M. Caelio*	*In Defense of Marcus Caelius*
Cat.	*In L. Catilinam*	*Against Catiline*
Man.	*Pro lege Manilia* (De Imperio Cn. Pompei)	*In Support of Manilius' Law*
Marc.	*Pro M. Marcello*	*On Behalf of Marcus Marcellus*
Mur.	*Pro L. Murena*	*In Defense of Lucius Murena*
Phil.	*In M. Antonium Oratorio Philippica*	*Philippic Oration*
Pis.	*In L. Calpurnium Pisonem*	*Against Lucius Calpurnius Piso*
Verr.	*Actio secunda in C. Verrem*	*Against Verres* (Second Speech against Verres)

In referring to speeches in the notes and the Biographical Index, section numbers are given for each speech (e.g., *Mur.* 66 means section 66 of *In Defense of Lucius Murena*) preceded (when appropriate) by the number of the book or speech (e.g., *Verr.* 4.25 means section 25 of the fourth book of *Actio secunda in C. Verrem*, and *Cat.* 2.5 means section 5 of *Second Speech against Catiline*).

Some Other Works of Cicero Cited in This Volume

ad Att.	*Epistulae ad Atticum*	*Letters to Atticus*
ad Fam.	*Epistulae ad familiares*	*Letters to Friends*
de Or.	*De Oratore*	*On the Orator*
Leg.	*De legibus*	*On Laws*
Off.	*De officiis*	*On Duties*
Tusc.	*Disputationes Tusculanae*	*Tusculan Disputations*
[n/a]	*Brutus*	*Brutus*
[n/a]	*Orator*	*Orator*

Map 1: Italy and Sicily

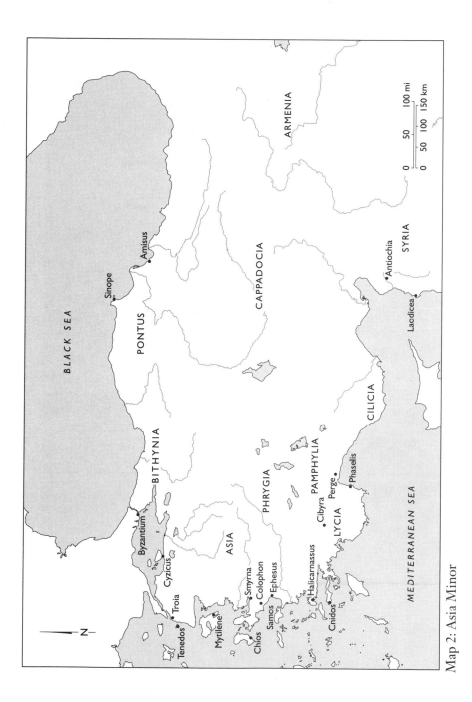

Map 2: Asia Minor

Map 3: Greece

1

Against Verres

On the Theft of Works of Art

The trial of Gaius Verres in 70 BCE was Cicero's only important prosecution;[1] it was also an important stage in his political career. Cicero had had forensic successes before this, and he was certainly proud of his successful speech in defense of Roscius of Ameria on a charge of murder in 80. In that speech, and in his (lost) subsequent defense of a woman from Arretium, he had presented himself as critical of certain elements of the Sullan settlement: in the defense of Roscius, the role of Sulla's freedman Chrysogonus and the more general misuse of the proscriptions for personal gain or revenge; in the case of the woman from Arretium, Sulla's vindictive restriction of the citizen rights of Etruria. Those cases may have been a reason for his withdrawal from Rome in 79 on a tour of study in the Greek east; in any case, he returned to Rome after Sulla's death and in 76 was elected one of the twenty quaestors for 75 and thus became a member of the senate.

It was his service as quaestor that led directly to the prosecution of Verres. As quaestor, Cicero was assigned to the western half of Sicily under the governorship of Sextus Peducaeus;[2] he performed his task with enough honesty and fairness that, when the Sicilians wanted to prosecute Verres for extortion, in January of 70 they asked Cicero to represent them in the trial. Verres was somewhat older than Cicero; as quaestor in 84, he had been a member of the anti-Sullan regime in Rome, but he had subsequently switched sides at an opportune moment (taking his consul's military funds with him) and had gone on to a career of constant treachery, greed, and corruption, if we can believe Cicero. He reached the office of praetor in 74, serving as urban praetor, the chief legal officer of Rome; he followed that year of judicial misconduct in Rome with not

---

1. His only other known prosecution is that of Lucius Munatius Plancus (successful) in 52 BCE, twenty-eight years later, near the end of his forensic career.

2. Unlike the other Roman provinces, Sicily, as a vestige of its having been acquired in two stages, had two quaestors, one east, one west.

one but three years (73–71) as governor of Sicily, an unusually long term
extended because his prospective successor was called on to deal with a
more urgent problem, the slave revolt of Spartacus. In Sicily, Verres acted
as an unchecked tyrant with unmitigated greed, extorting, as Cicero tells
us in great detail, huge amounts of money and looting every good work
of art from the entire province. The Sicilians decided to prosecute him,
estimating the amount of their losses at 40 million sesterces.

Even with what looks like an open-and-shut case, it was no simple
matter for provincials to seek redress from a corrupt governor. The court
established to deal with cases of provincial extortion (res repetundae,
literally, "property to be reclaimed") was the oldest tribunal (quaestio)
in Rome set up to deal with a specific crime; it was authorized by the
Calpurnian law of 149 BCE. By the time of Verres' trial, the law in force
was that established by Sulla. The jury consisted only of senators, and the
long and cumbersome procedure was very clearly weighted in favor of the
defendant and against the provincials.

The process began when someone—necessarily a Roman citizen, and
preferably one of some standing—applied to the praetor in charge of the
extortion court for the right to prosecute on behalf of the province. Before
permission could be given—and long before a trial could take place—there
was an opportunity for other potential prosecutors to seek to replace the
initial applicant; in the trial of Verres, Quintus Caecilius Niger, who had
been Verres' quaestor in Sicily, sought to replace Cicero. In Cicero's view,
this move was collusive; by putting up a friend to prosecute him, Verres
counted on Caecilius deliberately to present an unconvincing case. But in
the hearing (divinatio), Cicero won decisively, and Caecilius was not even
permitted to assist in the prosecution.

At that point, the prosecutor requested a specific amount of time
to gather evidence and witnesses. Cicero asked for 110 days to go to
Sicily, collect his materials, and return, but in fact he did his job much
more rapidly than that. Even so, another obstacle remained. Verres had
organized the prosecution of a different governor, in which a shorter time
for discovery was requested; as a result, even though he returned rapidly,
Cicero had to wait several months before the actual trial of Verres could
begin. Furthermore, when the trial began in early August, there had been
important developments: Verres' chief advocate, Quintus Hortensius
Hortalus (the leading orator in Rome at the time), had been elected consul
for 69, and his colleague in office was to be Quintus Caecilius Metellus, a
strong supporter of Verres. What is more, Metellus' two brothers were also
in a position to influence the trial; Lucius was governor of Sicily in 70 and
did all he could to hinder Cicero's collection of evidence, while Marcus
was elected praetor for 69 and was selected by lot to preside over the
extortion court. The defense pursued the obvious tactic. If the trial could

be delayed into the next year, it would be possible to bring strong pressure in favor of acquittal.

The cumbersome procedure of the extortion court, moreover, lent itself to delaying tactics. As was not the case in other criminal proceedings, extortion trials required two hearings rather than one. In the first hearing (Actio prima), it was customary for the prosecution to give a lengthy explanation of the charges, accompanied by a full presentation of the witnesses and evidence; the defense replied in kind. After an adjournment, there was then a second hearing (Actio secunda), in which the two sides again presented their cases and evidence: déjà vu all over again. In the case of Verres, as it happened, much of the second half of the year was taken up by holidays on which the court was not in session; had Cicero proceeded in the normal fashion, with a lengthy presentation of the case and perhaps an even longer rebuttal by Hortensius, it was very likely that the trial could not be finished by the end of the year and would instead be concluded in the next year under circumstances much more favorable to Verres. That Cicero himself had been elected one of the plebeian aediles for 69 (despite the active bribery and intimidation used by Verres' allies to defeat him) would make relatively little difference with such powerful opposition.

The solution Cicero adopted was to forgo the lengthy presentation of his case in the first hearing; his brief extant speech (the first actio*) concentrated on attacking the tactics of Verres' defense and was immediately followed by the full presentation of the large and damning body of evidence. Hortensius was not given any case to reply to, and in fact no serious defense was mounted. The first hearing ended only ten days after the trial began, leaving ample time for the second* actio*, but Verres saw that conviction was inevitable and retired rapidly to a life of comfort and oysters in Marseilles, taking his stolen art collection with him. Ironically, it was his love of art that killed him: in 43 Mark Antony demanded that Verres surrender his Corinthian bronzes, and when Verres refused Antony proscribed him and took the bronzes anyway.*

Given that the second actio *never took place, Cicero's speech is a remarkably substantial document; indeed, it is Cicero's longest extant work of any kind. It is, in fact, a fictional speech. While it obviously resembles what Cicero would have said if Verres had stayed for the second half of the trial, he did not give such a speech, and all the references in the extant text to Verres' presence—beginning from the opening paragraph (2.1.1–2) marveling that he has stayed for the second* actio*—are merely intended to give verisimilitude to what the first audience certainly, and most readers as well, would know was not a real speech. To the best of my knowledge, it was the first work of its kind in Rome—a vivid recreation of a scene that never happened. Its very fictionality,* *however, is what allows Cicero such scope for development; it is hard to believe that any real jury would endure a speech, even one by Cicero, more than four hundred pages long.[3]*

The mundane and obvious reason for making the speech public—and in fact Cicero very rapidly made the set of seven texts (divinatio, first actio, five books of second actio) public as a group—is not to allow such intensive work and collection of evidence to go to waste, and at the same time to make clear to all that Verres fled because he was in fact guilty. But the Verrine orations are more than that: not only are they a demonstration of Cicero's legal and rhetorical skill, but they also portray him as a wise and reforming statesman and the legitimate heir to the best traditions of Rome. The Verrines are about Cicero almost as much as they are about Verres.[4]

*The Second Speech against Verres in its five books has both an order and a structure. Insofar as Verres' early career, up to his urban praetorship, is dealt with in Book 1, before beginning on the Sicilian material, it is chronological; within the Sicilian section, it moves from Verres' administrative misbehavior as governor in Book 2, through his financial manipulations of the grain supply in Book 3, to his thefts of works of art from individuals and cities in Book 4 (the portion included in this volume), to his disastrous conduct of military and naval affairs and his executions of Roman citizens in the final book.[5] The last story told is the pathetic tale of Gavius of Compsa, crucified in Messana while still plaintively repeating "I am a Roman citizen"—*civis Romanus sum. *The speech builds to a climax, moving from mere administrative and financial cruelty to religious violations (the works of art) to treason, torture, and the violation of the rights of Roman citizens.*

---

3. Cicero suggests (*Verr.* 1.25) that there was a time limit on speeches, and in fact the extortion law of 59 BCE placed a limit of six hours. The Second Speech against Verres is well beyond that. Many modern accounts speak of the second *actio* as if it were five *speeches*, but in fact it is one speech divided into five *books*—an arrangement that itself draws attention to the fiction and to the speech as one to be read rather than heard.

4. Very little has been written about the interpretation of the Verrines as a whole, but see the valuable account of Vasaly (2002) 87–103. There are some excellent studies of particular aspects; see especially Butler (2002) and Vasaly (1993).

5. Cicero claims that the military aspect of Verres' governorship would be the basis of the defense; in fact, military affairs were quite important at the time, because of the revolt of Spartacus just across the Straits of Messina (the modern spelling of Messana).

In reading this massive and emotional indictment, filled with vivid and powerful narratives of Verres' crimes, one is tempted—Cicero wants you—to forget about the cool and practical question that any jury should be considering: what, of the terrible things Verres did, is actually a crime under the law against provincial extortion? And the answer almost certainly has to be "not very much." In the first place, Verres' most horrendous acts, the execution of Roman citizens, were not strictly speaking illegal—and certainly did not fall under the law against extortion. A magistrate with imperium in a province had the right of life and death over all under his control, even citizens, and while it was customary to extend to citizens the rights to a trial that they would have in Rome, it was not formally necessary. And what about the thefts? Some of them were clearly illegal, but perhaps not as many as Cicero wants the reader to believe; over and over, Cicero has to admit that many of the works of art were purchased rather than stolen. True, the price was ludicrously low, but that was not illegal, and Cicero would not have spent so much time pointing out the gaps in Verres' accounts if proof of sale were not significant evidence. As for Verres' military failures—the pirates sailing into the harbor of Syracuse—they may be evidence for incompetence or even treachery, but not for extortion. The fairly loose rules governing the behavior of magistrates in the provinces were gradually tightened over the course of the first century, but at the time of Verres' governorship of Sicily, they were very much a work in progress.[6] The charges most likely to be both true and punishable were the very technical ones about the manipulation of tithes and taxes, described in detail in Book 3, but tricky bookkeeping does not excite a jury, and hence Cicero moves from that to less criminal but more outrageous behaviors.

The procedure in extortion cases was heavily weighted against the prosecution, and the jury would naturally be inclined—and in other cases Cicero makes extensive use of that inclination—to favor Romans over defeated peoples who spoke odd languages. Hence, more than in other trials, the facts of the case mattered less than the emotions of the jury, and Cicero places his emphases accordingly. Above all, Cicero stresses the loyalty of the Sicilians to Rome; even more, he regularly describes Verres' victims as either close friends of important Romans or as Roman citizens themselves. Indeed, he makes the Sicilians sound like Romans, particularly in their morality, religiosity, and seriousness. It is religion, above all, that he stresses; the first book begins by drawing attention to Verres' violations of temples and religious works of art, and the last book ends with a long prayer to the thirteen divinities whose shrines Verres has most grievously

---

6. On trials under the extortion laws, see Riggsby (1999) 120–50; for a skeptical reading of one episode, see Steel (2001) 233–51.

violated.[7] *In the fourth book, although the topic is nominally the theft
of works of art, from the very beginning it is only objects and statues of
religious significance that Verres stole. The first half discusses objects taken
from individuals, culminating in the theft of the candelabrum of Prince
Antiochus supposed to be dedicated to Jupiter Optimus Maximus on the
Capitol in Rome, and the second half deals with statues and artifacts taken
from cities and temples, beginning with the statue of Diana at Segesta,
dwelling on the sanctuary of Ceres and Proserpina at Enna, and ending with
the robberies from the temple of Athena at Syracuse. The constant refrain
of the Sicilian victims, as reported by Cicero, is that they have no interest in
the money, that all they want back is their gods and their ritual implements.*

*The other important emphasis is the incessant contrast between the
vile behavior and character of Verres and the nobility of the great Roman
generals, Marcellus and Scipio, whose dedications he stole. Over and over,
it is the Sicilians who respect Rome's heroes, while Verres is completely
uninterested in maintaining the morals and standards of Rome's past.
Cicero goes further than that, portraying Verres as a Greek, and a corrupt
and decadent one at that, while the Sicilian Greeks, who are supposed
to be corrupt and decadent, are in fact the bearers of Roman moral
standards. By making the Sicilians Roman and the Roman governor Greek,
Cicero dramatically reverses the relationship between the provinces and
Rome. Past and present, Greek and Roman switch places: Verres deserves
conviction not because of his specific misdeeds but because he has
assaulted a people who embody the values he has betrayed.*

*In portraying Verres as someone who has perverted Roman values,
Cicero implicitly sets himself, not the Sicilians, as the arbiter of what
Roman values are. Indeed, it is not just implicit; Cicero very deliberately
shows himself as the heir to those great Romans whose heritage Verres has
destroyed. That is clearest in the story of the statue of Diana at Segesta.
It had been taken from Segesta by the Carthaginians, returned by Scipio
Aemilianus after the destruction of Carthage in 146, and taken again by
Verres—who also had to remove the statue base naming Scipio as the
donor. At 4.79–81, Cicero turns to another Publius Scipio, this time one
of Verres' advocates, and berates him for not defending the gift of his
ancestor (who, in fact, was a distant and collateral relative) and expresses
his regret that he, Cicero, has to take the place of Scipio's (degenerate)
descendant and defend him.*

*The moral that Cicero draws is clear and explicit. He, the new man,
better embodies the values represented by a Scipio or a Marcellus in
the past than do their biological descendants. It is one of the clearest
statements of what has been called the ideology of the new man—that*

7. It is also the longest sentence in extant Latin literature.

virtue (in both the military and moral meanings of that word) matters more than ancestry; that the ancestors of the nobility were once not yet noble and had to gain eminence through the qualities now represented by the Ciceros of this world. This claim returns at the end of Book 5, where Cato the Elder is extolled for his virtues, the qualities of courage, hard work, and honor that made Rome great. Cicero, like old Cato, is the true heir of the Roman aristocracy, even if none of his ancestors had ever held office in Rome.[8]

With the subjects of aristocratic decline and the vigorous virtue of men such as Cicero comes a third, more technical subject, which is discussed most clearly in the first actio but is implicit throughout, and that is the composition of juries in the criminal courts. That had long been a bone of contention between the senate and the knights, and juries had alternated between equestrian and senatorial since the first extortion law of 149. Sulla, in his conservative reorganization of Roman government during his dictatorship, had firmly placed the juries in senatorial hands (although he also enlarged the senate). But in 70 Pompey and Marcus Crassus as consuls deliberately undid the more reactionary elements of the Sullan plan, restoring to the tribunes the powers Sulla had removed and, later in the year, supporting a new arrangement of juries, dividing their composition among three groups: the senate, the knights, and the so-called tribuni aerarii or "treasury tribunes," another group of wealthy nonsenatorial men.

The jury reform was complex and almost certainly took some time to formulate and to gain the acquiescence of as many interested groups as possible—and in fact this jury system lasted until the end of the Republic. But in the first actio and the opening of the second, Cicero threatened the senate with the loss of control of the juries if they failed to convict a man, particularly a senator, so obviously guilty as Verres. By August, when the trial took place, jury reform will have been well known and expected; Cicero's threats are misleading.[9] Far from trying to shame the senate, he is contributing to his own image as a reasonable reformer, one who rejects the corruption of the present system while still supporting senatorial control, but who is willing to support the new compromise if the senate refuses to reform itself. In all these areas, Cicero shows himself to be a statesman rather than a politician, a man who may not be genetically a Roman aristocrat but who embodies the grand values of fairness, hard work, common sense, and integrity.

The fourth book of the Second Verrine, more than any other part of the speech and more than any other early speech, shows Cicero walking

---

8. On the ideology of the new man, see Wiseman (1971) 107–16.
9. On this, see Mitchell (1986) 11.

a series of tightropes: between attacking the aristocracy and appearing as their uncritical supporter; between the values of Romans and the values of provincials; between the national interest and individual rights; between Greek culture and Roman virtue. It is this last theme that preoccupies him in this text, and it is one that he presents both here and in later speeches with considerable irony and humor. In claiming not to know or care much about Greek culture or values, he nods to Roman know-nothingism, but at the same time he reveals that in fact he has a vast knowledge of Greek culture. The book begins by his forgetting the name of Polyclitus; it ends with him giving a speech to the Syracusan senate in Greek. For that he is criticized by Verres' supporter and successor in Sicily, Lucius Metellus, but the very source of that criticism taints it. Throughout his oratorical career, and in many of the speeches included in this volume, Cicero simultaneously claims to support old Roman values while buttressing them with his obvious intellectual achievements and knowledge of Greek art, rhetoric, and literature.[10] The prosecution of Verres was a crucial step in Cicero's careful and complex self-definition.

Actionis in C. Verrem Secundae Liber Quartus

[1] I come now to what Verres calls his enthusiasm, his friends call mental illness, and the Sicilians call highway robbery.[11] I'm not sure what word to use; I'll tell you what happened, and you examine its substance, not its name. You should first learn how to classify it, members of the jury; after that it may not be hard to figure out what name you think you should give it. I assert that in all Sicily, a province of such wealth and age, with so many towns and so many wealthy families, there was not a single silver vessel, a single piece of Corinthian or Delian bronze,[12] a single precious stone or pearl, a

---

10. On this topic, see Zetzel (2003).

11. The speech begins abruptly as it is only one section of the (fictional) Second Verrine. Cicero's emphasis on naming here is not casual; much of the legal case turns on whether Verres' appropriations of Sicilian property were theft in a legal sense. In many cases, as both Verres' accounts and those of his victims showed, he "bought" works of art at scandalously low prices, but what is unethical is not always illegal. Hence Cicero urges the imagined jury not to be swayed by arguments about definition.

12. Corinth and Delos were the source of some of the most prized bronzes in antiquity.

single object made from gold or ivory, a single statue (bronze, marble, or ivory), a single painted picture or tapestry that Verres did not seek out, appraise, and, if he liked it, steal. **[2]** This sounds like a sweeping statement; but listen to what I have to say. I don't say "everything" as an empty word or to exaggerate the charges; when I say that he left behind nothing of this kind in the whole province, I'm talking plain Latin, not prosecutorese. I'll make it even clearer: there was nothing in anyone's home, not even in those of his hosts; nothing in a public place, not even in temples; nothing belonging to a Sicilian, nothing belonging to a Roman citizen—*nothing* that came to his eyes or his knowledge, nothing private or public, nothing sacred or profane in all Sicily that he left behind.

[3] What better place to begin than with the city that was your particular love and joy, or with what group but the people who have sung your praises? It will be easier to see how you behaved among people who hated you—the ones who have accused you and prosecuted you—once it's clear you robbed your own dear Mamertines so viciously.[13]

Gaius Heius is a Mamertine (everyone who's been to Messana knows that), far and away the richest man in the city. His house is just about the finest in Messana; it's certainly the best known and the most open and welcoming to Roman visitors. Until Verres got there, that house was fitted out so well that it was an ornament to the city, too; Messana itself, although adorned by its location and walls and harbor, is entirely empty, stripped bare of the things which turn Verres on.[14] **[4]** In Heius' house there was a shrine of great distinction, very old and passed down by his ancestors. In it there were four statues of great beauty, of extraordinary workmanship and nobility; they could bring pleasure not only to a man of Verres' wit and wisdom but to any one of us, people he calls amateurs.[15] One of

---

13. The people of Messana were called Mamertines—an army of Oscan mercenaries from Italy who had captured the city in the third century BCE. All Sicilian place-names will be found on Map 1.

14. "Richest," "fitted out so well," "ornament," and "adorned" are in Latin all from the same root, *orno*, "to adorn": the similarity in the qualities of person, house, and city is not easy to convey in English. The language used to describe Verres' love of objects is frequently erotic rather than aesthetic.

15. *Idiotae*, the same term Cicero later has Piso use of nonphilosophers (see *Against Lucius Calpurnius Piso*, n. 109).

them was a marble statue of Cupid made by Praxiteles—I've had to learn the names of the artisans while conducting this investigation.[16] I'm pretty sure the same artisan made a similar Cupid which is now at Thespiae, and is the reason for going to Thespiae; there's no other reason to go there. And in fact the great Lucius Mummius,[17] when he liberated the statues of the Muses of Thespiae (which are now at the temple of Felicitas in Rome) and all the other nonsacred statues in the town, did not lay a hand on this marble Cupid, because it was a religious dedication.

[5] But let me get back to that shrine. There was the marble statue of Cupid I mentioned, and on the other side a beautifully made bronze statue of Hercules. They say it's by Myron, and I'm pretty sure that's right. Also, in front of these gods were small altars, from which anyone could recognize the religious character of the shrine. There were two other bronze statues, very pretty if not really outstanding, of girls dressed modestly, holding in upraised hands ritual objects resting on their heads, in the manner of Athenian girls; they were called Canephoroe.[18] The artisan who made them they said was—What's his name? Who? Thank you—Polyclitus. Any Roman who came to Messana used to go to see them—they were open daily to public viewing; the house was an adornment as much to the city as to the owner.[19] [6] Gaius Claudius, whose tenure of the aedileship is well known for its great splendor, borrowed this Cupid for only as long as he had the forum decked out for the everlasting gods and the Roman people; since he had a relationship with the family of Heius and was a patron of the people of Messana, he was as careful to return it as they had been generous in lending it.[20] But not long ago—but

---

16. Cicero's claims of ignorance about the names of the most famous Greek sculptors and his general tone of condescension about Greek cultural interests are clearly ironic. His contemporary Varro said that everyone with any claim to culture knew the name of Praxiteles.

17. The destroyer of Corinth in 146 BCE.

18. "Basket-carriers." Cicero uses the Greek form, something more common in this speech than in his other orations. Statues of this kind used as architectural supports are most familiar from the porch of the Erechtheum on the Acropolis in Athens.

19. See above, n. 14.

20. Gaius Claudius Pulcher was aedile in 99 BCE; putting on games (for which he borrowed the statue) was part of the position.

why "not long ago"? in fact, very recently—we saw nobles like this adorn the forum and the basilicas not with what they had plundered from the provinces but with elegant possessions belonging to their friends, with loans from their hosts, not criminal thefts. And in any case they returned to their owners the statues and ornaments; they did not, under the guise of doing their jobs as aediles, for the sake of four days' display, lift them from the cities of our allies and friends and then take them home to their country estates. **[7]** All these statues I've mentioned, members of the jury, Verres stole from Heius' shrine. He left, I say to you, not one of them, nothing but one very old wooden statue. I think it was the statue of Good Luck—something Verres didn't want in his house.

By all that's honorable among gods and men, what's going on here? What kind of case is this? What kind of shamelessness does he display? The statues I'm talking about: before you stole them, no magistrate came to Messana without going to see them. So many praetors, so many consuls were in Sicily in peace and even in wartime; so many men of every sort—forget about honorable, honest, scrupulous men; so many greedy, wicked, audacious men. None of them thought he was so tough, so strong, so noble that he dared demand or steal or touch anything in that shrine. Will Verres get away with stealing everything beautiful, wherever it is? Can't anybody else keep anything? Will his one house swallow up so many great houses? Did all his predecessors leave this statue untouched for Verres to steal? Did Gaius Claudius Pulcher bring it back so Verres could carry it off? But that statue of Cupid wasn't looking for a pimp's house and a whore's rules; he was happy to be held in that ancestral shrine; he knew he was left to Heius by his ancestors in a sacred inheritance. He didn't go looking for a whore's heir.[21]

[8] But why am I ranting like this? A single word defeats me. "Bought," he says. Holy heaven, what a great defense! We sent a peddler to the province with the full authority of Rome so he could buy up everything—statues, paintings, all the silver, gold, ivory, and precious stones—and leave nothing to anyone! This defense of his, that he bought it, seems to work for everything. But first, let me grant you what you want, that you bought it—since this is the single defense you'll use for this whole category of things—and then I ask

---

21. Verres was named heir by his mistress Chelidon (see also sec. 71 below).

you this: what kind of courts did you think there were in Rome, if you thought anyone would allow you, while you held the power and office of governor, to buy up from the whole province so many valuable objects, in fact every object that was worth anything?

[9] Look how careful our ancestors were. They had no suspicions of anything like this, but still they were careful to be ready for what could happen on a smaller scale. They didn't think anyone who went to a province as a magistrate or ambassador would be so crazy as to buy silver, since it was supplied from public funds, or clothing, which was supplied by law. They thought he might buy a slave, since we all use them and they're not supplied by the people, so they made a rule that no one could purchase a slave except to replace one who died. If one died at Rome? No, only if one died out there. They didn't want you to use your province to furnish a household, just to fill your needs in the province. [10] And why did they so thoroughly bar us from provincial purchases? Because, members of the jury, they thought that when a seller has no choice about selling, it should be called pillage, not purchase. They understood that in the provinces, if a person with official powers wanted to buy something from anyone and it was legal, then he would take what he wanted whether or not it was for sale, and at whatever price he wanted.

Someone will say: "Don't treat Verres that way. Don't measure his actions by the ancient standards of virtue. Don't penalize his purchases, so long as he bought fairly—not using his official powers, not from someone unwilling, not unjustly." That's what I'll do: if Heius had something for sale and sold it for the amount he thought it was worth, then I'll stop asking if you bought it legally.

[11] So what are we supposed to do? Are there arguments appropriate to something like this? I suppose we should find out whether Heius was in debt and was selling off his goods; if he was, whether he was so short of cash, so poor, so financially strapped as to plunder his own shrine and sell his ancestral gods. But I see that he had no auction; he never sold anything except his crops; not only was he not in debt at all, but he is, and always has been, rolling in cash. And even if everything I'm saying is the opposite of the truth, then still, he wouldn't have sold things that had been in his household, in his ancestral shrine, for so many years. "What if he was persuaded by a huge offer?" It's unlikely that a man as rich and as honorable as he would put cash ahead of his religion and the memorials of his ancestors. [12] "All well and good, but a hefty price often seduces men

from their principles." Let's see how much money it was that could drag Heius—a man whose wealth is as great as his greed is small— away from his humanity, his respect for his family, his religion. This is what he wrote in his accounts—at your orders, I believe: "All these statues by Praxiteles, Myron, and Polyclitus were sold to Verres for 6,500 sesterces."[22] That's what it says; recite from the account book. It tickles me that these famous artists' names, which people like Verres praise to the skies, have so fallen in his estimation. A Cupid by Praxiteles for 1,600! That must be where the proverb comes from, "Better to buy than to borrow."

[13] Someone will say, "What's all this? Do you put a big price on that stuff?" For my own purposes, no; but I think you should be aware how much people who collect these things think they're worth—how much they sell for, how much these specific things would fetch if they were available on the open market, and in fact how much Verres himself thinks they're worth. If he thought that statue of Cupid was worth only four hundred denarii, he would never, because of it, have let himself become the object of public speech and of so much attack. [14] Who here doesn't know how much these things are worth? Haven't we seen a bronze statue of average size fetch 40,000 sesterces at auction?[23] If I wanted to, I could name men who've bought them for no less or for even more. In this kind of thing, the limit is set by greed; you can only stop the price of art going up if you stop drooling over it. What I see is that Heius was brought to sell these statues not because he wanted to and not because he had some temporary difficulty and not because he was offered so much money, and that you, with a dummy sale, used force, intimidation, and the power and weapons of your office to rob and pillage a man whom, along with the rest of our allies, the Roman people had entrusted not just to your power but to your protection.

[15] In making a charge like this, members of the jury, what could be better than to have Heius himself make this statement? Nothing at all, but let's not wish for what's hard to get. Heius is a Mamertine; the city of the Mamertines publicly, by vote of the senate, is the only

---

22. A ridiculously small amount, as becomes clear below. On currency: 4 sesterces = 1 denarius.

23. Note that Cicero does not ascribe value to the artist, merely to the size and material.

one to offer praise for Verres. All the other Sicilians hate him; he's loved by the Mamertines alone; and the leader of the embassy sent to praise him is Heius. He is, after all, the first man in the city, and I'm afraid that in carrying out his public instructions he may be silent about his private injuries. [16] Although I knew this and believed it, members of the jury, I left it up to Heius; I brought him forward at the first hearing, and I did so without any risk. What could Heius have answered if he were a wicked man, unlike the man he is? That the statues were in his house, not in Verres'? Who could say anything like that? If he were completely sleazy and the biggest liar in the world, he would say that he put them up for sale and got his price. This is the most noble man in his city; he desperately wanted you to have the right idea about of his religiosity and his worthiness, so he first said he was praising Verres in a public capacity, because those were his instructions, but then that he had not put these things up for sale and, if he had his choice, he could never have been induced to sell objects in a shrine that had been left to him, passed down by his ancestors.

[17] Don't just sit there, Verres. What are you waiting for? Why do you say there's a vast conspiracy to crush you by Centuripae, Catina, Halaesus, Tyndaris, Henna, Agyrium, and the other cities of Sicily? Your second homeland, as you used to call it, Messana, has conspired against you: your Messana, I repeat, the city that was your accomplice in crime, the witness of your lust, the receiver of your stolen goods. Here's the most substantial man in the city, sent as an envoy from home for this trial, the leader of the delegation sent to praise you. He praises you in public—because he was ordered and instructed to do so. But when he was asked about the cargo ship,[24] you remember his answer—that it was built by public workers under public compulsion and that a Mamertine senator was publicly in charge of building it. Heius came to you in private, members of the jury, to seek refuge; he makes use of the law under which this court is established, a fortress to protect all our allies. And even though the law concerns the recovery of stolen money, he says he isn't trying to recover money; although it was stolen, he doesn't really want it. It's the sacred objects of his ancestors he wants to recover, his ancestral gods he demands back from you. [18] Have you no sense of decency,

---

24. See below, sec. 19. The cargo ship the Mamertines built for Verres is more fully discussed at *Verr.* 5.44–48.

Verres? No scruples, no fears? You took up residence in Heius' home in Messana and saw him perform religious observances before those gods in his shrine almost every day. Money doesn't matter to him and he isn't even looking for the objects that were ornamental. Keep the Canephoroe; give back the statues of the gods. And since he said this, and since in the time allotted he made his complaint before the judges in a measured fashion as an ally and friend of the Roman people, and since he remained true to his religious beliefs not only in seeking to recover his ancestral gods but also in giving evidence under oath, you should know that one of the members of the embassy was sent by Verres back to Messana—the one who was in public charge of building his ship—to ask the senate to deprive Heius of his civic rights.

[19] What kind of lunatic has ideas like that? Did you think you'd get anywhere? Didn't you know how much his fellow citizens valued Heius, how much respect they had for his authority? But suppose you had gotten what you wanted, suppose the Mamertines voted some serious penalty against Heius; how much authority do you think their praise for you would have if they punished the one man who obviously gave true witness? And what sort of testimonial is it anyway, when the person giving it has to damage your case under questioning? In fact, aren't the men who bring praise for you witnesses for me? Heius gives a testimonial, and he's seriously damaged you. I'll call the others—they'll be happy to keep quiet about what they can, but even if they don't want to they'll say what they must. Are these friends of yours going to deny that a huge cargo ship was built at Messana? Let them deny it, if they can. Are they going to deny that a senator of Messana was publicly put in charge of building the ship? If only they could deny it! And there's more, but I prefer to keep it all in reserve, to give them as little time as possible to plan and organize their perjury. [20] Is this how praise of you is supposed to go? Will the influence of these men help you out? Even if they could help you, they shouldn't; even if they wanted to, they couldn't. In private, you heaped on them a heavy load of injury and insult; in their city you brought permanent disgrace on many entire families through your sexual assaults. "But there were public benefits." Not without a huge cost to our country and to the province of Sicily. The Mamertines were obligated to buy 60,000 bushels of grain and give them to the Roman people, and they did so; by you alone was the obligation

remitted.[25] Our country was harmed because you diminished our imperial rights for this one city; the Sicilians were harmed because this amount was not deducted from the total obligation of grain but passed on to the people of Centuripae and Halaesa, exempt cities,[26] and this additional imposition was more than they could bear.

[21] The treaty required you to demand a ship from Messana. You remitted the obligation for three years; for all those years, you never demanded a single soldier. You acted the way pirates do: even though they're enemies of all humankind, they still select some friends whom they not only spare but also make rich with plunder. They choose in particular people who live in the right place for ships to land. Publius Servilius captured the famous city of Phaselis.[27] In the past, it was not the city of Cilician pirates; the Lycians, a Greek people, lived there. But its location and its being on a promontory often made pirates setting sail from Cilicia land there, and the same was true on the return trip. As a result, the pirates annexed the city for themselves; first they traded with one another, then they became partners. [22] Before Verres, the city of Messana was not evil; in fact, it was hostile to criminals, and it sequestered the property of Gaius Cato, the former consul.[28] And what a man he was! Very well known and very powerful; but despite his having been consul, he was condemned. Gaius Cato was the grandson of two men of great fame, Lucius Paullus and Marcus Cato,

---

25. Verres' extortionate manipulation of the required contributions of grain (crucial to the Roman food supply) is discussed in detail in *Verr.* 3.

26. The various cities of Sicily (and of other provinces, for that matter) had different formal relationships with Rome. In this case, Centuripae and Halaesa were "free" cities and exempt from the grain tax, while Messana (like most Sicilian cities) had obligations to supply both grain and military contributions.

27. Publius Servilius Vatia Isauricus, proconsul in Cilicia from 78 to 75 and a member of the jury in this case. The southern coast of Asia Minor was a stronghold of pirates from the second century until their extermination by Pompey in 67. For the geography, see Map 2.

28. There are some doubts about the text of the passage about Cato, which is both repetitive and obscure. It is unclear what Cato did in Messana, or why he was there, and this event is otherwise unknown. Cato was consul in 114 and was involved in several disreputable incidents; the penalty described here was for extortion from the province of Macedonia, which he governed after his consulship.

and the son of Publius Africanus' sister; when he was condemned, in the days when verdicts were harsh, the damages were assessed at 8,000 sesterces.[29] The people of Messana were angry at him, but they've often ordered a dinner for Timarchides that cost more than the damages against Cato.[30] [23] But Messana was a Phaselis for this Sicilian pirate; this is where everything was brought and kept. They kept hidden the things that needed to be concealed; they loaded contraband for him and smuggled it out. And, not least, he had them build a huge ship for him to send to Italy with what he'd stolen, and in return he gave them remission of all expenses, of required labor, military service, and everything else. For three years they were the only people, not only in Sicily, but at this time, as far as I can see, the only people in the whole world who were free and clear, released and excused from all expenses, all troubles, all obligations. [24] This is where the Festival of Verres was created, the banquet where he ordered Sextus Cominius to be dragged in: he tried to hit him by throwing a cup with his own hand, and ordered him to be dragged by the throat from the party and locked up in chains in a dungeon.[31] This is where that cross was placed, the cross on which he hung a Roman citizen in the presence of a crowd, a cross he didn't dare erect anywhere other than among the people with whom he shared all his crimes and thefts.[32]

---

29. A tiny amount. Cicero's point is that even minor infractions were severely punished in the good old days. The damages in Verres' case were assessed at 40 million sesterces. Cato's grandfathers were Lucius Aemilius Paullus and Marcus Porcius Cato the Censor (see Biographical Index); his mother Aemilia was the biological sister of Publius Cornelius Scipio Aemilianus Africanus. Throughout the speech, Cicero refers to him as Africanus to emphasize his military rather than his cultural importance; in modern accounts he is normally called Scipio Aemilianus.

30. Timarchides is one of Verres' freedmen; a fuller account of him appears at *Verr.* 2.134–36.

31. The Festival of Verres (*Verria*) was Verres' substitute for the traditional festival in honor of Marcus Claudius Marcellus, the conqueror of Syracuse in 212 BCE. The *Verria* appear again in the last section (151) of this book and were discussed (and contrasted with the *Marcellia*) at 2.52, 114, and 154. The story of Cominius is otherwise unknown.

32. The crucifixion of the Roman citizen Publius Gavius (punctuated by the victim's refrain "I am a Roman citizen") is Verres' ultimate outrage and is treated with high pathos at the very end of the Verrines, 5.158–71.

So you're coming to sing someone's praises? On what authority? Is it the influence you ought to have with the senate or with the Roman people? **[25]** What city is there, not just in our provinces but even at the ends of the earth, that is so powerful, so independent, or so horrendously barbarous, or what king is there, who would not welcome a senator of the Roman people into his house and home? Such an honor applies not just to the man but above all to the Roman people, by whose good will we've become members of this order, and secondly to the authority of the order. If this isn't taken very seriously by our allies and by foreign nations, what will happen to the name and standing of our empire? The people of Messana did not issue a public invitation to me. And when I say "me," that's minor, but if they failed to issue an invitation to a senator of the Roman people, then they diminished an honor owed not to the person but to the order. Cicero the individual was welcomed at the wealthy and splendid home of Gnaeus Pompeius Basiliscus; even if you had issued a public invitation, I would have stayed there anyway. There was also the house of the Percennii, now also named Pompeius. It's a very honorable home, and my cousin Lucius received their warm welcome and stayed there.[33] But as far as you were concerned, a senator of the Roman people spent the night in your town in the public street. No other city has ever done this. "But you were prosecuting our friend." Are you going to take my private concerns as an excuse for diminishing the honor of the senate? **[26]** But if it ever comes up in the senate—the order that you alone have treated with contempt— I'll voice my complaints then. And how brazen must you be to show yourselves in the sight of the Roman people? Before you came to Rome, before you came into this assembly, did you rip out that cross, which still now reeks with the blood of a Roman citizen, which is set up at the harbor of your city, did you hurl it into the sea, and did you purify the entire place? In the soil of Messana, an allied and friendly city, there is a monument to Verres' cruelty. Was your city chosen so that when people came from Italy they would see the cross that held a Roman citizen before they saw any friend of the Roman people? You like to display it to the people of Regium (a city you envied) and

---

33. Both Basiliscus and the Percennii received Roman citizenship through the agency of Pompey; Basiliscus, as was customary, took the first two names of his patron. Lucius Tullius Cicero was Cicero's first cousin and assisted him in this case.

to the Roman citizens that live among you, so they will think less of themselves and despise you less, when they see the rights of citizenship have been sacrificed with such torture.

[27] But, Verres, you say you bought these works. What about those "draperies of Attalus" woven with gold,[34] renowned throughout Sicily—did you forget to "buy" them from Heius? You could have done it the same way as with the statues. What happened? Were you worried about wasting paper? But this lunatic never thought about it; he thought what he stole from the cupboard would be less obvious than what he stole from the chapel. And what about the way he stole it? I can't speak more plainly than Heius himself spoke to you. When I asked whether any other property of his had reached Verres, he answered that Verres had sent a message that he was to send the draperies to him at Agrigentum. I asked if he'd sent them; he answered as he had to, that he obeyed the praetor and sent them. I asked if they made it to Agrigentum; he said they had. I asked how they had come back to him; he said they hadn't yet. Everyone laughed; you were all astonished. [28] Didn't it occur to you to give instructions to record that he sold them to you for 6,500 sesterces? Were you afraid your debts would grow if you had an obligation of 6,500 for something you could easily sell for 200,000? Believe me, it would have been worth it. You would have a defense, nobody would ask the price; if you could have said you bought them, you could easily have made your case about what happened. But now you have no way to untangle yourself from those draperies.

[29] Next there's Phylarchus of Centuripae. He's a rich aristocrat, who owned harness ornaments of exquisite workmanship, said to have belonged to King Hiero.[35] Did you steal them or buy them? When I was in Sicily, what I heard from the people of Centuripae, as from others—it wasn't exactly hidden—was that you'd stolen the ornaments from Phylarchus of Centuripae just as you'd stolen equally fine ones from Aristus of Panormus and a third set from Cratippus of Tyndaris. And in fact, if Phylarchus had sold them, you wouldn't

---

34. The invention of weaving with gold thread was ascribed to Attalus, king of Pergamum (which Attalus is unclear); these materials were used as coverings for banquet couches.

35. *Phalerae* were disks of precious metal (often decorated) attached to the harness of cavalry horses. Hiero II (Hieron in Greek) ruled Syracuse from 270 to 216 BCE.

have promised (after you were accused) to return them. Since you saw that a lot of people knew about it, you thought that if you returned them to him, you would have less but the affair would be no less well known. So you didn't return them. Phylarchus said in evidence that because he knew about this illness of yours—to use your friends' word—he wanted to hide the ornaments from you. When he was summoned by you, he said he didn't have them, and that he'd put them in safe keeping with someone else so they wouldn't be found. But you were so clever that you used that person to spy out where they were kept, and once he was caught he couldn't deny it. So the ornaments were taken from him for free, against his will.

[30] At this point, members of the jury, it's worth understanding Verres' usual method for sniffing out and inspecting all these objects. Tlepolemus and Hiero are two brothers from Cibyra;[36] I think one of them did modeling in wax, and the other was a painter. When the citizens of Cibyra suspected them of having looted the temple of Apollo, I think they were afraid of being prosecuted, convicted, and punished, so they went into exile. They knew Verres was a lover of their kind of workmanship, and when Verres, as you learned from witnesses, came to Cibyra with phony letters of credit, they presented themselves to him as exiles from their home when he was still in Asia. He kept them with him at this period and made extensive use of their advice and assistance in the theft and plunder that marked his service as legate. [31] They are the men Quintus Tadius mentions in his accounts, that he gave money "to the Greek painters" at Verres' orders. They were already well known and well tested when he took them to Sicily with him. And once they got there, they were amazing at sniffing out everything—you could call them hunting dogs—and made a thorough search to discover where everything was in any way they could. They found one thing by threats, another by promises, one thing through people's slaves, another through their children, one thing through a friend, another through an enemy. And whatever they liked, the owner had to lose. When people's silver was requisitioned, they prayed for nothing except that Hiero and Tlepolemus not like it.

[32] What I'm about to tell you is true, members of the jury. I remember Pamphilus of Lilybaeum, my friend and host, telling me

---

36. In Phrygia. Tlepolemus was (or claimed to be) a Roman citizen, called Cornelius Tlepolemus (3.69).

that when Verres had used his powerful position to take from him a hydria made by Boethus[37]—a fine piece of work, and very heavy—he went home very unhappy and upset that such a vase, which he had inherited from his father and his ancestors and which he regularly used on religious occasions and for the arrival of friends, had been stolen from him. "As I was sitting at home in sadness," he said, "one of the temple slaves of Venus came running up:[38] he ordered me to bring my figured drinking cups to the praetor right away.[39] I was very upset," he said. "I had a pair; I ordered both to be brought out, to avoid anything else bad happening, and to be brought with me to the praetor's house. When I got there, the praetor was resting, but the brothers from Cibyra were there, strolling about. When they saw me they asked, 'Where are the cups, Pamphilus?' I sadly displayed them, and they praised them. I began to complain that I would have nothing left of any value if the cups were stolen, too. And when they saw me being very distressed, they asked: 'What's it worth to you not to have them taken?' To make a long story short, they asked me," he said, "for 1,000 sesterces, and I agreed to pay it. Meanwhile, the praetor called out, and demanded the cups." And they then began to tell the praetor that they had thought what they heard was true, that Pamphilus had some valuable cups, but in fact they were junk, not worthy of being in Verres' collection. And Verres agreed. So Pamphilus took his superb cups home.

[33] I knew it was no big deal to understand this stuff, but before this I used to be amazed that Verres had any sense about such things, since I knew that otherwise he bore no resemblance to a human being. But then I understood for the first time that that was the purpose of the boys from Cibyra, that he would steal with his own hands but would see through their eyes. He so wanted this great reputation of being thought an expert on such matters that not long ago—look at how crazy he is—after the first hearing was adjourned, when Verres was already as good as convicted and dead, on the morning of the circus games, when he was at the house of

---

37. A silver water jug. Boethus of Chalcedon (late third century?) was famous for his work in silver.

38. The temple slaves of Venus of Eryx were used by Verres as if they were his own.

39. *Scyphos sigillatos:* drinking vessels with figures in relief.

Lucius Sisenna,[40] a fine man, when the dinner couches had been set out and the silver was displayed throughout the house, when the house was packed with men of distinction, in accord with Sisenna's position, Verres went up to the silver and began to study every piece of it carefully and calmly.[41] Everyone was amazed at how stupid he was. Some people thought he was just plain dumb in the middle of his trial to be increasing everyone's suspicion that he was as greedy as he was accused of being. Others thought he was crazy, that after the first hearing had been adjourned, when a crowd of witnesses had already spoken against him, he still had any interest in such things. I'm sure that Sisenna's slaves (who had heard the testimony given against him) never blinked while they were watching Verres, and their fingers never let go of the silver. **[34]** A good judge can use the evidence of small things to draw a conclusion about anyone's greed or self-restraint. This defendant, a defendant after the adjournment of his trial, when in fact and in common opinion he was as good as convicted, in a large gathering couldn't keep himself from fondling and examining Sisenna's silver. Does anyone think when he was praetor in his province he could keep his greed or his hands off the Sicilians' silver?

[35] But my speech has moved away from Lilybaeum, and it's time to return. There's a man named Diocles, called Popilius, the son-in-law of the Pamphilus from whom the hydria was stolen.[42] Verres stole every piece of silver that was set out on his sideboard. He can say he bought them, and in fact I think it was because the theft was so huge that there was a receipt. He ordered Timarchides to give an estimate for the value of the silver, understating it as people do for gifts to actors.[43] But I suppose I've been off the track for some time, spending so long talking about your purchases and asking whether or not you bought them, how, and for how much; I can get through all that in one word. Tell me in writing what silver you acquired in Sicily, where each item came from, and what you paid for it. **[36]** Is there a

---

40. Lucius Cornelius Sisenna, a supporter of Sulla, praetor in 78, possibly governor of Sicily in 77, and one of Verres' advocates in this trial.

41. It is not clear whether the anecdote is true; Verres went into voluntary exile after the first hearing.

42. Diocles is using the Roman name Popilius as a cognomen; he is clearly not a citizen.

43. There were strict limits on the value of the gilded wreaths given to performers that could only be evaded by false understatements of worth.

problem? I shouldn't have to ask you for a statement; I should already have your accounts and be displaying them. But you say you kept no accounts for the last few years. Write down what I'm asking about the silver, and we'll see about the rest later. "I don't have it in writing and I can't produce it." So what will happen? What do you think the jury will make of it? Even before you were praetor your house was full of beautiful statues, there were a lot on display at your country houses, many were in safe keeping with your friends, many were given away to others; but your accounts show no record of any purchase. All the silver was carried off from Sicily, and nobody there has anything left he wants to call his own. Verres invents an immoral defense, that as praetor he bought all that silver—but there's no proof to be had in his accounts. If the accounts you produce have no record of how you possess the things you possess, and you produce no accounts at all for the period when you yourself say you bought most of these things, isn't it inevitable that you be proven guilty by both the accounts you produce and those you don't produce?

[37] Marcus Coelius is a Roman knight, a fine young man;[44] from him you stole what you wanted at Lilybaeum. Gaius Cacurius is energetic, industrious, and very engaging: you didn't think twice about stealing all his furniture. Quintus Lutatius Diodorus, who was made a Roman citizen by Sulla through the favor of Quintus Catulus[45]—with the full knowledge of everyone at Lilybaeum, you stole a huge and very beautiful table of citrus-wood from him. I don't criticize your having robbed and cheated of all his fine silver a man whose character matches yours, Apollonius, the son of Nicon of Drepanum, now known as Aulus Clodius; I'll keep quiet about that. In fact he doesn't think any outrage was committed against him, because you rescued the awful man as he was putting his neck in a noose, when you split with him the inherited property he had stolen from the orphans of Drepanum.[46] I'm even glad that you stole from him; it's the best thing you ever did. On the other hand, you certainly shouldn't have stolen the statue of Apollo from Lyson of Lilybaeum, one of the leading citizens at whose home you stayed. You'll say you

---

44. The name is possibly to be corrected to Cloelius.

45. Quintus Lutatius Catulus, consul in 78 and a judge in this case.

46. In fact, only one orphan (*Verr.* 2.140); Verres' successor, Lucius Caecilius Metellus, made Clodius (there called Claudius) give it back.

bought it. You bet, for 1,000 sesterces. "To the best of my recollection." I know it, I tell you. "I'll produce written evidence." Still, you
shouldn't have done it. From Heius the orphan (Gaius Marcellus is
his guardian)[47] you grabbed a huge amount of cash; are you going
to say that his cups decorated with figures[48] at Lilybaeum were purchased or will you admit they were purloined?

[38] But what's the point of collecting his minor outrages? They
concern only his thefts and the losses of the people he stole from.
Members of the jury, please attend to an incident that lets you see not
just his greed but also his utter insanity and madness.

Diodorus has already given evidence before you; he comes from
Malta and has lived at Lilybaeum for many years. He's a member
of the aristocracy in Malta, and he's eminent and influential where
he lives because of his character. Verres was told he had some fine
examples of relief work, including some cups called Thericlean,
very skillfully made by Mentor.[49] As soon as Verres heard this, the
flames of desire, both to see and to steal, so consumed him that he
summoned Diodorus. Diodorus, who wasn't sorry he owned these
objects, answered that he didn't have them in Lilybaeum but had left
them in Malta with a relative. [39] Instantly, Verres sent trusty men
to Malta and wrote to some people there to seek out these objects;
he asked Diodorus to write to his relative; it seemed an eternity to
him until he could see the silver. Diodorus, a thrifty and careful man
who wanted to hang onto his own possessions, wrote to his relative to
tell the men sent by Verres that he had sent the silver to Lilybaeum
a few days past.

Meanwhile, Diodorus beat a retreat: he preferred to spend some
time away from home rather than stay home and lose this very fine
silver. But when Verres heard this, he was so upset that nobody had
any doubt he'd gone completely mad with rage. Because he couldn't

---

47. Gaius Claudius Marcellus, governor of Sicily in 79, and a judge in this
case. On the use of his statue to torture Sopater of Tyndaris, see secs. 86–87
below.

48. *Emblemata* (also *sigilla*) were high-relief figures made separately and
attached to cups.

49. Mentor (fourth century BCE) was renowned for his work in metal; the
origin of the name Thericlean was disputed in antiquity. These cups may
have been forgeries (as much of the metalwork ascribed to Mentor in antiquity was), but neither Verres nor Cicero is aware of that.

himself snatch the silver from Diodorus, he said this fine silver had been snatched from him; he threatened Diodorus in his absence, he shouted, and he even sometimes wept. We know about Eriphyle from plays; when she saw a necklace—which I suppose was made from gold and jewels—she was so inflamed by its beauty that she betrayed her husband's life.[50] Verres' greed was like that, and all the more fiercely insane because she lusted after what she'd seen, while Verres' lust was aroused not just by what he saw but even by what he heard. **[40]** He gave orders for Diodorus to be hunted throughout the province; but Diodorus had already packed up his household and moved away.

Verres wanted somehow to get him back to his province, and so he thought up this plan—if you can call it a plan rather than the ravings of a disordered mind. He got one of his bloodhounds to say that he wanted to accuse Diodorus of Malta of a capital crime. At first, everyone was surprised to see Diodorus as a defendant. He was a very retiring man, a completely improbable suspect for the smallest infraction, let alone a major crime. Then it became clear that all this was happening because of the silver. Verres didn't think twice about ordering Diodorus' name to be put down for trial; it was, I believe, the first time he started proceedings against a man who wasn't there. **[41]** It was well known throughout Sicily that greed for engraved silver was bringing men to trial on capital charges, and not only bringing them to trial but also trying them in absentia. Diodorus was at Rome; he put on the soiled garb of a defendant and ran around to his patrons and friends telling the story. Verres' father sent him an angry letter, and so did his friends: he should be careful about what he did to Diodorus and how far he let things go; the story was widely known, and hateful, that Verres was out of his mind and would be done in by this case if he didn't look out. Verres still thought of his father as a fellow human being, if not as a parent, and he was not yet fully prepared to take the case to trial. It was his first year in the province and he was not, as in the case of Sthenius,[51] already stuffed with cash. And

---

50. Eriphyle was bribed by a necklace (of divine workmanship, to be sure) to reveal the hiding place of her husband Amphiaraus, who was fated to die (and did) in the war of the Seven against Thebes. Their son Alcmaeon killed her in revenge.

51. The story of Sthenius is at *Verr.* 2.82–118; he was tried and convicted in absentia by Verres, the year after the case of Diodorus. Verres' father failed to influence him toward sense (or mercy) at 2.97–100.

so he kept a rein on his lunacy for a while—not from shame but from fear. He didn't dare condemn Diodorus in absentia, and so he took his name off the list of defendants. Meanwhile Diodorus, while Verres was praetor, had to stay away from his province and his home for nearly three years. **[42]** Everyone else, not just Sicilians but Roman citizens, too, had reached the conclusion that since Verres was so far gone in his greed, there was nothing anyone should expect to keep safe at home, if it was at all pleasing to Verres. But after they learned that although the province was yearning for the arrival of Quintus Arrius (a brave man), he wasn't going to take over from Verres, they concluded they could have nothing so locked up or hidden that wouldn't be completely open and accessible to Verres' greed.[52]

Next comes Gnaeus Calidius, a Roman knight of substance and standing, whose son is a Roman senator and judge. Verres knew that, but he still stole the fine silver drinking horns[53] that had belonged to Quintus Maximus. **[43]** I'm sorry, members of the jury, I wasn't thinking. He didn't steal them, he bought them. I'm sorry I said it; he'll boast and prance around on those drinking horns. "I bought them, I paid ready money." You bet. "Bring out the account books." It's worth it: give me the accounts. You can explain away this charge concerning Calidius, so long as I can see the accounts. But still, why did Calidius complain at Rome that in all his years doing business in Sicily, you were the only one who treated him badly, that he was so dishonored that he was robbed along with the rest of the people of Sicily, if in fact you had bought them? Why did he say he would try to recover the silver from you, if he had willingly sold it to you? But how could you not return them to Calidius, particularly seeing that he is such a good friend of your advocate Lucius Sisenna and seeing that you returned things to all Sisenna's other friends? **[44]** I don't suppose you'll deny that you returned his silver to Lucius Curidius, a respectable man, but of no higher standing than Calidius, through your friend Potamo.[54] In fact, Curidius made everyone else's case with you harder. Even though you'd acknowledged you would return

---

52. Quintus Arrius (praetor in 73) was supposed to replace Verres in Sicily in 72, but became involved in the war with Spartacus, where he died.

53. *Eculeus* is a drinking horn ending with the figure of an animal head. The metaphor of riding in the next sentence suggests that these had horses' heads. Which Quintus Fabius Maximus is meant is unclear.

54. Lucius Papirius Potamo, Verres' scribe.

their property to a number of people, once Curidius gave formal evidence that you had in fact returned his property to him, you stopped returning things, because it dawned on you that, even if the plunder slipped out of your grasp, you still couldn't avoid the testimony. As far as every other praetor was concerned, Gnaeus Calidius, a Roman knight, was welcome to his finely crafted silver; he was welcome, whenever he invited a magistrate or some other higher-up, to use his private resources to make his banquet grand and elegant. Many people who had authority and military power came to Calidius' house, but none was lunatic enough to steal such famous and noble silver; there was nobody brazen enough to demand it, nobody shameless enough to insist that he sell it. [45] It is tyrannical, members of the jury, it is unacceptable for a praetor in his province to say to a man of standing, wealth, and substance, "Sell me your engraved silver." That's the same as saying, "You don't deserve to have such fine work, but I do." You're more deserving than Calidius, Verres? I won't draw comparisons between your life and your reputation and his—there isn't any comparison. But I can compare the area where you think yourself better than him. Because you gave 300,000 sesterces to bagmen so you could be elected praetor, and 300,000 more to keep a potential prosecutor from making trouble,[55] is that a reason for you to scorn and despise the equestrian order? Is that a reason for you to believe that Calidius doesn't deserve to have something that appeals to you?

[46] Verres has been puffing himself up about Calidius for a long time; he tells everyone he bought the silver. But what about Lucius Papinius, a leading citizen, a wealthy and honorable Roman knight? You didn't pay for his incense burner, did you? He stated in evidence that you demanded to see it and returned it to him with the attached figures ripped off. That shows you that our Verres has intelligence, not greed, that he lusted after the workmanship, not the silver. And it's not just in the case of Papinius that he showed such forbearance—that's how he behaved with every incense burner in Sicily. It's unbelievable how many there were, and how beautiful they were. In the days when Sicily was flourishing and wealthy, I think there was a great deal of fine workmanship on that island. Before Verres was praetor, there wasn't a single home of even moderate wealth that didn't have such things, even if there was no other silver: a large

---

55. Money paid (unsuccessfully) to keep Cicero from being elected aedile.

platter with relief figures of the gods, a libation bowl for women to use in religious rituals, an incense burner. And these were all old, all of outstanding workmanship. That leads me to suspect that at one time the Sicilians had an equivalent amount of other silver objects, but that fortune had taken away a lot, while the objects important for religion stayed behind. **[47]** I said, members of the jury, that there were many, and they were in almost every Sicilian home; I now state that there's not a single one left. What's going on? What is this monstrosity, this deformity that we have sent into a province? Doesn't it look to you as if he was trying to satisfy not just one person's desire, not just his own eyes, but every lunacy of every insanely greedy person when he got back to Rome? The minute he reached any town, the hounds from Cibyra[56] were instantly let loose to sniff out and find everything. If there was any large game, any grand vessel, to discover, they happily brought it to Verres; if they couldn't hunt out anything of that kind, they went after the small fry as if they were tasty little bunnies—platters, bowls, incense burners. And can you imagine the wailing and mourning of the women over such things? It may seem a small thing to you, but it stirs up a big and bitter pain, particularly for women, when someone snatches out of their hands the vessels they've been using for divine sacrifice, which they've inherited from their relatives, which have always been in their families.

[48] Now don't expect me to go through these charges retail, like a door-to-door salesman—that he stole a bowl from Aeschylus of Tyndaris, a platter from Thrason, who was also from Tyndaris, an incense burner from Nymphodorus of Agrigentum. I'll give you Sicilian witnesses, and he can pick anyone he wants me to ask about platters and bowls and incense burners. And it's not just that no town was untouched—there's no house of any substance that escaped his assault. As soon as he came to a dinner party, members of the jury, if he saw any engraved metalwork, he couldn't keep his hands off it. Gnaeus Pompeius (formerly Philo) comes from Tyndaris. He gave Verres a banquet at his villa in the territory of Tyndaris, and he did what Sicilians didn't dare do. Because he was a Roman citizen, he thought he could get away with it. He put a platter that had fine seals on it in front of Verres. As soon as Verres saw it, he had no qualms about lifting from the table of hospitality the particular possession of the gods of house and hospitality; but still, as I said before about

---

56. See note 36 above.

his self-restraint, after he had ripped off the figures he abstemiously returned the rest of the silver. **[49]** And then there's Eupolemus of Calacte, a noble of his city, the host and close friend of the Luculli, a man who is now with Lucius Lucullus' army.[57] Didn't Verres do the same thing to him? He had dinner at Eupolemus' house; Eupolemus put out undecorated silver to avoid being left completely without decorations himself. He did put out two cups, small but with attached figures. And Verres, like a party entertainer who doesn't want to leave the banquet without his wreath, had the figures ripped off while the dinner guests watched.

I'm not trying to list everything Verres did. There's no need and it's completely impossible. I'm just bringing up for you typical examples of each variety of his wickedness. He didn't behave in these matters as if he would someday have to give a reckoning, but as if he would never be brought to court—or that the more he stole, the less danger he was in of conviction. The things I'm reporting he did neither in secret, nor through his friends and agents, but openly, using the public power and authority of his position.

[50] Verres had come to Catina, a rich, respectable, prosperous town. He had Dionysiarchus the Speaker (that's the chief magistrate there) summoned.[58] He openly ordered him to see that all the silver that anyone had in Catina was gathered up and brought to him. And didn't you hear the testimony under oath of Phylarchus of Centuripae, the first citizen of his town in birth, character, and wealth? He swore that Verres gave him orders to gather up all the silver from the people of Centuripae—the grandest and richest city of all Sicily—and bring it to him? The same pattern at Agyrium: all the Corinthian vessels, by Verres' orders, were sent to Syracuse by Apollodorus, whose testimony you have heard.

[51] But the best story of all is this: when our hardworking and careful praetor came to Haluntium, he didn't want to go into the town itself because it involved a steep and difficult climb. So he ordered Archagathus of Haluntium, a man who is the most noble not only in his own town but in all Sicily, to appear before him. He instructed him that whatever engraved silver or Corinthian vessels there were in Haluntium should all be brought down to the seashore

---

57. In the Third Mithridatic War; see *In Support of Manilius' Law*.

58. The title is *Proagorus*, used only in *Verr.* 4: it presumably indicates the officer presiding over the assembly and the senate.

from the town as soon as possible. Archagathus went up into his town. This noble man, who wanted to be held in esteem and affection by his fellow citizens, was very distressed that Verres had given him this responsibility, but he had no idea what to do. He announced the orders he'd received; he ordered everyone to bring out what they had. Everyone was terrified. The tyrant was not far away; he was lying in his litter near the seashore below the town and waiting for Archagathus and the silver. [52] Can you imagine the crowd in the town, the shouting, the wailing of women? Anyone watching would say that a Trojan Horse had been brought in and the city captured. Vessels were brought out without their cases; some were wrenched from the hands of the women; people's doors were broken down and their storerooms broken open. What would you expect? If there's a war or an invasion, shields are requisitioned from private citizens; even though they know it's for the common safety, men are still reluctant. So you shouldn't think that people didn't experience great suffering in bringing out their engraved silver from their homes for someone else to tear from their hands. Everything was carried down. The Cibyra brothers were called. They rejected a little; from the things they approved of, the bands of relief decoration or the attached figures were ripped off. And so the people of Haluntium had the objects of their delight torn from them, and they went home with their silver plain.

[53] Has any province ever been swept out like this, members of the jury?[59] It was common enough to divert something from the public funds in secret, with the help of a local magistrate, and when they sometimes stole something from a private citizen in secret, they were still condemned. If you ask (to be modest about my own accomplishments), I think the real prosecutors were people who hunted out by scent or by faint tracks the thefts of men like this. As for me, what is there to do in the case of Verres? I found him from tracks he made by rolling his whole boar-body in the mud. It's a really big job to prosecute someone who has his litter put down for a little while, doesn't use trickery but gives a single order from a position of power, and just in passing rips off an entire town house by house. But at least he wanted to be able to say he bought everything, and so he gave orders to Archagathus to give a few coins for the sake of appearances to the people whose silver it had once been. Archagathus found a few people

---

59. Puns on Verres' name: "swept out" is *everriculum*, and *verres* is a boar.

who were willing to take it, and he gave them the money—but Verres never paid Archagathus back. Archagathus wanted to make a claim against him at Rome, but Gnaeus Lentulus Marcellinus convinced him not to, as you have heard him say. Read the testimony [EVIDENCE OF ARCHAGATHUS AND LENTULUS].[60]

[54] You shouldn't think Verres wanted to heap up such a huge pile of ornaments without good reason: pay attention to how much he cared about you, about the opinion of the Roman people, about the laws and the courts, and about these witnesses from Sicily. After he had gathered such a vast quantity of ornaments that nobody had a single one left, he set up a huge workshop in the palace.[61] He commanded every craftsman to assemble, the engravers and the silversmiths, and he had quite a few of his own. He shut them in, this whole crowd of men. For eight straight months they worked continuously, making only vessels from gold. Then all the ornaments he had ripped from platters and incense burners he had so cleverly riveted to gold cups, so neatly soldered to gold vessels, that you'd say they were born for it. And the praetor, who says that peace reigned in Sicily because of his vigilance, spent most of the day sitting in the workshop, wearing a dingy tunic and a Greek cloak.

[55] I wouldn't dare bring all this up, members of the jury, if I weren't afraid that you could say you heard more about him from other people's gossip than from me in court. Who hasn't heard about his workshop, the gold vases, Verres' Greek cloak? Pick any solid citizen among the Romans living in Syracuse, and I'll bring him forward. There's nobody who won't say he heard about it or saw it. [56] What's happened to our morals? I'm not going to mention something ancient; quite a few of you knew Lucius Piso, the father of the Lucius Piso here who was praetor.[62] When he was praetor in Spain (where he was killed), somehow, while he was doing military exercises, his gold ring was broken in pieces. He wanted to have a

---

60. As in a few other places (see *Cael.* 19), Cicero omits in the published version some of the technical evidence. The oddity here is that this speech was never given, hence there was no oral version to include the section that he here marks as omitted.

61. The former palace of the kings of Sicily was used to house the Roman governor.

62. The elder Lucius Calpurnius Piso Frugi governed Spain in 113 or 112; his son was praetor at the same time as Verres in 74.

ring made, so he ordered a goldsmith to be called to his tribunal in the forum at Corduba and weighed out the gold in public; he ordered the man to put his bench in the forum and make the ring in front of everybody. Someone might say he was too scrupulous, but that's the only thing that can be criticized. But it made sense for him: he was the son of the Lucius Piso who carried the first law against provincial extortion.[63] **[57]** It's a joke for me now to speak about Verres after talking about Piso Frugi, but pay attention to the difference between them. Verres made enough gold vessels for a great many sideboards, and he didn't care what people would say about him, not just in Sicily but in a Roman court as well; Piso, in the matter of a half-ounce of gold, wanted all Spain to know where the praetor's ring came from. So just as Verres proved the truth of his family name, so Piso proved the truth of his cognomen.[64]

There's no way for me to remember or to report all Verres' actions, but I want briefly to touch on the broad categories, as Piso's ring has just now reminded me of what had completely slipped from my mind. How many rings do you think Verres stole from the fingers of respectable men? He never hesitated, whenever he was attracted by someone's precious stone or ring. I'll tell you something unbelievable, but so well known I don't think Verres himself will deny it. **[58]** When a letter was brought to Verres' interpreter Valentius from Agrigentum, Verres happened to notice the seal pressed in the clay. He liked it; he asked where the letter came from; Valentius answered, "From Agrigentum."[65] Verres sent letters to the usual suspects to have the ring brought to him as soon as possible. As a result, Lucius Titius, a Roman citizen and the head of a family, had his ring pulled from his finger.

Here's another story of Verres' unbelievable greed. Even if he wanted to have thirty dining couches for every dining room in all his houses at Rome and elsewhere, and to have them all beautifully covered to go with all the other fittings of a banquet, he would still seem to have collected too many; there was no prosperous home in Sicily where he didn't set up a tapestry studio. **[59]** There's a very rich and noble lady at Segesta named Lamia; she had her house filled

---

63. The Calpurnian law of 149 BCE.
64. Verres presumably as a pig; Piso's cognomen Frugi meant "thrifty."
65. Aulus Valentius was Verres' translator and accomplice.

with looms for three years making coverings for him, everything dyed with purple. And then there's Attalus, a rich man at Netum, Lyson at Lilybaeum, Critolaus at Aetna, Aeschrion, Cleomenes, and Theomnastus in Syracuse, Archonidas at Helorus—I'll run out of daylight before I run out of names. "Verres supplied the purple himself, his friends just supplied the labor." Yes, indeed; but I'm not going to make all the charges I could. As if it weren't enough for a charge that he had so much purple to give, that he wanted to export so much, and finally, what he admits, that he used his friends' slaves in work of this kind. **[60]** Did anyone make couches sheathed in bronze or brass candlesticks for anyone except Verres for three years at Syracuse? "He bought them." Sure he did. But I'm only letting you know, members of the jury, what he did as praetor in his province, so that nobody should think he was too easygoing, or that, since he had the power, he paid inadequate attention to equipping and supplying himself.

My next topic is not theft, not greed, not desire, but a crime in which every evil quality is rolled up in one: the everlasting gods were violated, the reputation and the authority of the name of the Roman people were diminished, the laws of hospitality were battered and betrayed, all the kings who were most loyal to us were alienated by his crime, together with the nations under their royal control. **[61]** You know that the royal princes of Syria, the sons of King Antiochus, were recently in Rome. Their mission was not about the kingdom of Syria, which was undoubtedly theirs, inherited from their father and their ancestors, but about the kingdom of Egypt, which they believed belonged to them and to their mother Selene.[66] Political conditions at Rome shut them out, and they went back to Syria, their ancestral realm, when they couldn't conduct the business they wanted to before the senate. One of them, named Antiochus, wanted to travel via Sicily, and so he came to Syracuse when Verres was praetor. **[62]** That made Verres think he'd just inherited a pot

---

66. Antiochus X had been expelled from his kingdom (and possibly killed) by Tigranes, king of Armenia, in 83; Lucullus restored Syria to his sons, Antiochus (XIII) and Seleucus. They came to Rome (either 75–73 or 73–71) to try to regain a larger realm, particularly Egypt, to which they had a claim through their mother, Cleopatra Selene, from the Egyptian royal family. The senate was otherwise occupied during their embassy (wars against Mithridates, Sertorius, and Spartacus), and they gave up and went home.

of gold. Someone he'd heard, and suspected, had a lot of beautiful
things with him had come into his kingdom and his clutches. He
sent Antiochus fairly generous gifts for his household use—oil, a
decent supply of wine, what he thought was enough grain from his
tithe.[67] And then he asked the prince to dinner. He did up the dining room in full and fancy style; he put out a lot of beautiful silver
vessels (he had more than enough), since he hadn't yet made the gold
ones I just mentioned. He made sure that the banquet was arranged
and prepared in every respect. To be brief: the prince went home
thinking Verres was very well equipped and that he had been honor-
ably welcomed. Then he invited the praetor to dinner. He set out
everything he had, a lot of silver and quite a few cups made of gold;
as is the custom among kings, particularly Syrian kings, they were
decorated with glorious jewels. There was even an implement for
wine, a ladle carved from a single huge jewel with a golden handle;
you've heard Quintus Minucius, an appropriate and significant witness in my opinion, testify about it.[68] **[63]** Verres picked up each
and every vessel; he praised them, he admired them. The king was
delighted that the banquet was so pleasant and enjoyable to the praetor of the Roman people. And after the party was over, Verres could
think about nothing else than the obvious—how to send the prince
out of the province stripped and plundered. He sent to ask for the
most beautiful vessels he'd seen in the prince's collection, and said he
wanted to show them to his engravers. The prince didn't know him,
and so he sent them happily, with no suspicions. And Verres even sent
to ask for the ladle made from a jewel, because he wanted to examine
it more closely. And that, too, was sent to him.

[64] Members of the jury, pay close attention to the rest of the
story. You've heard about it before, and it's not the first time the
Roman people will hear of it; it's spread through foreign countries
to the most distant lands. These princes I'm talking about brought
with them to Rome a candelabrum created with astonishing skill
from the most brilliant precious stones. They intended to place it
in the temple of Jupiter on the Capitoline, but because they found

---

67. A reminder of Verres' extortions connected with the grain tithe, discussed at length in *Verr.* 3.

68. Appropriate because Antiochus was staying in Minucius' house; see
below, sec. 70.

the temple wasn't yet finished, they couldn't dedicate it;[69] and as they didn't want to bring it forth and display it to the crowd—they wanted it to seem even more glorious when at the right moment it was placed in the sanctuary of Jupiter Optimus Maximus and even more brilliant when its beauty reached men's eyes as something new and previously unknown—they decided to take it back to Syria with them and they planned, as soon as they heard the statue of Jupiter Optimus Maximus had been dedicated, to send ambassadors who would bring this striking and beautiful gift, along with other presents, to the Capitol. **[65]** I don't know how this news reached Verres' ears; the prince had wanted to keep it secret, not because he feared or suspected anything, but to avoid having too many people catch sight of it before the Roman people did. Verres asked the prince for it; he made urgent requests that he send it to him. He said he wanted to examine it and wouldn't let anyone else see it. Antiochus had the mind both of a child and of a prince; he had no suspicion of Verres' wickedness, and he ordered his people to wrap it up and take it to the praetor's residence as secretly as possible. After they brought it and set it up with its wrappings removed, Verres began to exclaim that it was a thing worthy of the kingdom of Syria, worthy to be a royal gift, worthy of the Capitol. And in fact it shone as much as something made from the most brilliant and most beautiful jewels should; it displayed such variety of workmanship that there seemed to be a contest between artistic skill and range of materials, and it was of such a size that it was easy to understand that it was made not for human adornment but for the enhancement of the grandest of temples. And when Verres seemed to have looked at it enough, they began to pick it up to take it back. But he said he wanted to look at it again and again; that he hadn't had nearly enough; and he ordered them to leave, leaving behind the candelabrum. And so they went back to Antiochus empty-handed.

[66] At first the prince had no fears or suspicions. One day went past, a second, more; it wasn't brought back. Then he sent his people to ask that it be returned, if it were convenient. Verres ordered them

---

69. Quintus Lutatius Catulus, consul in 78 (and a member of the jury in this case), was given the responsibility for restoring the temple of Jupiter that had been destroyed by fire in 83; it was dedicated in 69, and Catulus' name appeared on it as the magistrate in charge of rebuilding.

to come back later. That surprised the prince. He sent again; it wasn't returned. He addressed Verres himself, asking for its return. And here you can observe Verres' brazenness and amazing lack of shame. He knew, since the prince had told him, that it was to be dedicated on the Capitol; he saw it was being kept safe for Jupiter Optimus Maximus and for the Roman people; but he still began to ask that it be given to him and to seek it in the most urgent way. When the prince said he was bound by his vow to Capitoline Jupiter and by his reputation among men, since many nations were witnesses to the work and to the gift, then Verres began to make savage threats against him. When he saw the prince was moved no more by threats than by requests, he suddenly ordered him to leave the province before nightfall; he said he had learned that pirates were on their way from his kingdom to Sicily. **[67]** In the forum of Syracuse, in a huge crowd[70]—and nobody should think I'm talking about an obscure crime or making something out of mere suspicion—in the forum at Syracuse, I repeat, the prince wept and called on the witness of gods and men; he began to shout that the candelabrum made from jewels, which he was going to send to the Capitol, which he wanted to be a monument to the Roman people, in the greatest temple, of his friendship and alliance—that Gaius Verres had stolen it from him. He wasn't worried about his other objects made of gold and jewels that Verres had, but that it was awful and shameful for this to be taken from him. Before now, it had been consecrated only in his and his brother's minds and thoughts, but now, in the presence of this gathering of Roman citizens, he gave, presented, dedicated, and consecrated it to Jupiter Optimus Maximus, and he called Jupiter himself as witness to his intention and to his vow.[71]

Who has the voice, the lungs, the strength to be able to utter the lament owed to such a crime? Prince Antiochus, who had been in Rome before all our eyes for nearly two years with his royal entourage and state, was a friend and ally of the Roman people. His father had been our close friend, as had his grandfather and his ancestors, kings of great antiquity and fame. He was from a rich and powerful kingdom—and now he was hurled headlong from a province of the Roman people. **[68]** How do you think foreign nations will receive

---

70. Cicero calls it a *conventus*, which is specified later in the chapter as the assembly of Roman citizens in Syracuse.
71. Cicero uses the formal language of Roman religious dedications.

this? With what effect will the report of your deed reach other kingdoms and the most distant lands, when they hear that a prince was assaulted in a province by a praetor of the Roman people, that a guest was robbed, that a friend and ally of the Roman people was expelled? Your name and that of the Roman people, know it well, members of the jury, will be greeted with bitter hatred in foreign lands if this great outrage should go unpunished. Everyone will think, particularly when the report of the greed and avarice of our people becomes more widespread, that this is the crime not of Verres alone but of those who have condoned it. Many kings, many free cities, many wealthy and powerful private individuals have it in mind to provide adornment for the Capitol as the dignity of the temple and the name of our empire deserve. If they learn you have treated harshly the misappropriation of this royal gift, then they will believe their enthusiastic gifts will be received with gratitude by you and the Roman people. But if in the matter of such a noble prince, such an extraordinary object, so vicious an outrage they hear you have been negligent, they will not be so crazy as to spend their effort and care and money on things they don't believe will be received with gratitude.

[69] And now, Quintus Catulus, I call upon you; I am speaking about your most glorious and beautiful monument. With such a charge, you should put on not just the sternness of a judge but something like the vehemence of a personal enemy or a prosecutor. It is your public responsibility that is hallowed along with that temple, thanks to the favor of the senate and the Roman people; it is your name whose memory is hallowed for all time together with that temple. It is for you to take up this concern, to assume this burden, that the Capitol be more sumptuously adorned than it was, just as it has been restored more grandly than it was, so that the fire may seem to have arisen divinely, not to destroy the temple of Jupiter Optimus Maximus but to insist on a temple more glorious and grand. [70] You have heard Quintus Minucius say that Prince Antiochus stayed at his home in Syracuse, that he knows the candelabrum was taken to Verres, that he knows it was not returned. You have heard and will hear men from the association of Roman citizens in Syracuse, men who will say that in their hearing the candelabrum was dedicated and consecrated to Jupiter Optimus Maximus by Prince Antiochus. If you were not a member of the jury and this affair were reported to you, then you in particular would have the obligation to avenge, to accuse, to prosecute. For that reason I have no doubt about the attitude you

should have as a judge of this crime, since before a different judge you
ought to have been a much more fierce prosecutor than I.

[71] But for you, members of the jury, what can possibly seem
more degrading or less tolerable than this? Will Verres have in his
home the candelabrum of Jupiter, finely made from jewels and gold?
Its gleam ought to shine on and make bright the temple of Jupiter
Optimus Maximus; will it be set up in Verres' house for parties that
are themselves inflamed with sex and sin? Will adornment for the
Capitol be set out together with the decorations he inherited from
Chelidon in the home of this filthy pimp? What will ever be sacred to
this man, what do you think has ever been holy to him—a man who
does not recognize that he has now implicated himself in such a great
crime, who comes to a trial in which he cannot even pray to Jupiter
Optimus Maximus and ask his aid as all other defendants do? Here
is a man from whom the everlasting gods demand restitution of their
property, in a court that was established for men to seek restitution
of their property. Is there any surprise that Verres assaulted Minerva
at Athens, Apollo at Delos, Juno at Samos, Diana at Perge, and many
other gods throughout Asia and Greece,[72] when he could not keep
his hands off the Capitol? A temple to which private individuals give
offerings and will continue to do so is not permitted by Gaius Verres
to receive an offering from kings.

[72] Once Verres had conceived this unspeakable crime, there
was nothing in all Sicily he thought of as sacred or holy, and so for
three years he behaved in his province in a way to make you think
he'd declared war not just on humans but even on the everlasting
gods.[73] Segesta is an ancient town of Sicily, members of the jury,
which they claim was founded by Aeneas when he fled from Troy on
his way here.[74] Therefore the people of Segesta think they're bound
to the Roman people not just by a permanent alliance and friendship

---

72. Verres' visits to (and thefts from) the famous shrines of Greece were
described in *Verr.* 1.1.

73. The last item in the series of thefts from individuals (Antiochus) turns
into a sacrilegious theft from Jupiter. This marks a transition to the second
half of the book, which concerns thefts from gods and cities. At the same
time, Verres' attacks on Sicily increasingly involve attacks on the memory
of Rome's great heroes, Marcellus and Scipio Aemilianus.

74. The mythic connection between Rome and Segesta was of long standing
and is important in Book 5 of the *Aeneid.*

but by family ties as well. Long ago this city, when it was fighting on its own behalf and by its own decision against the Carthaginians, was captured by them and destroyed; everything that could adorn the city was taken from there to Carthage.[75] There was in Segesta a bronze statue of Diana of great antiquity and holiness and perfected by unique artistic skill. When it was taken to Carthage it changed only its place and its people, but it preserved its original religious significance: because of its outstanding beauty, even enemies thought it deserved to be worshiped with great religiosity. **[73]** Several centuries later, Publius Scipio captured Carthage in the Third Punic War.[76] He was a man of scrupulous morality: your delight in home-grown examples of outstanding morality should make you regard Verres' unbelievable rapacity with even greater hatred. On the occasion of his victory, he called together all the Sicilians, and because he knew Sicily had been ravaged long and often by the Carthaginians, he ordered everything to be brought together and promised he would take great care in returning to each city everything that had belonged to them. I've spoken before about the things once stolen from Himera and returned to the people of Thermae;[77] some things were returned to the people of Gela, others to the people of Agrigentum, including the famous bull into which Phalaris, the most cruel of all tyrants, is said to have put living men and tortured them by heating the bull with fire. When Scipio returned the bull to the Agrigentines, they say he said they should consider whether it was better for the Sicilians to be enslaved to their own people or to comply with the Roman people, since they now had a single monument both to native cruelty and to Roman decency.

[74] At that time, this particular Diana I'm talking about was given back to the people of Segesta with great attentiveness. It was taken back to Segesta and put on its original foundations to the greatest satisfaction and joy of the citizens. In Segesta it was placed on a

---

75. It is not clear what war is meant here.

76. Scipio Aemilianus destroyed Carthage in 146 BCE. In this passage Cicero calls him either Publius Scipio or Publius Africanus to link him, in one direction, to the great Africanus who defeated Hannibal, and in the other, to the young Publius Cornelius Scipio Nasica (below, sec. 79), a very distant relative who was a supporter of Verres.

77. Discussed previously at *Verr.* 2.85–88. Himera had been destroyed in the fifth century and was restored with the name of Thermae.

very high pedestal, on which in large letters the name of Publius Africanus was carved with the statement that he had returned the statue after the capture of Carthage. The citizens cherished it; all visitors went to see it; when I was quaestor,[78] it was the first thing they showed me. It was a large and tall statue in a robe, but large as it was, it had the appearance and dress of a young woman; a quiver of arrows hung from her shoulder and she held a bow in her left hand, while in her right she held out a blazing torch. **[75]** As soon as this highwayman, the enemy of everything sacred and holy, saw it, it was as if he'd been struck by her torch itself. He began to burn with mad desire; he ordered the magistrates to take her down and give her to him; he made it clear that nothing would gain his gratitude more. They said it was immoral for them, that they were bound both by their great religious awe and by their fear of legal retribution. Verres began by making requests to them, then he threatened them; at one moment he gave them hope, at another fear. They, meanwhile, raised the name of Publius Africanus against him and said the statue belonged to the Roman people; they had no authority over something that a great general, after the capture of an enemy city, had intended as a monument to the victory of the Roman people. **[76]** Verres didn't let up, and in fact he became daily more violent. The matter was taken up in the senate, and there were violent objections on all sides. And so at that moment, on his first arrival, he didn't get anywhere. But later, whatever burden there was in drafting sailors and oarsmen or in the exaction of grain, he placed on the people of Segesta more than on the rest, a lot more than they could stand.[79] Along with that, he summoned their magistrates, commanding the best and most noble citizens to attend him; he dragged them around all the towns of the province; he announced to each of them individually that he would be their doom; and to all of them he threatened he would overturn their city from its foundations. Eventually, the people of Segesta were defeated by their many troubles and their great fear; they decided they had to obey the praetor's command. With great grief and mourning throughout the city, with much weeping and wailing of every man and woman, a contract for moving the statue of Diana was issued.

---

78. In 75.

79. Verres' manipulation of the burdens on the Sicilians of grain and service is the subject of Book 3.

[77] Now see how deeply religious the people of Segesta were. You should know, members of the jury, that not a single person, neither free nor slave, neither citizen nor foreigner, dared touch that statue. You should know that non-Greek laborers were imported from Lilybaeum;[80] since they were ignorant of the whole affair and its religious significance, they took the money and removed the statue. When it was carried out of the city, how great do you think was the throng of women, how much did the old people weep? Some of them still remembered the day when that same Diana came back from Carthage to Segesta and announced with its return the victory of the Roman people.[81] The difference between this day and that! Then a general of the Roman people, a man of great glory, carried back to the people of Segesta their ancestral god, recovered from the city of their enemies; now a praetor of the same Roman people, a man of great filth and foulness, was carrying off from an allied city that same god in a sacrilegious crime. What is better known in all Sicily than that all the mothers and daughters in Segesta gathered when Diana was being carried from the town? They anointed her with unguents, they covered her with garlands of flowers, they followed her with burning incense to the border of their territory. [78] This great sense of religious awe—even if because of your shameless greed you didn't fear it while you were in office, aren't you now terrified of it when you and your children are in such danger? What help can you expect from any man against the wishes of the everlasting gods, or from a god when you've done such violence to their worship? In a time of peace and tranquillity, didn't that Diana affect you with any religious feeling? She has seen the two cities where she had been established captured and burned; she has been saved twice from the fire and weapons of two wars. When she changed places after the Carthaginian victory, she did not lose her religious significance, and by the military virtue of Publius Africanus she recovered her worship together with her proper place. After this crime, the statue base with the name of Publius Africanus carved on it was empty, and it seemed shameful and unbearable to everyone that not only had their religion been violated, but the glorious deeds of the great Publius Africanus, the memory of his military virtue, the memorials of his victory had

---

80. Lilybaeum, at the western tip of Sicily, had Punic inhabitants.
81. A very long memory, nearly seventy-five years.

been removed by Gaius Verres. **[79]** And when someone told him about the statue base and the inscription, he thought men would forget the whole business if he removed the base, too, as if it were a witness to his crime. And so at his command, the Segestans issued a contract for removing it; the contract of hire was read to you in the previous hearing from the public records of the people of Segesta.

But now it's you, Publius Scipio, a young man of great ability from a distinguished family, it's you I call on: I ask, I demand from you the sense of obligation that is owed to your family and your name.[82] Why are you fighting for Verres, a man who has stolen the glory and honor of your family? Why do you think he deserves a defense, while I perform your role? Why do I take up a duty that is yours? Why does Marcus Tullius look out for the monuments of Publius Africanus, while Publius Scipio defends the man who stole them? It's a custom handed down from our ancestors, that each person should defend the memorials of his ancestors so actively that he not permit them to be decorated with anyone else's name; so why are you supporting Verres, who didn't just block one side of a monument of Publius Scipio but completely destroyed and removed it? **[80]** In the name of the everlasting gods, who's supposed to protect the memory of the deceased Publius Scipio, the monuments and witnesses to his virtue, if you abandon and desert them, and not only permit them to be plundered but even defend the man who plundered and vandalized them? The people of Segesta, your clients, are here, allies and friends of the Roman people. They tell you that Publius Africanus, after the destruction of Carthage, restored the statue of Diana to their ancestors, and that it was placed and dedicated in Segesta in the name of the general; that Verres had seen to its being taken down and taken away, and to removing and destroying completely the name of Publius Scipio. They beg and pray that you restore to them their sacred statue, and to your family its praise and glory; the statue they recovered from an enemy city through Publius Africanus they want to preserve from the highwayman's home through you.

Do you have any honorable response to them? Do they have any honorable action available other than to beg you to display good

---

82. Publius Cornelius Scipio Nasica, a very distant relative of Scipio Aemilianus, was one of Verres' advocates in this trial; he was perhaps twenty-five at this time. He was adopted by Metellus Pius and became Quintus Caecilius Metellus Pius Scipio Nasica; he was consul in 52.

faith? Here they are; they're begging you. You have the opportunity, Scipio, you can preserve the splendor of your family's glory. You possess everything in yourself that either fortune or nature bestows on humans; I'm not trying to poach the rewards of your sense of duty; I'm not looking for praise that belongs to another; my own sense of decency doesn't allow me to claim to be the defender and protector of the monuments of Publius Scipio while a Publius Scipio, in the flower of his youth, is alive and well. **[81]** For that reason, if you undertake the defense of your family's glory, I will feel obliged not only to keep silent about your monuments but even to rejoice that the fortune of the deceased Publius Africanus is such that his honor is defended by members of his own family and needs no external assistance. But if you're hindered by friendship with Verres, if you think what I ask of you isn't relevant to your sense of duty, then I'll step up as a substitute for the task you should do, I'll take a role I thought wasn't mine. And then let that glossy nobility of yours stop complaining that the Roman people are happy, and have always been happy, to give public office to new men who work hard. You shouldn't complain, because virtue is the most important thing in a country that rules over all nations because of its virtue. Let others have a wax mask of Publius Africanus; let others deck themselves in the virtue and the name of a dead man. He was a man of such quality, he served the Roman people so well, that he should be entrusted not to a single family but to the entire nation. I have some responsibility in this, as a man who belongs to the nation that Africanus made splendid and famous and glorious, especially because I work hard to be actively engaged in the area in which he was the leader: fairness, hard work, self-control, the defense of the helpless, hatred of the wicked. This kinship in interests and behavior is not much less a bond than the one of family and name that gives you such pleasure.[83]

[82] I demand from you, Verres, the return of the monument of Publius Africanus. I set aside the cause of the Sicilians that I've taken up; for the moment let's not consider the extortion trial; let's ignore the outrages to the people of Segesta. Let the statue base of Publius Scipio be restored, let the name of the unconquerable

83. The whole paragraph is a stirring evocation of the ideology of the new man: Cicero is (morally) descended from the great Scipio and must act on his behalf, since Scipio's (biological) relatives have declined from the old standard and fail to respect his memory.

general be inscribed on it, let the beautiful statue captured from Carthage be replaced. It's not the defender of the Sicilians making this demand, not your prosecutor, not the people of Segesta, but a man who has undertaken to protect and defend the glory and reputation of Publius Africanus. I'm not afraid that Publius Servilius, the juror, won't approve of my sense of moral duty:[84] he's accomplished great deeds and is right now working hard to set up monuments to his own accomplishments. He'll certainly want to hand them on, to be protected not just by his own descendants but by all brave men and responsible citizens, not vandalized by evil men. I'm not afraid that you, Quintus Catulus, whose monument is the grandest and most glorious in the world, will frown on the idea that there should be as many guardians of monuments as possible, and that all responsible citizens should believe the defense of other people's glory is part of their moral duty. **[83]** For my own part, I'm moved by Verres' other thefts and crimes to think they deserve censure; but at this one I'm affected by such anguish that there's nothing that seems more degraded or less endurable. Will Verres use the monuments of Africanus to decorate his house—a house filled with sexual misconduct, filled with immorality, filled with disgraceful behavior? Will Verres take the monument of that man of great self-control and sanctity, the statue of the virgin Diana, and put it in a house where there are incessant immoral acts of whores and pimps?

[84] But this is the only monument of Africanus you defiled. Really? Didn't you also take from the people of Tyndaris a beautifully made statue of Mercury placed there by the gift of Scipio? And, by the everlasting gods, his methods! What boldness, what lusts, what a lack of shame! You've heard just now the envoys from Tyndaris who are men of great honor and leaders of their state. Mercury is worshiped by them in annual rituals with great devotion; he was given to the people of Tyndaris by Publius Africanus after the capture of Carthage as a monument and witness not just of his victory but of their fidelity as allies; he was removed by Verres' violent and criminal abuse of his official power. As soon as he reached the town, as if it were not only right but necessary that it happen this way, as if the senate had given instructions and the Roman people had ordered it, he immediately commanded that the statue be pulled down and taken

---

84. A member of the jury (as is Catulus below); see sec. 21 above.

to Messana. **[85]** People who were there thought it was degrading, people who heard of it thought it was unbelievable; as a result, he didn't force the issue on his first visit. As he left he gave instructions to Sopater, their Speaker[85] (whose evidence you've heard), to have it pulled down; when he refused, Verres threatened him violently and immediately left town. Sopater brought it before the senate; there were violent objections on all sides. To be brief, Verres came back a while later and immediately asked about the statue. He was told that the senate hadn't given permission, that it had been made a capital offense to touch the statue without orders from the senate; its religious status was also mentioned. Then Verres said: "Why are you talking to me about religion or penalties or a senate? I won't leave you alive: you'll be whipped to death if the statue isn't handed over to me." Sopater, in tears, went back to report to the senate and described Verres' greed and threats. The senate gave Sopater no answer but went home in a state of great disturbance and agitation. Sopater was summoned by the praetor's messenger, described the state of affairs, and said that there was no way it could be done.

[86] All this—and I don't think I should leave out any element of his shamelessness—took place while he was on official business, in public, from the praetor's seat on a platform. It was deep winter; the weather, as you have heard Sopater himself testify, was freezing and it was raining hard. Verres ordered his lictors to take Sopater from the portico where Verres himself was seated, throw him headlong into the forum, and tie him up naked. He'd hardly finished giving orders when you could see Sopater stripped and surrounded by the lictors. Everyone thought the poor, innocent man would be beaten; but everyone thought wrong. Would he beat a friend and ally of the Roman people for no reason? He's not so wicked as that; one person doesn't contain every vice. Verres was never cruel. He treated Sopater gently and generously. There are equestrian statues of the Marcelli in the middle of the forum, as is true of most of the towns of Sicily.[86] Verres selected the statue of Gaius Marcellus, whose services to the city and to the whole province were the most recent and most

---

85. For the title, see sec. 50 above.

86. The family of the Marcelli had been patrons of Sicily since the conquest by Marcus Claudius Marcellus in 212; the statue selected is that of Gaius Marcellus, governor of Sicily in 79 (and a member of the jury). See above, note 47.

extensive; on that statue, he ordered Sopater—a man who was a noble
in his own town and held the chief magistracy—to be tied down with
his legs around the horse. **[87]** We must all feel acutely the tortures
he suffered, strapped naked to a bronze statue, in the freezing rain.
This vicious assault didn't come to an end until the entire populace
was roused by the savagery of Verres' action and by pity for Sopater
to force the senate by their shouts to promise the statue of Mercury
to Verres. They shouted that the gods would take their own revenge,
but meanwhile an innocent man shouldn't die. The senate then went
in a body to Verres and promised the statue. And so Sopater, nearly
frozen stiff, was taken down barely alive from the statue of Gaius
Marcellus.

Even if I wanted to, I couldn't deliver an organized and orderly
accusation of Verres; it requires not just talent but also a remarkable level of skill. **[88]** This charge, concerning the Mercury of
Tyndaris, seems to be a coherent unity, and I'm presenting it that
way; it consists of quite a few charges, but I simply don't know how
to break them down and divide them up. There's the charge of extortion, because he took from our allies a statue of considerable value;
there's the charge of misappropriation of public funds, because he
had no qualms about carrying off a statue that's the public property
of the Roman people, from booty taken from the enemy, which
was set up in the name of our commander; there's the charge of
treason, in that he dared to pull down and carry off monuments
of our empire and our glorious military accomplishments; there's
the charge of sacrilege, in that he grossly violated religious sanctions; there's the charge of cruelty, in that he invented a new and
unique variety of torture to use on an innocent man, your friend
and ally. **[89]** What the charge is, or what name I should give to
his use of the statue of Gaius Marcellus for this torture, I can't say.
What's going on here? Is it because Marcellus was a patron of Sicily?
What's the point of that? As a patron, is he supposed to bring help
or disaster to his clients and friends? Or was it to show that patrons
provide no protection against Verres' use of force? Who wouldn't
know that there's much greater force available in the official power
of a wicked man who's present than in the support of good men
who aren't? Does this action indicate your unmatched haughtiness,
stubbornness, and tyrannical behavior? Apparently you thought
you could diminish a little the eminence of the Marcelli; and so
now the Marcelli are no longer patrons of the Sicilians, but Verres

has replaced them.[87] **[90]** What virtue or worth did you think you possessed that was so great you tried to transfer the patronage of such a glorious and famous province to yourself and take it away from its oldest and most consistent patrons? With your wicked, dumb, lazy ways, can you protect as your client not all of Sicily but even one miserable Sicilian? Did you use the statue of Marcellus as the gallows for the clients of the Marcelli? Were you trying to use an honor given to Marcellus as a means to torture the people who had honored him? Look ahead: what did you think would happen to your own statues? Maybe just what did happen. The people of Tyndaris, as soon as they heard a successor to Verres had been appointed, knocked down Verres' statue, which he had ordered to be placed on a higher pedestal next to the Marcelli. The good fortune of the Sicilians has now given you Gaius Marcellus as a judge, so we can give you over, bound and tied, to the sacred judicial oath of the man to whose statue the people of Sicily were tied under your praetorship.[88]

[91] What Verres said at first, members of the jury, was that the people of Tyndaris had sold this statue of Mercury to Marcus Marcellus Aeserninus here, and he hoped that Marcellus himself would support his case.[89] That never seemed likely to me, that a young man of such family, a patron of Sicily, would lend his good name to Verres and accept a transfer of guilt.[90] Even so, I was prepared for it and took careful precautions so that, even if he found someone eager to take on his criminal guilt, he still wouldn't get anywhere. I brought witnesses and documents so compelling that nobody could have any doubts about what Verres did. **[92]** There are official documents to the effect that the Mercury was taken to Messana at public expense; they state the cost, and that Poleas was officially entrusted with this

---

87. As in the replacement of the Festival of Marcellus by the Festival of Verres.

88. The text of this sentence is corrupt, but its general sense is clear.

89. This Marcus Claudius Marcellus Aeserninus is otherwise unknown; he is presumably the son of Marius' legate Marcus Marcellus, who gained the cognomen Aeserninus for defending Aesernia during the Social War.

90. "Transfer of guilt" (*translatio criminis*) is the technical term for one of the four fundamental defense arguments, the assertion that someone else is responsible (the others are denial of the fact, denial of its criminality, and justification).

responsibility—"Really? Where is he?" Here he is, a witness—at the orders of Sopater the Speaker. "Who's that?" The man who was tied to the statue. "Really? Where is he?" You've seen him and heard his evidence. Demetrius, the head of the gymnasium, was in charge of pulling it down, because he was in charge of the place it stood. "Really? Did I say that?" In fact he was there in person. And recently Verres himself promised he would return the statue to the envoys if the formal evidence on the subject were eliminated and it was stated in writing that they would not testify. That's the evidence given to you by Zosippus and Ismenias, men of great nobility and leaders of the city of Tyndaris.

[93] Let's talk about Agrigentum. Didn't you remove from the holy shrine of Aesculapius another monument of Publius Scipio, a remarkably beautiful statue of Apollo on whose thigh, in tiny silver letters, is inscribed the name of Myron?[91] That, members of the jury, he did in secret, using for this criminally wicked theft some evil men as guides and assistants. The city was profoundly disturbed. At one and the same moment the people of Agrigentum lost the sign of Africanus' benevolence, their own religious observances, an adornment of the city, a record of victory, and evidence of their alliance with Rome. As a result, the leaders of the city gave instructions to the quaestors and aediles that they should keep watch at night at all temples. In fact, probably because of the number of men involved and their courage, and because a great many Roman citizens, brave and honorable men, live and do business in the town in great harmony with the people of Agrigentum, Verres didn't dare make public demands or remove the things he liked.

[94] There's a temple of Hercules in Agrigentum, not far from the forum, a particularly holy and sacred shrine for them. There stands a bronze statue of Hercules, and I couldn't easily say I've seen anything more beautiful (although I don't know much about these things even if I've seen lots of them); it's so beautiful, members of the jury, that its mouth and chin have been worn away a little, because at times of prayer and thanksgiving they don't just worship it but kiss it, too. During the time Verres was in Agrigentum, a sudden attack by a gang of armed slaves was made on this temple in the dead of night under the leadership of Timarchides. The night watch and the keepers of the temple raised the alarm; at first they tried to resist

---

91. Myron also made one of Heius' statues; see above, sec. 5.

and defend the temple, but they were badly mauled by clubs and fists and beaten back. After that the hinges were torn apart and the doors were broken. They tried to pull the statue down and used crowbars to make it fall. Meanwhile, because of the alarm the rumor spread through the whole city that their ancestral gods were being assaulted, not because of the unexpected appearance of enemies or a sudden attack by pirates, but an armed band of runaway slaves had come from the home and household of the praetor. [95] There was nobody in Agrigentum so old or feeble that he didn't get up that night because of this news, and every man snatched whatever weapon came to hand. And so in a very short time everyone came out of the city and rushed to the temple. A large body of men had already spent more than an hour struggling to take the statue down, but during that time the statue didn't give way on any side, even though some people tried to pry it up with crowbars while others wrapped ropes around it and pulled. Suddenly the people of Agrigentum appear: a lot of stones are thrown; the nighttime soldiers of this great general turned and ran. They did manage to remove two very small figures: they didn't want to return to Verres the pirate without some religious object. Things are never so bad for Sicilians that they don't have something funny and to the point to say: in this case they said that this huge Boar[92] belonged among the list of Hercules' labors just as much as the one from Erymanthus.

[96] The people of Assorus later imitated the courage of the people of Agrigentum, brave and honorable men, but from a city not nearly so large or so noble. The river Chrysas flows through the territory of Assorus; it's considered a god and worshiped with great religious feeling. His temple is in their territory, next to the road from Assorus to Enna; in the temple is a fine marble statue of Chrysas. Because the shrine was extremely holy, Verres didn't dare demand the statue from the people of Assorus: he gave the job to Tlepolemus and Hiero. They came at night with an organized and armed band; they broke down the doors of the temple. The temple staff and the guards noticed quickly; the signal that the neighbors knew was given by horn; men came running from the fields. Tlepolemus was tossed out of the temple and chased away, and nothing from the shrine of Chrysas was missing except one tiny bronze statue.

---

92. "Boar" = *verres*.

[97] At Engyon there is a shrine of the Great Mother (and now I not only have to be brief about each event, but I have to leave out a lot to get to his grander and more notorious thefts and sacrileges of this kind). In this shrine the great Scipio, a man of unique excellence, had placed armor and helmets of bronze engraved in Corinthian style together with large jars made with similar style and skill; he put his name up in an inscription. But why bother saying anything more about Verres or complaining about him? All those things, members of the jury, he stole; he left nothing in that holiest of shrines except the traces of his sacrilege and the name of Publius Scipio. The spoils of our enemies, the monuments of our generals, the decoration and adornment of temples—after this they will lose their great names and be reckoned among the furnishings and possessions of Verres. [98] You, I imagine, are the only person who enjoys Corinthian vases. You're the most discerning connoisseur of the blending of the bronze and the design of the engravings. The great Scipio didn't understand such things, a man of great learning and cultivation; but you, who have no skills and no culture, no brains and no education—you understand them and make judgments about them. Be careful: Scipio has conquered you, and those friends of yours who want to be thought elegant, not just in his moderation but in his intelligence, too. It's precisely because he understood how beautiful these objects were that he thought they were not designed for human self-indulgence but for the adornment of shrines and towns. He wanted them to be seen by our descendants as monuments to our religiosity.[93]

[99] Listen, members of the jury, to a story of Verres' unparalleled greed, rapacity, and lunacy, particularly in polluting sacred objects it was wrong for anyone not only to touch but even to think about harming. There's a sanctuary of Ceres at Catina, as sacred as the one in Rome, as in other places, as in more or less the entire world. In the innermost part of the sanctuary there was a very ancient statue of Ceres. Men didn't know what it was like, not even that it existed at all, since men aren't allowed to enter that sanctuary and the religious rites are performed by women and girls. Secretly, by night, Verres' slaves stole the statue from that place of great holiness and antiquity. The next day the priestesses of Ceres and the high priestesses in

---

93. The text of the last clause is probably corrupt, and some editors have wanted to delete it.

charge of the sanctuary, older women of honor and nobility, reported the matter to their magistrates. To all it was painful, degrading, and a source of grief. **[100]** At that point Verres became upset by the terrible effect of his own action; to dispel suspicion of the crime from himself, he instructed one of his friends to find someone to accuse of having done it and to make sure he was condemned for the crime so that Verres himself would not be thought responsible. No delay: when Verres left Catina a slave was accused; for the prosecution, false witnesses were produced. The whole senate acted as jury under the laws of Catina. The priestesses were summoned; they were asked in a closed hearing in the senate house what they thought had happened and how the statue was taken. They answered that slaves of the praetor had been sighted in the area. The whole thing (which was not exactly obscure before then) began to be as clear as day because of the priestesses' evidence. Deliberations began; the innocent slave was acquitted unanimously—which makes it even easier for you to be able to condemn Verres unanimously. **[101]** What do you want, Verres? What are you hoping for or waiting for? Who, god or man, do you think will help you out? Did you dare send slaves into a shrine to steal from it, where it was wrong for free men to go even to add adornment? Didn't you have any doubts about laying hands on objects which the laws of religion forbade you to lay eyes on? And it wasn't your eyes that lured you into such a wicked, evil crime. What you lusted after was something you had never looked at; you loved something you hadn't seen. Your ears were the source of a passion so great it couldn't be held back by fear, by religious scruple, by the force of the gods, or by the opinions of men. **[102]** But I suppose you heard about it from a respectable man who was a good source. How's that possible, if you couldn't hear about it from a man at all? So you heard about it from a woman, since men couldn't see it or know about it. And what kind of woman, members of the jury, do you think she was? How modest was a woman who would talk to Verres? How religious was a woman who would show him how to rob the sanctuary? No wonder religious rituals performed with supreme purity by men and women have been ravaged by Verres' criminal assaults.

So is this the only thing Verres wanted by hearing of it when he hadn't seen it himself? In fact, there are lots more, from which I'll select the stripping of a temple of great nobility and antiquity, one you heard witnesses talk about in the first hearing. At this point I ask you to listen closely and carefully just as you have so far.

[103] Malta is an island, members of the jury, separated from Sicily by a fairly wide and dangerous stretch of ocean. On the island there's a town of the same name. Verres never went there, but for three years it served him as a weaving factory for women's clothing. Not far from the town, on a headland, there's an ancient shrine of Juno. It's always been so holy that it's remained untouched and sacred not just in the Punic Wars, which involved naval actions and maneuvers in the area, but even with the present swarm of pirates.[94] In fact, there's a story that once the fleet of King Masinissa was driven to that spot, and the king's admiral stole some huge ivory tusks from the shrine, took them to Africa, and gave them to Masinissa.[95] At first the king was delighted by the gift, but when he heard where they came from, he instantly sent some trustworthy men in a warship to put the tusks back. As a result, it was inscribed on them in Punic letters that King Masinissa took them without knowing, and once he knew the story he made sure they were taken back and replaced. There was also a great quantity of ivory and many ornaments, including ancient ivory statues of Victory made with exquisite skill. **[104]** All this, to be brief, Verres had stolen and carried off in one assault, with one set of orders, using as agents temple slaves of Venus he had sent for that purpose.

Whom, by the everlasting gods, am I accusing? Whom am I pursuing through the laws and the courts? About whom will you vote on a verdict? The envoys from Malta make a public declaration that the temple of Juno was plundered, that Verres left nothing in that most sacred shrine. A place where enemy fleets have often landed, where pirates spend the winter almost every year, which no pirate has ever violated and no enemy ever touched, was so ravaged by this one man Verres that nothing at all is left. And we're calling him a defendant, or me a prosecutor, or this body a court? He's convicted by the charges; he's indicted by suspicions. We find that gods have been stolen, shrines have been ravaged, cities have been stripped naked, and for none of these things has Verres left himself any grounds to deny the charges or any possibility of defense against them. In all of them he's convicted by me, he's found guilty by the witnesses, he's weighed down by his own confession, he's caught red-handed

---

94. Pirates were a serious problem in the Mediterranean until they were defeated and suppressed by Pompey in 67–66.
95. King of Numidia from the Second Punic War until his death in 148.

in his evil deeds—but still he stays and reviews with me his deeds in silence.[96]

[105] I've spent too long, I think, dealing with one type of charge, and I recognize, members of the jury, that I have to counteract the bloated feeling in your ears and minds. That's why I'm leaving a lot out; but for what I'm about to say, members of the jury, I ask you to revive yourselves, in the name of the everlasting gods—the very gods about whose worship we've been talking for a long time—while I introduce my account of a crime of his that shook the entire province. And if in this case I seem to start from a long way back and describe the history of this cult, please forgive me; the scope of the subject doesn't allow me to give a brief glance at the horror of his crime.[97]

[106] There is an old belief, members of the jury, which is attested in the most ancient Greek writings and monuments, that the entire island of Sicily is sacred to Ceres and Libera. Other nations believe this, but the Sicilians themselves are so convinced of it that it seems to have been planted and born in their minds. They believe that the goddesses were born in this region and that agriculture was first discovered on their land; they also believe that Libera, whom they also call Proserpina, was snatched from the sacred grove of Henna, a place found in the center of the island and thus called the navel of Sicily. When Ceres began to search and hunt for her, they say she lit her torches with the flames that burst from the top of Aetna; she carried these torches before her while she wandered over the entire world. [107] Henna itself, where everything I'm talking about is supposed to have happened, is on a high and open place; at the top there is a flat plain and ever-running springs, and the whole place is

---

96. Part of the fiction of the Second Verrine: Verres was long gone.

97. The digression on Henna and the cult of Ceres and Proserpina (secs. 106–15) was famous; Cicero himself (*Orator* 210) speaks of its rhythmical style, and it is singled out by the rhetorician Quintilian in the first century CE (4.2.19 and elsewhere) and echoed by both Ovid (*Metamorphoses* 5.341–571 and *Fasti* 4.417–620) and Milton (*Paradise Lost* 4.268–72). It is the earliest extant identification of Persephone/Proserpina with Libera; in Rome she is part of the triad Liber-Libera-Ceres (equivalent to Dionysus, Persephone, Demeter), worshiped in an ancient temple on the Aventine Hill and associated with plebeian liberty (*liber* = "free"). Cicero is here working hard to adapt Greek religion to Roman; in fact, much of the narrative seems to have been drawn from the fourth-century Sicilian historian Timaeus.

steep on all sides. Around it are lakes and many groves and flowers that flourish throughout the year, a place that seems to announce the abduction of the maiden, just as we learned it as boys. There is, in fact, a cave nearby facing north and very deep; they say that Father Dis came out of it suddenly in his chariot and carried off the girl he had snatched, and just as suddenly, not far from Syracuse, went underground again in a place where a lake suddenly appeared, where to this day the people of Syracuse celebrate an annual holiday attended by a huge crowd of men and women.[98] The antiquity of this belief—that the traces and, in effect, the birthplace of these gods are to be found here—has led to an extraordinary worship of Ceres of Henna throughout Sicily, both public and private. In fact, there are many miraculous occurrences that display the force of her divinity; immediate help has been given to many people in dire circumstances, with the result that the island seems not only to be loved by her but even to be her dwelling and under her protection. **[108]** And the Sicilians aren't the only ones to show great devotion to Ceres of Henna; other peoples and nations do, too. In fact, if people are very eager to participate in the mysteries at Athens, where Ceres is said to have come during her wanderings and to have brought the cultivation of grain, how much greater should her worship be among the people where it's generally believed she was born and discovered the cultivation of grain?[99] So, too, at a critical and dangerous moment for our nation in the time of our fathers, when, after Tiberius Gracchus was killed and fear of great dangers was created by omens and portents, in the consulship of Publius Mucius and Lucius Calpurnius, the Sibylline books were consulted: there it was found that "the most ancient Ceres should be appeased."[100] Then, even though there was a splendid and beautiful temple of Ceres in Rome, priests of the Roman

---

98. Lago di Pergusa, south of the town of Enna (the modern spelling of Henna); modern festivals involve the racetrack now encircling the lake. A plaque on the main street of Enna commemorates Cicero's visit to collect evidence against Verres. Dis is the usual Roman name for the Greek Hades, the god of the Underworld.

99. There is a certain strain in Cicero's linking of the Eleusinian Mysteries and the cult of Demeter/Ceres at Henna.

100. The consuls of 133; given the fact that there was considerable military activity at Enna in 133 (see sec. 112 below), the embassy must have been later. The tribune Tiberius Sempronius Gracchus was killed by a mob led

people chosen from the distinguished Board of Ten[101] traveled all the way to Henna. Such was the authority and age of that cult that when they went there they seemed not to be going to the temple of Ceres but to Ceres herself. **[109]** I'm not going to beat the subject to death; in fact, I've been afraid for some time that my speech seems alien to the normal form of judicial proceedings and the language of everyday life. But I do say this: that this same Ceres, the most ancient, the most holy, the first of all cults among all the peoples of the whole world, was stolen by Gaius Verres from her temple and her home. Any of you who has been to Henna has seen the statue of Ceres made of marble and, in the second temple, one of Libera. They are very grand and beautiful, but they're not particularly old. There was one carrying torches, made of bronze, of moderate size and exquisite workmanship, extremely old, far the oldest of all the things in that shrine. That's the one he took. But he wasn't satisfied with that. **[110]** In front of the temple of Ceres, in a broad open space, there are two statues, one of Ceres and the other of Triptolemus, very beautiful, very grand. Their beauty put them in danger, but their size made them safe, because it seemed extremely difficult to pull them down and cart them off. But in Ceres' right hand there was a beautifully made, large statuette of Victory: Verres had that torn from the statue of Ceres and carted off.

What must be Verres' state of mind now, in recollecting his crimes, when I myself, in reporting them, am not only mentally distressed but physically trembling? There comes into my mind the image of the temple, of the place, of the ritual. The whole scene appears before my eyes, the day when I came to Henna and the priestesses of Ceres met me with ritual fillets and sacred boughs; when I addressed the gathered assembly of the citizens there was such wailing and weeping that the whole city seemed plunged in the deepest mourning. **[111]** Verres' orders about the tithes, his plundering of people's goods, his unjust judgments, his shameless passions, his violence, the insults and injuries that harassed and oppressed them—about none of this did they complain. But the divine authority of Ceres, the antiquity of their religion, the holiness of the shrine—these they wanted

---

by the *pontifex maximus*, Scipio Nasica; it is presumably Tiberius' murder that needed expiation.

101. The *decemviri sacris faciundis*, the board responsible for the conduct of religious ritual.

to be expiated by the punishment of that man of such immense and bold criminality. Everything else they said they would endure and ignore. Their anguish was such that Verres seemed another Dis come to Henna, one who hadn't carried off Proserpina but had stolen Ceres herself. In fact, that city seems to be not a city but a shrine of Ceres; the people of Henna believe that Ceres lives among them, with the result that everyone seems to me not a citizen of that city but a priest, and they are all neighbors and ministers of Ceres. **[112]** You dared steal the statue of Ceres at Henna, to rip from the hand of Ceres the statue of Victory at Henna, you tried to pull goddess apart from goddess? Men who were in all respects closer to crime than to the gods did not dare steal or even touch any of these things. In the consulship of Publius Popilius and Publius Rutilius the place was in the control of slaves, fugitives, barbarians, enemies,[102] but they were not slaves of their owners so much as you are a slave of your desires, nor fugitives from their owners so much as you from justice and law, nor barbarians in speech and origin so much as you in character and habits, nor enemies to humankind so much as you to the immortal gods. What plea for mercy is left for a man who surpasses slaves in degradation, fugitives in boldness, barbarians in crime, and enemies in cruelty?

[113] You have heard the envoys from Henna, Theodorus and Numenius and Nicasion, state publicly that they had the following instructions from their fellow citizens: to approach Verres and demand the return of the statues of Ceres and Victory. If they were successful, then they should preserve the ancient custom of the people of Henna and not give any public testimony against him, despite the fact that he had laid waste to Sicily, because this was their ancestral practice. But if he did not return them, then they should appear in court, inform the jury about Verres' outrages, and make particular complaint about matters of religion. Members of the jury, do not, by the everlasting gods, spurn their complaints; do not scorn and reject them! At issue are outrages to our allies; at issue is the power of our laws; at issue is the reputation and the truthfulness of our courts. All these are of great importance, but the greatest is this: the entire province is so tied to its worship, such religious dread has taken over the minds of every Sicilian because of Verres' action, that whatever

---

102. A major slave revolt (led by the Syrian Eunus) began in the region of Henna in 140 and was only suppressed in 132 by the consul Rupilius.

unfortunate events occur in public or in private are seen to be the result of his crime. **[114]** You have heard the people of Centuripae, of Agyrium, of Catina, of Aetna, of Herbita, and many others give public evidence of the desertion and desolation of the fields, the flight of plowmen, the abandonment, the lack of cultivation, the emptiness. This has happened because of the many and varied outrages Verres has inflicted, but in the minds of the Sicilians this one explanation is most important: they believe that because Ceres was violated, all the cultivation and crops of Ceres in that area have died. Heal the wounds to the religion of our allies, members of the jury, and preserve your own; this religion is not foreign or unfamiliar to you, and even if it were, even if you did not want to recognize it, you still ought to want to punish the person who violated it. **[115]** As it is, this is the shared worship of all peoples, and with regard to rites our ancestors summoned and adopted from a foreign people—and which they wanted to be called Greek, as they were—how could we be negligent or lax, even if we wanted to?

One city is the most beautiful and magnificent of all, Syracuse, and in bringing my speech on this subject to an end, I will recall its devastation and place it before your eyes, members of the jury. There's probably nobody here who hasn't heard the story of Marcus Marcellus' capture of Syracuse, and even read it in our histories. Compare this peace with that war, the arrival of this praetor with the victory of that commander, the filthy band of Verres with the unconquered army of Marcellus, the lusts of Verres with the self-control of Marcellus; you will say that the man who captured Syracuse founded it, the man who took it over as a well-established city captured it. **[116]** At this point, I'm leaving out all the things I will talk about and have talked about on many occasions: that the forum at Syracuse, which Marcellus in entering the city had kept undefiled by slaughter, at the arrival of Verres flowed with the blood of innocent Sicilians; that the harbor of Syracuse, which up to then had been closed to our fleets and to those of the Carthaginians, under Verres' praetorship was wide open to a Cilician pirate ship and its crew.[103] I'm setting aside the violence brought to bear on free people, the rape of married women, the things that were not perpetrated when the city was captured either by the enemy's hatred, or military license, or the custom of war, or the right of victors. I'm setting all that aside,

---

103. The incident is described fully at *Verr.* 5.95–100.

I repeat, all the things that Verres accomplished in three years; but I do want you to know about matters connected to the things I've already talked about.

[117] The city of Syracuse is, as you've often heard, the largest of the Greek cities and the most beautiful of all cities. And, members of the jury, what you've heard is true. Because of its location, it is not only protected but glorious to look at from all approaches, by land or by sea; it has harbors that are virtually enclosed in the embrace of the buildings of the city; and although they are entered from opposite directions, at the far end their waters are joined together. At the point where they meet is the part of the city called the Island;[104] it's separated by a narrow branch of the sea but is joined to the mainland by a bridge. [118] The city is so big that you could say it's made up of four large cities itself. One of them is the Island I just mentioned; surrounded by the two harbors, it extends into the mouth of each. That's where the house is that once belonged to King Hiero, and now is generally used by the praetor. On the Island are many sacred shrines, but there are two of particular importance. One is of Diana, the other—which, before Verres arrived, was highly embellished—of Minerva. At the end of the Island is a spring of fresh water named Arethusa. It's very big, full of fish, and would be completely covered by ocean if it weren't separated from the sea by a protective stone seawall. [119] The second city in Syracuse is named Achradina, where there's a large forum with beautiful porticos, a very ornate building for public officials, and a very large senate house. There's also an outstanding temple of Olympian Jupiter. The other neighborhoods of this city consist of private houses divided by one broad street and many cross streets. The third city is called Tycha, because that's where the ancient temple of Fortune was located; in it are a very substantial gymnasium and quite a few temples. It's the area with the greatest and most dense population. The fourth was the last to be built, and so it's called Neapolis.[105] At the top is the great theater, also two very fine temples—one of Ceres, the other of Libera—and a statue of Apollo called Temenites, very beautiful and very large. If Verres could have carried it, he wouldn't have hesitated to steal it.

---

104. Properly, Ortygia.
105. Neapolis = "new city."

[120] At this point, I'll return to Marcellus; I don't want this description of Syracuse to seem irrelevant. After Marcellus had taken this glorious city by military action, he didn't think it would add to the glory of the Roman people to destroy and eliminate such beauty, particularly as it seemed to hold no danger. And so he spared all the buildings, public and private, sacred and profane, as if he had come with his army to defend them, not to conquer them. In dealing with objects of art, he took account of having won the war, but he also took account of common human sentiment. He thought that as victor he could carry off to Rome many objects that could beautify Rome, but as someone with humanitarian sentiments he should not completely strip the city, particularly as he had chosen to preserve it.[106] **[121]** In this division of works of art, Marcellus as victor took for the people of Rome no more than his humanitarianism left for the people of Syracuse. What he took to Rome can be seen at the temple of Honor and Virtue and in other public places. There is nothing in his own house, nothing in his gardens, nothing in his country estate. He thought that if he refrained from putting ornaments for the city in his own house, then his own house would be an ornament for the city. At Syracuse, moreover, he left a great many marvelous objects; he harmed no god, he didn't even touch one. Compare him to Verres, not as if you were comparing one man to another—we shouldn't outrage such a great man after his death—but as if you were comparing peace and war, law and violence, the arrival and entourage of one with the army and victory of the other.

[122] There's a temple of Minerva on the Island, as I have already said. Marcellus didn't touch it but left it full of its ornaments. Verres ravaged and plundered it not even like an enemy who respects religion and customary law even in a war, but as if it had been sacked by barbarian pirates. A cavalry battle of King Agathocles was beautifully painted on panels; they covered the interior walls of the temple.[107] There was nothing grander than that painting, nothing more worth going to see in Syracuse. Even though his victory

---

106. Marcellus in this account is (to make the contrast with Verres sharper) much kinder and gentler than he is in Polybius or Livy, according to whom nothing was left after Marcellus' conquest except the shells of the buildings.

107. Agathocles was the first tyrant of Syracuse to become king of Sicily; the battle was his defeat of the Carthaginians in 305/4.

had deconsecrated everything, Marcus Marcellus was kept by his religious sensibility from touching those panels; but even though Verres had taken charge of them as holy and sacred objects because of the long peace and the loyalty of the Syracusans, he carried off all those panels and left the walls, whose decoration had stayed in place through so many centuries and survived so many wars, naked and ugly. **[123]** Marcellus had made a vow to dedicate two temples at Rome if he captured Syracuse, but even so he didn't want to decorate his planned construction with the objects he had captured; Verres, who owed vows not to Honor and Virtue like Marcellus, but to Venus and Cupid, was the one to try to strip the temple of Minerva. Marcellus didn't want gods to be beautified by spoils taken from gods; Verres moved the decorations of the virgin goddess Minerva to the house of a whore. He also stole twenty-seven beautifully painted panels from the same temple, containing images of the kings and tyrants of Sicily. These were delightful not just because of the painters' skill but because they recalled and identified the faces of these men. You should observe how much more savage a tyrant of Syracuse Verres was than any of his predecessors; whatever they were, they adorned the temples of the everlasting gods, while Verres stole their monuments and decorations.

[124] And then there are the doors of this same temple; what am I to say about them? I'm afraid that anyone who hasn't seen all these objects will think I'm embroidering my account too much, but I don't want anyone to suspect that I'm so eager for victory that I would want so many important men—particularly the ones judging this case—who have gone to Syracuse and seen these things, to catch me speaking bald-faced lies. I can certainly state, members of the jury, that there have never been doors grander than these, more exquisitely made from gold and ivory, on any temple. It's hard to believe how many Greeks have written about the beauty of these doors. Yes, Greeks perhaps admire such things too much and make too much of them; true enough. But it still brings more honor to our commonwealth, members of the jury, for our general to have left behind in wartime things that Greeks think beautiful than for our praetor to have stolen them in peacetime. The subjects portrayed on those doors were carved in ivory, made with immense care and skill; Verres had them all taken off. He tore off and stole a very beautiful Gorgon's head wreathed with snakes—but at the same time he showed he was moved as much by the price and the profit as by the workmanship.

He didn't hesitate to steal all the gold studs from the doors, and they were both numerous and heavy; it wasn't the workmanship he admired but the weight. And so he left those doors, designed long ago for the splendor of the temple, looking now as if they were made only for closing it.

[125] There are also the spears made of reeds[108]—and I saw you were moved on this score when a witness gave evidence about them. They were something it's enough to have seen once; no workmanship is involved and they're not beautiful, just incredibly long. It would be enough just to hear about them, and more than enough to see them more than once: did you want them, too?

[126] You have a fair excuse for taking the statue of Sappho from the magistrates' building, almost good enough to let it go and to pardon you. It was a work of Silanion, so exquisite, so elegant, so carefully made; surely nobody, either a private person or a nation, should have it rather than this man of great elegance and learning, Verres? There's nothing to say in response. Each of us, who aren't as well heeled as he is and can't be as refined as he is, if we want to see something like that, can go to the temple of Good Fortune, to the monument of Catulus, to the portico of Metellus;[109] we can try to get admitted to the Tusculan villa of one of Verres' friends, we can look at the statues in the forum, if Verres lends any of his to the aediles. But Verres can have them at home, Verres can have a house full of the ornaments of temples and of towns, he can have villas stuffed with them. But, members of the jury, are you going to put up with the artistic passions of this clod? His birth and education suit him, both body and mind, much more for carrying these statues than for carrying them off. [127] And the yearning that the theft of this statue of Sappho left behind can scarcely be expressed. It was beautifully made, and it also had a fine Greek epigram carved on the base; but this learned mini-Greek, a man of such refined judgment, the only man with understanding, surely would not have taken it if

---

108. In fact, bamboo.

109. The temple of Good Fortune (Felicitas) held the statues of the Muses brought back by Mummius (cf. sec. 4). The elder Quintus Lutatius Catulus (consul in 102) built a temple to the Luck of the Day (*Fortuna huiusce diei*), but we have no idea what art it contained. Quintus Caecilius Metellus Macedonicus (consul in 143) built a portico that held Lysippus' statue group of Alexander and his officers at the battle of the Granicus.

he knew a single letter of Greek.[110] As it is, the writing on the empty base announces what was there and shows it was stolen.

Item: the statue of Paean from the temple of Aesculapius, of outstanding workmanship, sacred and holy.[111] Didn't you steal it? Everyone used to come to see it because of its beauty, and to worship it because of its holiness. **[128]** Item: the statue of Aristaeus from the temple of Liber. Wasn't it removed at your orders in broad daylight? Item: the most sacred statue of Jupiter Imperator, from the temple of Jupiter, the one the Greeks call Ourios, beautifully made.[112] Didn't you remove it? Item: the beautiful sheep's head[113] from the temple of Libera. We used to go to see it; did you think twice about taking it? That statue of Paean was worshiped by the Sicilians with annual sacrifices along with Aesculapius; Aristaeus is said to have discovered the olive, and they consecrated him together with Father Liber in the same temple. And how much honor do you think was shown to Jupiter Imperator in his own temple? **[129]** You can get a good idea, if you want to remember the sanctity of the statue of the same shape and size that Titus Flamininus captured from Macedonia and placed on the Capitol.[114] In fact, there were three statues in the whole world of Jupiter Imperator, of the same type and of exquisite workmanship: the Macedonian one that we saw on the Capitol; a second, at the narrows at the mouth of the Black Sea; the third, the one that was at Syracuse before Verres became praetor. The first one Flamininus took from its temple in order to put it on the Capitol, the earthly home of Jupiter. **[130]** The one at the entrance to the Black Sea, even though so many wars have come out of that sea and so many have gone into it, has been kept safe and unharmed up to this day.[115] This third statue that was in Syracuse, which Marcus

---

110. "Not" is deleted by some editors. If it is kept, then "it" refers to the statue; if it is deleted, it refers to the base.

111. "Paean" is a cult title of both Aesculapius and Apollo; here it refers to a separate divinity. Aristaeus, a semidivine agricultural hero, is one of the central figures of Virgil's *Georgics*, Book 4.

112. Zeus Ourios, the god of favorable winds and good outcomes.

113. Peterson's conjecture. The manuscripts read *parinum*, which is clearly corrupt and has been variously emended.

114. Titus Quinctius Flamininus defeated Macedon in 197. The temple was burned in 83.

115. The temple of Zeus Ourios at Chalcedon on the Bosporus.

Marcellus, as an armed conqueror, had seen and left there because of its sanctity, which citizens and residents worshiped, and tourists used to not only visit but worship as well—it was stolen from the temple of Jupiter by Gaius Verres. **[131]** I keep coming back to Marcellus, members of the jury, for this reason: more gods have gone missing from Syracuse since Verres got there than men did when Marcellus defeated them. In fact, Marcellus is reported to have looked for the famous Archimedes, the scientific genius, and was extremely upset to learn he had been killed.[116] But whatever Verres looked for, he looked for not to save it but to carry it off.

There's a whole list of less important things I won't talk about: how he took marble Delphic tables, beautiful bronze mixing bowls, a huge number of Corinthian vases from all the temples in Syracuse. **[132]** The result, members of the jury, is that the guides who used to take tourists to show them all the sights—they call them mystagogues—have changed their tours: before, they used to show where everything was, and now they show the places from which everything was taken.

What follows from this? Surely you don't think the Syracusans were afflicted by only a mild agony? That's not how it is, members of the jury. In the first place, they're all deeply religious and they believe they should worship regularly the family gods they inherited from their ancestors and that they should keep them safe. Second, all this decoration, all these works of art and artifice, statues, painted panels—Greeks take inordinate pleasure in them. And so we can understand from their wailing that these events are truly painful for them, things we might think should be looked down on as trivial. But believe me, members of the jury, even if I'm sure you have yourselves heard the same thing. Even though our allies and dependent states have suffered many disasters and outrages in recent years, Greeks endure, and have endured, nothing with greater emotion than this kind of ransacking of temples and towns. **[133]** Verres can say he bought these things; that's what he usually says. But believe me, members of the jury, there isn't a single city in all of Asia and Greece that willingly sold any statue, any painting, any ornament of the city at all to anyone; unless you perhaps think that after we stopped having strict courts at Rome, the Greeks began to sell this stuff that

---

116. Cicero himself rediscovered the tomb of Archimedes when he was quaestor in 75; see *Tusc.* 5.64–66.

before then, when there were real trials, they not only didn't sell but even bought more. Or unless you think that really powerful men like Lucius Crassus, Quintus Scaevola, and Gaius Claudius, who celebrated their terms as aedile with great splendor, had no right to trade in such things with Greeks, while the men made aedile after the courts collapsed did have the right.[117]

[134] You should know, then, that this bogus fiction of purchase was much harder on those cities than if someone stole these things secretly or took them in broad daylight and carried them off. They think it's the worst disgrace to enter into the public accounts that the city was led by money, and a small amount of money at that, to sell and transfer to someone else objects inherited from their ancestors. In fact, the Greeks take an amazing amount of pleasure in this stuff we look down on, and so our ancestors were perfectly content to leave as much of it as possible with them. They left such things among our allies, so that through our rule they would be as magnificent and resplendent as possible; they left them with the people they made taxpaying and tributary, so that people who take pleasure in things we think are silly would have them as a source of pleasure and comfort in their slavery. [135] What do you think the people of Regium, who are already Roman citizens, would want to get in return for letting their marble Venus be carried off? Or the people of Tarentum to be deprived of Europa on the bull, or the Satyr that is in their temple of Vesta, or their other statues? What would the people of Thespiae take for their statue of Cupid—the only reason to go to see Thespiae[118]—or the people of Cnidus for their marble Venus, or the people of Cos for the painting of Venus, or the people of Ephesus for their Alexander, the people of Cyzicus for their Ajax or their Medea, the people of Rhodes for Ialysus, the people of Athens for their marble Iacchus or the painting of Paralus or Myron's bronze cow?[119] It would take a long time, and there's no point, to list all the

---

117. Lucius Licinius Crassus and Quintus Mucius Scaevola Pontifex were consuls in 95 and presumably aediles roughly a decade earlier; the aedileship of Gaius Claudius Pulcher is mentioned in sec. 6 above. Cicero claims that the Sullan transfer of the courts from equestrian to senatorial juries in 82 led to gross corruption and theft from provincials.

118. See sec. 4 above. Some editors delete the phrase as a repetition.

119. Not all these works of art are otherwise known, but some of them are (and were in antiquity) famous: the Venus of Praxiteles at Cnidus, the

things throughout Asia that are worth going to see in each place, but that's why I mention these things, because I want you to think that the people from whose cities these things were stolen suffered excruciating anguish.

[136] But let's leave out all the others and concentrate on the people of Syracuse. When I got there, at first I believed, as I had learned from Verres' friends at Rome, that because of his gift of Heraclius' inheritance,[120] the city of Syracuse was no less friendly to Verres than the Mamertines were because of their partnership with him in all his plunder and theft. At the same time, I was concerned that anything I found in the public documents of Syracuse would be countered by the influence of the beautiful and noble women under whose guidance Verres had conducted his governorship, together with that of their husbands, who had shown remarkable mildness in his direction, not to say open generosity. [137] As a result, at Syracuse I stayed among the Roman citizens, asked for their financial records, and learned about outrages to them. But whenever I had worked too long on this topic, I used to turn back, for rest and mental relaxation, to those wonderful accounts of Carpinatius and I unraveled, together with the Roman knights who were the most honorable of the group, all those entries about "Verrucius" that I've mentioned before.[121] But I expected no help from the people of Syracuse either public or private, and I didn't plan to ask for it.

While I was busy with all this, Heraclius came to me unexpectedly; he was then a magistrate in Syracuse, a noble who had been priest of Jupiter, the most honorable position in Syracuse.[122] He urged me and my cousin please to go to their senate; they were in the senate house in numbers, and he had come at the order of the senate to ask us to

---

Venus Anadyomene at Cos painted by Apelles, Myron's bronze cow on the Acropolis at Athens. Many of them were brought to Rome in the early empire.

120. Discussed by Cicero at *Verr.* 2.35–50; Verres had defrauded Heraclius, a rich Syracusan, of a huge inheritance and given it to the people of Syracuse as a bribe to overlook his other thefts.

121. *Verr.* 2.186–91. Lucius Carpinatius was the local manager of the company contracted to collect the tax on the use of public land for grazing (*scriptura*); he lent money to Sicilians to pay Verres, but he altered the entries in his accounts from "Verres" to "Verrucius."

122. Clearly not the same Heraclius as in the previous paragraph.

attend. **[138]** At first we were unsure what to do, but then we rapidly realized we shouldn't be avoiding their senate and senate house, and so we went there. They stood to honor us, and at the request of the magistrates we sat down. Diodorus the son of Timarchides—the man who was first in authority and age and, it seemed to me, political experience—began to speak, and his whole speech had this theme, that the senate and the people of Syracuse were deeply disturbed because, although in the other cities of Sicily I had told the people and senate about the usefulness and salutary effects of my visit, and although I had taken from all of them instructions, envoys, and documentary evidence, in Syracuse itself I had done nothing like that. I answered that in the meeting of Sicilians in Rome, when they sought assistance from me by the common agreement of all the embassies and the case of the whole province was being brought to me, there were no Syracusan envoys present, and that I was not about to demand that there be a decree against Gaius Verres in a senate house where I saw a gilded statue of Verres himself.[123]

[139] After I said that, they groaned so deeply at the sight and reminder of the statue that it was clear the statue in the senate house was a monument of Verres' crimes, not of his good deeds. Then, to the best of their ability as speakers, each of them began to tell me what I mentioned a little while ago, about the stripping of the city, about the plunder of temples, about the inheritance of Heraclius that Verres had assigned to the directors of the gymnasium but in fact had stolen most of it for himself; they said it was not to be expected that a man who had stolen the god who discovered the olive himself should also have affection for the people who use the *palaestra*. They said the statue was not paid for by public funds nor given as a public action, but that the people who had shared in the theft of the inheritance had taken steps to have the statue made and set up, and that those same people were the envoys to Rome, Verres' assistants in evil, his partners in theft, witnesses to his disgusting behavior. That should remove any surprise that they had failed to participate in the shared desire of the envoys for the well-being of Sicily.

[140] Once I recognized that their anguish at his outrages was not only no less than that of the other Sicilians but in fact greater, I explained to them my own attitude toward them. I explained the reasons for my plan and the structure of the whole case; I urged them to

---

123. The statues of Verres and his son are described at *Verr.* 2.50.

support the interests of the common cause and to withdraw the testimonial they said they had voted on in the past few days because they
were driven by the fear of Verres' violence. And so, members of the
jury, this is what the people of Syracuse, Verres' clients and friends,
did. They immediately brought out for me the public accounts they
kept hidden in their inner treasury, and they showed me that in those
accounts there was a complete record of the thefts I've talked about,
and even more than I was capable of reporting. The accounts were
written in this fashion: "WHEREAS THIS OBJECT AND THAT OBJECT
WERE MISSING FROM THE TEMPLE OF MINERVA"; "WHEREAS FROM THE
TEMPLE OF JUPITER"; "WHEREAS FROM THE TEMPLE OF LIBER"—it was
documented by each person who had been in charge of preserving
and protecting these objects—and when, in accordance with the law,
they had rendered their accounts and should have passed on to their
successors what they had received, they asked that they be pardoned
for the absence of these objects; as a result, they all went free and
they were all pardoned. I made sure that these records were sealed
with the official seal and removed.[124]

[141] Furthermore, they gave me this account of their testimonial
for Verres. First, when a message came from Verres about a testimonial shortly before my arrival, no decree was voted. But then, when
some of Verres' friends warned them that they ought to make such
a decree, they were shouted down with insults. Afterward, when my
arrival was getting closer, the person who held the highest power[125]
ordered them to make a decree; and the decree was written in a
way that their praise brought Verres more harm than good. I would
like to show you, members of the jury, just how that was so, as they
showed me.

[142] The custom at Syracuse is that if something is brought
before the senate, anyone who wants can state his opinion. Nobody
is asked by name, but even so the people who are most advanced in
age or career usually offer their views first, and the others allow that.
But whenever everyone is silent, then they are forced to speak in an
order determined by lot. This being the custom, the senate took up
the issue of a testimonial for Verres, and at first a great many people
interrupted the debate, so that there would be some delay. They said,

---

124. In other words, taken by Cicero as evidence in the case.
125. Verres' successor as governor, Lucius Caecilius Metellus.

concerning Sextus Peducaeus (who had done an excellent job for the city and for the whole province),[126] that when they had heard he was in some trouble, the public statement of praise in recognition of his many outstanding services they had wanted to issue had been blocked by Verres, and that it was not right, even if Peducaeus no longer had any need for their testimonial, not to issue the decree they had actively wanted to make before the one they were now being forced to make. **[143]** Everybody shouted their approval of that order of procedure. A motion was made concerning Peducaeus, and those who were most advanced in age and career spoke their views in order of rank. You can see that from the decree of the senate itself, since the opinions of the leaders are normally written out. Recite it. "WHEREAS A MOTION HAS BEEN MADE CONCERNING SEXTUS PEDUCAEUS . . ." and it gives the first people who spoke in favor of it. It was passed. Then the issue of Verres was introduced; but tell me, please, how it was done. "WHEREAS A MOTION HAS BEEN MADE ABOUT GAIUS VERRES . . ." What then? "AS NOBODY ROSE TO GIVE HIS OPINION . . ." What's going on here? "USE WAS MADE OF THE LOT." How come? Wasn't there anyone who wanted to praise your governorship, nobody to defend you in danger, especially when he could gain favor with the current governor? Nobody. Those dinner companions of yours, your advisers, your accomplices, your allies—none of them dared speak a word. There in the senate house stood your statue and a nude statue of your son, but since the province had been stripped naked, nobody there was aroused even by your naked son.[127] **[144]** They told me this, too, that those eulogists provided a senatorial resolution that everybody could understand as embodying not praise but derision, in serving as a reminder of Verres' disgusting and disastrous governorship. In fact, it was written as follows: "WHEREAS HE DID NOT HAVE ANYONE BEATEN WITH WHIPS"—that lets you know that men of great nobility and innocence were decapitated—"AND WHEREAS HE WAS VIGILANT IN HIS MANAGEMENT OF THE PROVINCE"—but all his wakeful nights were spent in adulterous sex—"AND WHEREAS HE KEPT PIRATES FAR

---

126. Peducaeus was governor of Sicily in 76–75; presumably there was a subsequent threat of prosecution for extortion. Cicero served under him as quaestor.

127. In contrast to Verres' almost sexual desire for art, the statue of a naked little Verres aroused no erotic interest even among Greeks.

FROM THE ISLAND OF SICILY"—but in fact he had received them in the harbor within the island of Syracuse.

[145] After I learned all this from them, I left the senate house with my cousin, so that they could make whatever decree they wanted without our being present. Their first, immediate decision was to extend public friendship to my cousin Lucius, because he had adopted the same goodwill toward the people of Syracuse as I had always had. They not only recorded that vote then but also had it carved in bronze and gave it to us. It's obvious that your Syracusans love you a whole lot, the people you mention so often; they think they have a good reason for forming a close bond with your accuser precisely because he's about to prosecute you and came to inquire about you. Then they decided—and it was no split vote, but pretty much unanimous—that the testimonial that had been voted on behalf of Gaius Verres should be rescinded. [146] At that point, when there had not only been a formal vote but it had been written and recorded in the city records, someone summoned the governor. And who was it who summoned him? One of the magistrates? None of them. A senator? Not that either. Some Syracusans? No again. So who called the praetor? The man who had been Verres' quaestor, Publius Caesetius.[128] What a farce! What a man, without friends, without hope, abandoned! There's an appeal from the decision of a Sicilian magistrate, trying to block Sicilians from passing a decree of the senate, to keep them from enjoying their own rights in accordance with their customs and their laws. This appeal is made not by one of Verres' friends, not by one of his hosts, not by a Sicilian at all, but by a quaestor of the Roman people to the praetor. Who has ever seen or heard of such a thing? This just and wise praetor[129] orders the senate to be dismissed. A huge crowd came running to me. First the senators shouted that they were being robbed of their rights and their freedom. The people praised the senate and thanked them; the Roman citizens never left my side. Thanks to my great efforts, nothing worse happened that day; nobody laid a hand on the man who called the praetor.

[147] When we went to court before the praetor Metellus, he discovered a brilliant way to make his decision. Before I had said a word, he rose from his seat and left. And so, as evening was coming,

---

128. Publius Caesetius was Verres' quaestor in western Sicily in 72–71 and was presumably still there when Cicero came to investigate in early 70.

129. Verres' successor, Metellus.

we left the forum. The next day I demanded from him that the people of Syracuse be permitted to give me the senatorial decree they had passed the previous day. He refused. He said that my speaking in a Greek senate was a disgraceful action, and that I had spoken Greek to the Greeks was completely intolerable. I answered him as I could, as I ought, as I wanted to. I remember a lot that I said, but this in particular, that it was easy to see how different he was from the great Numidicus, a trueborn Metellus. Numidicus had been unwilling to assist his brother-in-law Lucius Lucullus with a testimonial, much as he liked him, while this Metellus was gathering up testimonials through the use of force and intimidation for a man hated by the cities.[130] **[148]** But when I understood that recent dispatches and letters (not of introduction but of credit) had had a great deal of influence on Metellus,[131] on the advice of the Syracusans themselves I launched an assault on the tablets on which they had written the decree of the senate.[132] Suddenly there was a new crowd and a brawl: you shouldn't think that Verres was entirely stripped of friends and supporters in Syracuse. A man named Theomnastus started to cling to the tablets—a real lunatic; the Syracusans call him Theoractus.[133] He's the sort of man boys chase, the sort everyone laughs at when he starts to speak. His insanity is an object of ridicule to others but was a lot of trouble for me. While he was foaming at the mouth and with his eyes blazing and shouting at the top of his lungs that he was going to attack me, we came to court jointly. **[149]** At this point, I began to demand permission to seal the tablets and take them with me, but he spoke against me, denying that a decree about which the praetor had intervened was a true decree of the senate, and denying that it should be handed over to me. I recited the law, that I had

---

130. Quintus Caecilius Metellus Numidicus had governed Sicily in 111; his brother-in-law Lucius Licinius Lucullus (father of the Lucullus who fought Mithridates) fought against the slave revolt in Sicily in 102 but was convicted of theft on his return.

131. In other words, Cicero claims that Verres had had to bribe Metellus to get his support.

132. In other words, even if the praetor stopped the senate from voting, the written record of what they had planned to vote existed as a document that Cicero could demand as evidence.

133. Meaning "driven mad by the gods." Possibly the same Theomnastus mentioned in sec. 59.

access to all written documents; the lunatic insisted that our laws were irrelevant to him. The praetor, a man of great perception, said that he did not approve of my taking to Rome a decree of the senate that would not be held valid. I'll be brief. If I hadn't made strong threats against him, if I hadn't recited the sanctions and penalties of the law, I wouldn't have gotten hold of the tablets. But the lunatic, who had made such a violent speech for Verres against me, after he didn't get his way, gave me a pamphlet—I think he wanted to get into my good graces—listing all Verres' thefts from Syracuse, but I had already learned about them from others.

[150] So let the Mamertines praise you, since they're the only ones in the whole province who wish you well. But let them praise you so long as Heius, the leader of the embassy, is present; let them praise you so long as they're ready to answer my questions. I don't want to trap them, so I'll give them my questions in advance. Do they owe a ship to the Roman people? They'll admit it. Did they provide it while Verres was praetor? They'll deny it. Did they build a huge cargo ship at public expense and give it to Verres? They won't be able to deny it. Did Verres take grain from them to send to Rome, as his predecessors had? They'll deny it. How many soldiers or sailors did they supply over this three-year period? They'll say they supplied none. They won't be able to deny that Messana was the warehouse for all Verres' thefts and plunder; they will admit that a great many objects were exported in many ships, and finally that this huge cargo ship was given by the people of Messana to Verres and departed with him, fully loaded.

[151] So keep that testimonial from the people of Messana; we can see that the city of Syracuse has an attitude toward you that matches what you did to it, and your disgraceful Festival of Verres has been abolished. In fact, it was completely inappropriate for a man who had stolen statues of the gods to receive divine honors.[134] And it would really be a cause for deserved reproach to the people of Syracuse if after they had removed from their calendar a holy festival day of great games—the day when Syracuse was said to have been captured by Marcellus—they treated the same day as a holiday in Verres' name, when he had taken from the people of Syracuse all the things that day of calamity had left them. Look at the shameless arrogance of this

---

134. It was not rare for Roman magistrates to be honored as divine by Greeks, but in general magistrates did not initiate such worship themselves.

man, members of the jury. Not only did he establish this disgusting and absurd Festival of Verres using the money of Heraclius, but he ordered the abolition of the Festival of Marcellus. He wanted them to observe annual rites in honor of a man whose actions had led to their loss of the rites that had lasted for all time and the loss of their ancestral gods, and he abolished the festival of the family that had given them back all their other festivals.

2

In Support of Manilius' Law

Cicero's speech In Support of Manilius' Law *was delivered at a formal
public meeting in the forum (contio) early in 66 BCE.[1] The tribune Gaius
Manilius had proposed a bill to give Pompey an extraordinary appointment
to take charge of the war against Mithridates VI Eupator, king of Pontus,
concomitantly making him proconsul of the provinces of Cilicia and
Bithynia and giving him the right to appoint a large number of legates.
Cicero had recently taken office as praetor, and this was his first speech to
a* contio; *his intention was simultaneously to express his support both of
the law (and of the people's right to make such a decision) and of Pompey
himself. Pompey was extremely popular and there was never any doubt
that Manilius' law would be passed. Cicero's purpose in giving such a
speech was less to provide substantive aid to Manilius' proposal than it
was to be seen giving such aid and to display solidarity with the people
and the people's hero before a large and favorable public audience. It is, in
fact, the first major speech in Cicero's own campaign to be elected consul
for the year 63.*

*To take the positions that Cicero adopts in this speech was not
altogether comfortable. Pompey was resisted by the remaining Sullan
aristocracy (Catulus and Hortensius in particular), and there could be no
doubt that to add one more extraordinary military command to someone
whose entire career had consisted of extraordinary and sometimes
irregular military commands was to weaken even further the already
debilitated constitutional consensus. To attack, as Cicero does, both the
dominance of the oligarchy and the moral standards of Roman provincial
administration was not without risk in a political structure dominated by
the wealthy and aristocratic. As in the Verrine orations four years earlier,
Cicero presents himself as the candidate of good order, good sense, and
compromise—what was to crystallize in his consular year in the slogans*
concordia ordinum *and* consensus omnium bonorum *("harmony among
social classes" and "agreement among men of substance"). In a period
dominated by extremes, however, to aim for middle ground risked rejection
by all. And while Manilius' law was less controversial than the Gabinian*

---

1. On the *contio*, see Introduction, sec. 2 at note 21. The speech is also
known as *On Pompey's Command* (*De Imperio Cn. Pompei*).

law of 67 BCE (which had given Pompey command of the war against the pirates), Mithridates, and the choice of commanders against him, had been a sore spot of Roman public life for more than twenty years.[2]

When Cicero addressed the assembly in 66, only fifteen years had passed since Sulla's dictatorship—a violent and bloody attempt to shore up the power of Rome's narrow oligarchy against the genuine and valid pressures to loosen access to power or even to citizenship. And assaults had come from all directions: the Social War of 91–89 against Rome's Italian allies had forced the oligarchy to extend citizenship to most of Italy; the continuing disturbances of Marian remnants, even after the Sullan purges, disrupted Italy, Africa, and (for a long time, because of the skilled opposition of Sertorius) Spain; and the revolt of Spartacus in the 70s revealed the precariousness of Rome's control even of its slaves. Even more important was the warm welcome shown to Mithridates by almost all the Greeks subject to Rome when he invaded the province of Asia in 88 and ordered the simultaneous murder of every Italian and Roman in the province: Rome's leading source of revenue (the phenomenally wealthy province of Asia above all) was shown to be much less secure than anyone had suspected.

Mithridates himself is a figure of vast importance, the greatest threat to Roman power since Hannibal. As the ruler of a kingdom precariously balanced between the Hellenic (and rapidly being Romanized) western portions of the Anatolian peninsula and the Iranian culture to the east in Parthia and Armenia,[3] *Mithridates was himself thoroughly Hellenized— and yet his name, and the title "King of Kings" that he sometimes adopted, show his Asian allegiances as well. Coming to the throne in 120 BCE at the age of eleven after the assassination of his father, he first consolidated his position, then gradually extended his influence first to the east and north, and then, partly in response to Rome's having reduced the influence that Mithridates' father had had, moved to increase his power in Bithynia and Phrygia, two regions in which Rome already had a strong interest. As Anatolian, Iranian, and Greek, Mithridates plausibly represented himself as a unifying force in the region—and as a force consolidating opposition to the powerful interloper from the west, Rome. In 90 BCE, when friction between Rome and Mithridates began to turn to open hostility, Mithridates was a genuine alternative to the greedy, ambitious, and barbarous Italians. When war broke out in 89, it was provoked by the legate Manius Aquillius, without explicit authorization from Rome. Mithridates' response—killing*

---

2. For a good analysis of Cicero's argument, see Steel (2001) 114–56; more briefly, Vasaly (2002) 106–8.

3. Pontus is located on the northern coast of Anatolia, almost directly south of the Crimea. For the geography, see Map 2.

the captured Aquillius by pouring molten gold down his throat as a
symbol of Roman greed, butchering all the Italians in Asia, and sweeping
across not only Asia but Greece and most of the islands with little or no
resistance—required an immediate and violent response from Rome.[4]

Rome, however, was preoccupied with the Social War, and it is
plausible that Mithridates deliberately began his assault just then. Events
turned even more in his favor, however: disputes over the choice of a
commander led to Sulla's first march on Rome to defeat Marius and his
allies, and although Sulla decisively defeated Mithridates' forces in Greece
(First Mithridatic War, 88–84, including a ruinous siege of Athens in
87–86), the settlement negotiated (but never ratified by the senate) let the
king off very lightly. Sulla's first priority was to return to Italy to take power
as dictator (after a fierce fight against the Marian government), settle
accounts with his enemies, real or convenient, through the proscriptions,
and remodel the constitution to remove almost all popular checks on
senatorial control. After his departure from Asia, his successor Murena,
father of Cicero's client in 63, attempted further warfare against Mithridates
(Second Mithridatic War, 83–81) and was badly defeated, although to save
face (both Sulla's and his own) he was awarded a triumph for his efforts.
It was not until 74 that Rome renewed the war, when both consuls, Cotta
and Lucullus, were sent to the East to deal with Mithridates. Cotta fought
in Bithynia for several years, returning home in 70. Lucullus ultimately
pursued Mithridates as far as Armenia, but after unrest among his troops,
he was relieved of his command in 67, just as his legate Valerius Triarius lost
a major battle to Mithridates. Lucullus was succeeded by Manius Acilius
Glabrio, consul of 67, who did little; Mithridates returned to Pontus, and
after his near destruction by Lucullus he again became a danger to Rome.
It was at this point that Manilius proposed giving the command to Pompey.

The damage caused by Mithridates was real, and so was the danger he
posed even in 66 to Roman interests in Asia. But to resolve the situation
in the East posed dangers in itself, not least the choice of Pompey.
Mithridates was, as noted above, the excuse for, if not the cause of,
Sulla's brutal and reactionary dictatorship, and Sullan military operations
provided the context for the rise of Pompey. Cicero outlines his career
more than once, but he places in a favorable light actions that were open
to a less sanguine—and more sanguinary—interpretation. Pompey's first
major military initiative was to raise an army of his father's veterans to
support Sulla's return to Rome in 83. His control of an army led Sulla to
accept and use him rather than—as he generally did with those he did not
trust—eliminate him. Pompey was used to stamp out resistance, first in

---

4. On the origins of the Mithridatic War, see Morstein-Marx (1995) 250–59.
The molten gold may not be true, but the symbolism is in any case clear.

*Italy, then in Sicily and Africa, earning (or rather extorting) his first triumph
at the age of twenty-four, without ever having held formal office. Given
praetorian standing, after Sulla's death he was used by the conservative
Sullan government to suppress the anti-Sullan revolt of the consul Lepidus
in 78, then sent on to Spain to deal with Sertorius' strong and effective
Marian resistance. And conveniently, on his return to Italy in 71, he had
the good fortune to encounter the last organized remnants of Spartacus'
army and butcher them, thus being able to claim that he had ended the
slave revolt—despite the fact that it was Marcus Crassus who had done the
serious military work.*

*To this point, Pompey's entire career consisted not of war against
Rome's foreign enemies but in eliminating pockets of resistance not to
Rome, but (except for his minor part in suppressing Spartacus' revolt)
to Sulla and his followers. That is an element of his career that Cicero,
for obvious reasons, does not emphasize. Nor, in recounting Pompey's
military career, does Cicero need to say anything about the next phase,
when Pompey, returning from Spain to triumph over Sertorius, was freed
from the normal rules and permitted to be elected consul for 70 together
with Crassus. The two men disliked one another intensely, but they
collaborated long enough to shatter the last pieces of the reactionary
Sullan constitution, restoring the powers of the tribunate while the praetor
Lucius Cotta passed a law removing juries from the sole control of the
senate. Pompey's unquestioned military accomplishments gave him
considerable popularity; it is not unlikely that his estrangement from the
remaining supporters of the Sullan constitution served only to increase
it. In 67, over the violent objections of the optimates, the tribune Aulus
Gabinius passed a law giving Pompey an unlimited command against
the pirates—whose resurgence throughout the Mediterranean was yet
one more result of Sulla's incomplete war against Mithridates—with vast
powers and funds. And Pompey's astonishing campaign, which eliminated
the pirates in less than three months, set the stage for Manilius' proposal
the next year: Pompey was conveniently in the East, he already controlled
a large military force and an effective staff, and, from his point of view, it
was an opportunity for further glory through defeating Rome's greatest
enemy, not to mention the power and patronage to be derived from
reorganizing the Roman East.*

*Like the Gabinian law, Manilius' law was opposed by conservatives, in
this case Catulus and Hortensius (Cicero's opponent in the trial of Verres),
and the argument against it was clear: it entrusted one man (Pompey)
with too much power and left no one else remotely comparable in glory,
influence, and military strength. What is more, Sulla's return from the
East with a strong army and an even stronger desire for power in Rome
offered a disturbing precedent—and Pompey's career, from the very*

beginning, had been extraconstitutional and unprecedented. Cicero, in arguing for Manilius' law, could not entirely ignore the objections of the optimates, particularly in presenting himself as a representative of reason and moderation. He in fact acknowledges the irregularities of Pompey's career, and he even takes the extraordinary step of using Pompey's history of unprecedentedness as precedent for yet one more military command without precedent. Throughout the speech, Pompey is presented as completely unlike all other Roman generals, both in his speed and military genius and in his complete immunity to the seductions of the East; he is both skillful and lucky, a great general and a man with divine (or almost divine) assistance. He is so hyperbolically above the mere mortals in the senate—and above Sulla and all Sulla's followers—that he poses no risk at all, merely a great benefit to the Roman people who are in a position to profit from his remarkable and unique attributes.

The indictment of the optimates is not concealed, but it is generally polite. Cicero respectfully demonstrates their failure of judgment in opposing Gabinius' law the year before, but he goes much further than that. During the course of the speech, Cicero first opposes the incapacity or corruption of the optimates to the hard work and important contributions of the companies of publicani, the corporations of Roman knights who collected the taxes of Asia and thus provided the financial basis of Roman government; then he turns to the virtue and imperviousness to pleasure and corruption of Pompey himself; and finally he presents the authority of the Roman people itself as something both wiser and more powerful than that of Catulus and Hortensius. By portraying the conservatives as a small and ineffective part of the ruling class and by enhancing the abilities of all other parts of society, Cicero links himself to all sensible Romans—and to Pompey himself.

We do not normally think of Cicero as a populist, and indeed he is not. But in the period of his campaign for consul, he carefully presents himself as a reformer, as supportive of the legitimate demands of the people, and as beholden to them. The speech against Verres draws repeated attention to the corruption of the Roman aristocracy and the danger that it poses to Rome's empire. The year after the speech on the Manilian law, in defending the tribune Gaius Cornelius on charges of sedition, Cicero invoked the precedent of the secession of the plebs as an argument that the tribunes had a right to represent the needs of the people, even if it entailed some disorder.[5] The opening and closing of the speech for the Manilian law draw attention to his gratitude to the people for his election and make it clear that the speech itself—his finest example of epideictic oratory, and the only oration whose structure is so explicit and

---

5. Fr. 47–49 Crawford (1994). The speech is unfortunately fragmentary.

emphatic—in its style as in its content is a representation of that gratitude.
It is a command performance, a display of oratorical skill to delight and to
please the popular audience for and before whom it was spoken.

De Imperio Cn. Pompei ad Quirites

My fellow citizens:

[1] Even though I have always taken great pleasure in seeing you
gathered in numbers, even though this spot has always seemed to me
the most dignified place for magistrates and the most honorable place
for citizens to address the public, nevertheless, despite my desire,
the organization of my life from the outset has until now kept me
away from this avenue to fame, one that has always been available to
every citizen of worth.[6] Previously, indeed, I did not dare approach
this place of such influence. I decided I should bring nothing here
if it did not represent the summit of my talent and the perfection of
my labors. I believed I should devote all my time to the support of
my friends. [2] This spot has never been short of men to represent
your interests, and the efforts I put forth with honor and integrity
against threats to private citizens have received the most extensive
rewards from your judgment. Because the elections were broken off,
I was three times declared the praetor elected in first place by all the
centuries,[7] and so I readily understand, my fellow citizens, both what
you think of me and what you require of others. Now, since I have as
much influence as you wanted in assigning me this public office and

---

6. The elaborate and very self-conscious opening of the speech (secs. 1–2)
reflects its importance as Cicero's first *contio* and first public speech as praetor: his thanks to the people (and self-congratulation) for his election, an
account of his previous career, and a preview of the speech that is to come.
The speech not only declares his gratitude but is itself a gift in return: his
work as an advocate not only brought him the fame and fortune to gain election, it gave him the rhetorical power that, in this speech, he is displaying
as a reward to the people who elected him. The speech is unusually formal
for Cicero in its structure and regularity; that is because it is Cicero's most
explicit use of the conventions of epideictic oratory.

7. The elections were interrupted twice, but not before Cicero had each time
received enough votes to ensure his election in first place. Elections for praetor and consul were held in the (timocratic) centuriate assembly (see Roman
Institutions and Offices). We do not know the cause of the interruptions.

as much ability in public affairs as almost daily practice in the courts can give a man of energy, I will certainly use whatever influence I have in the presence of those who gave it to me, and whatever skill I have as a speaker I will display above all to those who judged that such skill deserved to be rewarded. **[3]** And I take particular and proper joy in observing that, in the unfamiliar role of speaking in this place, I have been offered a cause in which words could fail nobody. My task is to speak of the unique and outstanding virtue of Pompey, and in a speech like this it's harder to stop than to start. I have no need to look for the words; I need to find a limit.[8]

[4] Let me begin my speech where the problem begins. A major, dangerous war is being waged against your sources of revenue and your allies by two very powerful kings, Mithridates and Tigranes;[9] because one of them was not finished off and the other was provoked, they thought they had been offered the chance to seize the province of Asia.[10] Messages arrive daily from Asia to those most respectable men, the Roman knights, who have substantial capital at risk in the collection of your revenues; because I have close ties to that group, they approached me in the public interest and because of their private risk. **[5]** Many villages have been burned out in Bithynia, which is now your province; the kingdom of Ariobarzanes,[11] which abuts your sources of revenue, is entirely under the control of the enemy; Lucius Lucullus, after great military achievements, has left the war; his successor[12] is inadequately prepared for command in so great a war; there is one man who is sought and asked for to lead this war by

---

8. Cicero again hints at the epideictic nature of the speech, this time combining it with his first praise of Pompey.

9. On Mithridates, see the introduction to this speech. Tigranes (the husband of Mithridates' daughter Cleopatra) was king of Armenia. For fuller identification of individuals, see the Biographical Index.

10. The taxes of the Roman province of Asia (the western portion of Asia Minor) were collected by tax-farming companies (the *publicani*) controlled by Roman knights. For geographical locations, see Map 2. For political terminology, see Roman Institutions and Offices.

11. Ariobarzanes was king of Cappadocia in east-central Asia Minor, abutting the Roman province of Cilicia (south), Mithridates' kingdom of Pontus (north), and Armenia (east). The major source of revenue was not Cilicia but Asia.

12. Manius Acilius Glabrio, consul in 67.

every ally and citizen; this same man is the only one feared by the enemy. There is no alternative.

[6] You see what the problem is. Now consider what action should be taken. I must first speak about the type of war; then about its size; then about the choice of a general.[13] The type of war is one that ought greatly to arouse your spirits and set them ablaze with eagerness for victory. At issue in it is the reputation of the Roman people, handed down from your ancestors—glorious in all things, but particularly in military affairs. At issue is the safety of our allies and friends, for which your ancestors waged many major wars. At issue are the most assured and substantial revenues of the Roman people, without which you will lack both the enhancements of peaceful life and the means to pay for war. At issue are the goods of many citizens, which you must protect both for their sake and for that of the public. [7] And since you have always wanted glory and been eager for praise beyond all other peoples, you must eliminate the stain created by the last war against Mithridates, a stain that has set deeply in the name of the Roman people. The man who on a single day by a single messenger and a single message in all Asia, in so many cities, arranged the slaughter of every Roman citizen[14] has not only not yet received any punishment worthy of his crime but also, after twenty-three years, still reigns, and reigns in such a manner that he chooses not to skulk in hiding places in Pontus or even in Cappadocia but to come out of his ancestral kingdom and conduct a campaign in your revenue territories, that is, in the bright light of Asia. [8] And to this day, our generals have engaged with the king in such a manner that they bring home the tokens of victory rather than victory itself. Lucius Sulla triumphed over Mithridates, Lucius Murena triumphed over him—two men of great courage, great generals, but they triumphed in such a way that even though he was beaten and overcome, he still ruled. But those generals deserve praise for what they did and forgiveness for leaving him in power, since the commonwealth recalled Sulla to Italy from the war, and Sulla recalled Murena.[15]

---

13. Cicero follows this outline, although the true subject of every section is in fact Pompey.

14. In 88 BCE Mithridates ordered the simultaneous killing of every Roman and Italian in Asia.

15. Sulla and Murena both held triumphs in 81; Sulla had returned to Italy in 83, but the triumph was delayed by his reconquest of Rome, his "election"

[9] Mithridates, moreover, used all the time since then not to wipe out the memory of the earlier war but to get ready for a new one. After he'd built and fitted out a huge navy and gathered immense armies from whatever nations he could, pretending to make war on his neighbors the Bosporans,[16] he sent ambassadors with messages all the way to Spain to the generals we were then fighting. His purpose was that if there were war by land and sea in two regions very far apart, against two enemy forces coordinated by a single strategy, then you would be fighting to preserve the empire while distracted by a war on two fronts.[17] **[10]** But the danger on one front, against Sertorius and the Spaniards, who had much greater strength and resources, was dealt with by the superhuman wisdom and unique virtue of Pompey;[18] on the other front, affairs were so managed by that great man Lucullus that the great successes at the outset of the campaign were owed to his virtue rather than his good fortune, and the recent events to luck rather than to any fault of his. But I will have more to say later about Lucullus,[19] and what I say then, my fellow citizens, will neither diminish the praise he is truly owed nor exaggerate with false praise. **[11]** But about the respect and glory of your empire, the starting point of my speech, it is you, my fellow citizens, who must determine your own opinion.

Our ancestors often went to war when our merchants and traders were roughed up; what should your attitude be when so many thousands of Roman citizens were slaughtered at one signal? When our ambassadors were insulted, your forefathers decided to snuff

---

as dictator, and the butchering of his opponents. Cicero's language about Sulla is, as always, carefully chosen. Here (as later in his defense of the younger Murena) Cicero also passes discreetly over Murena's disastrous campaign against Mithridates.

16. The region of the Crimea on the north coast of the Black Sea.

17. Sertorius, the last major survivor of the Marian cause, resisted government forces for ten years (82–72). Cicero refers to the same attempt at an alliance in *Mur.* 32.

18. Pompey fought Sertorius for five years with mixed success; after Sertorius was assassinated in 72, Pompey succeeded in eliminating his remaining supporters. Note that "virtue" (*virtus*) has two distinct meanings in Latin (and in this speech in particular), military courage and moral excellence; in speaking of Pompey, Cicero deliberately blurs the distinction.

19. See sec. 20. Lucullus commanded the Third Mithridatic War, 74–66.

out Corinth, the brightest light of all Greece;[20] will you let off a king who used whips and chains and every kind of torture to put to an agonizing death a consular legate of the Roman people?[21] They didn't permit the liberty of Roman citizens to be infringed; will you neglect the taking of a life? They avenged verbal violations to the rights of our envoys; will you ignore the murder by torture of a legate? **[12]** For them, it was truly magnificent to hand on to you so glorious an empire: watch out that it not be just as truly disgraceful for you not to be able to preserve and protect what you have inherited.

Consider this: the safety of our allies has been placed at risk, in the highest danger. What should your attitude be in response? King Ariobarzanes, a friend and ally of the Roman people, has been driven from his kingdom; two kings threaten all Asia, kings who are profoundly hostile not just to you but to your friends and allies; all the cities throughout Asia and Greece must seek your aid because of the magnitude of the danger; they don't dare, particularly since you have sent them a different general,[22] demand a specific general from you, nor do they believe they can do so without the greatest risk. **[13]** They see and feel the same as you, that there is one man who has the most outstanding qualities, and the fact that he's nearby makes their lack of him all the more painful.[23] They know his arrival and his name alone, even though he came for the war at sea, checked and slowed the attacks of the enemy. Since they can't speak freely, they silently beg you to think them just as worthy of having their safety entrusted to such a man, all the more so because the generals we send into other provinces, even if they fend off the enemy, arrive in our allies' cities in a manner not very different from an enemy assault. But this man, as they used to hear before and now see before

---

20. Corinth was destroyed in 146 after an assembly of the Achaean League had shouted down (and possibly shaken up) Roman ambassadors. There were also more substantive reasons for the war.

21. Manius Aquillius, head of a commission to restore the kings of Bithynia and Cappadocia to their thrones, provoked an invasion of Pontus that, in turn, led Mithridates both to order the slaughter of the Romans and Italians in Asia and to torture Aquillius to death; see above, sec. 7.

22. Glabrio (above, n. 12).

23. Under the Gabinian law (67 BCE), Pompey was in charge of the war against the pirates; see below, secs. 31–35.

their eyes, is endowed with such moderation, such gentleness, such humanity that the longer he stays among people the more blessed they seem.

[14] On behalf of our allies, our ancestors, although not assaulted themselves, waged war with Antiochus, with Philip, with the Aetolians, with the Carthaginians:[24] how much more vehemently should you, who have been provoked by injuries, defend the safety of our allies together with the dignity of our empire, especially when your greatest sources of revenue are at risk? The revenues of other provinces, my fellow citizens, are hardly big enough to pay for defending the provinces themselves, but Asia is so rich and fertile that in the productivity of its fields and the variety of its crops and the size of its pasture lands and the quantity of its exports, it easily outdoes all other lands. And thus, my fellow citizens, if you want to maintain both military readiness and the comforts of peace, this province must be defended not just from disaster but even from the fear of disaster. **[15]** In other matters, loss follows disaster; in the case of revenues it isn't just the arrival of trouble but fear of it that brings disaster. When enemy troops aren't far off, even if there's no invasion, nevertheless flocks are abandoned, farms are deserted, merchants give up shipping. And so not from harbor dues nor from the tithe on crops nor from the rent of pasture land can revenues be maintained, and for that reason the profits of a whole year are often lost from one hint of danger and a single alarm of war.[25] **[16]** So what do you think is the attitude either of those who pay our taxes or of those who manage and collect them, when there are two kings with large forces nearby, when a single cavalry raid can carry off the revenues of a whole year in an instant, when the tax companies believe that the large staffs that they employ—for pastures,[26] for agricultural territory, for the harbors and guard posts—are in great danger? Do you really believe you can profit from all these if the

24. Against Antiochus III of Syria (192–188), Philip V of Macedon (200–197), the Aetolian League (191–189), and Carthage, most recently the Third Punic War (149–146).

25. The three sources of tax revenue are harbor dues, a tax on produce, and rent for the use of public land for pasture. The order is reversed from the previous sentence, and reversed again in sec. 16.

26. An emendation: the manuscripts (and Clark) read *salinis*, "salt-mines," rather than *saltibus*, "pastures."

people who are the source of your profit are not kept safe, not only, as I've already said, from disaster but also from the fear of disaster?

[17] Don't forget, moreover, the last topic I set for myself when I began to talk about the type of war, that it involves the property of many Roman citizens. You must think carefully about it, my fellow citizens, in a manner worthy of your wisdom.[27] The members of the tax companies, men of great honor and substance, have lodged their resources and investments in that province; their property and fortunes should certainly concern you. In fact, if we've always recognized that revenues are the sinews of the commonwealth, then it's only proper to say that the order that collects them is the foundation of the other orders. [18] What is more, some diligent and hardworking men of other orders themselves do business in Asia (and since they aren't here you should look after their interests), while others have large investments in that province. Your humanity should protect this great number of citizens from disaster; your wisdom should recognize that a disaster affecting a lot of citizens can't be isolated from the commonwealth itself. In the first place, it makes little difference that you can restore their lost revenues to the tax companies after a victory; the same men won't be able to bid for the tax contracts because of the disaster, and others won't want to do so because of fear. [19] Second, having learned from disaster we should remember the lesson that Asia and Mithridates themselves taught us at the start of the Asian war. At that time, when a great many people lost a lot of capital in Asia, we know that the failure of liquidity caused a collapse of credit at Rome. If many people in one state lose their property and their fortunes, they can't help dragging more people with them over the same cliff: that's the danger from which you must protect the commonwealth. Indeed (trust me—you can see for yourselves), the banking system that operates in the forum in Rome itself is closely tied to the Asian revenues; you can't destroy the second without causing the failure and collapse of the first. That's why you need to see that you mustn't hesitate to push on with a war in which the glory

---

27. Cicero's recognition of loss of revenue is ever more explicit and ever more closely tied to the income of the *publicani*. With virtual monopolies, the tax companies committed large resources and considerable staff to the provinces from which they gathered taxes. Cicero claimed a close connection to the financial class; his praise of them and support of their interests in this speech is evident.

of your name, the safety of your allies, huge tax revenues, and the fortunes of a great many citizens linked to the commonwealth are being protected. **[20]** Since I've spoken about the type of war, I will now say a few words about its size. It may well be said that the type of war is such that it's necessary to fight it, but its size is not such that we must greatly fear it. We have to be very clear about this: you must not think you can make light of things for which very careful preparation is needed. And since I want everyone to understand that I am offering Lucullus the praise that is owed to a brave and wise man and a great general, I say this: when he arrived,[28] Mithridates had huge armies outfitted with every conceivable resource; the most famous city of Asia, Cyzicus, one of our firmest allies, was oppressed and besieged by the king himself with a vast army; by his courage, diligence, and wisdom Lucullus freed it from the impending danger of the siege. **[21]** It was at the hand of the same general that a large and well-equipped fleet, rushing toward Italy, commanded by Sertorius' men, inflamed and motivated by hatred, was conquered and sunk.[29] What is more, great numbers of the enemy were destroyed in numerous battles, and Pontus, which had previously been closed to the Roman people from every direction, was opened to our legions. Sinope and Amisus, cities in which the king had homes adorned and crammed with all his goods, together with countless other cities of Pontus and Cappadocia, were captured by a single appearance of Lucullus; the king, despoiled of his ancestral realm, fled to other kings and other nations as a suppliant.[30] All these campaigns took place without destroying our allies and with the integrity of the revenue-producing provinces unimpaired. I believe, my fellow citizens, that this is sufficient praise, offered for you to understand that none of those who oppose this law and its purpose has given Lucullus as much praise from this platform.

---

28. In 74 BCE. Cicero is very cautious in speaking about Lucullus, who had been Sulla's quaestor in the First Mithridatic War and was his most loyal officer. Beginning in sec. 51, Hortensius and Catulus are treated with equal care, as devoted adherents both of Sulla and of Lucullus.

29. On this fleet, see secs. 9–10.

30. Tigranes, king of Armenia; Machares, Tigranes' son, king of the Bosporus; and subsequently Arsaces, king of Parthia.

[22] At this point, someone may ask how, since conditions are as
I've described them, there can be much left of the war. My fellow
citizens, listen: it's a reasonable question. First of all, Mithridates
fled from his kingdom in the same way that Medea of old is said to
have fled from the same kingdom of Pontus. They say that in her
flight she scattered the limbs of her brother in the places where her
father would pursue her so that the collection of his son's widespread
remains and parental grief would slow the speed of his pursuit.[31]
In the same way, Mithridates in his flight left behind in Pontus his
entire vast stores of gold and silver and all sorts of beautiful things,
some of which he had inherited from his ancestors, some of which
he had plundered from all Asia and collected in his kingdom during the previous war. While our troops were being too careful in
collecting all this, the king himself escaped their clutches. And so
Medea's father was slowed in pursuit by grief and our soldiers were
slowed by joy. [23] Mithridates in his fearful flight was received by
Tigranes, the king of Armenia, who reassured him when he doubted
himself, raised him up when he was afflicted, and restored him from
disaster. After Lucullus reached Tigranes' kingdom with his army,
even more nations rose up to oppose our general. Nations whom the
Roman people had never thought to provoke or assail in war began
to be afraid; another deep and violent suspicion filled the minds of
these barbarian tribes, that our army had been led to that region in
order to plunder a very rich and very sacred shrine.[32] The result was
that many great tribes were shaken up by a new and terrifying fear.
Our army, moreover, even though it had captured one of Tigranes'
cities and had been successful in battles, was still distressed by being
too far away and yearning for their own people. [24] I will say no
more here; the outcome was that our soldiers desired to come back
quickly rather than continue onward.[33] Mithridates, moreover, had

31. The story of Medea's dismemberment of her brother Absyrtus is alluded
to in Euripides' (and Ennius') *Medea* and told in fuller detail in Apollonius'
Argonautica.
32. The temple of Nanaea/Anaitis in Elymais (Luristan). Most unlikely: it's
in the wrong direction.
33. Lucullus' troops mutinied in the winter of 68–67, after Lucullus had
captured Tigranocerta (69), defeated the forces of Mithridates and Tigranes
at the battle of the Arsanias, and captured Nisibis in northern Mesopotamia.
Lucullus' command was transferred to Acilius Glabrio (consul in 67) by a law

already strengthened his forces, thanks to those who had come from his own kingdom to join him; he was also helped by significant additional support from many kings and nations. We can take this as a general rule: when kings experience ill fortune, they easily draw the resources of many to the side of pity, particularly those who are either kings themselves or live under a monarchy; to them, it seems, the name of king is great and holy. **[25]** Therefore, after being defeated, he was able to accomplish more than he dared hope for when he was unharmed. And so, when he returned to his kingdom, he was not satisfied with the unexpected result of reaching his homeland again after having been driven from it, but he launched an attack on our glorious, conquering army.

Permit me at this point, my fellow citizens, just as poets who write about Roman history usually do, to pass over our disaster; it was so huge that common rumor, not an official messenger from the battle, brought the news to the general's ears.[34] **[26]** Here, at the very moment of this disastrous defeat, Lucullus, who could perhaps at least have mitigated the calamity, was forced by your orders—since according to precedent you decided to place a limit on his command—to dismiss the portion of his troops who had already served their time and to transfer the rest to Manius Glabrio. I am deliberately leaving a lot out; but you can infer how great that war became: a war that was the joint effort of kings of great power, renewed by nations that had been aroused, undertaken by tribes previously uninvolved, and taken over by a new general of ours when the previous army had been beaten.

[27] It seems to me that I've said enough about how this war's circumstances make it necessary and how its size makes it dangerous. It remains for me to speak about the choice of a general for this war, a commander to take charge of such a massive effort. If only, my fellow citizens, you had such a large supply of brave and honorable men that you could think there was some difficulty in choosing a commander for such a great war! As it is, since Pompey is the one man who surpasses through his virtue not only the glory of men now living but even our recollections of antiquity, what could possibly cause anyone to have any doubts in our current situation? **[28]** In my

---

proposed by the tribune Gabinius—another of whose laws created Pompey's command against the pirates.

34. Lucullus' legate Valerius Triarius was defeated at the battle of Zela in 67 before Lucullus could return from Armenia.

own opinion, there are four attributes that make an outstanding general: knowledge of military affairs; ability;[35] authority; and good luck. Who has ever been or could be more knowledgeable than Pompey? Coming from school and the education of a boy, he set out in the midst of a great war against terrible enemies to his father's army and the education of a soldier.[36] At the end of his childhood he was a soldier in the army of an outstanding general; as he came of age he was himself the general of a great army.[37] He has more often fought our enemies than any individual has struggled with a personal adversary; he has fought more wars than others have read about; he has reduced more provinces than others have even hoped for. As a young man he was educated in military science not by the instruction of others but by his own commands, not by military defeats but by victories, not by years of service but by triumphs. What kind of war is there in which the fortune of the commonwealth has not made trial of him? Civil, African, Transalpine, Spanish (a war against a combination of citizens and very hostile tribes), a slave war, naval war.[38] The varied and disparate types of both wars and enemies, not only waged but completed by this one man, declare that there is nothing of military experience that could escape his knowledge.

------

35. The Latin is *virtus*—Cicero slips back and forth between the military and moral meanings. The word is often translated as "manliness" (its etymological meaning), which frequently makes little sense. Here it is translated as "ability," "courage," or "virtue" depending on the context.

36. In the Social War (against the Italians) in 89, when Pompey's father, Gnaeus Pompeius Strabo, was consul.

37. Pompey continued to serve in his father's army until the latter's death in 87; on Sulla's return to attack Rome in 83, Pompey raised a private army to support Sulla; he was appointed propraetor and fought for Sulla against the Marian remnants in Italy and Sicily in 82 and in Africa in 81, when he returned and successfully demanded a triumph (at the age of twenty-four), never having held elected office.

38. When the consul Marcus Aemilius Lepidus in 78 attempted to reverse Sulla's "reforms" and on failing turned to revolution, Pompey defeated him and killed his supporter Marcus Brutus at Mutina (78–77); he then went through Gaul to Spain, where he fought Sertorius (76–72), returning to Italy in 71 in time to take credit for the defeat of Spartacus' slave revolt. In 67, by the Gabinian law, he was given his extraordinary command against the pirates.

[29] Furthermore, what can I say that could match Pompey's outstanding ability? What could anyone add either worthy of him or new to you or unfamiliar to anyone at all? The virtues of a general are not only those commonly thought of as military—energy in operations, courage in danger, hard work in action, speed in accomplishment, wisdom in planning. All these are greater in this one man than in all the other generals we've seen or of whom we've heard. **[30]** Italy is a witness:[39] Lucius Sulla, himself the victor, admitted that Italy was freed by the aid of this man's virtue. Sicily is a witness: when it was encircled by many dangers, he liberated it not through war with its terrors but through his strategic speed. Africa is a witness: it was overwhelmed by large enemy forces but flowed with the blood of those enemies themselves. Gaul is a witness: the route of our legions to Spain was opened through exterminating the Gauls. Spain is a witness: over and over it has seen him conquer and lay low innumerable enemies. Italy is a witness again and again: when it was oppressed by a savage and dangerous slave revolt, it sought help from this man who was then absent; the war was diminished and reduced because he was expected, and it was done away with and buried by his arrival.[40] **[31]** And now every shore and every land, tribe and nation, indeed, every ocean, both as a whole and in every particular bay and harbor on each and every shore, is a witness. What place on the entire ocean in these past years either has had such strong protection that it was safe or was so remote that it was hidden? Who has taken ship without exposing himself to the risk of death or enslavement, having to set sail either in the winter or on an ocean filled with pirates? This war was so large, so disgraceful, so long-lasting, so widely scattered and dissipated—who would ever think it could be brought to a conclusion by all the generals in one year or in all time by one general? **[32]** What province, in recent years, have you held free from pirates? What revenue has been safe for you? What ally have you protected? Whom have you guarded with your fleets? How

---

39. The subsequent sentences provide a more hyperbolic list of the same wars described above in sec. 28.

40. A gross exaggeration: Marcus Crassus had nearly eliminated Spartacus and his troops before Pompey returned from Spain, coming across a group of five thousand survivors trying to escape to the north. He claimed credit for ending Spartacus' revolt—but even he could not claim credit for defeating him.

many islands do you think have been deserted, how many cities of
your allies have either been abandoned through fear or captured by
pirates?[41]

But I have no need to mention far-off events. Once upon a time,
once it was the custom of the Roman people to fight wars far from
home and to defend the fortunes of our allies, not our own homes,
with the forces of empire. Am I to speak of the ocean having been
closed to your allies in recent years, when your own armies never
crossed from Brundisium except in the depth of winter? Am I to complain that emissaries to you from foreign nations have been captured,
when legates of the Roman people have been held for ransom? Am I to
say that the ocean has not been safe for merchants, when two praetors
with the full regalia of office have been held by pirates?[42] **[33]** Am
I to mention the capture of such noble cities as Cnidus or Colophon
or Samos, as well as countless others, when you know that your own
harbors—and the very harbors through which you draw your life and
breath—have been in the power of the pirates? Don't you know that
the crowded harbor of Caieta, filled with ships, was plundered by the
pirates while a praetor was watching, that the children of the very
man who had previously waged war with the pirates were snatched
from Misenum by the pirates?[43] Why should I complain about the
embarrassment at Ostia and that stain and disgrace to the commonwealth when almost under your own eyes, a fleet commanded by a
consul of the Roman people was captured and sunk by the pirates?[44]
By the everlasting gods! The incredible and superhuman virtue of
one man has so quickly brought such light to the commonwealth that
you, who recently saw an enemy fleet at the mouth of the Tiber, now
hear that there is now not a single pirate ship within the mouth of

---

41. Partly as a result of Rome's civil disorders and Sulla's devastation of
the Greek East, piracy had greatly increased since the 80s. Plutarch (*Life
of Pompey* 24) gives an account of pirates' power and successes. Pompey was
not the first to be given an extraordinary command against them; Marcus
Antonius Creticus had held one from 74 to 71.

42. Sextilius and Bellienus, known only in this context.

43. The events mentioned in this paragraph are not all recent: Samos was
sacked while Sulla was still in Asia, and the praetor whose daughter (only
one child) was captured and ransomed was Marcus Antonius, consul in 99,
who had fought the pirates from 102 to 100.

44. Date uncertain.

the Ocean! **[34]** And although you see yourselves how fast all this was accomplished, I can't leave it out here. For was there ever anyone, in the zealous conduct of business or the pursuit of profit, who was able in so short a time to go to so many places and complete so many voyages as quickly as the expeditionary force under Pompey's command completed its campaign? Before the sailing season had begun, he went to Sicily, scouted Africa, and from there came to Sardinia with his fleet, and he fortified these three sources of grain with the strongest protection. **[35]** From there, after he had come to Italy, when he had secured the two Spanish provinces and Transalpine Gaul with garrisons and ships and had also sent ships to the shore of the Adriatic and to Achaea and all of Greece, he provided Italy's two seas with large fleets and strong garrisons; he himself, on day forty-nine after leaving Brundisium, added all Cilicia to the empire of the Roman people.[45] All the pirates anywhere were either captured and killed or surrendered themselves to the power of this one commander. He, too, when the people of Crete sent envoys to him all the way to Pamphylia seeking mercy, allowed them to surrender to him and required hostages of them.[46] And so this war, so great, so long-lasting, so widespread, a war that weighed upon all peoples and nations, Pompey organized at the end of winter, began at the start of spring, and completed by the middle of summer.

[36] Here is a general of superhuman and incredible qualities. As for his other virtues, which I started to talk about earlier, how great and how many they are! In a complete and perfect general, we look not only for military abilities; many other outstanding qualities go hand in hand. In the first place, generals must be upright; beyond that, how restrained must they be in all things, how trustworthy, how approachable, how intelligent, how humane! We should briefly consider these qualities in Pompey. In him they are all preeminent, my fellow citizens, but they can better be recognized and understood

---

45. Pompey's organization of the campaign was brilliant, but Cicero ascribes to him in person much that was in fact done by his many legates. The western Mediterranean was indeed cleared in forty days and the eastern Mediterranean in forty-nine.

46. Quintus Caecilius Metellus Creticus held a proconsular command against the pirates in Crete predating Pompey's command; apparently some Cretan cities hoped for better terms from Pompey. Cicero exaggerates the distance, even more so in sec. 46 below.

through comparison with others. **[37]** What general can we consider a general at all, in whose army positions as centurion have
been and still are being sold? What great or distinguished ideas
about public life can a man have who takes the money assigned from
the treasury for the conduct of war and either splits it up among
the magistrates because he wants to keep his province or leaves it
invested in Rome because he's greedy? Your murmurs, my fellow
citizens, seem to show that you know who did this. I'll name no
names; no one can be angry at me without accusing himself.[47] And
because of our generals' greed, who doesn't know what disasters our
armies bring with them wherever they go? **[38]** Remember the passage of our generals in recent years through the property and towns
of Roman citizens in Italy; then you'll have an easy time figuring
out what's going on in foreign territory. Do you think that, in recent
years, there have been more hostile cities destroyed by the weapons of your soldiers or allied states destroyed by quartering troops
on them in winter? A general with no self-control can't control his
army; no one can be a severe judge who wants other judges not to
be severe to him. **[39]** Should we be surprised that this man stands
out so much above all others? When his legions reached Asia, this
large army kept its hands off more than just the property of noncombatants; even its footprint was harmless. Every day we hear talk and
receive letters about how our soldiers behave in winter quarters. Not
only is no one mugged to spend money on our troops, but they aren't
allowed to pay even if they want to. Our ancestors wanted the homes
of our friends and allies to be a refuge from winter, not a refuge for
greed. **[40]** Notice also his restraint in other matters. Where do
you think he got such speed, such incredible rapidity? It's not that
his rowers were phenomenal or that his helmsmen had some secret
skill or that there was some new wind that brought him so quickly
to the ends of the earth. Instead, things that usually delay others
didn't slow him down. Greed didn't seduce him from his planned
route for plunder, nor sensuality for pleasure, nor charm for delight,
nor the nobility of a city for tourism, nor indeed toil for relaxation.
In sum, the statues and paintings and other ornaments of the Greek
cities that others think they have to steal, he had no interest in

---

47. Cicero's use of innuendo allows him to exaggerate the failings of (uncertain) other generals purely in order to exaggerate Pompey's virtues.

seeing at all.[48] **[41]** And so everyone over there looks on Pompey as someone not sent from Rome but descended from the heavens.[49] Now at last they begin to believe that there once really were Romans of such self-control, something that used to seem to other nations an unbelievable fiction; now the splendor of your empire has begun to bring light to those peoples; now they understand that their ancestors had good reason, at a time when we had magistrates of such restraint, to prefer to be enslaved to the Roman people rather than rule over others. What is more, access to him is said now to be so easy for private citizens, complaints about harm done by others so permissible, that a man who stands above the highest men in dignity seems equal to the lowest in accessibility. **[42]** The strength of his insight, the range and solemnity of his speech, which has in itself a kind of dignity appropriate to a general, you, my fellow citizens, have often observed from this very spot. And how much trust do you think our allies have in him, when all our enemies from every tribe have always judged him completely trustworthy? His humanity is so great that it's hard to say whether our enemies have been more afraid of his courage when fighting him or have loved his mildness when defeated. And will anyone still have any doubts about entrusting this great war to a man who appears to have been born according to a divine plan for bringing to an end all the wars of our time?

[43] And since authority is also extremely important in the conduct of war and in commanding troops, surely nobody doubts that this same general has the greatest capacities in this respect, too. And who doesn't know that it's highly relevant to the conduct of war what both enemies and allies think of our generals, since we know that rumor and report no less than careful logic affect men who are involved in affairs great enough to arouse fear or scorn or hatred or love? What name, then, has ever been more glorious throughout the world? Whose accomplishments are comparable? Is there any man to whom you have yourselves given so many and such visible signs of approval, a thing that confers particular authority? **[44]** Or do you believe that there is any coast anywhere so deserted that the report

---

48. Pompey was indeed highly disciplined, but Cicero is making a virtue of his complete lack of artistic sensibility.

49. Hints of Pompey's superhuman (and possibly divine) nature run through the speech; the description of a provincial savior as someone sent down from heaven has parallels elsewhere.

of that day hasn't reached it, when the entire Roman people, with the forum crowded and every temple from which this spot can be seen packed, demanded this one man, Pompey, as the commander of a war that concerned every nation?[50] And so I don't speak too long and don't use the examples of others to prove the importance of military authority, I'll use Pompey himself to supply instances of all his outstanding accomplishments. On the day you made him commander over the naval war, the price of grain dropped so far, after the greatest shortage and highest prices, that a long peace and abundant harvests could scarcely have caused it. **[45]** After the disaster in Pontus, the result of the battle I reluctantly mentioned to you a little while ago, our allies were in great fear, the resources and the spirits of the enemy had risen, the province had inadequate defenses; and you would have lost Asia, my fellow citizens, if the Fortune of the Roman people had not divinely brought Pompey to that region at the exact moment of crisis. Mithridates was puffed up with his unaccustomed victory, but Pompey's arrival brought him to a halt and slowed down Tigranes, who was threatening Asia with large forces. And will anyone have doubts about what a man who accomplished so much by his authority will accomplish by his courage, or how easily a man who defended our allies and revenues by his name and reputation will preserve them with the command of an army? **[46]** Tell me: what does it show about the authority of this man among the enemies of the Roman people that from such distant and dispersed locations in such a short time they all surrendered to him alone?[51] That envoys from the common council of the Cretans, even though we had a general and an army on their island, came to Pompey almost at the ends of the earth and said that all the cities of Crete wanted to surrender to him? Didn't Mithridates himself send an envoy to Pompey all the way to Spain? At least Pompey always thought he was an envoy, although people who were annoyed at his having been sent especially to Pompey wanted him to be thought a spy rather than an envoy.[52] Therefore, my fellow citizens, after his

---

50. The passage of the Gabinian law in 67 giving Pompey the command against the pirates.

51. Both this and the following sentence describe exactly the same incident as in sec. 35 above.

52. Cicero's hedging makes it clear that the ambassador is imaginary, whether or not he was a spy.

many great accomplishments enhanced by your own weighty judgments, you can now judge how great his authority will be with those kings and among foreign nations.

[47] What remains is to say a few words about his good fortune. No one can vouch for his own good fortune, but we can call to mind and speak about someone else's, just as it's right for men to speak briefly and cautiously of something within the power of the gods. I firmly believe that commands and armies were frequently entrusted to Maximus, Marcellus, Scipio, Marius, and the other great generals not just because of their virtue but also because of their luck.[53] There are some great men who had god-given good luck, which contributed to their grandeur and glory and their accomplishment of great deeds. In speaking of the good fortune of the man we're now discussing, I will be moderate. I won't say that good luck is in his power, only that we can hope that what is still to come will be like what has come before: may my speech not be hateful to the everlasting gods or display ingratitude to them. [48] And so I will not describe how much he's done with how much good fortune at home and on campaign, by land and by sea; how not only citizens approved of his wishes, allies supported him, and enemies obeyed, but even the winds and storms favored him. This I will say, very briefly: that there has never been anyone so shameless as to dare to ask from the everlasting gods so many and such great accomplishments as the everlasting gods have showered on Pompey. That this may remain his own for ever and ever,[54] my fellow citizens, both in the interest of the common safety and the empire and on behalf of the man himself, you should, as you do, both wish and pray.

[49] Therefore, since this war is so necessary that it can't be neglected, so large that it must be managed with the greatest attention, and since you have the power to place in command of it a general in whom there exists extraordinary knowledge of warfare, unique

---

53. Great heroes of the Roman past: Quintus Fabius Maximus and Marcus Claudius Marcellus in the Hannibalic War, Gaius Marius in the wars against Jugurtha and the German invasion at the end of the second century. "Scipio" is deliberately ambiguous and could refer to both the elder Publius Cornelius Scipio Africanus, who defeated Hannibal, and the younger Publius Cornelius Scipio Aemilianus, who destroyed Carthage and Numantia. Favorable reference to Marius is normal in speeches to the people but not elsewhere.

54. The formal language of prayer.

ability, the most outstanding authority, and remarkable good fortune, do you have any doubt, my fellow citizens, that you should apply this great good, offered and given to you by the everlasting gods, to the preservation and enhancement of the commonwealth? **[50]** If Pompey were a private citizen in Rome at this moment, he would still be the one to be chosen and sent to so great a war; but now, since to the other elements of his great utility is also added the advantage that he's in the area, that he has an army, that he's able to take over from other commanders at once, what are we waiting for? Or why, under the guidance of the everlasting gods, do we not entrust this war against the king to the same man to whom all the other wars have been entrusted with the greatest benefit to the commonwealth?

[51] And yet there are two men of great eminence, Quintus Catulus, a great lover of the commonwealth and the recipient of your most magnificent honors, and together with him Quintus Hortensius, a man who has reached the highest level of public office, good fortune, ability, and talent, who disagree with this argument.[55] I allow that their authority has had, and ought to have under many circumstances, a great weight in your minds; but in this matter, even though you recognize the opposing authority of men of great courage and distinction, we should be able to set authority aside and seek out the truth based on both fact and logic. That is all the easier because everything I have said so far is agreed by these men to be truth: that the war is necessary and important and that the highest qualities are to be found in Pompey alone. **[52]** What, then, does Hortensius say? If everything ought to be entrusted to one man, then Pompey is the most worthy; but everything should not be entrusted to one man. That argument has gotten old, refuted by events rather than words. It was you, Hortensius, who used the resources of your unique and extraordinary eloquence both to speak in the senate in a solemn and dignified manner against that brave man Aulus Gabinius, when he had proposed a law to choose one general against the pirates, and to say a great deal from this very spot against that law. **[53]** Well? If

---

55. Quintus Lutatius Catulus, consul in 78, was the senior senator (*princeps senatus*); Quintus Hortensius, consul in 69, was the leading orator in Rome before Cicero defeated him in the trial of Verres. Both were staunch Sullan conservatives; they favored Lucullus, who had been removed from the command against Mithridates, and feared—with some reason—the concentration of power and influence in the hands of Pompey.

at that time, by the everlasting gods, your influence on the Roman people had overcome the well-being and the true interests of the Roman people itself, then would we today still hang onto our glory and our empire over the world? Did this really seem to you to be an empire, when the envoys and quaestors and praetors of the Roman people were being taken captive, when we were blocked from both private and public commerce with all the provinces, when every ocean was so closed to us that we could engage in neither private nor public business overseas?

[54] What nation has there ever been in the past—I won't speak of Athens, which is said to have had broad control of the sea at one time; I won't speak of Carthage, which had a strong fleet and maritime success; I won't speak of Rhodes, the memory of whose naval skill and glory has lasted until our time—what nation, I repeat, has ever been so slight or tiny that it couldn't defend on its own its harbors and territory and some part of its coast? But, by god, there was a stretch of years before the Gabinian law in which the Roman people, to whose name no naval defeat had ever been attached, were deprived of a large part—the largest part—not only of useful supplies but even of its reputation and empire. [55] Our ancestors defeated King Antiochus and Perseus at sea, and in every naval encounter overcame the Carthaginians, a people who were extremely well versed and well prepared in naval matters—but we were nowhere able to stand up to the pirates.[56] In the past we not only used to hold Italy safe but could also guarantee the safety of all our allies on the most distant shores by the authority of our empire; then the island of Delos, located so far from us in the Aegean Sea, a center for merchandise and cargo from everywhere, filled with riches, small, unfortified, had no fears at all. But now we were deprived of not only our provinces and the coasts and harbors of Italy but even the Appian Way. And at those moments did it not shame the magistrates of the Roman people to mount this platform, since our ancestors had left it to us adorned with naval

---

56. There were naval battles in the war against Antiochus (192–189) and the First Punic War against Carthage (264–241). The praetor Gnaeus Octavius received a triumph for Perseus' surrender of his fleet in 168, but it was, as Livy (45.42) records, a victory "without captives and without spoils." The account of Roman naval invincibility, particularly against Carthage, is not entirely true: the consul Publius Claudius Pulcher was defeated by the Carthaginians in 249 BCE.

booty and the spoils of ships? **[56]** At that time, Hortensius, the Roman people believed that you and others who shared your opinion spoke with good intentions and sincerity; but still, in a matter of the common safety, the Roman people preferred to give heed to its own anger rather than to your authority. And so a single law, a single man, a single year not only freed you from that misery and shame but made you at last seem to have genuine power over all peoples and nations by land and by sea. **[57]** That makes it all the more unworthy to object—whether I should say to Gabinius or Pompey or both, which is in fact more accurate—to Gabinius' being made a legate to Pompey, who is making the request.[57] Is it the case that the person asking for whatever legate he wants for so great a war is not worthy of having his request honored, given that other men have taken the legates of their choice to plunder the allies and pillage the provinces, or is it that the very person by whose law safety and honor were given to the Roman people and all nations ought to be kept apart from the general and army established by his own plan and personal risk? **[58]** Is it the case that Gaius Falcidius, Quintus Metellus, Quintus Caelius Latiniensis, and Gnaeus Lentulus, all of whom I name with great respect, were eligible to be legates the year after they had been tribunes of the people,[58] but such scruples are appropriate in the case of Gabinius alone, who ought to have particular rights in the case of this war, waged under the Gabinian law, and with this general and army, which he established with your approval? I expect the consuls to refer the issue of his legateship to the senate. And if they have doubts or make heavy weather of referring the issue, I promise I will do so, and no one's hostility will keep me from defending your rights and your generosity. Unless a tribune intercedes, I will listen to nobody—and as to that, those very people who keep threatening it should think very carefully about what is permissible. In my opinion, my fellow citizens, Gabinius alone should be accounted Pompey's partner in

---

57. Gabinius could not be appointed a legate in the pirate war, since it was impermissible (although no longer seriously enforced) to receive office under one's own law; he was subsequently appointed a legate in the war against Mithridates under Manilius' law.

58. These men were still alive, but of uncertain identity and date. The argument is a red herring; unless they had proposed the laws under which they became legates, it was not illegal for a tribune to become a legate in the next year.

the maritime war and military accomplishments, since one of them offered that war to one man with your approval and the other took up what was offered and finished it.

[59] It remains to say something about the authority of Quintus Catulus and his opinion. When he asked you in whom you would place your hopes if something should happen to Pompey after you put everything in his hands, he received a great reward for his virtue and his distinction when you all, almost in unison, said he was himself the one in whom you would place your hopes. In fact, he's a man of such character that there's no task so great and so difficult that he couldn't manage it by his wisdom, shepherd it by his honesty, and accomplish it by his ability. But in this specific matter I disagree with him in the strongest terms. The less certain and the briefer is the life of men, the more the commonwealth ought, so long as the everlasting gods permit it, to make use of the life and talents of an outstanding man. [60] "But nothing unprecedented should be done contrary to the examples and the institutions of our ancestors." I won't say here that our ancestors were obedient to tradition in peace but to expediency in war, that they always made new plans to fit new emergencies. I won't say that two of our greatest wars, the Punic War and the Spanish War, were brought to an end by the same general and that the two most powerful cities that were the greatest threat to our empire, Carthage and Numantia, were destroyed by one and the same Scipio.[59] I won't mention that not long ago both you and the senate deemed it right to place the hopes of our empire in Gaius Marius alone, so that the same man commanded the wars against Jugurtha, against the Cimbri, and against the Teutoni.[60] But in the case of Pompey himself, about whom Catulus wants no new precedent established, you should remember how many innovations have been made regarding him with the enthusiastic approval of Catulus himself.

[61] What is so unprecedented as for a young man to raise a private army during a public crisis? He raised one. To command it? He commanded it. To wage a campaign successfully under his own leadership? He waged it. What is so untraditional as for a very young

---

59. In 146 and 133, respectively, at the end of the Third Punic War and the Numantine War.

60. Marius took over the Jugurthine War as consul in 107 and defeated Jugurtha in 105; as consul continuously from 104 to 100, to meet the German invasion he defeated first the Teutoni in 102 and then the Cimbri in 101.

man, who isn't nearly old enough to become a senator, to be given a
command and an army, to be put in charge of Sicily and Africa and
a war to be waged in that province? He behaved in those provinces
with unique integrity, seriousness, and virtue; he completed a great
war in Africa and brought home the conquering army. What is so
unheard of as for a Roman knight to hold a triumph? But that, too,
the Roman people not only saw but thought it should be witnessed
and celebrated with universal enthusiasm. **[62]** What is so unfamiliar as that, when there were two very distinguished and courageous
consuls, a Roman knight should be sent as proconsul to a huge and
fearful war? He was sent. And at that time, since a number of senators
said, "A private citizen should not be sent in place of a consul," Lucius
Philippus is said to have said that with his vote he was not sending
him in place of a consul but in place of both consuls.[61] There was
so much hope that he would serve the commonwealth well that the
function of both consuls was entrusted to the virtue of a single young
man. What is so remarkable as that by a vote of the senate he was
exempted from the laws and made consul before he was legally eligible
to hold any other office?[62] What is so unbelievable as that a Roman
knight should triumph twice with the approval of the senate? All the
innovations we have seen in all men in human memory are fewer
than the ones we have seen in the case of this one man.[63] **[63]** And
these so many examples, so great and so new, with regard to this man
have been based on the authority of Quintus Catulus and the other
distinguished men of the same rank.

   That is why they should be careful. It would be extremely unjust
and intolerable that their authority concerning distinctions awarded

---

61. The war against Sertorius in Spain. Lucius Marcius Philippus, the oldest living ex-consul (consul in 91), supported Pompey from an early stage.
Philippus' joke depends on the close relationship between the official title
"proconsul" and its meaning, "in place of a consul."

62. Pompey's first consulate was in 70 BCE, when he was thirty-six. He
was eligible for lesser offices, but Cicero is not to be held to constitutional
precision in this context.

63. In this extraordinary passage Cicero has turned Catulus' justifiable
doubts about Pompey's respect for constitutional procedure into praise of
the very irregularity of his career. Many of the specifics are referred to
above, secs. 28–30. His behavior in his early (Sullan) campaigns earned him
the title *adulescentulus carnufex*, "the boy butcher."

to Pompey should always have been approved by you, but that your judgment and the authority of the Roman people concerning the same man should be impugned by them.[64] That is all the more true because the Roman people can with justice defend its own authority in the case of Pompey against any disagreement, because it was over the objections of precisely these people that you chose this one man of all men to put in charge of the pirate war. **[64]** If you did that rashly and did not properly look out for the commonwealth, then they are right to try to guide your enthusiasm by their wisdom. But if at that time you had greater political vision, and against their objections you, acting on your own, brought respect to this empire and safety to the world, then it's time for those so-called leaders to admit that they and all others should yield to the authority of the united Roman people. And in this war in Asia against the king, my fellow citizens, it is not just Pompey's unique military virtue that is needed but also his many other outstanding qualities of mind. It's difficult for one of our generals to behave in Asia, Cilicia, Syria, and the kingdoms of the interior in such a way as to pay attention to nothing but the enemy and to act in a praiseworthy fashion. What is more, even if through a sense of shame and self-control they act with restraint, no one believes they actually are restrained because of the great number of men who are greedy. **[65]** It is hard to say, my fellow citizens, how much we are hated in foreign lands because of the greed and cruelty of the rulers we have sent them in recent years.[65] What temple in those lands do you think has been held sacred by our magistrates, what city holy, what home adequately closed up and fortified? Rich cities of many resources are sought out to make war on so as to provide an opportunity for plunder. **[66]** I would be happy to discuss this in public with Catulus and Hortensius, men of great accomplishment and distinction; they know the wounds to our allies, they see their disasters, they hear their laments. Do you think you're sending armies against the enemy on behalf of our allies or, with the

---

64. Cicero in this passage makes extremely effective use of the word *auctoritas* ("authority" or "influence")—a quality normally attributed to senators or the senate itself—and transfers it to the popular assembly. It is one of the most (apparently) populist passages in Cicero.

65. The indictment of Roman provincial government is powerful and largely justified; Cicero had documented one egregious instance in his prosecution of Verres four years earlier.

pretense of fighting our enemies, against our friends and allies? What city in Asia can satisfy the eager arrogance not only of a general or a legate but of a single military tribune? For that reason, even if you have someone who seems able to overcome the armies of the king in pitched battle, nevertheless, unless that same person can keep his hands, his eyes, his mind away from the money of our allies, from their wives and children, from the decoration of their temples and towns, from the gold and treasure of the king, he will not be suitable to be sent to fight the king in Asia. **[67]** Do you think there is any city at all at peace with us that is wealthy? Any wealthy city that such people think is at peace with us? The coast of the ocean, my fellow citizens, sought out Pompey not just because of his military glory but also because of his mental self-control. He saw that our praetors, with a few exceptions, enriched themselves every year with public funds, and that we accomplished nothing with our fleets (fleets in name alone) except that through the losses we incurred we seemed to be afflicted with greater disgrace. Now I suppose the men who think we should not entrust the whole problem to a single man are unaware of the greed with which men set out for the provinces after making large payments on harsh terms.[66] As if we don't see that Pompey is great[67] not only because of his own virtues but because of the vices of others! **[68]** For that reason, do not hesitate to entrust everything to this one man, a man who for so many years has been the only one to be found at whose arrival with an army in their cities our allies rejoice.

My fellow citizens, if you think this argument needs the support of authoritative figures, you have Publius Servilius as an authority, a man experienced in every sort of war and in affairs of great magnitude; his accomplishments on land and sea are so great that his opinion should have more authority for you than anyone else's in a debate on war.[68] Another is Gaius Curio; he is a man of the greatest

---

66. Candidates for office borrowed money for the campaign (and bribery) at high rates of interest; they needed to extract money from their provinces in order to satisfy their creditors.

67. Pompey's cognomen *Magnus*, "the Great," was bestowed on him by Sulla.

68. The figures named in this section are all senior consulars: Publius Servilius Vatia Isauricus, consul in 79, had fought the pirates in Cilicia; Gaius Scribonius Curio, consul in 76, had fought in Macedonia; Gnaeus

intelligence and wisdom, who has received great honors from you and accomplished great things. Another is Gnaeus Lentulus; you have awarded him high office and acknowledge his wisdom and seriousness. Another is Gaius Cassius, a man of outstanding integrity, truthfulness, and steadfastness. Thus you see that we can use these authorities to reply to what people who disagree have said.

[69] This being the case, Gaius Manilius, I offer praise for your law, both your intention and your expression of it, and I give you my strongest possible support. What is more, I urge you to stick to your opinion: you have the authority of the Roman people to support you and should have no fear of violence or threats from anyone. I believe in the strength of your character and courage, and when we see so great a crowd with such great enthusiasm as we see now, for the second appointment of this same man, why should we have any doubts about what to do or about our ability to do it? For my part, whatever energy, wisdom, effort, and talent I have; whatever powers I have as praetor through the gift of the Roman people; whatever I can accomplish by authority, honesty, and perseverance—all this I promise and offer to you and to the Roman people in aid of accomplishing this goal, [70] and I call to witness all the gods, particularly those who preside over this hallowed spot, the gods who see especially into the minds of those who take part in public life, that I do this neither at the request of any man, nor because I think to obtain the favor of Pompey through this action, nor because I seek from any great man either protection from danger or assistance in seeking office. Under the shield of innocence I will easily ward off danger, insofar as a man can make such a claim, and I will achieve office not through one man or from what I do in this one place but by that selfsame organization of my life of hard work, if your goodwill supports me.[69] [71] For that reason, whatever actions I have taken in this matter, my fellow citizens, I affirm that I have done so entirely for the sake of the commonwealth, and I am so far from seeking any favor that I understand that I have incurred much hostility, some hidden, some open. I could have avoided that, but it has its uses for you. But having been invested

---

Cornelius Lentulus Clodianus, consul in 72, was one of Pompey's legates in the pirate war; Gaius Cassius Longinus, consul in 73, was one of the many generals (including Lentulus Clodianus) defeated by Spartacus.

69. Cicero returns to the rhetoric and themes of the opening of the speech, as often emphasizing his own selflessness.

with this office and been the recipient of such benefactions from you, my fellow citizens, I have decided that it is my duty to put your desires and the honor of the commonwealth and the safety of the provinces and of our allies ahead of all my own interests and benefits.

3

Second Speech against Catiline

For most people, including Cicero himself, the single most memorable event of his public career was the conspiracy of Catiline in the last months of his consulship in 63 BCE. But although the conspiracy was real, it was also in large part created by Cicero himself. Cicero's creation has several aspects. In the first place, in campaigning against Catiline in 64 for the consulship of 63, Cicero invented a whole range of lurid stories about his opponent, stories that have been taken as (perhaps exaggerated) fact from Cicero's time until fairly recently. Second, Cicero's later writings about the events of his consulship inflated the importance of Catiline, for the obvious reason that to magnify the danger he defeated was to magnify his own accomplishment. Among those later writings, moreover, must be considered the four speeches collectively known as the Catilinarian orations. Cicero included them as part of the larger collection of his consular orations that he put together, in deliberate emulation of the public orations of Demosthenes, when faced with the real threat of exile three years later, a threat that was based on Cicero's execution of five conspirators on December 5, 63, and that actually happened in 58.

To say that the Catilinarian orations are a product of 60 BCE rather than 63 BCE is to oversimplify. Cicero obviously gave speeches very much like the extant set in 63, on the days and on the subjects of the extant speeches. On the other hand, the collection as it exists is clearly shaped after the fact. Throughout the speeches, Cicero dwells on the risks of his actions and on his willingness to sacrifice himself for the common good, emphases that are much more appropriate to his later worries than to the immediate issues in 63. He also, quite clearly, selected these speeches out of a larger number that he gave in the second half of 63 about Catiline and his conspiracy.[1]

---

1. Cicero certainly spoke in the senate against Catiline to have the elections for 62 postponed; there was probably a debate about the rising in Etruria on September 22; on October 21 Cicero revealed the existence of the conspiracy to the senate. It would also be surprising if Cicero had not given a speech in the senate comparable to the Second Catilinarian, as he obviously did before the Third Catilinarian.

Before a discussion of Cicero's version, the underlying events deserve
some attention.[2] Lucius Sergius Catilina was a slightly older contemporary
of Cicero who was, like Cicero, a candidate in the consular elections of
64. He was defeated on that occasion and again in the elections of 63,
and then he turned to conspiracy. He plotted an attack within the city
against the consul Cicero and other leaders of the senate combined with
an assault from without by a makeshift army of Sullan veterans and other
distressed elements of the rural poor led by the former centurion Gaius
Manlius. The conspiracy was unmasked by Cicero, who had an informant
among the plotters; Catiline left Rome in November, joined Manlius, and
was defeated and killed in battle in January of 62.

Not all the conspirators left with Catiline; those who were still in Rome,
planning fire and destruction, made the foolish mistake of attempting to
enlist the support of the ambassadors of the Allobroges, a Gallic tribe
seeking redress from Roman administrators and relief from debt. Although
the failure of their embassy made them feel less than enthusiastic support
for Rome, they chose to report the attempt to Cicero, who organized
a trap. Leading conspirators sent messages to Catiline carried by the
Allobroges; the party of travelers was caught and arrested as they crossed
the bridge leaving Rome. The conspirators, convicted by their messages,
were brought before the senate on December 3. After debate on
December 5, they were put to death by Cicero on the basis of the senate's
approval. Roman law prohibited the execution of citizens without trial, and
thus Cicero's execution of the conspirators without a trial was, depending
on one's point of view, either a recognition of the authority of the senate
and an act of high statesmanship or the murder of citizens. Within a week,
Cicero was attacked for his actions; five years later he was exiled for the
same reason.

Aside from these basic facts, however, not much is clear about Catiline
and his conspiracy. Cicero is, directly or indirectly, our sole source, and
not just in the four Catilinarians.[3] In these speeches, Catiline emerges as
a conspirator, murderer, and pervert of long standing, but these sterling
qualities are assumed rather than proven. A fuller exposition of the story
came in an earlier speech delivered in 64 that is now largely lost, the
oration In Toga Candida. This "stump speech" probably ensured Cicero's
victory and Catiline's defeat in the consular elections. Cicero encourages
us to believe that his political success was both proper and inevitable, but

---

2. On the history, see, in addition to biographies of Cicero, the succinct
account of Wiseman (1994a) 346–58.

3. The other major source for the conspiracy is Sallust's *Conspiracy of
Catiline*, written twenty years later and heavily reliant on Cicero. The most
thorough study of the evidence is Hardy (1924).

in fact it was not. Cicero was not an aristocrat; his family had not been involved in Roman public life for centuries; he was not a great general; and he was not, it appears, accustomed to using bribery to win elections, as were many of his contemporaries. Catiline, on the other hand, was a patrician: his family traced its ancestry back to one of the men who left Troy with Aeneas (and his candidacy was supported by Gaius Julius Caesar, a descendant of Aeneas himself). He had a long military career, dating from service with Pompeius Strabo in the Social War. Unlike Cicero, he had governed a province (Africa); and although he was prosecuted for extortion in 65 (forcing him to postpone his candidacy for the consulship), he was also acquitted. He probably bribed the jury, but that was scarcely uncommon, and his case was good enough that Cicero himself at one point thought of defending him.

But Catiline had his unsavory side, and Cicero in his stump speech in 64 made the most of it. Catiline had been prosecuted for extortion and was deeply in debt; he had also been prosecuted for having sex with a Vestal Virgin. As later with the extortion charges, he was acquitted, and in both cases he had the support of senior members of the aristocracy. Cicero went further, however. He claimed that Catiline had been a brutal torturer at the time of the proscriptions; that he had murdered one or more of his relatives; that he had vile and indiscriminate sexual appetites; and, most important, that he had, along with various shadowy figures, conspired in 66 to murder the consuls of 65 on their first day in office. None of this was true—although the "first conspiracy" was long accepted as fact—but it was apparently plausible enough for the electorate to pick Cicero and Gaius Antonius (an ally of Catiline) as consuls.[4]

His electoral loss in 64 left Catiline in a desperate position. He was deeply in debt and needed to become consul (and subsequently to govern a province) in order to have the opportunity to make enough money to pay his debts. The election of 63 was his last chance, and he set about bribing the electorate so vigorously that a new law tightening the rules was passed (and used to prosecute Murena). Like his apparent friend Julius Caesar, another impecunious patrician, Catiline presented himself as the champion of the downtrodden, calling for debt reform and land reform. Shortly before the expected date of the election, he gave a speech in his house to supporters, saying that only someone who was himself in debt could understand the plight of the poor. Such a position frightened both Cicero and the senate. The elections were postponed, and Catiline's speech was debated in the senate. Catiline himself then gave another unsettling speech, claiming "that the commonwealth had two bodies, one tottering with a weak head, the other strong but headless; but if it

---

4. On the "first conspiracy," see Seager (1964) and Syme (1964) 83–101.

was worthy of him, that second body would not lack a head so long as he lived."[5] *When the election finally took place in September, Cicero presided wearing armor under his toga (deliberately not well concealed) as if his life were in danger. Catiline lost. Decimus Junius Silanus and Lucius Licinius Murena were elected—and Murena had to be defended by Cicero on (almost certainly true) charges of electoral corruption.*

Only beginning in October of 63 is there credible evidence for a conspiracy. On October 18 Marcus Licinius Crassus, the former consul and future partner of Caesar and Pompey, brought Cicero anonymous letters he and others had received warning them to leave Rome, that Catiline was planning to have them killed ten days later. News of Manlius' planned revolt in Etruria was received within a few days, and the senate, at Cicero's urging, passed the so-called senatus consultum ultimum, *"final decree of the senate," that the consuls should see to it that "no harm come to the commonwealth." Troops were sent to deal with Manlius.*

But in Rome nobody was assassinated, and there were no obvious signs of conspiracy; this was something of an embarrassment to Cicero, who had expected to be able to use the senate's decree against a more tangible threat. But Cicero's spy among the conspirators brought him news on November 6 of a meeting to plan Cicero's own assassination and other violent actions within Rome. Cicero blocked the men who (at least, so he claimed) had come to his house on the morning of November 7 to kill him. It was at this point that Cicero summoned the senate once more and delivered the speech we know as the First Catilinarian.

The four Catilinarian orations were organized, as noted above, in 60 BCE as part of Cicero's attempt to shape the interpretation of his actions as consul.[6] *The speeches were circulated as part of a larger collection of twelve consular orations: four (of which all or part of three survive) in opposition to the proposed agrarian law of the tribune Rullus at the beginning of the year; four against Catiline at the end of the year; and four others in the middle, all of which were intended to bolster his credentials as a strong supporter of senatorial rule and the status quo and a strong opponent of any measure designed to alleviate the desperate conditions of the Italian poor. Rullus' law was in the tradition of Gracchan land reform, an attempt to distribute public land in Campania to the urban poor: Cicero*

---

5. *Mur.* 51. The only evidence for Catiline's actions before the election is this speech, *In Defense of Lucius Murena*, delivered in November of 63; and while this report seems genuine, some uncertainty remains.

6. On the collection of consular speeches, see most recently Cape (2002). The letter from which we know of this collection (*ad Att.* 2.1) also discusses the various narratives of his consulship that Cicero wrote (Greek prose; Latin prose and verse) and those he tried to get others to write.

attacked it as leading to tyranny. He included his speech defending the
elderly Rabirius who was accused of treason because of his participation
in the riots that killed the tribune Saturninus thirty-seven years earlier;
again, he opposed tribunician agitation and at the same time supported
the legality of the senatus consultum ultimum *(which he was to use a
few months later)* as an instrument of senatorial control against popular
agitation. He also included a speech in support of the law reserving the
front rows at the theater for the equites *(scarcely a popular measure)*,
one supporting the Sullan law banning the children of men who had
been proscribed from public life *(again, a deeply conservative, not to say
reactionary, position)*, and one in which he gave up his proconsulship
in Gaul for the next year, part of his effort to detach his fellow consul
Antonius from the support of Catiline.[7] The entire collection presents
Cicero as a committed conservative, and it places his actions against
Catiline in the context of his support of senatorial power and the rights of
property. He omitted speeches, such as his defense of Murena, that did
not contribute to this edifying self-portrait.

The four Catilinarians themselves are a selection of speeches that
marked significant moments in Cicero's victory over Catiline. The first is
the one delivered in the senate in Catiline's presence on November 7
or 8, described by Cicero as "the speech in which I threw Catiline out"
(qua Catilinam emisi); the second, included here, was delivered to the
people on the next day, after Catiline had left.[8] The third was given before
the people on December 3, telling the story of the Gallic ambassadors
and the capture of the conspirators; the fourth, given in the senate
on December 5, was Cicero's summary of the debate leading to their
execution. Throughout, Cicero presents himself as the leader, the organizer,
the statesman; throughout, he emphasizes the support of the gods for his
actions; throughout, he shows himself as courageous, selfless, and placing
the good of the country before his own safety. And while there can be no
doubt that Cicero actually did give speeches resembling the present ones
at these times, it is very unlikely that the originals were quite so relevant to
Cicero's self-defense.

---

7. Under the usual procedure of assignment by lot, Cicero had received
Macedonia; Antonius, Cisalpine Gaul. Cicero bribed Antonius by ceding
Macedonia (a much more profitable province) to him, and his abdication of
his own province (which he did not want in any case) was a public sign of his
own commitment to deal with problems in Rome.

8. There is some dispute about the exact dates of the first two speeches:
either November 7 and 8 or 8 and 9, depending on one's interpretation of a
single ambiguous phrase in the first speech. It makes little difference.

*Catiline, moreover, deserves a slightly more sympathetic glance. If,
indeed, he organized a plot to attack the city from within and without, that
was something new and very dangerous. But by 63 BCE unrest in Italy was
not exactly novel. Setting aside the monstrous savagery of Sulla (in which
Catiline probably participated to some degree), there had been the revolt
of Lepidus against the Sullan system in 78 and the slave revolt of Spartacus
slightly later. At the time of Manlius' rebellion, we know that there were
several others, in Campania and possibly in Apulia. The complete failure
of the senatorial aristocracy, the heirs of Sulla, to deal with the genuine
economic problems of rural Italy was reason enough to rebel even without
Catiline.*

*The four Catilinarian orations are famous; they are powerful and
emotional speeches, but they are neither complicated nor subtle; there
is high rhetoric but little else.[9] Hence, although it is customary to edit or
translate the four as a group, only one is included here, the first of the
two given to the people, explaining the danger that had been expelled
and the danger that remained. In the first speech, to the senate, Cicero
had portrayed himself as a conservative hero along the lines of Opimius,
who had led the mob against Gaius Gracchus in 122, or the senators
who similarly disposed of Saturninus in 100. The Catilinarian conspiracy
is described as yet one more vicious attack on the virtuous government
of the senate, and Jupiter himself (in whose temple the first speech
was given) is made to support the senatorial position. Nothing of that
appears when Cicero is addressing the people in the second speech.
The core of the speech is a fascinating explanation of the motives of
those who support Catiline, all of which are moral and personal (debt,
corruption, softness of character) and none acknowledges the economic
problems of the urban or Italian poor or the political corruption of the
senatorial class against which one might reasonably rebel. What had
been political becomes moral—perhaps because the audience would
have had little sympathy for the reactionary politics of the first speech.
The politics of the Second Catilinarian are much closer to the position of
In Support of Manilius' Law than to that of the First Catilinarian, because
Cicero's rhetoric is always attuned to the audience he is addressing.[10]
Throughout the consular orations, Cicero expressed strong support
for the senatorial status quo, and in his dealings with the conspiracy
he acted on the belief that senatorial authority and national security*

---

9. The speeches most studied for their technique and effect are the first
and third. On the former, see Batstone (1994); on both, see Vasaly (1993)
40–87.

10. On the difference between *contio* and senatorial speeches against
Catiline, see Morstein-Marx (2004), esp. 251–52.

overrode individual rights and legal protections. The problem—posed in the late Republic most acutely by the constitutional status of the senatus consultum ultimum—was not new when Cicero confronted it, and it is not unfamiliar today. Cicero's solution is no less unsatisfactory than some more recent ones.

In L. Catilinam Oratio Secunda

My fellow citizens:

[1] Finally, after so long, we've driven Catiline from our city; we've let him out, we've followed him with our words as he left—Catiline, a man gone mad with his arrogance, panting crime, toiling in evil to build disaster for the country, brandishing fire and sword against you and this city. Gone, departed, snuck away, escaped. No further disaster for our walls will be organized within the walls themselves by that monstrous creature. There's no doubt that we've conquered at least this one leader of this internal war. No longer will that blade be twisted between our ribs: not in the campus, not in the forum, not in the senate house, and, last but not least, not within our own houses will we be afraid. He lost his place to stand when he was pushed out of the city. From now on, we'll wage a just war openly against our enemy, with nothing standing in our way. No question: we've brought the man down; we've conquered him gloriously by hurling him from his hidden ambush into banditry in broad daylight. [2] But he didn't succeed in taking with him a sword stained with blood; he left while we still live; we tore the weapon from his hands; he left our citizens unharmed and our city still standing. How great do you imagine is the grief that now has dragged him down and flattened him? He lies prostrate, my fellow citizens, he knows he's been knocked down and tossed away; certainly he turns his eyes back to the city often, the city he mourns has been snatched from his jaws. And to my eyes the city rejoices, because it has spat out and expelled such a plague.

[3] At this point, any right-minded person might attack me strongly for exactly the same thing that brings joy and triumph to my speech: why didn't I arrest this mortal enemy instead of sending him off? That's not my fault, my fellow citizens, but the fault of the times. Long ago, Catiline should have been killed, terminated with prejudice: ancestral practice and the rigorous standards of our empire and the interests of our country demanded it of me. But how

many people do you think there were who didn't believe my reports? How many people who defended him? How many who because of stupidity didn't think at all? How many who supported him because of their own wickedness? If I'd decided that removing him would drive all danger away from you, then I would have removed him at the cost of being hated and at the risk of being killed. **[4]** But I realized that even if I put him to death as he deserved, some of you would still not be convinced, and I would be assailed by ill will and unable to pursue his henchmen. That's why I brought the whole thing to this point, so you could openly fight against an enemy you could clearly see. And you'll understand how greatly I think we must fear him when he's outside the city, my fellow citizens, when you see how upset I am that so few people left the city with him. If only he'd led all his troops out with him! I'm glad he took with him Tongilius, his lover since he was a teenager; he took Publicius and Minucius, whose overdue bar bills couldn't cause any trouble for the commonwealth;[11] but what men he left behind! How deeply in debt, how strong, how noble! **[5]** So in comparison with our legions from Gaul and the draft that Quintus Metellus has just held in Picenum and Gaul,[12] and in comparison with the troops we daily enroll—in comparison with these I have great contempt for that army consisting of desperate old men, dandies of the countryside, bumpkin bankrupts, and men who chose to jump bail rather than desert from his army. I don't need to show them our army in battle array: the praetor's edict is enough to make them collapse.[13] The ones I see flitting around the forum, standing around near the senate house, even coming into the senate; the ones who are slippery from unguents and gleaming with purple—those are the ones I wish he'd taken with him as his troops. If they stay here, remember that we don't need to fear his army so much as those who deserted his army. And they're all the more to be feared because they recognize that I know what they think, and it makes no difference to them. **[6]** I see who's been allotted Apulia,

---

11. None of them is otherwise known. Cicero's point is that the people who left were nobodies, while those who stayed were potentially dangerous.

12. "Gaul" here means Gallia Cisalpina (on Map 1), together with the adjacent region of Picenum. Quintus Caecilius Metellus Celer (consul in 60) was praetor in 63 and had been assigned Cisalpine Gaul as his province for 62.

13. The praetor's edict governed civil actions at law (including debt collection).

who has Etruria, who has the Picene territory, the Gallic territory, who's become a fifth-columnist using fire and slaughter within the city. They know that all their plans of the night before last were brought to me. I made them public in the senate yesterday.[14] Catiline himself was in great fear; he fled. What are the rest waiting for? They're making a big mistake if they expect that my usual mildness will last forever.

I have now achieved what I've been hoping to: that all of you see that there was an open conspiracy against the country—unless there's somebody who doesn't think that people like Catiline think like Catiline. There's no more room for gentleness; the circumstances themselves demand harshness. Even now I will give them one last chance: let them leave; let them depart; let them not permit poor Catiline to fester from his desire for them. I'll give them directions: he left by the Aurelian Way, and if they want to hurry, they can catch him by sunset. [7] The nation would be fortunate indeed to throw this slop out of Rome! By flushing this one Catiline away, the commonwealth seems to me relieved and restored. What wickedness or crime can be imagined or invented that he didn't think of? In all Italy, can you find a poisoner, a gladiator, a bandit, a cutthroat, a patricide, a forger of wills, a swindler, a glutton, a spendthrift, an adulterer, a hooker, a child molester, a corrupt or immoral person who doesn't admit that he lived with Catiline on terms of the greatest intimacy? Has there been any murder in recent years without him? Any perversion without him? [8] Has there ever been a man as good as he is at seducing boys? With some of them he performed unspeakable sex acts himself; for others he was a filthy pimp; to some he promised the consummation of their desires; others he promised the death of their parents,[15] not just by egging them on but even by lending a hand! But now, how fast he's gathered a huge number of depraved characters, not just from the city but from the countryside as well. There's no one in Rome laboring under a burden of debt, no one in a single corner of all Italy, who hasn't been enrolled in this unbelievable criminal organization. [9] There's another way to look at his variety of interests: there's nobody in the gladiators' schools who's eager for crime who doesn't proclaim his intimacy with Catiline; there's

---

14. In the First Catilinarian.
15. For the sake of an inheritance.

nobody of the more frivolous and disreputable sort of actor who doesn't announce that he's been Catiline's bosom buddy. Catiline's sexual and criminal activity has made him able to endure cold and hunger and thirst and doing without sleep;[16] so he's praised by his friends for his bravery, even though he's worn away in sex and rapacity the resources that come from hard work and the tools that are part of virtue. **[10]** If his friends follow him, if the filthy herds of men without hope leave the city, then blessed are we, fortunate is the nation, and great will be the praise of my consulship! The desires of these men have no bounds, their rapacity is inhuman and unendurable. They think about nothing but murder, arson, and plunder; they've wasted what they inherited, their money's been sequestered. Their property deserted them long ago, and now their credit's on the way out; but they want just as much as when they were rich. If they limited themselves to brawls and whoring during their drunken gambling, then they would be beyond help but endurable; but who can endure these slugs plotting against Rome's finest; idiots against men of great wisdom, drunks against the sober, the sleeping against the wakeful? Look at them: stretched out on banqueting couches fondling hookers, sodden with wine, stuffed with food, tied up in garlands and smeared with unguents, limp from their sexual misadventures! As they talk they belch out the slaughter of respectable people and the burning of the city. **[11]** I'm absolutely certain that some fated punishment has long been hanging over their heads, a punishment owed to their wickedness, their evil, their crimes, and their lust. It's almost here, it's growing closer. And if my consulship eliminates what it can't heal, then it will extend our national existence not for a short span but for many centuries. There's no nation for us to fear, no king capable of making war on the Roman people. Every foreigner has been pacified on land and sea by a single man's outstanding qualities.[17] What is left is civil war: treachery is within, danger is locked within, the enemy is

---

16. Catiline's physical stamina was well known, and Cicero refers to it more than once (Sallust, *Conspiracy of Catiline* 5.3 also follows Cicero). Only here does Cicero ingeniously suggest that Catiline used sexual gymnastics to enhance his physical powers.

17. Cicero is careful to include praise of Pompey's achievements (in this case, the settlement of the East) to temper his self-praise. The logic of the argument (since foreign wars are over, only civil war remains) is less than compelling.

within. We must struggle against decadence, against insanity, against crime. This is the war for which I offer myself as leader, my fellow citizens: I accept the enmity of men who have no morals. What can be cured I will cure by whatever means works; what needs to be cut off I will not allow to remain to infect the state. So let them either leave or subside or, if they stay in the city with the same intentions, let them await what they deserve.

[12] But some people, my fellow citizens, say I've driven Catiline into exile. If I could do it with words alone, I would drive out the people who talk this way. I suppose the man is so shy and retiring that he couldn't take the voice of a consul: as soon as he was ordered into exile, he obeyed. Yesterday, my fellow citizens, after nearly being murdered in my own home, I summoned the senate to the temple of Jupiter Stator and reported everything to them;[18] when Catiline came, what senator addressed him? Who greeted him? Who even looked at him as if he were a citizen in disgrace rather than the most vicious enemy? The leaders of the senate even left bare and empty the section of seats where he had gone. [13] This is when I, forceful consul that I am, who sends citizens into exile with a single word, asked Catiline whether or not he'd been at the nighttime meeting in the house of Marcus Laeca.[19] Even though he's incredibly arrogant, he kept quiet at first from a sense of his own guilt, and I revealed the rest: I explained what he'd done that night, where he'd been, what plans he'd made for the next day, how the strategy for the whole war had been laid out. When he faltered, when he was trapped, I asked him what doubts he had about leaving for the place he'd long had ready, since I knew he'd sent ahead weapons, the *fasces* with axes, trumpets and military standards, and the famous silver eagle for which he'd built a shrine in his house.[20] [14] Was I sending into exile someone I saw had already started a war? I suppose Manlius the centurion, who set up a camp near Faesulae, declared war on Rome on his own and that camp is not now waiting for Catiline to become

---

18. What follows is a summary of the First Catilinarian, delivered on the previous day in the senate, in the presence of Catiline himself.

19. Marcus Porcius Laeca, a senator implicated in (and exiled for) the conspiracy and otherwise unknown.

20. Catiline treasured a silver eagle that had been Marius' standard in the war against the Teutoni and Cimbri.

their leader, and he is going to Marseilles as an outcast exile, as they say, and not to his camp.[21]

How appalling are the conditions not just for managing the commonwealth but even for trying to save it! Suppose Catiline, once he's been trapped and weakened by my plans and toils and dangers—suppose he suddenly takes fright, changes his mind, deserts his men, abandons his plans for war, and switches from the path of crime and war to the road to flight and exile: then they'll say that it wasn't that he was stripped of his weapons and hostility, stunned and terrified by my efforts, not that he was driven from his hopes and his plans, but that he was an innocent cast into exile without trial by a consul using force and intimidation. There will be people, if he does this, who would want him to be seen not as evil but as wretched, and me not as a consul working very hard but as the most cruel of tyrants! **[15]** It's worth it to me, my fellow citizens, to endure the storm of false and unjustified hatred as long as you are protected from the danger of this terrible and criminal war. Let them say I threw him out—as long as he goes into exile. But believe me, that's not where he's going. I would never seek to reduce hatred of me, my fellow citizens, by praying to the everlasting gods that you hear news of Catiline's military activity at the head of a hostile force—but that's what you'll hear within a few days. I'm much more afraid of hatred arising from my having let him go than from my having thrown him out. But since there are men who say that when he left he was really thrown out, what would they say if he were killed? **[16]** The people who keep saying that Catiline is on his way to Marseilles aren't complaining about it so much as they're afraid of it. None of them pities him so much as to want him to go to Marseilles instead of to Manlius. And as for Catiline, by Hercules, even if he'd never before imagined what he's doing now, he would still rather die as a bandit than live as an exile. But now, since the only thing that's happened contrary to his hopes and wishes is that he left me alive in Rome, let's hope he goes into exile instead of complaining about it.

[17] But why talk so much about one enemy, an enemy who admits he's an enemy and whom I don't fear because (as I've always wanted) there's a wall between us? Why do we say nothing about the men

---

21. Gaius Manlius, a former centurion in Sulla's army, is known only from his Catilinarian activities. There seems little doubt that his insurrection in Etruria (Faesulae = modern Fiesole) was in fact part of the conspiracy.

who disguise their intentions, who are still in Rome, who are still among us? If it were at all possible, what I want is not so much to take revenge on them as for them to cure themselves, to make peace with the commonwealth; and I don't understand why this can't happen, if they want to listen to what I have to say. So I'll explain to you, my fellow citizens, the types of men who are Catiline's recruits; after that, I'll offer each group a cure, if I have one, contained in the advice I'm giving.

[18] Type 1 is the people who own more than they owe, but they love what they have so much they can't settle their debts. These people are extremely honorable on the surface—they're rich—but their desires and goals are entirely shameless. You're decked out abundantly with land and buildings and silver and slaves and everything else, and you have doubts about selling some of what you have to shore up your credit? What are you waiting for? War? What happens then? When everything is destroyed do you think your property will be sacrosanct? Your accounts wiped clean? People who expect that from Catiline are off the mark. I'll be generous about bringing out new accounts, but they'll be the accounts of the auctioneer. There's no other way for the people with property to save themselves. But if they'd wanted to do it in good time and not to be idiots and try to balance farm income against interest due, then they would be both richer men and better citizens. But I'm not seriously afraid of these men: they can be made to change their opinions or, if they keep them, they seem to me more likely to make vows for the fall of the commonwealth than to carry weapons.

[19] Type 2 is the people who are deep in debt but still hope to get power. They yearn to get control of things, they think that in troubled times they can reach the offices that are beyond their hopes under a settled government. This is the instruction they need, one and the same advice as for all the others: they should give up hoping to get what they aim for. In the first place I'm wide awake, I'm here, I'm looking out for the commonwealth; second, the men of substance have great courage, there's great harmony among huge numbers, and we also have lots of troops; finally, the everlasting gods will bring aid to this invincible people, the most glorious of empires, the most beautiful of cities, against the great violence of this present crime. And if they get hold of what, in their terminal insanity, they are yearning for, surely they don't expect to become consuls or dictators or even kings in the ashes of the city and the blood of its citizens, the things

that they've longed for in their wicked and criminal hearts? Don't
they see that if they get what they want, they'll have to surrender it
to some runaway slave or gladiator?

[20] Type 3 is people who are old but still hearty from exercise.
That Manlius Catiline has gone to is one of them. They're men from
the colonies set up by Sulla; and although as a whole I recognize that
they're made up of the best and bravest of citizens, these people are
the settlers who squandered their sudden and unexpected windfall
on luxury and excess. They build like fat cats, they get a thrill from
fancy sedan chairs and large gangs of slaves and lavish dinners; but
they got into so much debt that if they want to come out all right,
they'll need to raise Sulla from the dead. And these people have
pushed a lot of poor and needy farmers into the same old hope of the
plunder they once had. I put both these groups into the same type of
bandits and housebreakers, but I offer this advice: they should stop
being crazy and dreaming about proscriptions and dictatorships. The
nation was branded by so much agony in those times that not just
men but not even cattle won't put up with such things any more.

[21] Type 4 is a motley, mixed, and unruly group. They've been
weighed down for a long time and never surface for air; partly because
they're lazy, partly because they're no good at business, partly because
they're on shaky ground piling new expenses on old debts. A lot of
them are worn out by foreclosures and judgments and auctions of
their property; the rumor is that they've left the city and their farms
and gathered at the camp. I think of them not as fierce soldiers but
as weak men running away from their lives. And if they can't stand
on their own, they should collapse as fast as possible—but so that not
even the neighbors, not to mention the nation, should notice a thing.
What I don't understand is why, if they can't live a decent life, they
want to die a disgraceful death. Why do they think their death will
be less painful with a lot of company than if they die alone?

[22] Type 5 is made up of patricides, cutthroats, and all the criminals; I'm not calling them back from Catiline. They can't be separated from him; let them die as bandits since there are too many of
them to fit in jail. The last type is last in number and in character and
in way of life; they're the ones who really belong to Catiline; they're
his special choice, and in fact he hugs them tight. You see them with
slick and coiffured hair, smooth-faced or with well-trimmed beards,
wearing tunics with cuffs coming down to their ankles, swathed in
awnings rather than togas. They spend all their efforts, all the toil

of wakefulness, in banquets that last until dawn. **[23]** To crews like this are attached all the gamblers, the adulterers, the foul and the filthy. These boys are so sparkling and gay; they've learned not just to love and be loved, not just to dance and sing, but even to brandish daggers and spread poisons. If they don't leave, if they don't die, even if Catiline dies, you must remember that this will be the seedbed of future Catilines in Rome. But what do these wretches want for themselves? Are they going to take their girlfriends to join the army? How can they do without them, now that the nights are getting cold? And how on earth will they survive life in the Apennines with all that frost and snow? But maybe they think they'll put up with the winter more easily because they're used to dancing naked at parties.

[24] What a terrifying war, with Catiline's bodyguard turning tricks! Get your defenses and your army ready, my fellow citizens, against Catiline's whorious army! First, match up your consuls and generals against that worn-out and wounded gladiator; then draw up the flower and strength of all Italy against that feeble band of exiled wrecks. The cities of Italy, our colonies and towns, will match up against Catiline's woodland hummocks. There's no need to compare the rest of your supplies, resources, or defenses with that bandit's poverty and need. **[25]** But if we set aside all the things we have and he doesn't—the senate, the Roman knights, the people of Rome, the city, the treasury, the tax revenues, all Italy, all the provinces and foreign nations that support us—if we set all this aside and choose to compare the opposing causes, that itself can show us how low their standing really is. On our side fights modesty, on theirs self-assertion; on our side decency, on theirs deviance; on our side good faith, on theirs fraud; on our side duty and respect, on theirs criminality; on our side steadfastness, on theirs madness; on our side honor, on theirs disgrace; on our side self-restraint, on theirs lechery; and finally on our side fight fairness, moderation, courage, foresight, and all the virtues against unfairness, decadence, sloth, and rashness, attended by all the vices. And last, abundance struggles against starvation, well-ordered reason against depravity, sanity against lunacy, decent expectations against despair in all things. In such a battle, such a contest, isn't it true that even if human support dwindles, the everlasting gods themselves should cause such great and such abundant vices to be conquered by these outstanding virtues?

[26] In these circumstances, my fellow citizens, you must, as I've said before, defend your homes and be alert in guarding them; for my part, I've made certain by my preparations that there's adequate protection for the city without your being disturbed and without any upheaval. I've informed all the members of colonies and towns about Catiline's midnight ride, and they will easily defend their towns and their territory. The gladiators, the troops he thought would be most firmly on his side, even though they're more loyal than a segment of the patricians, will be held under our control. Since I saw what was coming, I sent Quintus Metellus in advance to Picenum and further north; he will either crush Catiline or stop all his disturbances and attacks. As for making further decisions, forming plans, and acting on them, I will consult the senate, which you see is now coming into session.

[27] As for those who have stayed in the city and in fact were left in the city by Catiline to act against the safety of the city and of you all, even though they are enemies, they were still born as citizens, and over and over I want to give them my warning. If my mildness so far has seemed too lax to anyone, I was mild in the expectation that what was hidden would burst forth. For the future, I can't forget that this is my country; that I'm consul of these people and must either live with them or die for them. There's no guard on the gates, no watcher on the road; if anyone wants to leave, I can look the other way. But if anyone stirs things up in the city, when I find out not only about some action but even about any plan or attempt against the country, he will know that there are in this city consuls who are wide awake, magistrates who are outstanding, a senate that is brave. There are weapons, and there is a prison that our ancestors wanted to be a place of vengeance for wickedness and criminals caught in the act.[22]

[28] All this, my fellow citizens, will be done in such a way that matters of critical importance will be resolved with the least disturbance; the greatest dangers will involve no upheaval; the cruelest and greatest internal war in living memory will be settled by me alone as a leader and general in a toga. I will do this, my fellow citizens, if it's at all possible, so that not even a criminal in the city will suffer any punishment for his crime. But if the violence of their audacity is exposed, if the danger brooding over the Republic necessarily dislodges me from my accustomed mildness, then I will certainly do this: even though one can scarcely hope for it in a great and treacherous war, no

---

22. There were no prisons in Rome for long-term incarceration; they were used for executions.

responsible citizen will lose his life, and by the punishment of a few men you will all remain safe. **[29]** I make this promise to you, my fellow citizens, not on the basis of my own planning, relying not on human wisdom but on the many clear indications from the everlasting gods under whose leadership I've reached this hope and belief. They are not far away defending us from a foreign and distant enemy, as used to be the case, but they are present here, protecting with their power and aid their own temples and the buildings of the city.[23] You, my fellow citizens, should pray to them, worship them, beseech them thus: that, now that all external enemies have been defeated by land and by sea, they should defend this city, which they wished to be the most beautiful and flourishing and powerful of all, against the criminal wickedness of its own most abandoned citizens.

---

23. The actual presence of a god was requested in (and a necessary element of) prayer.

4

In Defense of Lucius Murena

Among the speeches in this volume, this is the first example of what was in fact Cicero's most important oratorical activity, legal advocacy. Before In Defense of Lucius Murena *of November 63 BCE, we know of twenty-four law cases in which Cicero took part, from which nine speeches survive.[1] Except the* Verrines, *however, none of these speeches shows the complex combination of legal and political considerations demonstrated by the speech for Murena. Cicero had previously appeared before the standing criminal courts (*quaestiones perpetuae*) as a defense advocate, to our knowledge, in only nine cases; of these three survive. While Cicero consistently tried to link the defense of his client to larger political or social issues, genuinely political cases increase along with his own political success. Enough fragments remain of his defense of the tribune Cornelius in 65 on a charge of treason to show how powerfully Cicero could use a trial to publicize his political views—and use political arguments to gain sympathy for a defendant.[2]*

---

1. There is a convenient list of Cicero's legal speeches on which I base these figures in Powell and Paterson (2004) 417–22. Despite their bulk, I count the Verrines as a single speech, even though they represent three appearances (*Divinatio against Caecilius*, First and Second Verrines), because they are all part of one case, the prosecution of Verres for extortion.

2. The nine earlier cases are defenses of Roscius of Ameria (80), Varenus (77–76), Scamander (74), Fonteius (69), Cluentius (66), Manilius (66–65), Cornelius (65), Gallius (64), and Piso (earlier in 63). Other cases may have been before the permanent *quaestiones*, but the charges and venues are uncertain. Of the nine, four are homicide (Roscius, Varenus, Scamander, Cluentius), three are for extortion (*repetundae:* Fonteius, Gallius, Piso), one is for treason (*maiestas:* Cornelius), and one is either extortion or treason (Manilius). Among these the defenses of Roscius and Cluentius exist complete, and that of Fonteius is largely extant. For the fragments of the defense of Cornelius—which Cicero made public, and which was extant in antiquity—see Crawford (1994) 65–144. One other major case was heard not by a court but by the assembly, the extant defense of Rabirius for treason

The defense of Murena should be placed in several different contexts— legal, political, and intellectual. The facts of the case itself are fairly clear, and (as usual in the written versions of Cicero's speeches) most of them can be inferred from the speech itself. In the consular elections in the summer of 63 there were four candidates: Lucius Licinius Murena, Lucius Sergius Catilina, Decimus Junius Silanus, and Servius Sulpicius Rufus. Of these, the patrician Catiline has been discussed earlier. Sulpicius, also a patrician, was a renowned legal expert and was supported by Cicero.[3] Murena, the defendant, was an experienced and successful military commander. Very little is known about Silanus. The two men elected were Murena and Silanus. The election was marked by perhaps even more corruption and bribery than was usual in the late Republic. Agitation (by Sulpicius, and perhaps others) had led first to a senatorial vote setting tighter rules about campaign spending and then to the passage of a law (Lex Tullia de ambitu, named after Cicero, the magistrate bringing it forward) including both rules about spending and increased penalties on conviction;[4] it is that law under which Murena was tried. Even before the election had taken place, Sulpicius apparently despaired of overcoming the electoral expenditures of the other candidates and announced his intention to prosecute one of the winning candidates if he were himself defeated, and he selected Murena. Cato, it should be noted, had promised prosecution of any candidate guilty of corruption, but he failed to prosecute Silanus, who was, not coincidentally, his brother-in-law. The case of Murena came to trial in late November of 63. There were four speakers for the prosecution: Sulpicius himself; a younger Servius Sulpicius Rufus (probably not the son of the other Sulpicius), about whom nothing else is known; a candidate (who either withdrew or was defeated) for the praetorship of 62 named Gaius Postumius;[5] and, perhaps most important, Marcus Porcius Cato, at the time recently elected tribune of the people and already renowned for his rectitude and Stoic severity.

---

early in 63. A very political and peculiar case, it has very little to do with crime and a great deal with the complex political maneuvering of 63.

3. Patrician status mattered in consular elections, as no more than one of the consuls could be patrician. In the end, the two elected were both plebeians.

4. Other than what this speech tells us about the law, it is known to have contained a clause barring presentation of gladiatorial games by candidates in the biennium preceding the election; see Crawford et al. (1996) 2:761–62.

5. Postumius' praenomen is uncertain in the manuscripts. As Sulpicius' wife was named Postumia, he was (like the younger Sulpicius) presumably part of the prosecutor's extended family.

*Cicero had two collaborators in the defense. Quintus Hortensius
Hortalus was recognized as the greatest orator in Rome just prior to
Cicero. As consul-elect in 70 he spoke as Verres' advocate against Cicero,
but the two gradually became closer and worked together in at least six
other trials; Cicero's description of him in* Brutus *(317–29) is eloquent
and moving. Marcus Licinius Crassus, consul with Pompey in 70, had
supported Catiline (and thus opposed Cicero) in the election of 64;
in 60 he became, with Caesar and Pompey, one of the so-called First
Triumvirate. Hortensius and Crassus defended Murena almost certainly
because, given their distrust of Pompey, it will have appealed to them
to have a former legate of Lucullus as consul when Pompey returned
to Rome, as expected, in 62. Hortensius spoke first, Cicero (as was his
custom) last. Murena was acquitted and duly took office as consul on
January 1, 62.*

*In terms of political background, the looming shadow of Pompey's
return may have influenced Hortensius and Crassus to defend Murena,
but that was not relevant to Cicero; he had a more pressing motive in
the conspiracy of Catiline.[6] One of the virtues, for Cicero, of Murena's
election was that he could be expected to contribute to the defeat of
Catiline; in the speech (secs. 78–80) Cicero emphasizes the importance
of having an experienced soldier as consul to oppose Catiline in the
field, if necessary. The trial took place between Catiline's departure from
Rome to join Manlius at Faesulae in early November and the unmasking
of the aristocratic conspirators in Rome in early December. The situation
at that moment was unclear and highly volatile; the argument of part of
the speech is, essentially, that it was more important to have two consuls
in office on January 1 than to enforce the strict letter of the law. It is an
argument from expediency, not from legality.*

*The law, of course, is the second important aspect of the case. Even
though the specific* Lex Tullia *under which Murena was prosecuted was
very new, both electoral corruption and laws attempting to control it
had a long, if not noble, history:[7] a permanent court had been set up
to deal with charges of corruption sometime before 115 BCE. In age,
it was second only to the court for extortion by provincial governors
(*res repetundae*) set up in 149 BCE; the connection between the two
crimes—one for spending money improperly, one for stealing it—is fairly
evident. There were apparently at least two further laws on the subject
between the original law and Cicero's law of 63. Then as now, the
definition of electoral corruption and the proper means of punishing it are
notoriously uncertain. To what extent is it corrupt to give food, drink, and*

---

6. See the introduction to *Second Speech against Catiline.*

7. On the history of *ambitus* (and on this case), see Riggsby (1999) 21–49.

entertainment to potential voters? To give presents? Where is the line to
be drawn between voluntary manifestations of support for a candidate
and purchased enthusiasm—and what is wrong with organizing rallies to
support a candidate? The Romans passed ever stricter laws and increased
the punishments with equal regularity; but (then as now) nobody in a
fiercely contested election could get anywhere without spending a great
deal of money, whether it be on advertising (as now), on largesse, or in
the straightforward purchase of votes. If Murena was guilty—as, by the
letter of the law(s), he fairly obviously was—so was virtually every other
candidate for every consular election for fifty years and more. After the
2008 exorbitantly expensive presidential election, I cannot help wondering
whether Sulpicius was shocked by Murena's corruption or merely jealous
and angry that Murena raised and spent his funds more effectively.

The genuine difficulty of drawing a clear line between corruption and
effective politics gave Cicero the opening for one of the most brilliant
passages of the speech, his parody of Cato's Stoicism: the rigidity of
the unrealistic philosopher makes him incapable of understanding the
necessary flexibility of political morality. But the parody of Cato is part
of a larger element of Cicero's defense, a contrast between the practical,
military experience of Murena and the un-Roman eggheadedness of both
Sulpicius and Cato. The two related questions of the speech, as Cicero
treats it, are whether Sulpicius or Murena ought to have won the election,
and whether Murena won it honestly. The first of these contrasts the
bookish and petty life of the law with the grand and manly world of the
Roman soldier: virtus in its etymological sense of "manliness" is elevated
over the learning of the lawyer. Cicero even argues that the law itself,
as generally handled, is so trivial that he could master it in three days.
The second question is again a contrast between the real world and the
world of the mind. Cato has swallowed the most ridiculous form of Stoic
rigor, recognizing only absolutes of good or evil; as a result, he is totally
incapable of dealing with the flexibility and ambiguity of politics. If he
had had the sense to follow Aristotle rather than Zeno, he (and Rome)
would be much better off. The first part dealt with virtus as "manliness";
the second deals with virtus in its Hellenizing sense of "moral excellence."
Cicero first contrasts Greek ideas of excellence with Roman ones, then one
set of Greek ideas (Stoic) with another (Aristotelian). The entire argument
can be read (and is meant to be read) as both valid on the surface—
particularly appropriate in defending a military man such as Murena—and
deeply ironic: Cicero, as his audience would have known, had even as a
young man a deep respect both for legal learning and for the serious study
of Greek philosophy. Cicero's irony also reflects the intellectual conditions
of Rome in the period after Sulla, when ever-intensifying Hellenism (in
poetry, philosophy, and in the articulation of intellectual disciplines)

cohabited uneasily with the traditional military and social values of
aristocratic culture.[8]

Given the fact that we lack the first two-thirds of Murena's defense
(the speeches of Hortensius and Crassus) and that Cicero claims (sections
48, 54) that the formal defense against charges of corruption had been
discussed by the others, there is no way to tell whether the entire defense
was as unconcerned with formal legalities as Cicero's own speech is.
Cicero outlines the case against Murena (section 11) as having three
main arguments: one about Murena's character, one about the relative
merits of Murena and Sulpicius as candidates, and one about the formal
charges of corruption. The weight placed by Cicero on the first two of
these, arguments from character and from circumstance rather than from
guilt or innocence (arguments that would not be permitted in a modern
criminal trial), is not surprising. Much forensic strategy in both Athens and
Rome rested on the argument that "X did not do Y, because X is not the
kind of person to do Y"; what Cicero calls the "comparison of worthiness"
(contentio dignitatis) is what opens the way for his great attack on lawyers.
The careful structure is matched by Cicero's mastery of styles. He moves
from a solemn and prayerful beginning in grand style to the parody of legal
argument to the satirical imaginary dialogue and colloquialisms of the attack
on Cato to the high pathos of his final plea for Murena. In its range of styles
and its complexity of argument, it is one of Cicero's most brilliant speeches.

Pro L. Murena Oratio

Members of the jury:

[1] On the day I took the auspices and reported to the voting
assembly[9] the selection of Lucius Murena as consul, I made a prayer to
the immortal gods according to the traditional custom of our ancestors: that this result should be successful and fortunate for me in the
faithful conduct of my office and for the citizens and people of Rome.
I now make that same prayer to these same immortal gods: that this
same man should safely enter the office of consul; that your will and
verdict should agree with the wishes and votes of the Roman people;

---

8. On the increased presence of Greek intellectual life (and Greek intellectuals) in Rome in the post-Sullan period, see Rawson (1985) 3–99.

9. The *comitia centuriata*, the more plutocratically organized of Rome's
assemblies, used for electing consuls and praetors. The taking of omens
by the presiding magistrate was a prerequisite for almost all governmental
action.

and that the result should confer on you and on the Roman people peace and calm, civic order and harmony. And if that ritual prayer at the elections, a prayer hallowed by the auspices taken by a consul, has as much effect and religious power as the dignity of the commonwealth demands, my prayer then, too, was that the result should also be fortunate, prosperous, and successful for those men who received the consulship while I presided over the elections. **[2]** That being the case, members of the jury, and since the power of the immortal gods has either been wholly transferred to you or at least shared with you, the same person entrusts a consul to your good faith as previously to the immortal gods, so that the man who has been declared consul and defended in court by one and the same voice may preserve and protect the favor conferred by the Roman people together with your well-being and that of all citizens.[10]

But since the enthusiasm of my defense in a matter of personal obligation, and even the fact that I have undertaken this case at all, are criticized by the prosecution, I must say a few words on my own behalf before speaking on behalf of Lucius Murena: not because I believe defending my sense of obligation more important than defending his well-being but so that the approval my actions receive from you may bring me greater authority to ward off the attacks of Murena's enemies on his office, reputation, and fortunes.

[3] My first response about my sense of obligation is to Marcus Cato, a man who directs his life according to the strict rule of reason and weighs all moral duties in the balance with the greatest precision. Cato says it wasn't right for me, as consul, as the man who carried a law about electoral corruption, and as one whose consulship was characterized by strictness, to take the case of Murena.[11] Cato's criticism moves me greatly, members of the jury. I want to gain not only your approval, which I genuinely need, for my course of conduct, but even that of Cato himself, a man of profound seriousness

---

10. The logic of this extraordinarily elaborate and contorted opening seems to be that (a) the prayer at the elections is for the safety of Rome; (b) the safety of Rome depends on Murena's being in office; (c) as Cicero is playing the same role in both the election and the trial, the jury must play the role of the assembly that elected Murena; and (d) as the election prayer essentially transfers divine power to the assembly, so too the jury must be seen as representing the gods in the trial.

11. On the *Lex Tullia de ambitu*, see the introduction to this speech.

and integrity.[12] But tell me, Cato, by whom can a consul more fairly be represented than by a consul? Who in public life either can or should be closer to me than the man to whom the commonwealth is being passed on to be kept going just as I, by making great efforts and enduring great dangers, have kept it going? If in disputes over the sale of property the guarantor of the title is the one who faces legal action,[13] then it is even more suitable in the trial of a consul-designate for the consul who declared him consul both to take responsibility for the gift of the Roman people and to defend him against this danger. **[4]** And if, as in many nations, an advocate were appointed publicly in such a case, then in a matter involving the highest office the defender to be assigned would be one who had reached the same office and would bring no less authority than ability to the case. People who have just reached port are generally happy to advise those who are just setting out to sea about storms, pirates, and dangerous places; it's only natural for us to look kindly on people approaching the same dangers we have gone through. What attitude, then, should I have, as I see the shore after being violently tossed around at sea,[14] toward a man who I know will have to face huge storms in the public arena? For that reason, as a good consul must not only see what's happening but also foresee what will happen, I'll explain later how much it matters to the well-being of the community that there be two consuls in office on January 1.[15] **[5]** That being so, my obligation to defend the fortunes of a friend should not be what moves me so much as the commonwealth itself calling me to defend the well-being of the community. As to the law on electoral corruption, I did indeed carry it, but that didn't revoke the law I had previously imposed on myself, to protect citizens from danger.

---

12. Three years later, fed up with Cato's sanctimonious and priggish politics, Cicero wrote to his friend Atticus that "he offers his opinion in the senate as if he were in Plato's republic, not among Romulus' dregs" (*ad Att.* 2.1.8).

13. In the formal kind of sale known as mancipation, the seller in the presence of five witnesses guaranteed the validity of his title to the purchaser and was responsible should title be disputed by a third party.

14. Cicero refers to the conspiracy of Catiline in particular, but the metaphors of storm and voyage are common in describing the perils of political life.

15. One part of the penalty on conviction of corruption is disqualification from the office in question.

If I admitted that bribery had been used and if I argued that it was properly done, then indeed I would be doing wrong, even if the law was someone else's; but since I will argue that nothing was done contrary to the law, then why should my sponsorship of it stand in the way of my acting for the defense?

[6] Cato asserts that I don't demonstrate the same rigor in having used my words and almost the power of my office to drive Catiline out of the city[16]—a man who was plotting the destruction of the commonwealth from inside its walls—and now speaking on behalf of Murena. I have, in fact, always been happy to play the part of mildness and mercy that nature herself wrote for me; I have never sought the role of stern severity but have taken it when the commonwealth cast me in it, just as the majesty of this empire demanded at a time of the greatest danger to its citizens. And if, when the commonwealth needed force and severity, I overcame my nature and was as forceful as I needed to be, not as I wanted to be, now, when every aspect of the case summons me to be merciful and humane, how much more eagerly should I obey my natural character and habits? Perhaps I'll need to say more later in my speech about the obligations underlying my defense and the reasons underlying your accusation.

[7] For my part, however, members of the jury, I'm no less moved by the lamentation of Servius Sulpicius, the wisest and most distinguished of men, than by Cato's attack: Sulpicius said he had the deepest and most bitter feelings about my forgetting our close relationship to take Murena's side against him. Members of the jury, I want to explain myself to him and to have you decide between us. A true accusation from a friend is a serious matter, but even a false accusation shouldn't be ignored. I believe, Sulpicius, that because of our close connections I owed you all my support and assistance in your candidacy, and I believe that I provided them. During your campaign for the consulship nothing was lacking on my part that should be asked from a friend, from a man of influence, or from a consul. But that was then. Things have changed. It's my opinion and firm belief that I owed you as much help as you could ask against Murena's candidacy; against his well-being I owe you nothing. [8] I supported you when you were going after the consulship;[17] that

---

16. Cicero is referring to the first speech against Catiline.
17. Part of this clause is conjectural; there is a gap in the text.

doesn't mean I ought to help you in the same way when you're going after Murena himself. It's not admirable, it's not even tolerable for us not to defend even complete strangers just because our friends are prosecuting them. But Murena and I, members of the jury, have a long and deep friendship that, in a case involving civic status, is not to be obliterated by Sulpicius just because he lost an election to Murena. Even if I had no such reason, still either Murena's honorable standing or the importance of the office he's achieved would have branded me as infamously proud and cruel if I'd rejected the case, involving such danger, of a man who has achieved high standing by his own distinction and by distinctions awarded by the Roman people. It's no longer possible or honorable for me not to contribute my efforts in relieving men in danger: since I've attained such great rewards for hard work in this area as have been given to no man before, I believe it would take a tricky and ungrateful man to work hard to get elected and then stop working when he wins.[18] **[9]** If I have permission to stop, if I have your authority for it, if it incurs no disgrace for sloth, no disrepute for arrogance, no blame for inhumanity, then I'm truly happy to stop. But on the other hand, if to shirk toil shows laziness, to spurn suppliants shows haughtiness, to neglect friends shows wickedness, then in fact this case is of the kind that no hardworking or merciful or dutiful person could possibly abandon. You, Servius, can very easily understand this from your own efforts. If you think you're obliged to give legal advice even to the opponents of your friends when they consult you, and if you think that when you're present as an advocate it's disgraceful for your adversary to bungle his case,[19] then don't be so unjust as to think that my resources should be barred to my friends when yours are available even to your enemies. **[10]** In fact, if my friendship for you had removed me from this case, and the same had happened to these distinguished men Quintus Hortensius and Marcus Crassus, if the same had happened to all the other people who I know value your goodwill greatly, then in a state where our ancestors wanted nobody, even the lowest of the low, to lack a patron, the consul-designate would have no defender. For my own part, members of the jury, I would think myself wicked if I failed a friend, cruel if

---

18. There is a gap in the text, and part of the last clause is conjectural.

19. Servius is so concerned with the integrity of the law that he will correct a procedural error by his opponent in court. Examples of sloppy advocacy of this kind are given by Cicero at *de Or.* 1.166.

I failed someone deserving pity, arrogant if I failed a consul. For that reason, Servius, I'll give generously of what should be given to friendship. I'll act toward you just as if it were my brother, who's very dear to me, in your place; I'll temper whatever is due to obligation, good faith, and religious feeling so as to remember that I'm speaking against the interest of a friend on behalf of a friend in danger.

[11] As I understand it, members of the jury, there were three components of the prosecution's case: one involves criticism of Murena's private life, the second the comparison of the candidates' worthiness, the third the formal charges of bribery. Of these three the first, the one that should have been most serious, was so feeble and insubstantial that some sort of "rules for prosecutors" rather than a true talent for slander compelled them to say something about Murena's way of life. Asia was thrown in his face; but he headed to Asia not for its fleshpots and luxury but to travel through it on military duty. If he hadn't gone to serve as a young man under his father's command, then he would give the impression of having been afraid either of the enemy or of his father's command, or of having been rejected by his father. When men hold triumphs, their sons who aren't yet of age frequently ride on their father's horses; should Murena have shunned enhancing his father's triumph with his own military honors, almost sharing in his father's triumph, after a war they had waged together?[20] [12] The defendant, members of the jury, was in Asia; he was a great support to his father, a man of great courage, in moments of danger; he was a comfort in toil and a source of pride in victory. And if Asia carries with it a whiff of decadence, then we shouldn't praise someone who's never seen Asia, but someone who's lived there with restraint. For that reason it isn't the name of Asia that should be cast in Murena's face—Asia is the source of praise for his house, remembrance for his family, honor and glory for his name—but only some dishonor or disgrace incurred in Asia or brought back from there. To have served as a soldier in the greatest, in fact, the only war the Roman people were waging at that moment is a sign of manliness; to have served eagerly under his father's command is a sign of filial respect; to have marked the end of his service with his father's victory and triumph is a sign

---

20. The elder Murena was one of Sulla's legates, left in command when Sulla returned to Rome in 84. He started, fought, and was badly defeated in the Second Mithridatic War (83–81), for which he was awarded a triumph by Sulla on his return in 81.

of good fortune. There is thus no room at all for insults because the story contains only praise.

[13] Cato calls Murena a dancer. If true, it's an insult from a hard-driving prosecutor; if false, from a quarrelsome slanderer. For that reason, Cato, given your authority, you shouldn't snatch an insult from the street corner or from idlers' mudslinging, and you shouldn't rashly call a consul of the Roman people a dancer. You ought to consider the other flaws of character affecting someone who could be the legitimate object of such an attack. Unless he's out of his mind, almost nobody dances sober; he doesn't dance alone, nor in respectable and decent festivities. At an elaborate banquet and in a pleasant place, dancing is the final step among many pleasures. Why do you snatch at what is inevitably the last in a series of vices and leave aside those without which this vice can't exist at all? There's no evidence of wild parties or love affairs or drunken revels or debauchery or extravagance; and since there's no sign of the things people call "pleasure" despite their immorality, do you expect to find the shadow of decadence in a man in whom you can't find decadence itself? [14] There can be no criticism of Murena's life, members of the jury, none at all. My defense of the consul-designate is that no deceit, no greed, no treachery, no cruelty, no insulting remark can be adduced in his entire life. Well and good: that's the basis of my defense. I haven't yet delivered my own praise of him (that will come later), but I can almost defend this good and upright man on the basis of the prosecutors' admissions. Having established that, it's even easier to move on to the comparison of worthiness, the second part of the accusation.

[15] In you, Sulpicius, I see the greatest worthiness in terms of family, honesty, hard work, and all the other qualities it's reasonable to rely on in undertaking a campaign for the consulship. I recognize similar qualities in Murena, and so similar that he can neither be surpassed by you nor overcome you in worthiness. You expressed scorn for Murena's ancestry and praised your own. On that score, if you mean that nobody who isn't a patrician is of good ancestry, you'll make it seem as if the plebeians should secede to the Aventine again.[21] But if respectable and honorable plebeian families exist, Murena's great-

---

21. The Aventine (or the Mons Sacer outside Rome) was where plebeians traditionally seceded to protest injustice or oppression by the patricians. The first secession in 494 BCE led to the creation of the tribunate of the plebs.

grandfather was a praetor, as was his grandfather;[22] and in ending his praetorship with a very grand and noble triumph, his father made it all the easier for Murena to take the next step to the consulship: the son was seeking what was already owed to the father. [16] Your own nobility, Sulpicius, is of the highest sort; but even so, it's well known to scholars and historians but fairly obscure to the voting public.[23] Your father was of equestrian rank; your grandfather wasn't famous for anything outstanding or glorious. The record of your nobility is not the subject of recent discussion but has to be dragged out of ancient chronicles. For that reason I always tend to consider you one of us,[24] because your virtue and hard work made you seem worthy of the highest distinction even though you were the son of a Roman knight. It never seemed to me that Quintus Pompeius, a new man and a man of great courage, had less virtue than Marcus Aemilius, a man of the highest nobility.[25] In fact, it shows the same talent and cast of mind to pass on to one's descendants, as Pompeius did, a distinction he had not inherited, as to renew by one's own virtue, like Scaurus, the almost extinct memory of his family. [17] Indeed, members of the jury, I have long thought that my own efforts had ensured that lack of nobility would no longer be cast in the face of brave men, through my speaking about not only earlier heroes, such as Curius, Cato, and Pompeius, but also recent ones, such as Marius, Didius, and Coelius.[26] And since after such a long lapse of time I had broken through the locked gates of the nobility, so that in the future, as

---

22. The precise dates of their praetorships are unknown but are earlier than 146 and earlier than 100 BCE, respectively.

23. Sulpicius was a patrician but one whose family had not held high office for centuries.

24. A "new man"—the first in his family to hold the consulship. The ideology of the new men (best represented in Cicero by the account of the elder Cato at *Verr.* 5.180–82) contrasted their virtue and hard work with the nobility's resting on the accomplishments of their ancestors.

25. Quintus Pompeius was a new man, consul in 141. Marcus Aemilius Scaurus was consul in 115; although a patrician, no one in his family had held office for three generations.

26. The three early consuls are Manius Curius Dentatus (290, 275, 274), Marcus Porcius Cato (195), and Quintus Pompeius (141); the more recent ones are Gaius Marius (consul in 107 and six times thereafter), Titus Didius (98), and Gaius Coelius Caldus (94).

among our ancestors, access to the consulship would be as open to
virtue as to nobility, I didn't believe that when a consul-designate of
an old and distinguished family was defended by a consul who's the
son of a Roman knight the accusers would say anything about "new-
ness of family." It happened that I was myself a candidate along with
two patricians, one very wicked and bold, the other very self-effacing
and good: I defeated Catiline in worthiness and Galba in prestige.
And if that should be a charge against a new man, then I certainly
would have lacked neither enmity nor envy. **[18]** So let's stop talking about family, as both men have great worth in that regard. Let's
move on to the rest.

"We were candidates for the quaestorship together and I came in
ahead."[27] Not everything deserves an answer. None of you is unaware
that while many people may be equally worthy, only one can come
in first. Order of worth isn't the same as the order of the election
results: election results have to be ranked, but all the candidates are
frequently equally worthy. But your quaestorships had more or less
equal fortune. Murena, according to the Titian law,[28] had a quiet
and inactive province; you had the quaestorship at Ostia. When that
post is allotted, it generally gets an outcry because it has less scope
for favor and glory than for toil and trouble. Neither one's reputation
rose in the quaestorship, because the lot gave you no field in which
virtue could speed ahead of the pack and be recognized.

[19] They go on to make a comparison of the following period,
which the two of them handled very differently. Servius soldiered
on here with us, giving legal opinions, writing, and advising—an
occupation full of worry and irritation. He studied the civil law, he
worked late a lot, he toiled, he came to the aid of a lot of people, he
suffered the stupidity or arrogance of a lot of people, he sucked up
their unpleasantness: he lived in accordance with others' wishes, not
his own. Men offer great praise and thanks that there is one man who
toils in a branch of learning that is useful to many. **[20]** Meanwhile,
what about Murena? He was a legate to Lucius Lucullus, a man of
outstanding courage and wisdom, a great general.[29] As legate he led

---

27. Murena and Sulpicius were quaestors in 74; Murena's province as
quaestor is unknown.

28. Otherwise unknown.

29. Murena served as Lucullus' legate in the Third Mithridatic War from
73 to (at least) 69, in charge for a time of the siege of Amisus, and serving

an army, he engaged in battle, he fought in close combat, he defeated large enemy armies, he captured some cities by force, others by siege, he behaved in Asia—the Asia of opulence and decadence—in such a way that he left there no trace of greed or luxuriousness. His actions in a great war were such that he accomplished many great deeds without his general, but his general accomplished none without him. And even though I say this in Lucullus' presence, still, to avoid seeming to invent things with his permission because Murena's in danger, everything is witnessed by public documents, in which Lucullus awarded him more praise than an ambitious or envious general ought to allow another as a share of his glory.

[21] Each of these men has the highest reputation and the highest worthiness; and with Servius' permission, I'll award their worthiness equal praise. But he gives me no such permission: he goes on about military experience, he attacks Murena's whole service as legate, he thinks the consulship belongs to diligence and daily drudgery. "You were in the army," he says; "for many years you didn't set foot in the forum; you were away for such a long time, and when after a long gap you came back, you claim worth equal to people who've lived in the forum?" In the first place, Servius, you fail to recognize how sick and tired people get of this diligence of ours. For me, it's been extremely useful to have my prestige visible to the public eye, but I, and perhaps you, too, have had to work very hard to overcome people's tedium. Certainly to have people miss us would have done neither of us any harm. [22] But setting that aside, let's go back to the comparison of interests and skills. Who can possibly doubt that military glory brings a lot more worthiness for election to the consulship than does the glory of the civil law? You stay awake at night to give advice to your clients; he stays awake to bring his army into position promptly. The cock's crow is your reveille; the trumpet's sound is his. You draw up lawsuits; he draws up lines of battle. You defend your clients from being caught; he defends cities and encampments from being captured. He understands and knows how to deal with enemy troops; you know how to deal with damage from rainwater.[30]

---

with Lucullus in Armenia in 69. The statement that Lucullus accomplished nothing without Murena is untrue.

30. Problems of drainage and rainwater are part of a standard list of legal trivia in civil law; cf. also *de Or.* 1.173. This passage is perhaps a model for Ovid's detailed comparison of military and amatory service in *Amores* 1.9.

He has experience in extending our borders, you in surveying them. In truth—and I have to say what I believe—military virtue stands above all other kinds. This is what has brought the Roman people its reputation; this is what has brought this city eternal glory; this is what has forced the whole world to obey our rule. All the affairs of the city, all these grand studies of ours, the glory and hard work of this forum, take shelter under the watchful protection of military virtue. The minute there's a murmur of conflict, our skills at once fall silent.

[23] And since you seem to me to hug your legal expertise as if it were your daughter, I won't permit you to linger in the false belief that what you've worked so hard to learn, whatever it is, is something magnificent. It's for other virtues—self-discipline, seriousness, justice, good faith, and the rest—that I've always judged you eminently worthy of the consulship and of every other office. In learning civil law, however, I won't say you've wasted your effort, but I will say this: that discipline of yours offers no yellow brick road to the consulship.

All the arts that bring to us the enthusiasm of the Roman people ought to possess a worth deserving admiration and a utility deserving gratitude. [24] The greatest worthiness belongs to men outstanding in military glory. They preserve and defend, we believe, everything in our empire and constitution; so, too, the greatest utility belongs to them, since by their wisdom and their danger we're able to have full enjoyment of both the commonwealth and private wealth. Ability as an orator, too, is serious and worthy: the power to move the minds of the senate, the people, and the courts by thoughtful speech has often had an effect on the choice of a consul. One looks for a consul who's able on occasion to check the agitation of tribunes, to turn aside the aroused emotions of the people, to resist calls for a dole. No surprise, then, if because of this capacity even men who aren't noble have often reached the consulship, particularly since this same capacity creates a great deal of prestige, powerful bonds of friendship, and the greatest goodwill.

Of all this, Sulpicius, in your field of expertise there's nothing at all. [25] In the first place, there's no possibility of worthiness in such a slight field of knowledge: the issues are small and practically turn on single letters and punctuation marks. Second, even if there was anything in your field of study in the days of our ancestors that was worthy of admiration, once your mysteries were revealed it's become despised and rejected. At one time, only a few people knew whether there was the possibility of legal action; the calendar was not generally available. The legal experts had great power, and the legal calendar was sought from them as from astrologers. But one scribe turned up, Gnaeus Flavius, who stuck the crows in the eye and by learning one day at a time gave the people a legal calendar and stole their wisdom from those cautious legal experts.[31] So they got angry, since they were afraid that once the legal calendar was generally understood people could go to law without their help, and they made up some mumbo-jumbo so as to get a piece of every case. **[26]** It would have been just fine to say, "The Sabine property is mine." "No, it's mine," followed by a trial, but they didn't want that.[32] "THE PROPERTY," he says, "WHICH IS IN THE TERRITORY KNOWN AS SABINE." Lots of words; what comes next? "I ASSERT THAT IT IS MINE ACCORDING TO THE LAW OF THE ROMAN PEOPLE." What comes next? "THENCE AND THERE I SUMMON YOU FROM THE PROCEEDING AT LAW TO ENGAGE THE ISSUE."[33] The person against whom the claim was being made had no idea what to say to such a wordy plaintiff. So the legal expert crosses the stage like a Latin flute-player.[34] "FOR THE REASON FOR WHICH YOU SUMMONED ME TO ENGAGE THE ISSUE IN ACCORDANCE WITH THE LAW, FOR THE SAME REASON IN THAT PLACE I SUMMON YOU IN RETURN." Meanwhile, so as not to let the praetor think he's sitting pretty and to say something on his own, a jingle has been made up for him that is particularly ridiculous in this: "IN THE PRESENCE OF WITNESSES FOR

---

31. Gnaeus Flavius, aedile in 304 BCE, made public the formulas for legal actions and the calendar of days on which legal actions were permitted. Until then, knowledge of legal procedure was limited to patricians and to priests in particular.

32. The procedure ridiculed here is the *legis actio sacramento in rem* ("action in law by oath concerning property"), a procedure that had long been obsolete in Cicero's day, having been replaced by the more flexible formulary system. On the procedure, cf. Gaius, *Institutes* 4.16–17, and Gellius, *Attic Nights* 20.10. Cicero expresses similar ideas about jurists' obfuscations at *Leg.* 2.47.

33. The interpretation here is that of Crawford et al. (1996) 2:599. The procedure is the move from proceedings before the praetor (at law = *in iure*) to proceedings before a judge.

34. The accompanists in drama were traditionally Latins, not Roman citizens.

BOTH PARTIES I POINT OUT THE PATH: FOLLOW IT." The wise man on the spot showed them how to follow the path. "COME BACK ALONG THE PATH." With the same guide they came back. Even our bearded ancestors thought that absurd, I believe, for men standing just in the right place to be ordered to go away and immediately to come back to the place they had left. The whole lot of it is steeped in the same kind of stupidity: "SINCE I SEE YOU AT LAW" and "MIGHT YOU DECLARE THE BASIS FOR YOUR CLAIM?" As long as all these things were secret, they had to be sought from the men who held them; but after they became public and were widely studied, it was discovered that they were completely empty of wisdom but completely full of deceit and stupidity. **[27]** Many things were brilliantly established by the laws, but the same things were largely corrupted and distorted by the talents of the legal experts. Our ancestors wanted all women to be under the power of guardians because of their feebleness of mind; the experts discovered varieties of guardian who were controlled by the power of women.[35] They wanted family cults not to die out; the experts' cleverness discovered old men to make civil marriages to kill off the cults. In every aspect of the civil law they abandoned equity but held onto the literal meaning of words to such an extent that, because they found a dummy name in someone's law books, they thought that every woman making a civil marriage should be called "Jane Doe."[36] And I think it's pretty remarkable that so many men of such intelligence, after so many years, still can't make up their minds whether to say "on the third day"[37] or "the day after tomorrow," "judge" or "arbitrator," "dispute" or "suit." **[28]** And so, as I said, a branch of learning that is entirely composed of fictions and inventions has never entailed the worthiness to be consul, much less the required prestige. Something open to all and as available to my adversary as to me can never be a source of prestige. As a result, you long ago lost not only the expectation of conferring benefits but even the good old "can I

---

35. The subject is collusive marriages between women with familial religious obligations and elderly men who are paid to take over the obligations and return the property to which the obligations were attached. On their death (without heirs) the family and thus the cult obligations would be extinct.

36. "Gaia." The wedding formula "as I am Gaius, you are Gaia" is preserved by Plutarch, *Roman Questions* 271de.

37. The Romans used inclusive reckoning; we would say "on the second day."

ask your advice?" Nobody can be considered truly wise in an area of knowledge that has no relevance outside Rome—nor even within Rome if the court's in recess. Nobody can be considered an expert because there's no room for disagreement about a subject that everybody knows. Furthermore, the fact that the subject is contained in a very small number of texts that aren't particularly obscure doesn't make people think it difficult. Indeed, if you get me mad, extremely busy though I am, I'll promise to become learned in the law in three days flat. For instance: issues that involve interpretation of a written text are all written, but nothing is so tightly written that I can't tack on "CONCERNING THE OBJECT OF THE SUIT."[38] There's also very little risk in giving opinions on matters brought for advice: if you give the appropriate opinion, then you will be seen to give the same opinion as Servius; if otherwise, you will be seen to recognize and deal with disputed points of law. **[29]** That's why not only is military glory to be ranked ahead of your phrases and forms of action, but, as far as being elected to office is concerned, even the practice of oratory is way ahead of that rote learning of yours. As a result, it seems to me that many people start out by greatly preferring oratory, but when they can't make it that way, they generally slide down in your direction. As they say about Greek musicians, people who sing with a piper are the ones who couldn't sing while playing the lyre;[39] so, too, we see that people who can't make it as orators are reduced to studying law. Oratory involves great effort and serious issues, great distinction and a very great deal of influence. People look for something helpful from you but for salvation from orators. What's more, your opinions and decrees are often overturned by oratory and can't stay secure without oratorical support. If I were better at it than I am, I would say less in praise of it; as it is, I'm not saying anything about myself, only about those who are or have been great orators.

[30] There are, then, two areas of expertise that can raise a man to the highest rank of distinction: one is that of the general, the other of the good orator. The orator preserves the refinements of peace, the general prevents the dangers of war. All the other virtues

---

38. A standard phrase in judicial formulae (e.g., *Digest* 43.24.1pr.).

39. The latter requires much more coordination than the former. Cf. Lyndon Johnson about Gerald Ford: "So dumb he can't fart and chew gum at the same time" (*Columbia World of Quotations*, http://www.bartleby.com/66/1/31101.html. Accessed March 28, 2009).

individually have a great deal of importance—justice, good faith, modesty, self-control—and everybody knows that in these respects, Servius, you're outstanding. But I'm talking now about the areas of expertise that lead to public office, not about each person's natural virtue. All those studies of ours are knocked from our hands once some new disturbance begins to sound the trumpet of war. In fact, as an intelligent poet—and very good writer—says,[40] "once battles are started, from the middle is driven"—not just your wordy imitation of wisdom but even that ruler herself of life, "philosophy. Force rules; the orator is spurned," not only the one who is a hateful and wordy speaker but even "the good one; the rough soldier is loved," and your field of expertise is totally ignored: "not by engaging the issue in accordance with law, but by steel," he says, "is property recovered." And that being the case, Sulpicius, in my opinion the courts should give way to the camp, leisure to soldiering, the pen to the sword, shade to sun; first importance in the state should belong to what has made the state itself the first of all.

[31]   And yet Cato shows that in my words I'm making too much of all this, that I've forgotten that the whole war against Mithridates was a girly war. Members of the jury, I differ from him greatly. I'll explain it briefly, since it isn't essential to the case. If all the wars we've waged against Greeks deserve scorn, then we should laugh at the triumph of Manius Curius over King Pyrrhus, of Titus Flamininus over Philip, of Marcus Fulvius over the Aetolians, of Lucius Paullus over King Perseus, of Quintus Metellus over the counterfeit Philip, of Lucius Mummius over the Corinthians.[41] But if these wars were very worrisome and the victories in them very welcome, then why do you sneer at the nations of Asia and this enemy in particular? On the contrary, I see from the records of ancient history that possibly the greatest war waged by the Roman people was against Antiochus.[42] The victor in that war, Lucius Scipio, gained glory equal to that of his brother Publius; and as Publius displayed the glory of defeating Africa in

---

40. Quintus Ennius, *Annals*, fr. 247–53 Skutsch (1985).

41. Victories over Greeks in chronological order from the defeat of Pyrrhus at Beneventum in 275 to the sack of Corinth in 146.

42. Antiochus III of Syria was defeated in three battles in 191–190 BCE; Lucius Cornelius Scipio was given the cognomen Asiaticus for the defeat of Antiochus, as his brother Publius had received the cognomen Africanus for his defeat of Hannibal.

his cognomen, so Lucius gained the same glory for himself from
the name of Asia. **[32]** In that war, the outstanding excellence of
your great-grandfather Marcus Cato shone forth;[43] and as I imagine
him to have been like you, he would never have set out with Scipio
if he thought it was a girly war. Nor, indeed, would the senate have
arranged for Africanus to go out as a legate to his brother, when
(having driven Hannibal from Italy, thrown him out of Africa, and
crushed Carthage) he had recently freed the Republic from the greatest of dangers, if that war had not been thought fierce and important.
What is more, if you examine carefully Mithridates' capacities and
accomplishments and character, you'll certainly rank him ahead of
everyone against whom the Roman people have waged war. Sulla,
with a huge and powerful army and a general who was aggressive,
fierce, and (to say no more) not inexperienced, after Mithridates
brought war to all Asia, let him go in peace.[44] Lucius Murena, the
father of this Murena, harassed him with great force and vigor but
left him largely subdued rather than suppressed.[45] Mithridates, after
taking a few years to reconstruct his government and military forces,
was so powerful in his hopes and undertakings that he thought he
could link the Atlantic with the Black Sea and the troops of Sertorius
with his own.[46]

[33] Two consuls were sent to that war so that one could pursue
Mithridates while the other protected Bithynia.[47] The disastrous
conduct of one of them by land and sea significantly enhanced
the resources and the reputation of the king; Lucullus' actions, by

---

43. The elder Cato served as military tribune in the battle of Thermopylae
in 191.

44. The treaty of Dardanus in 85 was less a marker of decisive victory than
the result of Sulla's having more interest in conquering Rome than in conquering Mithridates.

45. A generous description, as the elder Murena was badly beaten. See
above, n. 20.

46. On Mithridates' dealings with Sertorius in Spain, see *Man.* 21.

47. Both consuls of 74 BCE, Lucullus and Marcus Aurelius Cotta, were sent
to Asia in 73. Cotta was badly defeated and had to be rescued by Lucullus
from being besieged in Chalcedon. Lucullus, however, attacked and defeated
Mithridates while he was besieging Cyzicus, leading to Mithridates' flight
back to Pontus. The chronology of events is disputed; I follow Broughton
(1950–1986) 3:121–22.

contrast, were so successful that no greater war can be remembered
nor one waged with greater wisdom and courage. The whole thrust
of the war had come to a halt before the walls of Cyzicus; Mithridates
thought that city to be the door to Asia and believed that once it was
shattered and torn from its hinges, the whole province would lie open
to him. But then Lucullus organized everything for the defense of
that city, one of our most faithful allies, and all the king's troops
were worn down by the length of the siege. And what about the naval
battle off Tenedos? The enemy fleet under savage leaders was speed-
ing toward Italy puffed up with hope and courage; do you think that
battle was some mild contest with minor fighting? I set aside battles,
I pass over towns taken by storm. Finally, at long last, when the king
was driven from his kingdom, he still had enough intelligence and
influence to recover himself through an alliance with the king of
Armenia and his fresh resources and troops. And if it were now my
task to speak about the accomplishments of our army and our general, I could name many important battles—but that's not my topic
here. **[34]** What I say is this: if this war—this enemy, that king—
had deserved contempt, then the senate and Roman people would not
have found it necessary to undertake it so seriously, Lucullus would
not have waged it for so many years with such glory, and the Roman
people would not so eagerly have entrusted Pompey with the task
of bringing it to an end.[48] Of all his countless battles, I think the
most fiercely contested was the one he fought against the king. And
when Mithridates escaped from that battle and fled to the Crimea
where our army couldn't follow him, even at the end of his luck and
his flight he kept the title of king. As a result, Pompey himself, after
taking possession of his kingdom and driving the enemy away from
every inch of familiar territory, still placed such weight on the life of
one man that although victory had given him everything Mithridates
had held or attacked or hoped for, still he didn't judge the war to be
over until he had driven him from life itself. Is this the enemy, Cato,
whom you hold in contempt? A man so many generals fought for so
many years in so many battles, a man whose life, even when he had
been driven out and driven away, was of such importance that only

---

48. Cicero, here as elsewhere (*In Support of Manilius' Law, In Defense of the
Poet Archias*), glides delicately over the hostility between Lucullus and his
supporters (including Hortensius) and Pompey and his. Pompey defeated
Mithridates at the battle of Nicopolis in 66.

when his death was reported did they believe the war was finally over? It's in this war that Lucius Murena was a legate whom we claim to have been recognized for the highest courage, the greatest wisdom, and the most outstanding effort; his work in this regard has no less worthiness for gaining the consulship than our own efforts in the forum.

[35] "But Servius came in ahead of Murena in the praetorian election." Are you still trying to negotiate with the people as if you had a contract? If they've given someone a rank in election to office once, do they owe him the same rank for the rest of his career? What strait or narrows do you think has so much ferment, so many heaving and turbulent waves, as the roiling tides of elections? The passage of a day or a night often upends the whole thing, and a slight breath of rumor often changes everyone's opinion. Something unexpected frequently happens for no obvious reason, so that the people themselves are often as surprised as if they weren't the ones who did it. [36] There's nothing more mobile than the crowd, nothing more hidden than men's wishes, nothing more treacherous than the conduct of elections. Who believed that Lucius Philippus, with his great talent, efforts, prestige, and nobility, could be defeated by Marcus Herennius? Or Quintus Catulus, a man of outstanding benevolence, wisdom, and honesty, by Gnaeus Mallius? Or Marcus Scaurus, a man of great consequence, an outstanding citizen, a senator of great courage, by Quintus Maximus?[49] Not only was none of these expected, but even when it happened nobody could understand why. Storms often arise after some weather sign in the sky, but often they're unexpectedly stirred up, with no clear explanation, from some hidden cause. So too, in the popular storm of the elections you can often see what roused it, but the cause is often so hidden that it seems to have been stirred up by chance. [37] But if you must have an explanation, two things that later helped Murena greatly in the consular elections were sorely lacking for his praetorship: one was the anticipation of games, encouraged by rumors and the enthusiastic suggestions of his competitors; the other was that the people who had witnessed his generosity and excellence in his province and his legateship had not yet returned. Fortune kept both of these in reserve for his campaign for the consulship. The army of Lucullus, which had assembled for

---

49. In reverse chronological order: the consular elections for 93, 105, and 116, respectively.

his triumph, was present for Murena's election,[50] and the magnificent games that had been missing in his campaign for the praetorship were supplied by his praetorship itself. **[38]** Surely you don't think the support and assistance for his becoming consul given by the goodwill of the soldiers and the votes of the army are trivial? Their voting has a great deal of effect because of their numbers, and they do more than influence their friends: in the selection of a consul they have broad authority with the entire Roman people. Generals, not commentators, are chosen at consular elections. That's why words like these have a great effect: "He saved me when I was wounded; he gave me booty; he was the leader when we captured their camp and joined battle; he never demanded more effort from his soldiers than he took on himself, and not only is he brave, he has luck with him, too." How much do you think this is worth toward reputation and goodwill among men? In fact, if there is so much superstition in these elections that the omen of the first vote has always been right, why should it be surprising that the widespread reports of his good luck worked for Murena?[51]

But even if you trivialize matters like this, which are in fact of great significance, and even if you place more weight on the votes of city dwellers than on those of soldiers, you still shouldn't have such scorn for the elegance of Murena's games and their theatrical magnificence: they did him a lot of good. There's no need to say that the people and the uneducated crowd are delighted by the games; no surprise there. But it's quite enough for this case; the elections belong to the people and the crowd. For that reason, if the magnificence of the games gives pleasure to the people, there's no surprise that it helped Murena among them. **[39]** But if people like us who are too busy to share in the common pleasure and who can find many other pleasures in our work itself, if even we enjoy the games and find them enticing, then why should you be surprised about the untutored mob? **[40]** Lucius Otho, a man of courage and a good friend of mine, restored to the knights not only their position but their pleasure, too.[52] And so this

---

50. Although Lucullus was replaced in 67, his triumph was delayed until 63.

51. The first century of the first (wealthiest) class to vote was selected by lot, and its choice was regarded as an omen.

52. The law of Lucius Roscius Otho, tribune in 67, returned the first fourteen rows of the theater to the knights; Sulla had removed the privilege—and

law about the games is highly appreciated, because along with the restoration of its glory, that most honorable of orders received the rewards of pleasure. Believe me: the games give men pleasure, even those who conceal it and not just those of us who admit it; I was aware of this when I was a candidate. I, too, had a competitor's display, and if I who had given three sets of games as aedile was still worried by Antonius' games,[53] do you, who by chance had given none yourself, do you really think that Murena's silvery display, which you sneer at, roused no opposition to you?

[41] But let's suppose all these things are comparable: work in the forum and work as a soldier; the votes of soldiers and the votes of city dwellers; giving really splashy games and not giving any at all. What then? Do you really think there was no difference between your lot and his in the conduct of the praetorship itself?[54] He was allotted the position that all your close friends wanted for you, in charge of the administration of law, a position in which the extent of the business brings fame and the distribution of justice brings favor. In that position, a wise praetor like Murena avoids offending people by the fairness of his decisions, and he acquires goodwill through mildness in administering justice. It's a fine sphere of responsibility, just right for gaining the consulship: the praise of his fairness, honesty, and affability was rounded off at the last by the pleasure given by his games. [42] And what about your position, the gloomy, harsh court trying cases of embezzlement of public funds, filled on one side with tears and squalor, on the other with accusers and witnesses? The reluctant jurors have to be dragged in and held against their will; the condemnation of a scribe brings the hostility of the whole order; the criticism of gifts made by Sulla offends many brave men and in fact a good chunk of the state;[55] the harsh assessment of penalties is forgotten by the man it pleases but remembered by the one it pains.

---

the people at large did not approve of the law. Cicero included his speech supporting Roscius in the collection of his consular speeches.

53. Cicero's three sets of games were given in his aedileship in 69, Gaius Antonius' as praetor in 66. Both men were elected consuls for 63.

54. Responsibilities of the praetors were chosen by lot; Murena became urban praetor, in charge of civil trials, and Sulpicius presided over the court dealing with embezzlement (*peculatus*).

55. Sulla as dictator had given his troops lands he had seized; people attempting to reclaim stolen property would bring a charge of embezzlement.

And, finally, you didn't want to take charge of a province. I can't criticize in you what I approved of in myself after my praetorship and after my consulship. Nevertheless, Murena's province brought him a great deal of goodwill and an excellent reputation.[56] As he set out, he drafted troops in Umbria; the commonwealth gave him the chance to be generous, and he used it to attach to himself many tribes that incorporate the towns of Umbria.[57] In Gaul, through his fairness and diligence, he made it possible for our men to collect money that had been given up for lost. Meanwhile, back in Rome, you were certainly a support to your friends, I admit it; but you should contemplate the fact that the enthusiasm of quite a few friends often dims in the case of a man whom they understand to reject his province.

[43] Members of the jury: I have now shown that Murena and Sulpicius brought equal worthiness to the campaign for the consulship but that their luck in provincial affairs was unequal. I will now speak more openly about the area in which my good friend Servius was worse off, and now that he's lost his chance I'll say before you things I often said to him in private while he still had it. I often told you, Servius, that you had no idea how to campaign for the consulship; I used to tell you that in precisely those areas where I saw you act and speak with a grand and brave spirit, you seemed to me more a powerful prosecutor than a wise candidate. In the first place, the intimidation tactics and threats of prosecution you used to use daily are the mark of a strong character, but they make people turn away from the hope of victory and weaken the enthusiasm of supporters. Somehow it always happens this way; it's been noticed not in one or two cases but in quite a few. As soon as a candidate is seen to think about prosecution, he seems to have given up on winning office. **[44]** "How so? Don't you approve of responding to injury?" Indeed, I do approve, strongly: but there's a time for campaigning and a time for responding. I want a candidate, particularly a candidate for the consulship, to be escorted to the forum and the campus[58] with great hopes, great spirits, and a great throng. I don't approve of the kind of questioning of a candidate that is an early

---

56. Murena governed Transalpine Gaul in 64 and the first part of 63.

57. The "tribes" are the thirty-five tribes that made up the *comitia tributa* at Rome.

58. The Campus Martius (Field of Mars) is where elections took place.

clue to defeat, nor of the balancing of witnesses instead of voters,
nor of threats instead of compliments, nor of subpoenas instead of
greetings—especially since by modern custom everyone runs around
to all the homes of the candidates and from their expressions guesses
at the level of their spirits and resources. **[45]** "Do you see him
looking sad and downcast? He's low; he's lost his confidence, he's
thrown in the towel." This kind of rumor spreads. "Did you know
he's thinking about filing charges, he's investigating the other candidates, gathering witnesses? Let's elect someone else if he's given
up on himself." Rumors of this kind undermine even the closest
friends of the candidates; they lose their enthusiasm; they either give
up the whole thing or keep their efforts and influence in reserve for
the prosecution and trial. Even more, the candidate himself can't
devote his whole mind and all his efforts to the campaign; he's also
thinking about the prosecution, which is no small thing but in fact a
huge job. It's a big job to collect material to use in driving someone
out of the Republic,[59] particularly someone who's not resourceless
and not feeble, who's defended by himself, his relatives, and even by
strangers. We all run to fight off dangers, and anyone who isn't an
open enemy offers the enthusiastic support of a very good friend to
the most distant people when civic status is at risk in a trial. **[46]** For
that reason, from my own experience of the difficulties involved in
seeking office and in legal defense and prosecution, I've concluded
that enthusiasm is the most important quality in running for office,
a sense of obligation in defending and hard work in prosecuting. And
so I've determined that it's completely impossible for one and the
same person to prepare and organize carefully both a prosecution
and a campaign for the consulship. There are few people who can
manage one of these; nobody can do both. In turning yourself aside
from the course of the campaign and transferring your attention to
prosecution, you believed that you could do a reasonable job in both,
but you couldn't have been more wrong. Was there a day, after you
made known your intention to prosecute, on which you weren't completely tied up in that project? You demanded a law against bribery,
which you already had: the Calpurnian law was very strict.[60] But
people accommodated the wishes of someone of such worth. That

---

59. Ten years' exile was part of the penalty for electoral corruption.

60. The previous law on electoral corruption, passed in 67.

whole law might have given your prosecution weapons—if you had a guilty defendant—but it worked against your campaign. **[47]** You were heard demanding a harsher penalty against the people; the anger of the lesser folk was aroused.[61] You wanted exile as a penalty against our order; the senate gave in to your demands, but it wasn't happy to follow your proposal to establish a harsher treatment for us all. A penalty was imposed on excuses of ill health; that offended the goodwill of many people who have to work hard to the detriment of their health or, because they're debilitated by disease, have to give up the other pleasures of life, too.[62] "Well, then, who sponsored all this?" Someone who yielded to the authority of the senate and to your wishes; someone to whom it was in any case of no benefit. The provisions the full senate—with my complete approval—rejected: do you think the damage they did to you was minor? You demanded a shuffled order of voting; the revival of Manilius' law;[63] the equalization of influence, of prestige, of votes. Honorable men, men who had influence in their own neighborhoods and towns, did not take kindly to having such a man strive to eliminate all distinctions of prestige and influence. You also wanted the juries to be selected by nomination so that the secret hatreds of citizens now limited to silent discontent might burst forth against the fortunes of every man of distinction.[64] **[48]** All this paved the path to prosecution; it blocked that of election.

That was the greatest blow of all suffered by your campaign, and I didn't keep quiet about it; on that score, a great deal of weighty

----

61. In fact, almost certainly directed against the *divisores* (bribery agents) and only marginally against the people at large. Cicero exaggerates both Sulpicius' viciousness and the potential resentment against him, and his account of the provisions of the law is somewhat suspect.

62. Again, almost certainly exaggerated. Then as now, defendants used the excuse of poor health to postpone trials, and Sulpicius may have done no more than ask for some proof of illness.

63. The text is uncertain. As tribune in 66 BCE, Manilius had tried to redistribute freedmen among all thirty-five tribes instead of just the four urban tribes. The rest of the sentence makes it seem that Sulpicius was demanding a wholesale revision of Roman electoral procedure, something highly unlikely.

64. That is, to have jurors selected by the prosecution (with rejection by the defense) rather than chosen by lot from a list.

comment has been made by my brilliant and eloquent colleague Hortensius. I've been allotted a tougher place in the order of speaking. Since both Hortensius and Crassus—a man of the greatest eminence, responsibility, and eloquence—have spoken before me, I come at the end and am not to argue a particular part of the case but to give my impression of the whole thing. The result is that I'm dealing with pretty much the same subjects they did, but as far as I can, members of the jury, I will try not to make you feel overstuffed. But, Servius, what kind of deathblow do you think you dealt your campaign when you made the Roman people afraid that Catiline would become consul while you threw away your campaign in favor of organizing a prosecution?[65] **[49]** As it was, they saw you making investigations, looking grim yourself, your friends mournful; they observed surveillance, depositions, witnesses being drawn aside, conferences with coprosecutors—all certainly things to make the expectations of candidates seem pretty dim.[66] At the same time, there was Catiline, alert and happy, surrounded by his chorus of young men, fortified with spies and assassins, puffed up with the hopes of his soldiers and the promises (at least according to him) of my colleague; surrounded by an army of colonists from Arretium and Faesulae; a crowd marked by a few men of a very different sort, those devastated by the disasters of Sulla's time. His own face was suffused with madness, his eyes with crime, his words with arrogance, just as if his consulship was already wrapped up and safe at home. He was scornful of Murena, and he counted Sulpicius as his prosecutor, not his rival; he warned him of violence and uttered threats against the Republic. **[50]** Don't ask me to remind you of the fear that affected all responsible citizens and of the great despair of the commonwealth if he had been made consul; you can remember it for yourselves. You remember when the people learned what that evil cutthroat is reported to have said in a meeting in his home: he said that no faithful defender of the suffering was to be found except someone who himself suffered; that the wounded and wretched should not trust the promises of the whole and happy; and therefore that those who wished to replace what had been spent, to take back what had been snatched from them, should observe what he owed himself, what he

---

65. Sulpicius' virtual withdrawal would leave Catiline much higher odds (2:3 rather than 1:2) of being selected.

66. Reading *spes* rather than *ipsi*.

possessed, what he dared to do; the man who was to be the future leader and standard-bearer of those who had been damaged should himself be without fear and should have suffered the most damage. **[51]** At that point, when you'd heard this, you remember there was a decree of the senate on my motion, that the elections should not take place on the following day so that we could discuss these matters in the senate. And on the following day, in a packed senate, I provoked Catiline and ordered him to speak if he wanted to about the matters that had been reported to me. He was, as always, very frank; he didn't claim innocence but gave evidence against himself and took on his own guilt. It was then he said that the commonwealth had two bodies, one tottering with a weak head, the other strong but headless; but if it was worthy of him, that second body would not lack a head so long as he lived. The packed senate groaned, but their decision was less severe than his disgusting behavior deserved: some of them were insufficiently firm in reaching a decision because they didn't feel any fear; others weren't firm because they were terrified. He burst forth from the senate triumphant in joy, a man who shouldn't have left that place alive at all, especially since in the senate a few days earlier he had told Cato, who bravely threatened him with the law and denounced him, that if a fire were set against his fortunes he would put it out not with water but with destruction. **[52]** All this left me in turmoil. Since I knew Catiline was already deploying conspirators with swords in the campus, I went down to the campus with a very strong guard of courageous men and with that broad and conspicuous breastplate: not to protect myself (since I knew Catiline usually aimed not at the chest or belly but at the head and neck) but so that, as in fact happened, all respectable citizens could see and, when they saw the consul in fear and danger, would rush to his support and defense. And since they thought that you, Servius, were too lax in your campaigning and that Catiline was inflamed with hope and greed, everyone who wanted to expel that monster from the Republic instantly came over to Murena. **[53]** A sudden shift of support in a consular election matters a lot, especially when it settles on a good and responsible candidate with many other qualities in his favor. Murena's father and ancestors were men of distinction; he was extremely temperate as a young man; his service as legate was distinguished; his praetorship met with approval of his behavior in legal affairs, with goodwill from his games, and with honor from his province. He worked hard on his campaign, and throughout he neither gave way to threats nor made threats against anyone else. Is it any surprise that Catiline's sudden hopes were a great aid to Murena in attaining the consulship?

[54] The third topic of my speech remains, concerning the charge of electoral corruption. Although it's been thoroughly cleared up by the previous speakers, at Murena's request I'll deal with it again. On this subject I'll answer my friend the distinguished Gaius Postumius[67] concerning the evidence of the bribery agents and the cash that was seized; I'll answer this clever and upright young man Servius Sulpicius concerning the centuries of the knights; and I'll answer Marcus Cato, a man who's exceptional in every virtue, concerning his accusation, the decree of the senate, and the commonwealth in general. [55] But before I go on, I must briefly express my sorrow concerning Murena's situation. In the past, members of the jury, on the basis of other people's sufferings and my own daily toils and worries, I often considered fortunate those men who pursued a life of leisure and serenity far from the occupations of political ambition; but such great and unexpected dangers as Murena's have affected my emotions so greatly that I'm not able properly to express my compassion either for the fate we all share or for Murena's present misfortune. Starting from the offices held by his family and his ancestors successively, he attempted to rise one step higher in position. In so doing he came in danger of losing both what he inherited and what he had gained for himself; through eagerness for new glory he has even been led to put his previous good fortune at risk. [56] That's bad enough, members of the jury, but most painful of all is that his accusers are not people who undertook the prosecution from hatred and hostility but who sank to the level of hostility from their enthusiasm to prosecute. I set aside Servius Sulpicius: I recognize that he is moved not by some assault from Murena but by the competition for office. But Gaius Postumius is prosecuting him, a friend of his father's and, as he says himself, Murena's neighbor and close acquaintance of long standing; he gave many reasons for their closeness but could name none for his animosity. Servius Sulpicius, the son of Murena's colleague, is prosecuting him;

---

67. Clark, following the manuscripts, reads "Postumus" rather than "Postumius," but the latter is almost certainly right. He was one of the prosecutors; see sec. 56 below.

his talent ought to be devoted to protecting his father's friends.[68] Marcus Cato is prosecuting him; he's never been estranged from Murena in anything, and it's my understanding that he was born in this Republic, so his resources and talent should provide protection for many, including strangers, but should not act destructively even toward an enemy. **[57]** So I'll answer Postumius first. As a candidate for the praetorship attacking a consular, he seems to me somehow like a stunt rider who jumps from one chariot to the next. If his own competitors did nothing wrong, he acknowledged their worthiness when he abandoned his campaign; but if one of them gave bribes, then Postumius is the kind of friend one looks for, since he's going after someone else's injury rather than his own.

[ON POSTUMIUS' ACCUSATIONS AND ON
THOSE OF THE YOUNGER SERVIUS][69]

[58] I come now to Marcus Cato, the firm foundation of the whole prosecution. He's such a serious and powerful prosecutor that I'm much more afraid of his influence than I am of his charges. In the case of this prosecutor, members of the jury, I will start by praying that Murena not be harmed by Cato's stature, by the expectation of his becoming tribune, by the grandeur and seriousness of his whole life—in sum, that the good qualities Cato has acquired in order to help people not be a source of harm to Murena alone. At the time he prosecuted Lucius Cotta, Publius Africanus had been consul twice and had destroyed two cities that caused terror in our empire, Carthage and Numantia.[70] He was outstandingly eloquent, trustworthy, and honorable; his authority matched that of the empire of the

---

68. As with Postumius (probably a relative of Sulpicius by marriage), so with the younger Sulpicius, Cicero obscures what must be a close family relationship to the prosecutor. He is described as the son of a *sodalis* of Murena, which ought to mean some kind of collegial position or partnership; is it possible that the partnership is the shared offices (quaestorship and praetorship) of Murena and Sulpicius, and that the younger Sulpicius is in fact the son of the elder? That may carry Cicero's disingenuousness too far.

69. As in a few other speeches, Cicero left out a technical portion of his speech in the written version and included the heading instead.

70. The prosecution for extortion was probably in 138, and hence Scipio had not yet conquered Numantia. By Africanus here Cicero means the man usually referred to as Scipio Aemilianus.

Roman people that his labors protected. I often heard older men say that this extraordinary effectiveness and stature of the prosecutor was in fact a help to Cotta: the jury at that time consisted of men of great wisdom, who didn't want anyone to lose his case in such a way that he seemed beaten by the excessive strength of his opponent. **[59]** Another instance: didn't the Roman people, as tradition has it, save Servius Galba from your great-grandfather Cato, that man of enormous courage and energy, when he was trying to destroy him?[71] In this state both the people at large and judges who are wise and show great foresight have always resisted excessive resources in an accuser. I do not want a prosecutor to bring his power into court, or excessive force, or outstanding authority, or too much favor. All those things should work to protect the innocent, to support the powerless, to aid the suffering, but they should be rejected when they are used to endanger and damage our citizens. **[60]** If somebody should say that Cato would never have stooped to prosecution if he hadn't decided the validity of the case in advance, then, members of the jury, he will be establishing an unjust law and wretched rules for men at risk if he thinks that the prosecutor's judgment against the defendant ought to determine the verdict in advance.

For my own part, Cato, because of my own judgment about your extraordinary virtue, I'm unable to criticize your plan; but perhaps I might shape it and slightly improve it. "You don't make many errors," said the old teacher to the great warrior, "but you make errors; I can straighten you out."[72] I can't straighten you out: in absolute truth, I'd say that you make no errors nor are you in any way at all the kind of person who needs to be corrected. You just need to be made a little more flexible. In terms of honor, seriousness of purpose, moderation, greatness of mind, justice—in terms of all the virtues—nature shaped you to be a great and lofty human being. But to that nature was added a dogma that's neither measured nor mild; rather, as it seems to me, it's a little more rigid and more harsh than either truth or nature can endure. **[61]** And since I'm not giving this speech to the uneducated masses or to some bunch of farmers, I'll speak a little more boldly about the liberal studies that are known to, and give

---

71. Not a formal trial, but an accusation of mass murder of the Lusitanians by Servius Sulpicius Galba in 150.

72. Clearly Phoenix to Achilles, presumably from an unknown tragedy.

pleasure to, both me and you.[73] In Cato here, members of the jury, you must know that the divine, unique excellence that we see is all his own; what we occasionally find wanting comes not from nature but from his teacher. There was once a man of great intelligence, Zeno; those who imitate his discoveries are called Stoics.[74] His aphorisms and instructions go like this: the Wise Man is never moved by favor; he never forgives anyone's failings; only an insignificant fool feels pity, while a real man is not susceptible to entreaty or appeasement. Only Wise Men, even if they are hideously deformed, are beautiful; if they are beggars, they are rich; if they are slaves, they are kings. Those of us who are not Wise Men they call runaways, exiles, enemies—in short, lunatics. All faults are equal; every failing is an unspeakable crime, and the man who unnecessarily kills a rooster is no less criminal than someone who smothers his father. The Wise Man does not have mere opinions; he regrets nothing; he can be deceived in nothing; he never alters his judgment. **[62]** Now Cato is a very smart man, and under the influence of very learned authorities he snatched all this up—and not, as most of them do, as topics for argument, but as a way of life. The tax collectors have a request. Make sure that favor plays no part in the decision. Some suppliants turn up, wretched victims of disaster. You're a wicked criminal if you do anything under the influence of pity. Someone admits he made a mistake and asks pardon for his error. "It's wicked to pardon a crime." But it's just a misdemeanor. "All faults are equal." You made a random statement. "It's fixed in stone." You were moved by opinion rather than the facts. "The Wise Man never has opinions." You got something wrong. He thinks it's slander. This

---

73. Similar flattery introduces Cicero's mocking discussions of Greek culture in *Defense of the Poet Archias* and *Against Lucius Calpurnius Piso*. See the introductions to those speeches. Cicero loathed the living Cato, however much he may later have expressed admiration for him as a martyr for the Republic; Cato was likeable only posthumously. See above, n. 12.

74. Zeno of Citium (335–263 BCE), inventor of Stoicism. Cicero's version of the philosophy and of Cato is parodic, based on the so-called Stoic paradoxes. The theme of Roman misunderstanding of Greek philosophy is taken up in *Against Lucius Calpurnius Piso*, this time concerning Epicureanism. Capitalized "Wise Man" indicates the technical use of *sapiens* by the Stoics to describe the perfect sage—who may never have existed even in their beliefs.

education is the source of things like this: "I said in the senate I would bring charges against a consular candidate." You were angry when you said it. "Never does the Wise Man get angry," he replies. You said it for the moment. "Only a wicked man deceives by lying," he says; "it's disgraceful to change your views; it's a crime to be moved by prayers; it's disgusting to show pity." **[63]** But the philosophers I follow—and forgive me, Cato, when I was young I too distrusted my own intelligence and sought the support of dogma— my people, I say, those in the line from Plato and Aristotle, moderate and measured men, say that sometimes the Wise Man can be moved by favor; good men do show pity; there are different kinds of crimes and different penalties for them; a man of constancy has room for pardon; even the Wise Man himself often has opinions about things he doesn't know. He sometimes gets angry, he can be swayed and appeased, he occasionally changes what he said if it seems right, he sometimes departs from his stated views; all virtues need to be tempered in accordance with some middle ground.[75] **[64]** If some chance, Cato, had brought you to these teachers, given your character, you wouldn't have been a better man nor braver nor more moderate nor more just—that's impossible—but slightly more inclined to mildness. Without having any personal enmity to spur you on, provoked by no injury, you wouldn't bring a prosecution against a man of great decency who has the greatest worth and respectability. You would have thought, since fortune had put both you and Murena in charge of the same year, that you were bound to him by the link of public service;[76] the savage things you said in the senate you either would not have said or, if possible, you would have them understood in a milder way. **[65]** And in my opinion, as far as I can predict, although now you're spurred on by a certain excitement, carried away by the force of your own natural talent, on fire from your recent studies with your teachers—experience will make you pliant, time will make you milder, age will soften you. Even your teachers and instructors in moral excellence seem to me to have extended the bounds of obligation somewhat further than nature would wish, so

---

75. By "middle ground" Cicero invokes the Aristotelian idea of the virtues as occupying a mean between extremes. The views given here are purely Aristotelian, not Platonic; the invocation of Plato probably reflects the syncretistic history of philosophy common in the first century.

76. Murena as consul, Cato as tribune for 62.

that, although we stretch ourselves as far as possible in our minds, we should still stop at the appropriate point. "You should show no pardon." Well, for some things, but not everything. "You should do nothing for the sake of acquiring goodwill." Well, you should resist favor, when duty and honor demand it. "You should not be moved by pity." True, if it means a loss of strict standards; but being humane deserves some praise, too. "You must stick to your declared views." Yes, unless another and better view overcomes the first. **[66]** That's how Scipio was,[77] a man who was not ashamed to do as you have, to maintain a great scholar, Panaetius, in his home; although his ideas were the same as those that delight you, Scipio wasn't made harsher by his instruction but, as I've heard from my elders, very mild. Who was more affable than Gaius Laelius, who more pleasant emerged from these studies of yours, who was more serious or wiser than he? I could say the same thing about Lucius Philus and Gaius Galus, but it's time to bring you home. Who do you think was more accommodating, more accessible, more moderate in all aspects of humane behavior than your great-grandfather Cato?[78] When you spoke, both truthfully and seriously, about his exceptional virtue, you said you had in your home an example to be imitated. You do indeed have that example for yourself at home, but while hereditary likeness to him is more relevant to you, his descendant, than to any one of us, he's a model to be imitated as much for me as for you.[79] But if you added a pinch of easiness and amiability to your seriousness and solemnity, then while your outstanding qualities couldn't be better, they might be better seasoned.[80]

---

77. Scipio Aemilianus. The names that follow are of his friends and associates, sometimes wrongly described as "the Scipionic Circle." Laelius and Philus were his close friends (and appear with him in Cicero's later dialogue *On the Commonwealth*), Gaius Sulpicius Galus (consul in 166) was an expert on astronomy, and Panaetius of Rhodes was the head of the Stoic school and closely associated with members of the Roman aristocracy.

78. Although Cicero's presentation of the elder Cato as an affable old man in *On Old Age* in 44 may have been unironic, it is certainly a joke here: the younger Cato's greatest resemblance to his great-grandfather was in their sheer unpleasantness as human beings.

79. On Cato as the exemplary new man, see above, n. 24.

80. There is a play on words here between *condita* ("based, founded") and *condîta* ("seasoned").

[67] For that reason (to go back to my starting point), remove the name of Cato from this case; set aside his forcefulness; do without his authority, which in a trial should either have no influence or should influence in favor of innocence. Join me in engaging with the charges themselves. What's your accusation, Cato? What are you bringing to court? What are you attacking? You prosecute corruption; I'm not defending it. You criticize me for defending what I would punish by my law. I punished corruption, not innocence; if you want, I'll even join you in prosecuting corruption itself. You said a decree of the senate was entered on my motion that it would be deemed a violation of the Calpurnian law if people were paid to go to greet candidates; if people were hired as an entourage; or if places to watch the gladiators were broadly distributed to each tribe and similarly if meals were broadly distributed. So the senate decided that these things should be deemed illegal—if they were done: a completely pointless decision, but it's what the candidates wanted. The important question is whether or not they were done; if they were, nobody can possibly question their illegality. **[68]** This is ridiculous: to leave uncertain something that is doubtful, to make a judgment about something that can be doubtful to nobody at all. The decree was passed at the request of all the candidates, so that nobody could know from the senatorial decree in whose interest it was or against whom it was directed. So show me that Murena did these things; then I'll admit they were done illegally.

"Many people came out to meet him on his return from his province." That's normal for someone running for consul: is there anyone people did *not* go to meet on his return? "What was that crowd?" First, even if I can't tell you exactly, what's the surprise in lots of people going to meet such a man on his arrival, a candidate for consul? If it hadn't happened, that would be a bigger surprise. **[69]** I'll even add to that something else customary, that many people were invited to come. Surely that isn't criminal or even surprising. In a city where we often used to be asked to come from the far side of the city before dawn to escort the sons of men from the lowest levels of society,[81] why should men make heavy weather about coming out to the Campus Martius in broad daylight, especially when asked in the name of such a great man? So what if all the tax-companies came, companies of which many of these jurors are members? So did many

---

81. To accompany a client's son on his coming of age.

senators of great distinction. So did that most assiduous group that allows nobody to enter the city without honor, the whole tribe of political candidates; and, to end my list, my friend Postumius, who is prosecuting this case, came to meet Murena with his own huge crowd—so what's the surprise in such a large mob? I leave out clients, neighbors, members of the same tribe, the whole army of Lucullus, which had just arrived for his triumph: I will simply say this, that in performing this duty unpaid crowds have never shortchanged any man of worth—or even any man who just wanted followers.

[70] "But he had a large entourage." Show me they were paid, and I'll admit it's criminal. But without that, what are you carping at? "What need," he says, "for an entourage?" You ask me why someone needs what we've always had ourselves? This is the only way for men of slight resources to earn or repay the favor of senators: working for us and accompanying us when we're campaigning for office. It isn't possible, nor should we or Roman knights be asked, to follow candidates, even close connections, for days on end: if they fill our houses in the morning, if from time to time they escort us to the forum, if they show respect to us by walking one length of the basilica with us, we're seen to be attended and cultivated carefully. Our lesser friends and people who aren't busy attend us regularly, and a crowd of them usually surrounds good and benevolent men. [71] Do not, Cato, snatch this rewarding show of attention from the lower classes; permit people whose hopes rest entirely on us to have something to offer us in return. If there's nothing except their own votes, then these lesser folk, even if they vote, don't make much difference.[82] These people can't, as they often say, speak for us; they can't make legal agreements for us; they can't invite us to their homes. And yet they seek all these things from us, and they are unable to make a return for what they receive from us except by their physical efforts. For that reason they opposed the Fabian law about the size of candidates' entourages as well as the resolution of the senate passed in the consulship of Lucius Caesar.[83] There's no punishment, in fact, that could bar the respectful presence of men of lesser standing from this

---

82. The electoral assembly was weighted in favor of the rich, and the election stopped as soon as candidates had reached the necessary number of votes in their favor. A poor man's vote might never be counted at all.

83. 64 BCE. Nothing else is known of this resolution or of the Fabian law (date also unknown).

ancient customary way of discharging one's obligations. **[72]** "But he gave shows to each of the tribes and fed people wholesale." Even though this wasn't done by Murena at all, members of the jury, but was done by his friends according to custom and with restraint, still, since you remind me, I recall how many votes, Servius, your whining in the senate about this cost us.[84] In our own memory or in that of our fathers, when has there ever been a time when—whether you call it bribery or generosity—places were not given to friends and fellow tribesmen in the circus and the forum? These are the rewards men of lesser standing looked for from their fellow tribesmen by long-standing custom. . . .

[There is a gap in the text.]

[73] . . . {If it seems criminal for one of Murena's}[85] staff officers to have given seats once to the members of his tribe, then what will their verdict be against the leading citizens who have set up full bars[86] in the circus for their tribesmen? All these charges about entourages and games and meals are counted as excessive nit-picking on your part by the multitude, Servius, and in all of them Murena is defended by the authority of the senate. Consider this. The senate doesn't believe it's a crime for people to go out to greet someone, does it? "No, not unless they are paid." Prove that. A crime to have a large entourage? "No, unless they're hired." Show me. To give places at the games or invite people for a meal? "Not at all, unless it's widespread." What's "widespread"? "Offered to everyone." So if Lucius Natta, a young man of high birth—and we can already see what kind of person he is and what kind of man he'll become[87]—if Natta wanted to be amiable to the centuries of knights because of both the obligations of a close family tie and his looking to his own future, that won't be charged as a crime to his stepfather. And if Murena's close relative, the Vestal

---

84. By "us," Cicero is emphasizing his support of Sulpicius' candidacy.

85. Mommsen's supplement for the lost beginning of the sentence.

86. It is not entirely clear what *totas tabernas* here means; "blocks of seats" is another possibility, or perhaps "a bunch of skyboxes." The general point is in any case clear.

87. Lucius Pinarius Natta, who was also Clodius' brother-in-law and took part in Clodius' assault on Cicero in the 50s.

Virgin, wanted to give him her seat at the gladiatorial games, she didn't behave immorally, nor is Murena involved in some guilt. For people with close ties, such actions are duties; for people of lesser means, they're helpful; for candidates, they're expected.

[74] But here's Cato, playing the stern Stoic: he says that it's not true that goodwill can be gained by food; he says men's judgment in selecting magistrates shouldn't be corrupted by pleasures. So if somebody invites you to dinner as part of his campaign, should he be condemned? "Are you telling me that you're really seeking the highest power, the greatest authority, the helm of the commonwealth by playing to men's senses, softening their minds, providing pleasures? Are you asking for a job as pimp from a bunch of pretty young men, or are you seeking command over the whole world from the Roman people?" Tough stuff; but experience, life, custom, the state itself reject it. Not even the Spartans, the model for this kind of life and talk, who stretch out for their daily meals on wooden couches; not even the Cretans, none of whom ever ate a bite lying down, preserved their commonwealths any better than the men of Rome, who divide their time between pleasure and toil. The second bunch were destroyed by one visit of our army; the first use the protection of our power to preserve their discipline and laws.[88] [75] So, Cato, don't criticize with excessively harsh language the institutions of our ancestors: they've been proven good by the long duration of our empire.

In our fathers' generation there was once a man learned in the same discipline as you, a man who was honorable and noble, Quintus Tubero.[89] When Quintus Maximus was giving a great memorial banquet for the Roman people in the name of his uncle Publius Africanus, he asked Tubero (since Tubero was Africanus' sister's son) to organize

88. The Cretans were defeated in 68–67, but not so quickly as Cicero suggests. Sparta kept its peculiar institutions as a tourist attraction after the Roman conquest.

89. Quintus Aelius Tubero, the son of Scipio Aemilianus' sister, only reached the tribunate (by 130 BCE). He was a serious Stoic, to whom Panaetius and other Stoics dedicated books; Cicero says (*Brutus* 117) that his life, like his oratorical style, was "hard, uncivilized, and prickly." Quintus Fabius Maximus was also a nephew of Scipio Aemilianus. As before, "Africanus" is the younger Africanus, Scipio Aemilianus; he died suddenly and mysteriously in 129.

the dining arrangements. Tubero, a Stoic of great learning, spread Punic couches with goatskin covers and set out Samian pottery,[90] as if it was Diogenes the Cynic who had died, not a memorial for the godlike Africanus. When Maximus praised Africanus on the day of his funeral, he thanked the immortal gods that such a man was born in this commonwealth in particular, since it was necessary that whatever nation he belonged to would rule the earth. The Roman people took umbrage at the perverse wisdom that Tubero brought to bear on the ceremonies after Africanus' death, [76] and as a result that totally upright man, an outstanding citizen, the grandson of Lucius Aemilius Paullus and the son, as I said, of the sister of Africanus, because of those goatskin covers, lost the election for the praetorship. The Roman people hate private luxury but love public grandeur; they have no love for extravagant banquets but even less for stingy insensibility. They recognize distinctions among duties and occasions and the interchange between toil and pleasure. You say that men's minds shouldn't be enticed by anything other than worthiness in choosing a magistrate, but despite your supreme worthiness you don't keep to this rule yourself. Why do you ask anyone to support you or help you? You ask for my vote so as to rule over me, you ask me to entrust myself to you. But why? Should you be asking me such things, or shouldn't I rather be the one to ask you to undertake toil and danger on my behalf? [77] Don't you have a slave to remind you of people's names? That's a kind of deceit and deception: if it's right for you to call your fellow citizens by name, it's wrong that they're better known to your slave than to you. But if you know the names, why have them named by your prompter when you're campaigning, as if you were uncertain? Why, when you are prompted, do you still greet them as if you knew their names yourself? Why, after you have been elected, are you much less careful about your greetings? If you judge such things by the norms of society, that's fine and proper; but if you evaluate them by the teachings of your school, they may be found completely crooked. For that reason, the Roman people shouldn't be deprived of the enjoyment of the games, of gladiators, of parties, all of which our ancestors employed, nor should this kind of generosity be taken away from candidates. It indicates benevolence, not bribery.

---

90. It is not clear whether Carthaginian couches were as uncouth as the goatskins covering them. Samian ware is pottery rather than silver or gold.

[78] But the public interest led you to this prosecution. I'm sure, Cato, that you started in that state of mind and with that belief, but you've slipped from the path because you lack practical wisdom. I am doing what I am doing, members of the jury, in part because of my friendship for Murena and his worthiness, but also, I proclaim and call upon you to witness, on behalf of the peace and calm, harmony and liberty, the well-being and lives of us all. Listen, members of the jury, listen to a consul who (not to praise myself too much, but to say only this) spends whole days and nights thinking about the commonwealth! Catiline did not have so much scorn and contempt for the commonwealth as to think that with only the group he took with him he could crush this state. The infection of his crime is more widely diffused than anyone believes, and it involves more people. Within the city, within this very city, there is a Trojan Horse, but one that will never destroy you in your sleep so long as I am consul. **[79]** You ask me whether I have any fear of Catiline. None at all, and I've seen to it that nobody should fear him. But I do say that we must fear his troops that I see right here. It isn't the army of Catiline we should fear so much as those who are said to have deserted from it. They have not deserted; he left them here as spies and fifth-columnists, and they stand poised over our heads and necks. These people yearn to have an honest consul and good general, someone by nature and fortune closely linked to the salvation of the commonwealth, cast down by your votes from defending the city and pushed out of his post as guardian of the state. I turned aside their reckless weapons in the elections, I crippled them in my public speeches, I vanquished them frequently at my own home,[91] members of the jury; but if you hand over one of the consuls to them, they will have accomplished much more by your verdict than they could by their own swords. It makes a huge difference, members of the jury, that there be two consuls in the commonwealth on the first of January; that is something I have worked hard to accomplish despite much opposition. **[80]** You must not think these people use pedestrian plans or everyday methods. They're not looking for some wicked legislation, some destructive giveaway or some conventional means of damaging the commonwealth. They have undertaken a plan right here, members of the jury, to destroy the city, to slaughter its citizens, to blot out the very name

---

91. There was an attempt to murder Cicero at home on the morning of November 7. "Frequently" is something of an exaggeration.

of Rome. And these are citizens, citizens, I repeat—if I can even use that name for them—who are and have been making these plans about their own fatherland. I daily oppose their plans, I cripple their daring, I resist their crime. But hear my warning, members of the jury. My consulship is coming to an end. Do not steal from me my successor in diligence; do not take away a man to whom I desire to hand over the commonwealth in safety to be defended against these massive dangers.

[81] Members of the jury, don't you see what else accompanies these evils? Cato, I call on you: don't you foresee the storm of your year in office? In the public meeting just yesterday, the destructive voice of a tribune-designate, your colleague, thundered out;[92] against him your own wisdom took many precautions, as did all the responsible citizens who summoned you to seek the tribunate. Every disturbance of the past three years, from the time when, as you know, Catiline and Gnaeus Piso began their scheme for murdering the senate,[93] everything is bursting out in these days, these months, this time of crisis. [82] What place is there, members of the jury, what moment, what day, what night when I am not saved from their ambushes and the points of their daggers and escape not just by my own foresight but even more by that of the gods? It's not on my own account that they want me dead; they want to have a watchful consul removed from protecting the commonwealth. No less, Cato, would they wish to remove you somehow, if they could; and believe me, they're working and scheming for that result. They see your courage, they see your brains, they see your authority, they see your service in protecting the commonwealth. But when they see the power of the tribunate stripped of the authority and assistance of the consul, then they believe they will be able to crush you more easily when you're unarmed and weakened. They have no fear that a consul will be elected to replace Murena; they see this will be under the control of your colleagues. They hope that Decimus Silanus, an illustrious man but without a colleague; you yourself, without a consul; and the

---

92. Quintus Caecilius Metellus Nepos, who subsequently blocked Cicero from delivering a speech at the end of his term of office.

93. The so-called first conspiracy of Catiline in 65, a fiction invented by Cicero as part of his campaign for the consulship. Gnaeus Calpurnius Piso was given a command in Spain by the senate in 65; he was killed there in 64. His connection with Catiline is obscure at best.

commonwealth, without protection, will be served up to them on a platter. **[83]** In the midst of such great affairs and such dangers, it's up to you, Cato, you who always seem to me to have been born not for yourself but for your country,[94] to see what is going on, to keep as a supporter, a defender, an ally in public affairs a consul who is not greedy, a consul—what this crisis particularly demands—who has been shaped by his fortune to embrace peace, by his knowledge to wage war, and by his spirit and experience to complete whatever task you could wish.

In fact, however, the entire power to settle this matter, members of the jury, rests with you. In this case you hold in your hands the entire commonwealth; it is you who steer it. If Catiline, using as his council the evil companions he took with him, were to adjudicate this case, he would condemn Murena; if he could put him to death, he would. His plans require the commonwealth to be deprived of support, the supply of generals who can resist his insanity to be diminished, a greater opportunity to be given to the tribunes of the people to stir up sedition and discord once their opponent has been defeated. Are the most honorable and wisest men chosen from the highest orders in the state going to deliver the same verdict that the most destructive gladiator, that enemy of the commonwealth, would deliver? **[84]** Believe me, members of the jury, you'll be casting your votes in this case not just about Murena's well-being but about your own. We have come to the final conflict. There is nothing left to restore us, and once we have fallen there is nowhere left to stand. Not only are the supports we now have not to be reduced, but if possible we need to get new ones. The enemy is not at the Anio, which was the worst moment of the Punic Wars,[95] but actually in the city, in the forum and—what cannot, by the everlasting gods, be spoken without a groan of sorrow—some of them even in the inner sanctum of the commonwealth, the senate house itself; there are, I repeat, enemies even there. May the gods grant that my colleague in office, a man of great bravery, crush this criminal brigandage of Catiline with armed force! Wearing the garb of peace and with your aid and that of all responsible citizens, I will scatter and crush this danger spawned in

---

94. "We are not born for ourselves alone, but for our country" is one of Cicero's favorite tags, from Plato, *Ninth Letter* 358a.

95. Three miles from Rome; Hannibal's closest approach to the city in 211 BCE.

the heart of the commonwealth by my planning. **[85]** But what will happen if it slips from our hands to spill over into the following year? There will be one consul only, and he'll be kept busy not in conducting the war but in electing a replacement to be his colleague. Those who will be able to block him . . . that disastrous, monstrous danger of Catiline will break forth, and will threaten the Roman people.[96] He will quickly rush into the area around the city; madness will fill the city, fear will fill the senate house, conspiracy will fill the forum, armies will fill the Campus, devastation will fill the land. In every house and every place, we will fear fire and the sword. But all these things that have been organized, if the commonwealth has its proper protection, will easily be crushed by the wisdom of the magistrates and the concern of the citizens.

[86] This being so, members of the jury, first, on behalf of the commonwealth, which ought to take first place in our hearts, on the basis of my great efforts on behalf of the Republic, which are well known to you, I warn you; on the basis of my consular authority, I urge you; on the basis of the magnitude of the danger, I beseech you: act in the interest of civic order and peace and of the well-being and very lives of yourselves and all other citizens. Likewise, because of my obligation as a defender and a friend, I beg and beseech you, members of the jury, do not overwhelm with new lamentation the recent congratulations received by Murena, a man who is suffering and made weary by physical disease and mental anguish.[97] Just now he seemed blessed by fortune, having received the greatest favor given by the Roman people, because he was first to bring the consulship into an old family and an ancient town;[98] now he sits in rags and filth, worn by disease, lost in tears and grief. He is your suppliant, members of the jury, he calls on your good faith, he begs for your pity, he looks to your power and your resources. **[87]** Do not, by the everlasting gods, deprive him of this office, one he hoped would enhance his standing; do not deprive him in addition of all his previously won honors, his rank and his fortune. This, members of the jury, is Murena's prayer to you. If he has harmed nobody unjustly,

---

96. There are clearly words missing in this sentence, and some of what is printed here is conjectural.

97. Pathos, but perhaps not fact.

98. Lanuvium, a Latin town with ancient connections to Rome, about twenty miles from the city.

if he has never spoken badly about anyone or hindered their wishes, if he has never been an object of hatred (to put it mildly) to anyone either here or on active duty, may you offer room for humility, refuge for men who are downcast, aid for those who have decency. To have a consulship ripped away from someone ought to arouse great sympathy, members of the jury: everything is snatched away along with the consulship. The consulship itself at a time like this can arouse no envy. It is exposed to the public attacks of revolutionaries, the plots of conspirators, the weapons of Catiline; all alone, it is set against every danger and every injury. **[88]** Why Murena or anyone else should be the object of envy for attaining this wonderful consulship I do not see, members of the jury; all the things that deserve pity are before my eyes, and you too can see and identify them. If (and may Jupiter ward off the omen) you bring ruin upon him through your verdict, where is the wretched man to turn?[99] To his home? So he can see the image of that glorious man, his father, an image that a few days ago he saw wreathed in laurel to honor him, to see this same image twisted by shame and in mourning?[100] Or to his mother, that unhappy woman, who recently kissed her son as consul and is now tortured and worried that she may shortly see him despoiled of all honor? **[89]** But why do I name his mother or his house, when the new legal penalty deprives him of his home and his parent and the company and sight of all those dear to him? Is this unhappy man to go into exile? Where? To the regions of the East where he served as legate for many years, led armies, performed great deeds? But it makes for great pain to return in disgrace to a place you left in honor. Or should he hide on the opposite side of the world, so that Transalpine Gaul, which recently was happy to see him as supreme commander, should now see him in sadness and grief as an exile? And in that province, in what state of mind should

---

99. This passage of high pathos and emotion is drawn ultimately from Euripides' *Medea*, but more proximately resembles the last speech of Gaius Gracchus: "Where am I to go? Where to turn? To the Capitol? But it is dripping with my brother's blood. To my home? To see my wretched mother lamenting and downcast?" (fr. 61 Malcovati 1976).

100. Wax death masks of ancestors who had held office were kept in the atrium of Roman houses. The right to have such images came with holding the aedileship.

he see his brother Gaius Murena?[101] The pain of one, the grief of the other, the lamentation of both! How great the upheaval of fortune and of words, when in places in which a few days earlier messengers and letters had rejoiced at Murena's being made consul, places from which friends and companions had rushed to Rome to congratulate him—in these places Murena himself will suddenly appear as messenger of his own disaster! **[90]** If all this is bitter, if it is pitiable, if it causes grief, if it is utterly foreign to your civility and sense of pity, members of the jury, preserve the gift of the Roman people, give back to the commonwealth its consul, give this to his own modesty, give it to the memory of his dead father, give it to his family and household, give it even to Lanuvium, a distinguished town that you have seen present in numbers and grief throughout this trial. Do not drag from his ancestral cult of Juno the Savior, to whom every consul must sacrifice, its hometown consul.[102] With as much weight as my commendation has, as much authority as my support has, I as consul, members of the jury, commend him to you as consul. He longs in the highest degree for order, he is zealous on behalf of respectable citizens, he is a fierce enemy of revolution, a hero in war, a strong enemy of this conspiracy that now shakes the foundations of this commonwealth. Of that I give you my promise and oath.

---

101. Murena left his brother in charge of the province when he came back to campaign for the consulship.

102. Juno Sospita was the patron goddess of Lanuvium; this duty of Roman consuls is not otherwise attested.

5

In Defense of the Poet Archias

In 62 BCE one Grattius, otherwise unknown, brought a charge of illegal residence in Rome against the Greek poet Archias. The charge was brought under a law passed three years earlier, expelling from the city all aliens with no recognized domicile in Italy. For Archias to stay, therefore, he had to prove that he was a Roman citizen. Since he was a Greek born in Syrian Antioch and since his claim to citizenship was based on events twenty-seven years before the trial, that was not uncomplicated. The argument Cicero puts forward in the first part of his defense of Archias is that (a) Archias had been given citizenship by the allied city of Heraclea in Lucania; (b) nonresident citizens of allied cities were awarded Roman citizenship by a law of 89 BCE (Lex Papia Poppaea) on condition that they register with a Roman praetor within sixty days; and (c) Archias had duly registered with the praetor Quintus Caecilius Metellus Pius under the terms of the law and was therefore a Roman citizen entitled to residence in Rome.

The case of Archias is not a political trial like the case of Murena, but it has a political dimension. Archias, as Cicero's narrative makes clear, was closely attached to Lucius Licinius Lucullus and had written a long poem about Lucullus' campaign against Mithridates. Well before this trial, however, Lucullus had been replaced by Pompey (see In Support of Manilius' Law*), and the two men were not on friendly terms. It seems likely that Grattius was attempting to gratify Pompey by attacking Lucullus' pet Greek poet. Cicero, ever anxious to remain on good terms with all parties, presents Archias' poem about Lucullus as a poem about the war and about Roman glory; the unhappy end of Lucullus' command and his replacement go unmentioned, and the name of Pompey barely appears.*

But why harass a sixty-year-old minor Greek poet, even if he was connected to Lucullus? Several possibilities present themselves. That Greek poetic hangers-on were more significant than they appear seems very unlikely; that Archias had written offensively (to some) about Pompey seems more probable; and that he was a Syrian Greek poet made him vulnerable to Roman prejudices on several counts. Hence, the bulk of the speech—and the reason it is still widely read—is devoted to making Archias' poetic activities seem to be a significant contribution to the well-

*being and reputation of Rome.[1] But while it was probably necessary to
try to dispel prejudice, it remains true that the result is an extraordinary
argument:*

> Examine that inimitable, that immortal oration for Archias,
> and amidst that unbounded blaze of eloquence, with which
> it beams, observe the nucleus of argument, upon which it
> revolves. Archias was a Roman citizen, because he was a
> Greek poet. Were a counsellor in the courts of these states to
> start a train of reasoning like this, the judges would instantly
> arrest the career of his oratory, by calling for the certificate of
> naturalization.[2]

*So President (then Senator) John Quincy Adams in his lectures on rhetoric
in 1806–1808, stating the problem much more clearly than most modern
scholars. Cicero claims (somewhat disingenuously) that his client has
the equivalent of a certificate of naturalization, but he still feels obliged
to spend more than half the speech talking about the value of literature,
poetry, and Archias. As a result, this short and relatively unimportant
speech—not unimportant to Archias, of course—becomes a touchstone for
the examination of Cicero's technique, of the place of (Greek) intellectual
life in late Republican Rome, and for one's sense of the Roman court and
its procedures.*

*The style of the defense of Archias is, as Cicero himself says in the
prooemium, unusual. It is written in a much more flowery and lofty style
than most of Cicero's speeches; it is deliberately set out as a display
(epideictic) oration, designed to illustrate precisely what he claims to
have learned from Archias when he was a boy, and hence to provide a
justification of Archias' usefulness to society.[3] In speaking so ornately,
moreover, Cicero explicitly flatters the jury for their ability to appreciate
what he is doing—a technique he uses in the defense of Murena and
elsewhere to introduce elevated subjects—and thus implicitly argues that
the hard-nosed analysis of fact and argument that one expects in a court is
not really necessary. Archias is obviously a citizen and the legal elements
can be handled briefly. Cicero speaks of Archias repeatedly by his citizen
name, Aulus Licinius, and he calls him in his youth a* praetextatus, *using*

---

1. See Berry (2004) for a close analysis. On the intertwined issues of utility, empire, and patronage, see Steel (2001) 82–98.

2. Adams (1962) 1:294.

3. For a sentence-by-sentence analysis of the style of the speech, see Gotoff (1979).

Roman terminology for preadult males to suggest that Archias has been Roman from childhood.

At the same time, however, Adams' bald statement of the argument as "Archias was a Roman citizen, because he was a Greek poet" glosses over the complicated game that Cicero plays with the cultural context of Greek poetry in Rome. Even though some modern readers have seen it as a great appreciation of culture for its own sake, nowhere in the speech does Cicero offer an appreciation of poetry or of literature as important in themselves; it is only their instrumental value that matters.[4] Certain elements in Cicero's account of that value, moreover, make it hard to take his account as completely serious. If the jury is so cultivated that it can appreciate Cicero's display oratory, then what is the significance of his equation of literary study with gambling, ball-playing, and other leisure pastimes? Did the jury really need to be told that more people in the Roman world read Greek than Latin? And surely anyone with the least experience of poetry would recognize that the description of the bad poet's versification as "with every other verse just a little too long" is a satirical description of the normal elegiac couplet, alternating between hexameter and pentameter lines.

The range of ignorance imputed to the allegedly intelligent jury is, in fact, astounding. Not only do they not know anything about Greek or poetry, they are expected not to recognize that Cicero's account of what Archias wrote is highly tendentious. He equates an epic on Lucullus with the entire Mithridatic War, thus eclipsing Pompey; and he suggests a closeness between Archias and Marius that is, as Cicero himself seems to admit, far beyond what is credible. So, too, his comparison of Archias to Ennius, although it has convinced a great many scholars, is complete nonsense, and although a jury might not recognize it, Cicero knew that Ennius' grant of citizenship had nothing at all to do with his composition of the Annals.[5]

That comparison needs further scrutiny. Ennius was probably self-supporting; he is much less implicated in a patronage system than someone such as Archias, and hence he is much more independent. Archias, like many other Greek intellectuals in the two generations following him, came to Rome to make his fortune, or at least to earn a living. As an itinerant poet, he cultivated the ability to entertain those who could support him: according to Cicero's account (and we have no other), he was a hit as after-dinner entertainment because of his ability to extemporize multiple poems on the same subjects. He attached himself

---

4. Cf. Zetzel (2003), Berry (2004).

5. On the misleading comparison between Archias and Ennius, see Zetzel (2007).

to the nobility, particularly the family of the Luculli, in whose house he lived (as Cicero kept a blind Stoic philosopher in his house and his friend Marcus Pupius Piso a tame Peripatetic, and as, somewhat later, the poet Cinna kept the Greek poet Parthenius). In this connection he sang not only after supper but for it—notably his epic on Lucullus' military exploits. He also seems to have written poetry, perhaps only epigrams, on other great events. A number of poems ascribed to an Archias survive in the Greek Anthology, but it is unclear whether they are by the same poet or whether any of them are by this Archias. In any case, like most of the other Greek refugees in Rome, Archias had no independent social position, no independent income. He depended entirely on patronage, and he wrote what he thought (or was told) would please the people whose largesse supported him. For Cicero to exalt a hired versifier—who may have been competent but was certainly not inspired—to the level of Ennius or Homer is simply ludicrous, even if his description of the services rendered by Greek panegyrics to Rome's image in the East is probably fairly accurate.[6]

What effect (on either jury or readers) was Cicero aiming at with this elaborate praise of culture and Archias? Why did Cicero take the case, and why did he defend Archias in this extraordinary fashion? It is generally believed that (a) Archias was innocent, an innocuous elderly victim of the animosity between Lucullus and Pompey; and (b) Cicero chose to defend him because Archias both had been his teacher and would, if acquitted, write the epic on Cicero's consulship that he longed to have. Both views may be true, but in the absence of any external evidence, neither is unproblematic.

In the first place, Cicero's connections to Archias are not at all clear. We know quite a lot about Cicero's education from his other writings, and nowhere does the Greek poet appear as one of his teachers. What is more, the account at the beginning of the speech of just what Archias taught him is remarkably vague, gliding obscurely from grammar to rhetoric to perhaps elocution. Cicero may well have known Archias—he certainly knew some of the aristocrats with whom Archias is said to have been friendly—but in all likelihood the emphasis on Archias as teacher is simply part of Cicero's normal defense strategy, to link himself to the defendant in order to make his advocacy seem more heartfelt and personal.[7] As for the inchoate Ciceroniad of Archias, it was indeed undertaken and never finished, but again, Cicero may be exaggerating its importance and scope to make the epic on Cicero parallel to the epic on Lucullus. Both works praise (or were

6. The nature of Roman literary patronage (of both Greeks and Romans) is much debated. For a sample of views, see Wiseman (1982), White (1993), Damon (1997), and Zetzel (2007).

7. The classic treatment of this is Kennedy (1968); see also May (1981).

*to praise) individual leaders, but both redounded to the credit of Rome
as a whole. Cicero's identification of his own safety with Rome's makes it
likely that he actually believed this argument.[8]*

*And was Archias the completely innocent, frail old poet that Cicero
suggests? The case is far weaker than Cicero would have the reader
believe. If Archias had been made a citizen in so many Italian towns, why
did he base his claim of Roman citizenship on the one whose records
had been destroyed? Why were there no deputations from Regium or
Locri or the others? And how credible is the testimony of the embassy of
Heraclea to an event of limited importance twenty-seven years in the past?
There are other, smaller puzzles. What was Marcus Lucullus doing in Sicily
sometime in the 90s when he was too young to have an official position?
Is it possible that Archias came to Sicily and Heraclea after the Social
War rather than before? What is the value of Metellus Pius' notes taken
when he was praetor? Cicero himself admits that they were not an official
document, and his own anecdote shows that there had been changes in
them. While Cicero makes a convincing case, a case can be made for the
prosecution as well.*

*If it is allowed that the case for Archias was not so clear-cut, then
the choice of defense becomes even stranger. One line of explanation
emphasizes the fact that the president of the court was Cicero's own
younger brother, Quintus; while the president of a court had no vote
and could not directly influence the outcome, magistrates in office were
entitled to a certain amount of deference.[9] Another views the proposed
epic about the suppression of the conspiracy as Cicero's reason for
undertaking the defense and takes the style and the emphasis on the
importance of poetry as central to the claim for acquittal.[10] It is also
possible that the instrumentalist argument about Greek culture was indeed
intended to convince the jury that Archias deserved to be acquitted
(whether or not he was innocent).[11] But it is also possible to look at the
humor of this speech, of Cicero's presentation itself, as a means of gaining
the goodwill of the jury (and the reader) for himself and thereby for his
client as well.*

*Whatever interpretation of the case one adopts has its virtues and its
defects, and that is itself one of the most striking effects of the speech.
More than one reading of it is possible: Archias as innocent or guilty,
Cicero as serious or ironic, Greek culture as valuable in itself or merely*

---

8. For Cicero's identification with Rome, see Kaster (2006) 26–31.

9. See, for example, Gotoff (1979) 211–13.

10. See Dugan (2005) 31–47.

11. Berry (2004).

useful, the jury as boors or as men of culture. The success with which Cicero keeps so many issues in play is part of the fascination of the speech—and may explain why he chose to publish a speech of such little public significance.

Pro Archia Poeta Oratio

Members of the jury:

[1] Whatever native talent I have (and I recognize how slight it is); whatever experience as an orator (and I don't deny that I have a certain amount of practice); whatever understanding of this subject, based on the disciplined study of the highest forms of intellectual attainment (and I allow that no part of my life has been remote from that)—of all these things Aulus Licinius here has an almost legal right to claim the profits from me.[12] As I look back as far as my mind is able over the expanse of time gone by and summon up the furthest memory of my boyhood, even at this distance I recognize that this man was my guide in taking up this activity and in studying it scientifically. And if my voice, shaped by his encouragement and instruction, has from time to time brought help to many people, then the person from whom I received the skill through which to aid others and bring them safety is of course the person to whom, to the extent I am able, I have an obligation to bring aid and salvation.[13] [2] I don't want anyone

---

12. This extraordinarily careful and elaborate sentence sets the tone for the entire speech; ornate and balanced phrases convey the (specious) idea that Archias is responsible for Cicero's rhetorical training and skill. The three parallel clauses that begin the sentence refer to the three standard elements of oratorical success, respectively, talent (*ingenium*), practice (*exercitatio*), and the study of rhetorical theory (*ars*). The final clause uses a legal metaphor to describe personal relationships. As often, Cicero refers to Archias as Aulus Licinius, his Roman name, thus begging the question of Archias' civic status, which is the reason for the trial.

13. Archias gave Cicero the skill to help others; therefore, Archias should benefit from that skill. This essentially repeats the argument of the first sentence and is equally specious; Archias certainly did not teach Cicero rhetoric, and there is no other evidence that Archias ever gave Cicero formal instruction in anything. The technique of Ciceronian advocacy requires the establishment of a personal link, however spurious, between advocate and defendant.

to be surprised at my saying this, on the grounds that Archias has a rather different native talent from the study and practice of public speaking; I have myself never been exclusively chained to that sphere of activity. In fact, all the areas of learning that contribute to our humanity have a shared bond and are almost members of the same family. **[3]** And I don't want anyone to be surprised that in a public court duly constituted by law, when a case is being tried before a praetor of the Roman people, a man of singular qualities,[14] before a very strict jury, before a huge and crowded assembly of men, that I use a style of speaking foreign not only to the language of the courts but to all public speaking. I ask you to give me a certain amount of leeway in this case, a leeway suited to this defendant and, as I hope, not likely to bother you. I am speaking on behalf of a great poet, a man of great learning, before a large crowd of well-read men, before humane men such as you and the praetor presiding over this court; permit me to speak more freely than usual about the study of the humanities and of literature, and while I am playing a part that, because it belongs to leisured study, is rarely performed amidst the dangers of the courtroom, permit me to use a style of speaking that is unfamiliar and very new. **[4]** And insofar as I recognize that you have given me this leeway, I will demonstrate that Aulus Licinius here not only should not be severed from the citizen body, since he is a citizen, but you should think he would deserve to be made a citizen if he weren't one already.[15]

As soon as Archias moved away from boyhood and from the studies that shape the youthful mind toward civilized behavior, he enthusiastically began to be a writer. He started at Antioch, where he came from a noble family, a city once famous and rich and overflowing with men of great learning and cultivation; there he rapidly began to outpace all the rest through the fame of his talent. After that, in other areas of Asia and throughout Greece, there was so much excitement when he arrived that expectations outdid the reports of his talent, and his actual arrival and the awestruck

---

14. Cicero's brother Quintus was the praetor presiding over the trial.

15. The first half of the sentence introduces the formal argument about Archias' citizenship (secs. 4–11), while the second half paves the way for the subsequent long discussion of the value of Archias, poetry, and literature in general. The flattery of the jury here does not match the ignorance of almost everything that Cicero assumes in the second part of the speech.

reception he received outdid the expectations. **[5]** Italy, at that time, was filled with Greek letters and culture, and studies of this kind were pursued more enthusiastically even in Latium than they are now in the same towns; here at Rome, because civic life was calm, they were not neglected.[16] And so the people of Tarentum and of Locri and of Regium and of Naples presented him with their citizenship and other prizes, and everyone who had any discrimination at all in judging talent thought him worthy of acquaintance and hospitality. Since this great and exciting reputation of his was known even to people far away, he came to Rome in the consulship of Marius and Catulus.[17] Of the pair of consuls he first encountered, one could provide great accomplishments as a subject for Archias to write about, while the other could provide not only actions but even the interest and attention to listen. When Archias was still a teenager,[18] the family of the Luculli took him into their home, and he displayed not only the brightness of his intellect and literary talent but also his natural character, so that the same house that first smiled on his youth was his home in old age as well.[19] **[6]** In those days he was on friendly terms with the great Metellus Numidicus

---

16. Cicero slides elegantly from the area of Greek culture in southern Italy—where Archias would have been quite at home—to Rome itself, which was scarcely a cultivated Hellenic city at the end of the second century BCE.

17. Gaius Marius and Quintus Lutatius Catulus were consuls in 102, the year Marius defeated the Teutons. The Cimbri were defeated by Marius and Catulus together in 101. See sec. 19 below. Unlike the uncultivated Marius, Catulus knew Greek and wrote epigrams himself.

18. Cicero calls him *praetextatus*, wearing the striped toga worn by citizens before adulthood. Archias, obviously, was not entitled to wear such a toga. The Luculli here are the brothers Lucius Licinius Lucullus, consul in 74, whose war against Mithridates was the subject of a long poem by Archias, and Marcus Terentius Varro Lucullus (adopted by Terentius Varro), consul in 73. Their father had probably already gone into exile for provincial extortion by the time Archias came to Rome.

19. Pathos, not fact: if Archias was born c. 120 BCE, he was not yet sixty at the time of the trial, and he seems to have lived until at least 45 BCE. Cicero's language here also echoes the prologue of Callimachus' *Aetia* ("Causes," third century BCE; fr. 1.37–38), one of the most famous and influential Alexandrian poems.

and his son Metellus Pius;[20] his recitations were attended by Marcus Aemilius; he lived with Quintus Catulus, both the father and the son; he was cultivated by Lucius Crassus; and since he had close personal relationships with the Luculli and Drusus and the Octavii and Cato and the whole family of Hortensius, he received such respect that not only people who actually wanted to listen and to learn something cultivated him, but even people who pretended did so, too.[21] Meanwhile, after a fairly long time, when he had traveled to Sicily with Marcus Lucullus and left the province in the company of the same man,[22] he came to Heraclea.[23] That was a city bound to us by a fair and equal treaty, and he wanted to be enrolled as a citizen; since he seemed to deserve it on his own and also had the weight of Lucullus' influence behind him, he gained his request. **[7]** He received citizenship under the law of Silvanus and Carbo:[24] "Whatever persons had been enrolled in allied states if at the time of the passage of the law they had a domicile in Italy and appeared before the praetor within sixty days . . ." Since Archias had had a domicile in Rome for many years, he appeared before his

---

20. The list of Archias' "friends" (and Cicero is quite vague about what the relationships entailed) is a brilliant piece of name-dropping, including the leadership of the conservative oligarchy (at least, of the part of the oligarchy that might be accused of having any intellectual interests at all) both before and after the Social War and Sulla, moving gradually from figures of the late second century to Cicero's older contemporaries. Cicero's goal is to enhance Archias' respectability while simultaneously linking himself to the optimates whose support might be useful to him. For details of the individuals, see the Biographical Index.

21. In other words, it is Archias' connections to the aristocracy, not his talent, that won him an audience.

22. The chronology is slightly puzzling: in the 90s (when this must have happened), Marcus Lucullus was only in his twenties and could not have been going to Sicily as a magistrate, which is what Cicero's language suggests.

23. In Lucania. Before the Social War (91–89) and the granting of Roman citizenship to most Italians, many cities of Italy were in theory independent allies of Rome.

24. By the normal designation of laws, the *Lex Plautia Papiria* of 89 BCE. Cicero is avoiding technical language for the sake of elegance and ornament. Citizenship was given to most Italians by the *Lex Julia* of 90 BCE; this law must have covered a class of Italians not included in that law, that is, those resident in Italy but not where they were citizens.

good friend Quintus Metellus the praetor.[25] **[8]** If I'm to speak only about citizenship and the law, then I have nothing further to say: the defense rests. Can anything I've said, Grattius, be rebutted? Will you deny he was enrolled at Heraclea at that time? Present in court is a man of the highest authority, scrupulousness, and honesty, Marcus Lucullus: he states that he does not believe but knows, has not heard but seen, was not just present but took an active part in these events. Present also are envoys from Heraclea, men of great nobility, who have come for the sake of this trial with instructions and official testimony; they state that Archias was enrolled at Heraclea.[26] Are you now going to ask for the public records of Heraclea, which we all know were destroyed when their record office was burned in the Social War? It's absurd to say nothing to disprove the evidence we have and to seek evidence we can't have, to be silent about what men remember and to demand the memory embodied in documents, and, when we have the oath of a man of great honor and the sworn and trustworthy statement of a town of the highest integrity, to reject evidence that can't possibly be corrupted and to seek written records that you yourself acknowledge are often corrupted.

[9] Did Archias not have a domicile in Rome, a man who many years before the award of citizenship had located all his property and fortunes in Rome? Did he not appear before the praetor? In fact, his appearance is recorded in those records that are the only ones from this board of praetors to have the authority of public documents. The records of Appius were said to be carelessly preserved; the frivolity of Gabinius before he was convicted and his disastrous fall afterward undid any credibility of his records.[27] But Metellus, a man of such purity and the most self-effacing of them all, was so careful that he came to Lucius Lentulus the praetor and before the court to say he was upset because a single name had been erased.[28]

---

25. Quintus Caecilius Metellus Pius, praetor in 89 (in the list in sec. 6 above).

26. Note that these envoys (like Marcus Lucullus) are reporting on a minor event of twenty-seven years earlier, of which no documentary evidence survived.

27. Appius Claudius Pulcher (the father of Cicero's later enemy Clodius) was praetor in 89 and consul in 79; Publius Gabinius was praetor in 89 but was subsequently convicted of extortion while governor of Greece.

28. Lucius Cornelius Lentulus; the date of his praetorship is uncertain.

But here, in these records, you can see no erasure in the name of Aulus Licinius. **[10]** That being the case, what excuse do you have for doubting his citizenship, especially as he had been enrolled in other cities as well? In the Greek world they're used to giving citizenship freely to men of no great distinction, men who have either very modest talent or none at all. I suppose that the people of Regium or Locri or Naples or Tarentum were unwilling to give something they often give to actors to a man famous for his outstanding genius! And when other men, not only after the time citizenship was awarded but even after the passage of the Papian law,[29] somehow snuck into the records of these towns, is Archias to be refused, a man who doesn't even adduce the records in which he is named because he always wanted to be considered a citizen of Heraclea? **[11]** You ask for our census records.[30] Right. Is it hard to understand that at the time of the most recent census Archias was with the army, accompanying the great general Lucius Lucullus? At the previous census he was with Lucullus when he was quaestor in Asia; at the first possible census, when Julius and Crassus were censors, no significant part of the population was recorded. In any case, the census records don't confirm citizen status but merely report that the person being recorded claimed at that time to be a citizen. But at the times at which you claim the defendant deliberately chose not to act the part of a Roman citizen, he in fact frequently made wills under Roman law and accepted legacies from Roman citizens, and was reported to the treasury as the recipient of a donation by Lucullus as proconsul. Hunt up whatever arguments you can: neither his own judgment nor that of his friends will defeat him.

[12] You ask me, Grattius, why I take so much pleasure in this man. Because he supplies me a way for my spirit to be restored from the noise of the forum and for my ears to rest from the exhaustion of legal wrangling. Do you really think I would have the material to speak every day on such a range of subjects if I didn't cultivate my mind with learning? Do you think my mind could endure such stress if I didn't use that same learning for relaxation? I confess it: I

---

29. Only three years before this trial.

30. The census was supposed to take place every five years, but the censorship was very irregular in this period. The first census mentioned is in 89, the year of Archias' alleged enrollment; it was never completed. In 86 Archias was with Lucullus, then quaestor; in 70 he was with Lucullus during the Third Mithridatic War.

am devoted to this kind of studies. Other people should be ashamed if they have so buried themselves in books that they can't bring profit from them for the common good or for public inspection, but why should I be ashamed, members of the jury? My way of life for many years has been like this: my own relaxation has never drawn me away from any person's emergency or convenience; pleasure hasn't called me away nor indeed has sleep slowed me. **[13]** So who is to criticize me, or who has the right to be angry at me, if the amount of time other people are permitted to take for their own business or for the celebration of holidays or for other pleasures restoring mind and body, the amount of time they spend on social gatherings or on gambling or playing catch, if I spend the same amount of time for the renewal of my studies? And it's all the more appropriate to permit me this because it's from studies like this that my oratory has grown, that skill that, to the best of my ability, has never failed my friends when they were in danger. Some people may think it frivolous, but I still know the source from which I've drawn the best of my capacities. **[14]** If I hadn't persuaded myself from the time I was a teenager, based on what many people told me and I had often read, that there's nothing in life seriously worth seeking except praise and honor, and in the pursuit of that we should consider all physical torture, the danger of death and of exile, to be of small account—without that, I would never have hurled myself on behalf of your safety into so many and such great conflicts and against the present daily assaults of depraved men.[31] All the books, all the sayings of the philosophers, all past history are filled with models, but they would all remain in the shadows if literature didn't shine its light on them. How many images of the bravest men, not just to look at but to copy, have been left to us by writers both Greek and Latin! In my governance of the commonwealth I have always placed them in front of me and have shaped my mind and character by the contemplation of outstanding men.

[15] At this point, someone may ask: "Really? Those great men whose virtues are passed down in written texts—were they educated in the wisdom you praise to the skies?" It isn't easy to be certain about all of them, but the answer is clear. I admit there have been lots of men of outstanding mind and character who weren't learned and became measured and serious on their own through an almost divine natural

---

31. Both the Catilinarian conspirators in the previous year and those now attacking Cicero for putting them to death.

cast of mind. I'll add, too, that it's more frequent for nature without learning to attain praise for virtue than for learning to flourish without nature. But I also assert this: when the expertise and the shaping of knowledge is applied to a nature that is glorious in itself, then something of unique brilliance often comes into being. **[16]** From this company is the superhuman Africanus in the time of our fathers, from this company came Gaius Laelius and Lucius Furius, men of great judiciousness and self-control, from this company came that man of great courage and, for his day, great learning, Marcus Cato the Elder.³² If these men hadn't been aided in the recognition and cultivation of virtue by reading, they would never have undertaken such studies. If there were not so much benefit, and if it were only pleasure that was sought from these studies, you would still, in my opinion, consider this kind of mental relaxation something highly characteristic of free and civilized men. Other pleasures don't suit all times or ages or places, but these studies sharpen the minds of teenagers, give pleasure to old men, enhance success, and provide comfort and refuge when things go badly; they delight us at home and don't get in our way in public; they spend the night with us, they travel with us, they go to the country with us.

[17] And even if we don't have the capacity to feel these things or taste them with our own senses, we should still admire them when we see them in others. Who among us has such a crude and rustic mind that he wasn't moved by the recent death of Roscius?³³ Even though he was an old man when he died, it still seemed that on account of his outstanding skill and charm he shouldn't have died at all. He aroused all our love with the movements of his body; are we to neglect the amazing motions of the mind and the speed of the intellect? **[18]** How many times, members of the jury, have I seen

32. Africanus here is Publius Cornelius Scipio Aemilianus, traditionally the most cultivated aristocrat of the second century; he and his friends Gaius Laelius and Lucius Furius Philus are the main speakers of Cicero's dialogue *On the Commonwealth*. Marcus Porcius Cato the censor, consul in 195, is Cicero's ideal of the new man (an encomium appears at the end of *Verr.* 5), and Cicero consistently makes him seem more intellectually accomplished than the censor chose to appear himself.

33. Quintus Roscius, the greatest actor of his time, gave lessons to Cicero on delivery (and was represented by Cicero in a civil action); he was also the subject of an erotic epigram by the elder Catulus.

Archias here (and I'm relying on your goodwill, since you're paying such close attention while I speak in this unfamiliar style)—how many times have I seen him, without having written a single word, deliver extemporaneously a large number of fine verses on current affairs, and then, as an encore, speak of the same subject using different words and ideas! As for the things he's written with care and thought, I've seen them gain an approval that matches the praise of ancient writers. Am I not to cherish such a man, am I not to marvel at him, am I not to think he should be defended with every resource I have? Furthermore, as we learn from the greatest and most learned scholars, other areas of study are based on instruction in a body of material and a set of rules, but the poet is endowed by nature:[34] he is aroused through the force of his mind and is animated by an almost divine inspiration. That's why our own great poet Ennius rightly calls poets holy, because they seem to be recommended to us by a gift from the gods.[35]

[19] Therefore, members of the jury, you, as men of great cultivation, should hold the name of poet holy, a name no barbarous people has ever violated. Rocks and empty places answer our words, savage animals are often moved by song to stand still: are we, men who have received the finest education, not to be moved by the voice of poets?[36] The people of Colophon say that Homer was their own citizen; the people of Chios claim him as their own; the people of Salamis assert ownership; the people of Smyrna swear that he is theirs and have even dedicated a shrine to him in their city; and there are many other peoples who fight and argue among themselves about him.[37] So those

---

34. This is a standard contrast between *ars* (technical ability) and *ingenium* (native talent); in most discussions, true excellence as poet or orator requires both.

35. Quintus Ennius (d. 169) was Cicero's favorite Roman poet, author of both epic (*Annals*) and tragedy, as well as numerous shorter and more experimental types of poetry. Only fragments survive.

36. Cicero is playing a brilliant game. The mythical poets Amphion and Orpheus had power over rocks and animals, respectively, but in a more pedestrian context he is also referring to echoes and (for example) sheepdogs responding to whistles. For men to be "moved" means something quite different from either.

37. Homer's birthplace was a traditional subject of dispute. Cicero somewhat strangely describes it as a fight about a corpse.

people snatch at a foreigner, and a dead one at that, because he was a poet: are we going to spurn this living man who is by his choice and our laws one of us, particularly since Archias has focused all his earlier studies and his talent on enhancing the glory and honor of the Roman people? When he was young, he wrote about the war against the Cimbri and was on friendly terms with the great Marius himself, a man who seemed relatively impervious to such matters.[38] **[20]** But nobody is so hostile to the Muses that he doesn't readily permit his deeds to be heralded for all time in verse. They say that Themistocles, the great Athenian, when he was asked what sound or whose voice he most enjoyed hearing, replied, "The person by whom his greatness was best praised." Marius, too, was extremely fond of Lucius Plotius, because he thought his military accomplishments could be glorified by his talent.[39] **[21]** The war against Mithridates, a large and difficult war waged by land and sea with many unexpected turns, has been portrayed completely by Archias, and these books of his cast a bright light not only on Lucius Lucullus, a gloriously courageous leader, but on the name of the Roman people as well.[40] It is the Roman people who opened up Pontus under Lucullus' leadership, a land fortified both by the king's wealth and by the natural topography of the area. It was an army of the Roman people under the same general that with relatively small numbers routed the vast quantities of Armenian troops. It brings glory to the Roman people to have saved our close ally the city of Cyzicus using Lucullus' strategies and to have snatched it from all the king's attacks and from the jaws of war. It is our achievement, which will always be praised and glorified, that the enemy fleet was sunk and its leaders killed in combat against Lucullus at the great naval battle of Tenedus. The trophies are ours, the monuments are ours, the triumphs are ours. The men

---

38. Some careful obfuscation. Marius had saved Catulus' skin in the defeat of the Cimbri at Vercellae in 101, but after the Sullan obliteration of Marius' memory Catulus claimed the victory for himself. Which one was Archias writing for?

39. Lucius Plotius Gallus was the first teacher of Latin rhetoric, and as such was expelled from Rome by the censor Lucius Crassus in 92 BCE.

40. On the course of the Mithridatic War and Lucullus' role in it, see the introduction to *In Support of Manilius' Law*. Cicero is again treading delicately because of the hostility between Lucullus and Pompey: Archias' epic will have been about Lucullus, not about the war as a whole.

whose talent exalts these deeds are heralding the glory of the Roman people. **[22]** Our poet Ennius was loved by the elder Africanus; for that reason people believe that his marble statue was set up at the tomb of the Scipios. But his praises clearly adorn not just the man who is their subject but the name of the Roman people as well. The great-grandfather of Cato here is glorified; a great honor is added to the history of the Roman people. When all those heroes such as Maximus, Marcellus, and Fulvius are honored, we all share in the common praise. For that reason our ancestors admitted to Roman citizenship the man who had done all this, a man from Rudiae; are we going to cast out of our city this citizen of Heraclea who is sought after by many cities but is legally a member of this one?[41]

[23] If anyone thinks there's less profit to be harvested from Greek poems than from Latin, he's making a big mistake: Greek is read pretty much everywhere, while Latin is limited to fairly narrow boundaries.[42] For that reason, if our military achievements are defined by the parts of the earth that have seen them, then we should want our glory and reputation spread as far as our weapons have reached. Such rewards are important for the nations whose history is being recorded, but for the men who are fighting for their lives to gain glory, this is the greatest spur to enduring danger and toil. **[24]** How many chroniclers of his deeds is Alexander the Great supposed to have had with him? And yet when he stood at Sigeum in front of Achilles' tomb, he said, "Lucky young man, to have found Homer as the herald of your deeds!" He was right: if the *Iliad* didn't exist, the tomb that covered his body would have buried his name as well. What about our own Pompey the Great, whose excellence matches his good luck? Didn't he give Roman citizenship before a military assembly to Theophanes of Mytilene, who wrote the history of his deeds?[43] Didn't our men, who are brave but are also rustics

---

41. The whole paragraph is a carefully dishonest argument: even Cicero does not believe that Ennius' statue was among the tombs of the Scipios; Ennius mentioned all these leaders (for details, see the Biographical Index) but was not writing panegyric, while Archias was; Ennius was not given citizenship for writing the *Annals* but received it as a member of a Roman colony before the epic was even begun.

42. It is hard to imagine an upper-class jury not knowing this.

43. Theophanes was Pompey's tame historian, who accompanied him on campaign. Generals could confer citizenship for service in warfare;

and soldiers, moved by the sweetness of glory as participants in the praise of Pompey, give a loud shout of approval? **[25]** I suppose that if Archias weren't legitimately a Roman citizen, he couldn't get some general to give him citizenship. Sulla gave citizenship to Spaniards and Gauls; surely he wouldn't have spurned a request from Archias. We saw him ourselves, when a bad poet handed him up a leaflet from the crowd. He'd written an epigram about Sulla with every other verse a little too long, so Sulla instantly ordered him to receive a reward from the property being auctioned at that moment—but on condition that he never write anything again.[44] Wouldn't a man who thought a bad poet's effort worth at least some reward have sought out Archias' talent and skill and range as a writer? **[26]** Quintus Metellus Pius was Archias' very close friend, a man who gave citizenship to many people; couldn't Archias have gotten citizenship from him either by direct request or through the Luculli? He so wanted to have his deeds written about that he listened even to poets born in Corduba who spoke with a thick foreign accent.[45]

We shouldn't try to conceal what can't be hidden; it should be borne before us. We're all pulled along by the love of praise, and the better we are the more we want glory. Even the philosophers who write books about scorning glory put their names on the cover; in the act of claiming to despise praise and recognition they want to be praised and recognized. **[27]** Decimus Brutus, a great man and a great general, adorned the entrances of his temples and monuments with the poems of his close friend Accius.[46] The famous Fulvius who had Ennius in his entourage when he fought against the Aetolians

---

Theophanes' service was clearly not military. It should be noted that this is the only reference to Pompey in a speech praising a poet who worked for his enemy Lucullus.

44. Another passage of mock ignorance: "every other verse a little too long" describes the elegiac couplet normally used in epigrams. The auction (of the property of men who had been proscribed) dates the story to 82–81.

45. Cordoba in southern Spain. What poem Metellus Pius wanted, or who the Spanish poet was, is completely obscure. Note that Metellus as praetor did give Archias his citizenship by writing his name on a list of registrants.

46. Decimus Junius Brutus Callaicus, consul in 138; his temple to Mars had inscriptions written by Accius.

had no hesitation about dedicating the spoils of Mars to the Muses.[47] For that reason, in a city where generals who were dressed for war cultivated the name of poet and the temples of the Muses, in such a city judges wearing the garb of peace should not shrink from honoring the Muses and protecting poets.

[28] And since I want you to be enthusiastic about this, members of the jury, I'll indict myself and confess to my own love of glory; it may be too intense, but it's completely honorable. The actions I took in my consulship together with you, both for the safety of the city and empire and for the lives of citizens and for the nation as a whole— Archias has begun to write about them in verse.[48] When I heard this, because it's a grand and wonderful thing for me, I encouraged him to finish it. Virtue wants no other reward for toil and danger than the reward of praise and glory; and once you remove that, members of the jury, what reason is there, since the course of life is short and narrow, to wear ourselves out in work like this? [29] If the mind didn't anticipate the future and if the physical limits of our lives also marked the boundary of our consciousness, we certainly wouldn't batter ourselves on such great labors, or give ourselves pain from so much worry and wakefulness, or struggle so often for life itself. But every person of worth has within himself a virtue that night and day urges on the mind with the spurs of glory and warns us not to cast away the remembrance of our name at the end of life, but to make it last through all the generations to come. [30] Are all of us who take part in public life and its risks and toils so small-minded that, after having drawn throughout our lives no calm and restful breath, we think all this will die along with us? Many great men have been eager to leave behind statues and portraits, images not of our minds but of our bodies. But should we not have a much stronger desire to leave behind the image of our wisdom and virtues expressed and polished by men of great talent? In every action I have taken, even at the moment I was taking it, I thought I was spreading and sowing my eternal memory throughout the world. And whether this memory

---

47. On his return from defeating Aetolia, Marcus Fulvius Nobilior (consul in 189) dedicated a temple to Hercules of the Muses (*Hercules Musarum*) with statues of the nine Muses taken from their original home on Mt. Helicon.

48. Unfinished, and possibly unbegun. It serves Cicero's argument to conclude by linking himself to Archias, as he had started; and he certainly would not have minded a Greek epic on his defeat of Catiline.

will be imperceptible to my senses after death or, as the greatest philosophers have thought, will reach at least some part of my mind, right now I take great pleasure in that thought and hope.[49]

[31] For these reasons, members of the jury, preserve a man of such modesty, respected, as you see, by his friends both for his worthiness and for his age; a man of such genius as it's right to think a man has who is sought out by the judgment of our greatest men; a man whose case is such that it is proven by the support of the law, the authority of a town, the testimony of a Lucullus, and the records of a Metellus. And that being the case, members of the jury, insofar as the support for such great talent ought to come from the gods as well as from men, I ask you to give your protection to a man who has always brought distinction to you, to your generals, to the military achievements of the Roman people; a man who, in the recent domestic dangers that have affected you and me, promises to give us the eternal witness of praise, a man who is of that number who have always among all people been thought and called holy. Let him be seen to be raised up by your humanity rather than ruined by your harshness.

[32] I trust, members of the jury, that the things I have said in my usual fashion of brevity and simplicity have met with the approval of all. As for the things I have said in a style foreign to public life and the custom of the courts, both about Archias' own talent and about poetry in general, I hope that they have been received by you favorably; that they have by the president of this court, I know for sure.

---

49. Aristotle in particular worries whether events after our deaths can affect our happiness (*Nicomachean Ethics* 1.11).

6

In Defense of Marcus Caelius

The defense of Caelius is among Cicero's most widely read speeches, for good reason; it is an extraordinary tour de force of theatricality combined with sexual innuendo. It also intersects with the poems of Catullus—if the Clodia attacked by Cicero in the speech is the same Clodia Catullus addressed under the pseudonym Lesbia. Rhetorically, Cicero's speech for Caelius is a masterpiece of misdirection, defending a man who was almost certainly guilty (of something) by ignoring the real charges in favor of entertaining the jury and blackening the character of one of the witnesses.

1. The trial of Marcus Caelius Rufus for vis, seditious violence, took place on April 3 and 4, 56 BCE. Caelius was prosecuted by the young Lucius Sempronius Atratinus, whose father, Lucius Calpurnius Bestia, had been prosecuted by Caelius for electoral corruption.[1] That trial had taken place on February 11, with Cicero as Bestia's advocate. Bestia was acquitted, but Caelius planned to bring renewed charges. According to Cicero, Atratinus brought the charge of vis against Caelius to stop Caelius' renewed attack on Bestia, but there are good reasons not to trust what is said by any speaker in a trial. Of the other two speakers for the prosecution we know rather less. One, Publius Clodius, was presumably a relative of Publius Clodius Pulcher, the man responsible for Cicero's exile. The other, Lucius Herennius Balbus, was a senator and a friend of Bestia.[2] The first speaker for the defense was Caelius himself, followed by Marcus Licinius Crassus the triumvir and Cicero, who, as was his custom, spoke last.[3]

---

1. The difference of names indicates that Atratinus had been born a Calpurnius but adopted by Lucius Sempronius Atratinus.

2. For a reconstruction of the prosecution's case, see Alexander (2002) 218–43; on Cicero's treatment of the prosecution's speeches, see Gotoff (1986).

3. Both Crassus and Cicero also spoke in the defense of Sestius on the charge of *vis* only a few weeks earlier, another important trial dealing with the aftermath of Catiline's conspiracy and Cicero's exile. Cicero's speech for Sestius is a major document of his political beliefs and important evidence for the events of the period; see Kaster (2006).

Given that we have only a few fragments of the other speeches at the trial,[4] Cicero's speech is our only real source for the case, and it is not the best of evidence. Above all, it was only one of three speeches for the defense. Cicero says that Crassus had dealt with several of the charges, relieving Cicero of the necessity to do so. It is perfectly possible, indeed, that a serious defense on the major charges was given by Caelius and Crassus; Cicero's speech itself is singularly vague in this respect. What Cicero does say concerns what may have been only a small part of the case, namely, Caelius' alleged borrowing of money from Clodia to buy poison—to poison Clodia herself, as Cicero argues; to poison Dio, the ambassador from Alexandria, as most people believe.

Although Cicero in fact says very little about the intrigues involving the throne of Egypt that were swirling around Rome at this time, it is the Egyptian connection that must have formed the basis of a charge of vis. Rome did not take formal control of Egypt until 30 BCE, but there had long been Roman involvement. Early in the first century Ptolemy X Alexander had bequeathed his kingdom to Rome—a bequest that was not taken up for some time—in the context of dynastic disputes and declining Egyptian power. Ptolemy XII Auletes ("flute-player") came to the throne in 80 BCE, but his position was weak and he sought support from Rome. In particular, in 59 BCE, at the cost of a bribe to Pompey and Caesar of 6,000 talents, he was declared "friend and ally" of Rome. That did not, however, impress his subjects, who deposed him the next year. In 57—the year before the trial of Caelius—Auletes was in Rome seeking Roman aid for his restoration (which Pompey supported), but an embassy of one hundred Alexandrians, headed by the philosopher Dio, was also sent to oppose him. Ptolemy had the embassy attacked and killed; Dio (who survived the attack) was brought to Rome to explain his side of things and was killed there. One Publius Asicius was charged with the murder and acquitted, with Cicero speaking for the defense, shortly before the trial of Caelius.[5]

The restoration of Ptolemy and/or the annexation of Egypt was a political issue of no small importance, and involved potentially huge glory

---

4. There are three verbatim fragments of Caelius' speech, all quoted by the rhetorician Quintilian; we know nothing of Crassus' speech except what Cicero tells us. The fragments and other evidence are collected in Malcovati (1976).

5. The sequel, as far as the restoration of Ptolemy is concerned, was that the senate wanted to give the job to Lentulus Spinther, the proconsul of Cilicia; an oracle was discovered forbidding the use of force, and eventually, in 55, Gabinius, as proconsul of Syria, did in fact restore him—for a large payment. For the Egyptian side of these events, see Thompson (1994); for the Roman side, Wiseman (1994b).

and profit which would accrue to the invaders. Cicero passes over very lightly (in section 23) a set of events—very obscure to us—that must have to do with the troubles of the Alexandrian embassy: riots at Naples, an attack in Puteoli, the property of one Palla, otherwise unknown. He then comes to the central issue, which he carefully skirts, the murder of Dio in Rome. But despite Cicero's obfuscations, it is fairly evident that a charge of seditious violence must have involved significant public disturbance, and that has much less to do with Clodia than with Ptolemy and Dio. What is not clear is why Atratinus brought the charge. Cicero claimed that it was to ward off Caelius' second attempt at prosecuting Atratinus' father Bestia, but it is just possible that political disagreement or outrage at Caelius' violence had something to do with it.

　　2. Caelius and Crassus may have mounted a serious and detailed defense to the specific charges, but what little we know about their speeches suggests otherwise. According to Cicero, Crassus at least dealt with some of the charges, but he introduced the story of Ptolemy Auletes by quoting the opening phrase of Ennius' Medea, a passage that early on, like its Euripidean model, became a standard rhetorician's example of an argument begun from too far back: the troubles of Medea are traced back to the cutting of trees to build the Argo. In other words, Crassus appears to have been criticizing the prosecution for finding a ridiculously strained and distant motive for Caelius' actions. Cicero borrowed the quotation, fitting it to the story of Clodia; here, Caelius' troubles are traced to his renting an apartment near Clodia's house. There is tragedy in Caelius' speech, too—he referred to Clodia as "a two-bit Clytemnestra" and clearly made other attacks on her as well.[6] Cicero's speech draws together the strands of the earlier speeches, in making the attack on Clodia both central to the defense and, in fact, a repertory of Roman dramatic styles.[7]

　　The date of the trial, the Megalensia, plays a significant part in Cicero's defense and in the strategy of the defense as a whole. The Festival of the Great Mother in early April was one of the great occasions for dramatic performances, and Cicero commiserates with the jury on being stuck in a trial when everyone else is watching a play. In essence, he makes his speech a substitute for the plays the jury is not watching; along with

------

6. The puzzle of the case is that Atratinus is quoted as having called Caelius "a Pelias with curled hair"—perhaps to suggest that he was the orchestrator of a complicated plot that went awry. (It was Pelias who sent Jason to fetch the Golden Fleece.) Whatever he meant, it is clear that Atratinus unwittingly contributed an important element of the structure of the defense.

7. On the dramatic elements of the defense of Caelius, see particularly Geffcken (1973) and Leigh (2004).

the quotations from Ennius' tragedy Medea, he puts on a brilliant set
of dramatic scenes himself, first through his impersonations of Clodia's
ancestor Appius Claudius the Blind and her brother Clodius (sections
33–36), then through summoning up representative comic fathers from
Caecilius and Terence (sections 37–38). The prize, however, must go to
the famous scene in the baths, when supposedly Clodia's supporters failed
in the attempt to seize the poison and its bearer. It begins as slapstick
comedy—in which the poison carrier Licinius sticks out his hand with
the jar of poison over and over again in Cicero's repetitions—and ends,
explicitly, as the description of a mime, the lowest form of popular drama.[8]
The descent from tragedy through comedy to farce—a mad chase ended
abruptly by the curtain—succeeds, as Cicero surely wanted, in reducing
riot, violence, and attempted murder to the level of a dirty joke.

    3. At the center of Cicero's defense lies not Caelius but Clodia, one
of the witnesses for the prosecution, who claimed that Caelius had
borrowed money from her in order to buy poison. The strategy for
the defense required impugning her evidence, and Cicero does so by
impugning her character—standard procedure in a Roman court, and
in this case apparently not very difficult to do. Clodia was one of three
sisters of Publius Clodius Pulcher, the tribune of 58 and the author of the
bill sending Cicero into exile.[9] Clodius (along with his sisters) showed his
scorn for his patrician family by spelling his name Clodius (lower class)
rather than Claudius (upper class); he went on, more significantly, to have
himself adopted by a plebeian so that he could become tribune. The
relationship between Clodius and his sisters was (and is) the subject of
considerable speculation. He was accused of incest with at least one of
them, the wife of Lucullus, and Cicero makes the charge of incest with the
widow of Metellus Celer (the Clodia of this case) very vivid. Whether it is
all slander or the family were really that fond of one another is immaterial;
it allowed Cicero to attack her sexual morals, to blame her for whatever
relationship she and Caelius may have had, and thus to argue that she was
a completely untrustworthy witness.

    The story Cicero tells of the relationship between Caelius and Clodia
is a simple one. The innocent, honorable, ambitious young Caelius
moved to the Palatine Hill to be in the center of public life; he rented
an apartment in a building belonging to Clodius. There he met Clodia, a

---

8. In fact, mime was gaining literary pretensions in just this period, but
Cicero is treating it as low comedy.

9. On Clodius, see Tatum (1999). Roman women were referred to by family name alone, hence all the sisters would be "Clodia"; modern scholars
distinguish them by using their husbands' names.

woman of shameless and voracious sexual appetites, who seduced him, as she had seduced many other impressionable and handsome young men. Eventually, however, he tired of her and of the immorality and dumped her to renew his active engagement in public life. She was angry and took the opportunity of this trial to gain revenge.

All this makes a good story, but it should be pointed out that we have no evidence whatsoever of its truth. It gains belief not from what Cicero actually says but from the related, or perhaps overlapping, story to be gleaned from the poems of Catullus, written at just the same time as Caelius' trial. There, we find the young Catullus falling in love with a woman he calls Lesbia; she is unfaithful, they pass through various stages of reconciliation and separation, until, sadder and wiser, he renounces the whole relationship. The story here is a set of false biographical inferences from Catullus' poems, in which Lesbia is best seen as a figure used by the poet in his contemplation of love, honor, and political life (among other things). But because we know that the real name of "Lesbia" was Clodia, there is a strong temptation to identify Lesbia with the Clodia whose unhappy liaison with Caelius Cicero so vividly describes (and it does not hurt that Catullus' poems also include both a Caelius and a Rufus, who have some relationship with Lesbia).[10] Part of the identification of Lesbia turns on Catullus, poem 79, which puns on Clodius' name and suggests incest between Clodius and Catullus' Clodia; Cicero implies incest between Clodius and Caelius' Clodia. But unfortunately there is no reason to believe that Clodius was not equally attached to all his sisters.

The depraved and insatiable Clodia of Cicero's speech is a caricature and a monster. In fact, it is not even certain that the defense was consistent in its portrayal of her sexual appetites. One of the fragments of Caelius' speech, difficult to interpret, reads "in triclinio coam, in cubiculo nolam"; this ought to mean something like, "She says yes at dinner, but no in bed."[11] That suggests that Caelius argued that he never actually slept with her, which is very different from Cicero's argument. Whatever the real Clodia's sexual habits, it is clear that she was a woman of great intelligence and acumen, and in other contexts Cicero speaks of her very respectfully.[12] As a result, one should be as cautious about accepting

---

10. On the relationship of Catullus' characters with those in Cicero's speech, see, above all, Wiseman (1969, 1985a).

11. Fr. 27 Malcovati (1976). It is described as riddling by Quintilian, who quotes it: *coam* probably has to do with Coan silk, notoriously transparent, and *nolam* is a pun on the town of Nola and the verb *nolo* ("to be unwilling").

12. See Skinner (1983).

Cicero's attack on Clodia as one must be in reading his silence about the murder of Dio. The defense of Caelius may place Caelius and this Clodia in the milieu of Catullus, but arguments in this area are dangerously circular. All of them—Cicero, Clodius, Caelius, and Clodius' sisters—lived in the same social world and on the same hill. The defense of Caelius paints a compelling picture, but that is because Cicero was a great advocate, not because it is necessarily true.

4. What, finally, of Caelius himself? Whether or not he was guilty of complicity in the violence surrounding the Alexandrian embassy, it is fair to say that it was not an implausible accusation. Caelius was a very ambitious and volatile young man from the north; like Cicero, he was the first of his family to head for the bright lights of Roman public life. But although he began under Cicero's tutelage, Cicero's strained arguments show that Caelius was deeply involved with Catiline exactly at the time of the conspiracy in 63. A hothead, Caelius decided to make his name—and clear himself of Catilinarian suspicions—by prosecuting Cicero's fellow consul Antonius in 59 for provincial extortion, much to Cicero's embarrassment (not least because Caelius defeated Cicero in court), then prosecuting Bestia for electoral corruption in 56. After his acquittal, Caelius' public career continued, and he seems to have been more circumspect and more in harmony with Cicero. He was tribune in 52—a year of great violence, including the murder of Clodius by Titus Annius Milo, culminating in the sole consulship of Pompey and the conviction of Milo. Caelius supported Milo and Cicero unsuccessfully defended him in court; one of the other tribunes, the future historian Sallust, was on the other side. Caelius went on to become aedile in 50; it is in that period (from spring 51 to fall 50) that we know most about him, from the set of letters he sent to Cicero who was unwillingly away from Rome, governing the province of Cilicia. Cicero relied on Caelius for gossip and political intelligence; he respected Caelius' political judgment and his ability—amply demonstrated in the letters—to describe political activity in Rome. Book 8 of Cicero's Letters to Friends consists entirely of their correspondence, and the letters portray an active, impatient, clever man who enjoyed politics as a contact sport. After that, however, he took the other side from Cicero and supported Caesar in the civil wars. Appointed praetor in 48, his constant interference and radicalism resulted in his being expelled from office and leaving Rome; he was killed in an attempted revolt in southern Italy in 48.

Cicero's speech in defense of Caelius can be seen in many contexts. It is part of Cicero's vigorous renewal of his forensic career after his return from exile. Within the two months before the trial of Caelius, Cicero had defended Calpurnius Bestia (against Caelius), Sestius (in the extant speech), and Asicius (mentioned in this speech); he was shortly to defend

Cornelius Balbus, the close friend and ally of Pompey and Caesar. All these speeches also have a significant political element, partly supporting Pompey, partly attacking those who had exiled him, partly continuing his self-defense against attacks on his treatment of the Catilinarian conspirators. The most political is the defense of Sestius, but the underlying set of beliefs is very much the same. It is also one of the best examples of Cicero's forensic technique—his histrionic ability (quite literally in this speech), his often very sharp humor, and his structuring of a complex story that conceals or ignores the real facts of the case.

Pro M. Caelio Oratio

Members of the jury:

[1] If somebody were here who knew nothing about our laws, our courts, and our customs, he would certainly wonder what crime could be so vicious that on a holiday when public games are taking place, when all civic business is at a halt, this one court should be in session.[13] He would have no doubt that the defendant is charged with so massive a crime that to leave it unattended would result in the collapse of the state. Similarly, when he hears that there's a law requiring that this court must be in session every day to deal with criminals and revolutionaries who conduct an armed siege of the senate, who use force against magistrates, who assault the commonwealth, he wouldn't criticize the law itself, but he would find out what charge has come before the court. And when he hears there's no crime, no viciousness, no violence being prosecuted, but a young man of outstanding talent, application, and favor is being accused by the son of a man he's prosecuting and has prosecuted before,[14] but that the assault is backed by a woman who earns her living on her back, he wouldn't criticize Atratinus' devotion to his father, but he would think that a woman's sexual appetites should be controlled, and he would judge it very hard on you not to be on holiday when

13. Cicero's speech was given on April 4, 56, the first day of the *Ludi Megalenses* (in honor of the Magna Mater), one of the festivals when theatrical performances took place. The law on *vis* (public violence and sedition) required that trials not be postponed because of holidays. On the details of the trial and the case, see the introduction to this speech.

14. Caelius had prosecuted Lucius Calpurnius Bestia, the father of the prosecutor Atratinus; when he lost the case, he started a new prosecution.

everyone else is. **[2]** In fact, if you want to pay close attention and form a true judgment about this entire case, members of the jury, you will conclude that nobody would have stooped to this prosecution who had any choice, and once he had done so he would have no hope of success without the support of a certain person's overpowering lust and excessive hatred. But I forgive my friend Atratinus, a young man of great humanity and talent; he has the excuse of devotion to his father, or of necessity, or of his age. If he chose to prosecute, I attribute it to his devotion; if he was ordered to do it, to necessity; if he had any expectation of success, to his immaturity. But the other prosecutors deserve no forgiveness at all and deserve a pretty fierce response.

[3] To me, members of the jury, it's completely appropriate to Marcus Caelius' youth to begin my defense by first answering what the prosecutors have said to smear him and to rob him of his respectability. His father has been criticized, either because he's not sufficiently grand himself or because his son didn't treat him with enough devotion. Concerning his worthiness, even if I said nothing, the elder Caelius can easily respond to those who know him, to older people, without uttering a word. But on account of his age he hasn't been seen much in the forum for some time, and there are people to whom he's no longer so well known. People like that should know that he's always been considered extremely distinguished among Roman knights—and Roman knights can be extremely distinguished—and still is, not only by his own friends but by everyone who knows him for whatever reason. **[4]** Furthermore, it's not right, before this jury and this speaker for the defense, to consider it a crime to be the son of a Roman knight.[15] As for what you said about filial devotion, our opinions are just opinions, but his father has the final judgment. You will hear what we think from sworn witnesses; the feelings of his parents are declared by his mother's tears and profound grief, his father's disheveled dress and the sadness and mourning you see here before you. **[5]** As to the criticism that his fellow townsmen don't approve of him, the people of Praetuttium[16] have never given greater

---

15. The majority in criminal juries was of equestrian standing, as was Cicero's family.

16. A district in Picenum, north of Rome on the eastern side of the Apennines; its main town was Interamnia. The name is corrupt in the manuscripts, but the correction is fairly certain.

honors to anyone who was there than they did to Caelius when he was not. In his absence, they co-opted him into their senate; without his asking, they offered him things they refused to many people who did ask. And now they've sent distinguished men, both senators and Roman knights, as a mission to this court with an elaborate and solemn testimonial. That, it seems to me, is the foundation I have laid for my defense: it is strongest when it rests on the judgment of his own people. Indeed, nobody of his age could ever receive your approval if he displeased not only his father, a man of such distinction, but a town of such fame and importance. **[6]** As for me, my own career sprang from a similar source and carried me to fame, and my toil in the forum and the conduct of my life flowed more rapidly to men's good opinion because of the support and the approval of my own people.

As to the charges about immoral behavior that have been tossed around in what I will call not the accusations but the catcalls and slanders of the prosecutors, Caelius will never take them so hard that he regrets not having been born ugly. Slanders like that are only too common against everyone who had a pretty face and attractive appearance as a teenager. But it's one thing to slander, quite another to make an accusation. An accusation requires a formal charge to define its substance and identify the defendant; it should demonstrate the charge by arguments and confirm it by witnesses. Slander, on the other hand, has no purpose except injury. If it's really offensive we call it abuse; if it's done cleverly we call it urbane wit. **[7]** I was, in fact, quite surprised that this part of the prosecution was given to Atratinus, and I wasn't at all happy about it. It wasn't right, it wasn't appropriate to his age, and, as you could have seen, it placed too great a burden on the sense of shame of a fine young man for him to be caught up in talk like that. I wish one of you tougher types had taken on the trash talk; then I would have rebutted your lack of restraint and your vile language more freely and forcefully. But with you, Atratinus, I'll play a gentler part; your sense of shame tempers my language and I should preserve the goodwill I've shown you and your father.[17] **[8]** But I want to give you this piece of advice: first, that the impression everyone has of you should match the reality and that you stay as far away from crude speech as you are from crude behavior; second, that you not use words against someone else

---

17. Cicero had defended Bestia against Caelius' prosecution.

that make you blush when they are, even falsely, used against you. Is there anyone who can't go down that road? Is there anyone who can't slander young men at the beginning of their adult lives and their careers as rudely as possible? Even if there isn't a breath of suspicion, there is some plausibility. But the blame for your taking such a part belongs to the men who wanted you to play it; the fact that we could see you were speaking unwillingly can be credited to your sense of shame, while the fact that you spoke with such elegance and polish can be credited to your talent. **[9]** But the defense against this whole speech can be brief. For as long as Caelius' age could give room for such suspicions, it was protected first by his own sense of shame, second by his father's careful supervision. From the moment he gave Caelius here his adult toga—and I'm not going to say anything here about myself; think whatever you like. I will say this, that Caelius was brought to me by his father right away—nobody saw Caelius in the bloom of his youth unless he was with his father or with me or in the highly moral home of Marcus Crassus, when he was being educated in the most respectable branches of study.

[10] They accuse Caelius of having been close to Catiline, but that suspicion should be miles away from him. You know that when Caelius was a young man, Catiline was campaigning for the consulship at the same time I was.[18] If Caelius ever went near him, or if he ever left my side—although there were lots of respectable young men who supported that man, wicked and evil though he was—then let Caelius be thought to have been too close to Catiline. "But later on, we had ocular proof that he was one of Catiline's friends." No disagreement on that. But I'm talking now about that period of his life that is weak in itself and endangered by other people's lusts. He was constantly with me during my praetorship; he had no knowledge of Catiline, who was at that time in Africa as praetor.[19] The following year, Catiline defended himself on a charge of provincial extortion. Caelius was with me, and was never with Catiline, even

---

18. In 64 BCE. Since Cicero had made a point in his speeches of this period of accusing every enemy of having been a friend of Catiline, to defend a genuine friend of Catiline, as Caelius was, had its difficulties. Note particularly that Caelius was close to Catiline at a time very close to the conspiracy, that is, the elections of 63.

19. Cicero was praetor in 66; Catiline governed Africa in 67–66 before being prosecuted in 65 for extortion (when Cicero contemplated defending him).

as a supporter at his trial. The next year, when Catiline and I were both running for consul, Caelius never went near him and never left me. **[11]** After being active in public life for so many years without any suspicion or any disgrace, he supported Catiline in his second campaign for consul. So how long are young men of that age supposed to be kept locked up? For us, long ago, a single year was the established time for wearing your toga folded to keep your arm held in, and for games and exercises on the Campus Martius we wore tunics. If we began military service at that age, the same year of restriction applied on campaign.[20] At that age, anyone who didn't protect himself by his own seriousness and discretion both through the discipline of his household and through his natural qualities, such a person, no matter how well guarded by his people, couldn't escape deserved disgrace. But if anyone made it through that year untouched and unmolested, then nobody said a word about his reputation and modesty when he had grown up and become a man among men. **[12]** "But Caelius supported Catiline after he had already been in public life for some years." And as far as I can see, lots of men from every rank and of every age did the same. Catiline, as I think you remember, had a lot of signs of great excellence; not genuine signs but shadows of them. He enjoyed the services of many evil men, but he pretended to be devoted to the most responsible citizens. He had many enticements to arouse desire, but he also spurred people on to hard work and effort. He was on fire with the vices of passion, but his military skills were fully developed. I don't believe there was ever such a prodigy on earth, an alloy of such contradictory, divergent, and mutually opposed characteristics and desires.[21] **[13]** Who was ever, at one time, more amiable to men of distinction, or who was more tightly bound to men of low vices? What citizen was ever a more staunch conservative at times, who

---

20. Caelius was born in 88 or 87, and the year of restricted activity (at age eighteen or so) would have been well before Cicero's consulship. The arrangement of the toga was both to limit extravagant gesture in the beginning orator and to encourage the young to keep their hands to themselves.

21. The portrait of Catiline given here is similar to that given by Sallust in *Conspiracy of Catiline*—which is, of course, derived largely from Cicero. Elsewhere, Cicero paints Catiline as a more consistent villain, but here he needs to make Caelius' support of him more plausible.

was a more unspeakable enemy to this state? Who enjoyed nastier pleasures, who endured toil better? Who was greedier for plunder, who was more generous with gifts? He had, members of the jury, remarkable characteristics: he embraced many men in friendship, he was respectful and polite, he shared what he had with everyone, in time of need he assisted his friends with cash, influence, physical labor, criminal behavior if necessary, and daring; he could alter his character and direct it for the occasion, twisting and bending it in all directions. He behaved austerely with serious people, pleasantly with relaxed ones; he was solemn with old men, affable with young; daring with criminals, loose with the lecherous. **[14]** With this changeable and many-faceted character he had not only gathered together every bold and wicked man from every corner of the world, but he also kept a hold on many brave and respectable men through the counterfeit appearance of virtue. He could never have been the source of an attempt to destroy this empire if the vast hideousness of his multiple vices did not rest on a base of affability and endurance. That is why, members of the jury, this suggestion should be rejected, and the charge of having been a friend of Catiline should not stand. It's one that is shared with many people, some of them respectable. Even I, I say, even I was once almost deceived by him, as he seemed to me a responsible citizen and a strong, eager, and faithful friend of the most upstanding citizens. I recognized his crimes with my eyes before I believed them, I grasped them with my hands before I suspected them. If Caelius also was among the great throng of his friends, then he should be upset at his mistake, as I, too, often regret my own error about Catiline, more than he should fear a criminal charge based on that friendship.

[15] That's the way your oration slid from slanders about sexual misbehavior to creating guilt by association with the conspiracy. You stated, however hesitantly and briefly, that Caelius took part in the conspiracy as a friend of Catiline. But in that statement it wasn't just that the charge didn't stick, but the speech of this well-spoken young man scarcely stuck together. Is Caelius that crazy? Is his character or his property so badly damaged? And where, in the rumors about the conspiracy, was the name of Caelius ever heard? I'm saying too much about a topic on which there isn't any doubt, but I will say this: far from his being a participant in the conspiracy, unless he had not been a very strong enemy to the crime he would never have wanted to gain credit, as a young man, for accusing someone else of conspiracy.[22] **[16]** And since I've mentioned that subject, I don't know whether I should give a similar answer to their charges about bag men and political action committees.[23] Caelius would never have been so crazy as to accuse someone else of electoral bribery if he had tainted himself by spreading so much money around; he wouldn't have raised suspicion about someone else regarding the same things if he wanted a blank check for himself; he wouldn't, if he thought he was himself at risk of being accused of electoral corruption, himself have prosecuted another person twice for electoral corruption.[24] That was not a wise move, and it was over my objections, but he's so ambitious that he'd rather seem to persecute an innocent person than seem worried for himself.

[17] There are also charges of borrowing, criticisms of his extravagance, demands for his accounts; to all that my answer is short. Someone still under parental control does not have his own accounts.[25] He never borrowed money at all. Only one kind of expense is criticized, his rent—you said he paid 30,000 sesterces for housing. Finally, I understand. Publius Clodius is selling his apartment block; Caelius lives there, and the real rent, I believe, is ten thousand. But since you want to cater to Clodius, you've tailored your lies to fit his present needs.[26]

[18] You criticized him for moving out of his father's house. But he's a grown man, and that hardly deserves criticism. As a result of a public trial, he scored a victory that riled me but brought him glory,

---

22. Caelius prosecuted Cicero's consular colleague Antonius in 59 for provincial extortion; Cicero defended. Antonius was in fact an ally of Catiline, and presumably Caelius attacked him on those grounds as well as on the basis of more relevant evidence.

23. No specific instance of electoral bribery by or for Caelius is known.

24. Caelius had prosecuted Bestia for electoral corruption unsuccessfully two months earlier, and he was in the process of trying again when the charge of seditious violence was brought against him.

25. A technically true statement, but sons still under *patria potestas* (paternal authority, which lasted until the death of the parent) could have informal control of their *peculium*, the money that children and slaves were allowed to possess with the permission of their father/owner.

26. By inflating Caelius' rent from 10,000 to 30,000, Atratinus both inflates the value of Clodius' building and makes Caelius seem more extravagant. The Palatine Hill was fashionable, and Cicero also lived there.

and since he was of an age to run for office, his father not only permitted but even encouraged him to move out. And because his father's house was a long way from the forum, in order to be able to come to my house more easily and to enjoy the attentions of his own friends, he rented a house on the Palatine for a reasonable price. And about this I can say just what my distinguished colleague Marcus Crassus said a little while ago in complaining about the arrival of King Ptolemy:[27]

If only in the grove on Pelion had not . . .[28]

And I can extend the context of the poem further:

For never my wandering mistress

would have given us such trouble,

Medea sick in heart, wounded by savage love.

You will find, members of the jury, what I will demonstrate when I reach that point in my case, that this Medea of the Palatine and Caelius' move there were the cause of all his woes, or rather of all those rumors.[29]

---

27. Crassus (who spoke just before Cicero) referred to the arrival of Ptolemy XII Auletes in Rome in 58. He had been deposed and came to request reinstatement; the lucrative possibility of a campaign in Egypt aroused much interest and corruption. See the introduction to this speech.

28. Cicero (and Crassus) cited the opening verses of Ennius' tragedy *Medea* (adapted from Euripides), the single most famous passage of early Roman tragedy (Warmington 253–61 = Jocelyn 103): "If only in the grove on Mount Pelion the fir tree, axe-cut, had not fallen to the ground, and that the ship had not taken from there the start of its voyage, the ship now named Argo, because chosen Argive men sailing in it sought the ram's golden fleece from the Colchians by stealth, at the command of King Pelias. For then never would my wandering mistress have set foot outside her house, Medea, sick in heart, wounded by savage love." This proem (both in Euripides' version and in Ennius') was a famous example of taking a chain of causation excessively far back. Both Crassus (with the arrival of Ptolemy) and Cicero (with Caelius' move to the Palatine) are treating their own stories ironically.

29. In his prosecution speech, Atratinus had called Caelius "a cute little Jason," presumably in connection with the gold allegedly taken from Clodia.

[19] For that reason, since I can rely on your wisdom, members of the jury, I have no fear of all the things that I understood from the prosecutors' speech were being prepared and invented. They said one of the witnesses would be a senator who would say he was beaten up by Caelius at the elections for the priesthood. If he comes forward, I'll ask him, first, why he took no action right away, and second, if he preferred to whine about it rather than do something, why he was brought forward by you rather than coming forward on his own, why he prefers to whine so much later rather than immediately. If he has a sharp and clever answer for this, then I'll ask about the source from which that senator came. If he is self-motivated and self-starting, then perhaps I'll have some sympathy, as usual; but if he's trickling down from the real source of your prosecution, I'll be delighted that although your prosecution rests on so much influence and such great resources, there is only one solitary senator to be found who wants to give you pleasure.

[Concerning the witness Fufius][30]

[20] I'm not frightened, either, of that other kind of witness in the night. The prosecutors said there will be men who will say their wives were groped by Caelius while coming home from dinner. Serious men, those, who will dare to say this under oath, when they have to admit they never even sought a meeting or arbitration as a start to legal proceedings about such serious outrages.[31] But you can already see this whole type of attack coming, members of the jury, and when it's launched, you should repel it. Caelius, in fact, isn't being prosecuted by the same people who are attacking him. Weapons are being thrown at him in the open, but they're being supplied in secret. **[21]** My point in saying this is not to create hostility

---

The defense accordingly used tragedy, and particularly the *Medea*, to structure their case. On theatricality in Cicero's speech, see the introduction to this speech.

30. The senator unnamed just above is presumably Quintus Fufius Calenus, tribune in 61 and a friend of Clodius. Here and in two other places a heading indicates that the circulated form of the speech was abridged, possibly by Cicero himself.

31. The usual translation for the delict (tort) of *iniuria*, which punished actions damaging the standing or reputation of a person.

toward people whose actions even in this case ought to bring them honor. They're doing their duty, defending their own people, behaving as men of courage generally do: when injured they feel pain, when angered they're emotional, when provoked they fight back. But in your wisdom, members of the jury, the fact that brave men have an acceptable reason for attacking Caelius does not mean you should think it's an acceptable reason for you, too, to give more weight to someone else's pain than to your own oath as jurors. You see the throngs in the forum: what a range of people, what variety of interests and loyalties. In such a crowd, imagine how many there are who approach men of power, influence, and eloquence who seem to want something, offer their services, promise to give evidence. **[22]** There may be men like this who have gotten themselves into this trial, members of the jury, and you must use your wisdom to banish their greed. That's how you can be seen at one and the same time to have looked out for Caelius' safety, the sanctity of your oath, and the well-being of everyone against some dangerous and powerful men. For my part, I will minimize the importance of witnesses. I won't allow the real truth of this case to be subordinated to the desires of witnesses: they can very easily be manipulated and can be bent and turned aside with no effort at all. Our case rests on arguments; we will rebut the charges with logic that's clearer than day. Fact will fight with fact, case with case, argument with argument.

[23] In this connection, I'm relieved that the part of the case involving the riots at Naples, the assault on the Alexandrians at Puteoli, and the property of Palla was thoroughly explained by Crassus in his eloquent and serious speech.[32] I wish he'd done the same with Dio. But on this score, there's no more to be said.[33] The person who did it is unafraid and even admits his guilt; after all, he's

---

32. Precisely what these charges were is unclear, but they were presumably part of the larger accusation of violence. Dio was the ambassador of the Alexandrians (opposing Ptolemy), and the events at Naples and Puteoli (the northern end of the Bay of Naples) were probably attacks on the embassy on its way to Rome. Nothing is known about Palla or her property, although there may be a connection with the family of the prosecutor Sempronius Atratinus.

33. Dio was murdered at the house of Titus Coponius; Publius Asicius was accused of being the assassin, hired by Ptolemy Auletes, but he was acquitted (with Cicero as his advocate). It is likely that complicity in the murder and

a king. Publius Asicius, who is said to have been his henchman, was acquitted. What kind of charge is it when the criminal doesn't deny it, the one who denied it was acquitted, and Caelius here is afraid of being blamed, a man who has no connection with the act or even any suspicion of involvement? And if Asicius' case did him more good than ill will from the deed harmed him, why should your slander damage Caelius? He isn't tarnished by suspicion of having done this, not even by hostile rumors. **[24]** "But Asicius got off by a collusive prosecution." That's an easy answer, particularly to me who defended him. But Caelius believes that Asicius' case is strong; and strong or not, he thinks it has nothing to do with him. And Caelius isn't the only one who thinks so, but so do Titus and Gaius Coponius, these young men of great cultivation and learning, equipped with a fine and broad education.[34] They were the most affected by Dio's death; they were Dio's friends as well as his disciples. You have heard evidence that Dio lived with Titus, who was an acquaintance of his in Alexandria. What he or his distinguished brother thinks of Caelius, you will hear from their testimony, if they're called as witnesses. **[25]** So put all this aside so that, at long last, we can come to the real basis of the case.

I observed, members of the jury, that you paid close attention to the speech of my friend Lucius Herennius.[35] To a large extent, it was his talent and style of speaking that gripped you, but I worried at times that his carefully crafted accusation would slowly and gently gain a hold on your minds. He said a lot about luxury, a lot about sexual desire, a lot about the faults of young men, a lot about morals. For a man who's generally mild and enjoys indulging in the cultural pleasures that delight us all, he was in this case like some very grim uncle or censor or teacher. He scolded Caelius, as no parent ever did his son; he said a lot about lack of control and lack of moderation. To be brief, members of the jury, I understood your attentiveness, because I myself was frightened by such a grim and harsh style of speaking. **[26]** The first part had less effect on me, the fact that Caelius was on good terms with my friend Bestia; he had dinner with

---

other attacks on the embassy was a major part of the charge brought against Caelius in this trial, but Cicero minimizes its importance.

34. Nothing is known about them other than what is here.

35. Lucius Herennius Balbus, the final speaker for the prosecution. Cicero sometimes refers to him as Herennius, sometimes as Balbus.

him, he went to his home frequently, he supported him for praetor.[36] None of this affects me, because it's obviously false; in fact, he says that men had dinner together who are either absent or who have no choice except to agree with him. And it doesn't affect me, either, when he says that Caelius was a fellow member of the Luperci with him. The association of the true Luperci is a savage one, clearly rustic and rural. It was established in the woods before human society and laws existed, to judge from the fact that the members not only accuse one another but even make membership part of the accusation; they seem to be afraid that no one knows it![37] **[27]** But I'll set that aside and move on to what affected me more.

    Herennius' criticism of decadence was long and somewhat milder; it smacked more of the classroom than of savagery, which is why it was heard more attentively. For when my good friend Publius Clodius[38] was hurling himself around with great energy and seriousness and was on fire about everything, speaking with the gloomiest language in a booming voice, even though I admired his eloquence, I wasn't afraid; I've seen him in quite a few cases that he didn't win. But to you, Balbus, I'll answer with your approval, if I may, if it's right for me to defend someone who never turned down a party, who has been in pleasure gardens, who has used unguents, who has been to Baiae.[39] **[28]** I've seen and heard many people in this nation myself who not only tasted a small sample of this life and touched it, as they say, with the tips of their fingers, but even surrendered their entire adolescence to pleasure; they came out of it sooner or

---

36. The implication is that Caelius is hypocritical and ungrateful, turning on his former friend Bestia and prosecuting him.

37. If both Herennius and Caelius were members of the Luperci, then Herennius is disloyal to prosecute Caelius. The Luperci were said to antedate Romulus; on the day of the Lupercalia (February 15) they wore goatskin thongs and ran through the streets of Rome striking women with goatskin strips to encourage fertility. Cicero plays on the chronological and anthropological ideas of primitiveness.

38. Not the Publius Clodius who is attacked below beginning in sec. 36, but another person of the same name who was one of the speakers for the prosecution.

39. Baiae on the Bay of Naples was proverbial for its decadence and luxury. Cicero carefully described his own villa there as being in Puteoli, the next town.

later and returned, as they say, to a good harvest and became serious men of consequence. Everybody permits a certain amount of play to people of this age, and nature itself pours forth attractions for the young. And if they break out in a way that damages nobody's life, overturns nobody's household, then they're usually considered mild and tolerable. **[29]** But you seem to me to want to use the general bad reputation of the young to create guilt by association for Caelius. And so the extended silence that followed your speech is owed to the fact that although there's only one defendant, we were thinking about the vices of many others.

It's easy to attack luxury. The sun would set on me if I tried to dish out every possible view of that subject, about corruption, about sex, about shamelessness, about extravagance—it's endless. Even if you accuse no specific defendant, but the vices themselves, the topic leads to a weighty and fluent attack. But I rely on your wisdom, members of the jury, not to be distracted from this particular defendant. When the prosecutor has aimed the weapons of your ethical seriousness against vice, against bad character, against the times, don't fire them at this man, this defendant, who has become the object of an unjustified hatred not because of his own misdeeds but because of the faults of many. **[30]** For that reason, Herennius, I don't dare reply to your severity as it deserves. My natural tendency would be to ask for a certain space and leniency for teenagers. But as I say, I don't dare; I make no use of the excuses for his age, I cast aside all the rights permitted to everyone else. I ask only that whatever general resentment there may be at this time against the debts, the thuggishness, and the sexual excesses of young men—and I see that it's significant—I ask that other people's faults and the vices of their age and these times not harm this particular man. At the same time, in asking this I don't refuse to give a very precise response to the charges being brought against him.

There are two charges.[40] One involves gold, the other poison; in both of them one and the same person is concerned. The gold was

---

40. Perhaps Cicero's fellow advocates dealt with the real charges (to do with the murder of Dio) in more detail in their speeches; Cicero himself certainly distorts the case. Borrowing from Clodia and trying to kill her were not capital offenses, and in suggesting that they were the heart of the prosecution, Cicero deflects the jury's attention from the underlying serious crimes.

borrowed from Clodia, the poison was sought to give to Clodia—or
so they say. All the rest are not charges but slanders; they belong to
a violent quarrel rather than a public court. "Adulterer, degenerate,
graft-giver." That's brawling, not prosecution. There's no foundation
for these charges, no basis. They're fighting words thrown out hit
or miss by an angry prosecutor with no evidence. **[31]** Of these two
charges, I see the author, I see the source, I see a specific name and
origin. Caelius needed gold; he borrowed it from Clodia, he borrowed it with no witnesses, he held onto it as long as he wanted. I see
here a very strong sign of a really remarkable friendship. He wanted
to kill her; he sought out poison, he corrupted her slaves, he prepared
a potion, he picked a place, he brought the poison secretly. And now
I see the origin of a great hatred, with a really vicious breakup. In
this case, members of the jury, our whole dispute is with Clodia, a
lady not only prosperous but promiscuous—but I won't say anything
about her except to rebut the charges. **[32]** You have a great deal of
wisdom, Gnaeus Domitius, and accordingly you understand that our
business is with her alone.[41] If she denies she lent gold to Caelius,
if she isn't claiming that the poison was prepared by him to use on
her, then I behave rudely in naming a family woman in a manner
other than that which the sacred name of motherhood deserves. But
if, once that woman is removed, there's no charge and no backing
remaining for their attack on Caelius, what else am I supposed to do
as an advocate, except to fight off the attackers? And I would do it
more vigorously, if I didn't have previous enmities with that woman's
husband—I mean her brother; I keep making that mistake.[42] But as
it is, I'll behave with moderation and go no further than my own
honor and the case itself require. I've never thought I should conduct
hostilities with women, especially with a woman we've all always
thought of as loved by everyone rather than hated by anyone.

---

41. Gnaeus Domitius (whose identity is uncertain) was presiding over the
trial.

42. Cicero uses Clodia to attack her brother (Publius Clodius Pulcher,
one of Cicero's greatest enemies and the architect of his exile). Clodius was
reported to have slept with all three of his sisters; if this Clodia (the wife of
Metellus) is the same Clodia that Catullus addressed under the pseudonym
Lesbia, then Catullus, too, in poem 79 makes the same accusation. As the
sisters seem to have had similar tastes and character, the truth of the story
is not easy to discover.

[33] But first I have a question for her: does she want me to play the part of severity and solemn antiquity or the mild and gentle role of urbanity? If it's the stern manner and method of antiquity, then I'll have to raise up from the underworld one of those long-beards—not with the little goatee that she admires, but with the shaggy beard we see in old statues and portraits—to scold the woman, to speak for me, so she doesn't get angry at me. So let someone from her own family appear: how about the famous Appius Claudius the Blind?[43] Someone who can't see her will suffer less. If he should appear, I imagine, he would act and speak like this: "Woman, what business do you have with Caelius, what business with an underage boy, what business with someone who is not one of us? Why were you so friendly that you lent him money or so unfriendly that you were afraid of being poisoned? Didn't you see your father and uncle, didn't you hear that your grand-father, your great-grandfather, your great-great-grandfather, and your great-great-great grandfather had all been consuls? [34] Weren't you aware that your husband was Quintus Metellus, a man of great distinction and courage, a man of great patriotism, who only had to step outside to surpass almost every other citizen in virtue, glory, and honor?[44] Since you had married from a family of great distinc-tion into another of great glory, why was Caelius so tight with you? Was he a relative, a connection, a friend of your husband's? None of the above. What reason was there, then, except for the rashness of lust? If the portraits of the men in our family haven't aroused you, what about my daughter, the famous Quinta Claudia: didn't she urge you to compete with her in homegrown praise for a woman's glory? What about the famous Vestal Virgin Claudia, who held onto her father during his triumph and didn't permit him to be dragged from his chariot by a hostile tribune of the plebs?[45] Why did your

43. Appius Claudius Caecus ("The Blind") was consul in 307 and 296, and as censor in 312 was responsible for the construction of the Appian Way (the road from Rome to Capua) and the Appian aqueduct, Rome's first. As a blind old man in 280, he famously argued against Rome's making peace with Pyrrhus.

44. Clodia was married to Quintus Caecilius Metellus Celer, consul in 60, who died (suddenly) in 59 (see below, secs. 59–60). Neither he nor his brother Metellus Nepos (tribune in 62) was on friendly terms with Cicero.

45. Claudia Quinta demonstrated her virtue in 204 in freeing from a sand-bar the ship carrying the Black Rock (the sacred object of the Great Mother

brother's vices move you more than the good qualities of your father and grandfather, often reappearing in both men and women all the way back to me? Did I break up the peace with Pyrrhus so you could hook up daily in the most disgraceful love affairs? Did I bring water into Rome so you could use it for your disgusting purposes? Did I pave the Appian Way so you could go romping down it surrounded by a crowd of men who aren't our kind?"

[35] But why, members of the jury, did I bring in such a somber character? I'm afraid Appius will suddenly turn and start accusing Caelius with that censorial seriousness of his. But I'll see about that later, members of the jury, and I'll do so in such a way that I'm sure I will gain approval for Caelius' way of life among the strictest of judges. But you, woman—and now I'll speak to you without wearing a mask⁴⁶—if you expect to gain approval for the things you do, the things you say, the charges you make, the plots you contrive, the things you attack, then you must give an explanation for this close friendship and tight connection. The prosecutors go on about lust, love affairs and adultery, Baiae and beach parties, revels and drunken brawls, songs, musicians, party boats—and they hint that they're saying nothing against your wishes. I have no idea what unhinged condition of lunacy led you to want all this to be dragged into the forum and into court, but you should either refute it and show it's false or admit that neither your accusations nor your evidence deserve any belief at all.⁴⁷

[36] But if you want me to play a more sophisticated part, then how about this? I'll take away that old man, tough and nearly rustic, and I'll take someone from the modern world—the best is your little brother, the most sophisticated of them all. He loves you a lot;

Cybele) to Rome. The Vestal Virgin Claudia got in the chariot of her relative Appius Claudius Pulcher (consul in 143) to allow him to celebrate a triumph over the veto of a tribune. The Claudian family was notorious for its family pride, rudeness, and snobbery.

46. Throughout this section, Cicero blends two uses of masks: the mask of a character (*persona*) played by an actor in the theater and the portrait masks of the nobility worn by actors in the funeral processions of their descendants.

47. A brilliant use of the rhetorical figure of dilemma: if Clodia is a respectable woman, then what she says is false on the face of it; if she isn't, then what she says is untrustworthy because she is not respectable.

because he's fearful and has empty terrors in the night, as a little boy he always used to sleep with his big sister. Imagine him speaking to you: "What's the big deal, sis? Why act crazy?

> Why the fuss? You make a mountain from a molehill.
> What's the point?[48]

You saw a boy toy in the neighborhood. His fair skin, his height, his face, his eyes knocked you over; you wanted to see a lot of him; you were pretty often in the same gardens; noble woman that you are, you want to have this son of a frugal and grasping father bound tight by your cash. No go. He kicks back, he blows you off, he pushes you away, he doesn't think so much of your endowments. Find another. You have gardens along the Tiber, you deliberately got them in a place where all the young men come to swim; you can pick your partners every day. Why keep bugging someone who rejects you?"

[37] Now it's me again, Caelius, and I'm taking up the authority and sternness of a father. But I'm not sure what father it's best for me to adopt, some violent and harsh one out of Caecilius:[49]

> Now at last my brain is burning, now my heart is heaped
> with anger.

Or this one:

> Wretched man! You criminal!

Those fathers are made of iron:

> What am I to say, what to wish for? By your foul deeds
> You make all my wishes have no force.

Fathers of that kind are scarcely endurable. A father like that would say: "Why did you get so close to a hooker? Why didn't you flee these entrapments once you recognized them?

---

48. Clearly quoted from a comedy; author and play unknown.

49. The comic playwright Caecilius Statius was renowned for his character portrayals; it is unclear how many different fathers are represented in the quotations used here.

Why did you know someone else's wife? Scatter and
  waste,
I don't care. You can do it; if you're broke it's your pain,
  not mine.
There's enough left for me to please myself for whatever
  time I have left."

[38] To this stern and upright old man Caelius would answer that
no lust led him off the straight and narrow. Evidence? No expenses,
no losses, no borrowing. "But there was a rumor." Can anyone at all
avoid rumors in a city as slanderous as this one? Are you surprised
this woman's neighbor has a bad reputation when her own brother
can't avoid his enemies' gossip? But with a mild and forgiving father
like this one:[50]

He broke the doors; they can be fixed. He tore
Some clothes; they can be mended.

Caelius' case is clear as day. What can't he easily defend himself
about? I'm not saying anything against this woman, but if there were
some woman, not like this one, who was the common property of
everyone, who always had somebody in her sights, to whose gardens, whose house, whose home at Baiae every lechery in the world
migrated as if going home, who supported young men and made
up for their fathers' stinginess with her own resources; if a widow
lived loosely, a shameless woman flagrantly, a rich woman lavishly, a
wanton woman like a slut, am I supposed to think a man an adulterer
if he's greeted her with a little too much familiarity?
    [39] Someone will say: "Is this what you call discipline? Is this how
you train young men? Is this why his father trusted you and handed
his son over to you, so he could devote his youth to love affairs and
sweet delights, and so you could defend a life filled with pursuits like
these?" For my part, members of the jury, if there were someone
of such strength of mind and inborn virtue and self-control that he
could spit on every pleasure and live his whole life in physical toil and

---

50. Micio in Terence's *Adelphoe* ("The Brothers"), 120–21. The contrast
of stern and mild fathers (the brothers Demea and Micio) is central to the
play.

mental exertion—someone whom rest and relaxation, the pursuits of his contemporaries, games and parties did not please, who thought that nothing was worth seeking in life unless it were linked to glory and honor—a man like that, in my opinion, has been dressed out with the properties of a god. That's the model that produced men like Camillus and Fabricius and Curius and all those men who made all this so great from such tiny origins.[51] **[40]** But it's hard to find virtues like this even in books, not to mention in our own way of life. Even the pages that reported the stern manners of old have faded,[52] and not only among us, who follow this pattern of life in our actions more than in our words, but even among the Greeks, the most book-ish of men, who could talk and write with honor and grandeur even if they couldn't act that way—even among them, now that times have changed in Greece, different maxims for life have arisen.[53] **[41]** Some of them say that wise men do everything for the sake of pleasure, and even men of learning haven't shrunk from such foul language; oth-ers believe that honor and pleasure should be linked, so as to join together through their skill at speaking things that are opposite to one another; the ones who approve the one straight road to glory linked with toil are left almost alone in their lecture rooms. Nature herself has produced many allurements for us; they occasionally lull virtue to close her eyes in sleep. She shows many slippery paths to young men, on which they can scarcely stand or walk without slip-ping and sometimes falling;[54] she has given a variety of the most

---

51. The great and impecunious heroes of an earlier Rome. This is perhaps the only passage where Cicero seems to be making fun of the national myth of virtuous poverty.

52. A very similar image (without irony) a few years later at *On the Commonwealth* 5.1.

53. Cicero draws two comparisons here: one between Romans (who act rather than think) and Greeks (who think but don't act), the other between Greeks of the past—presumably of the fifth and fourth centuries—who at least had noble ideas and Greeks of the present—the Hellenistic schools of philosophy—who for the most part don't even have noble ideas. The three schools described in the next section are Epicureans, Peripatetics, and Stoics; the Academy (to which Cicero himself belonged) practiced skepticism and avowed no positive ethical theory of its own.

54. Cicero's language suggests some allusion to the choice of Heracles between the steep path to virtue and the slippery slope to vice.

delightful things that can ensnare not only young men but even men of a steadier time of life. [42] For that reason, if you find someone who closes his eyes to the beauty of the world, who is captivated by no smell, no touch, no flavor, who blocks from his ears every sweet sound, I, perhaps together with a few others, will think the gods smile on him, but most people will think they're angry at him. So let this path, which is deserted, overgrown, and blocked by branches and brambles, be abandoned. Let youth have some play; let young men live a little too freely. Not everything should be denied to pleasure; the true and straight philosophy should not always be victorious. Let desire and pleasure sometimes overcome reason, so long as there remains some limit and moderation in such things. Young men shouldn't be sexually active; they shouldn't force others to be sexually active, either. They shouldn't waste their family wealth, they shouldn't be savaged by usury, they shouldn't break into someone else's house and household. They shouldn't bring disgrace on the chaste, dishonor on the upright, shame on the good; they shouldn't frighten people with violence or take part in plots, they shouldn't commit crimes. Finally, after having followed their bodily urges and devoted some time to sport and the empty desires of adolescence, they should eventually resume their concern with the management of their own business and the business of the courts and the country; they should seem to have had enough of all the things they hadn't thought about rationally and to have rejected them on the basis of experience.

[43] There have been many men, members of the jury, in our own memory and in that of our fathers and ancestors, men of the highest standing, citizens of great distinction, whose outstanding qualities emerged when they reached maturity after the urges of youth had settled down. I won't indulge in naming names: you can remember on your own. I have no desire to link even the smallest slip of any brave, outstanding man to the great praise he is due. But if I wanted to, I could name many men of high standing and great eminence, some who were too wild as teenagers, some whose extravagant luxury, great debts, expenses, and sexual escapades could be mentioned; all this, because it's covered over by their many subsequent virtues, could easily be defended by the excuse of adolescence. [44] But in Caelius—I can now speak with more assurance about his honorable interests, since I have the courage to admit certain things openly relying on your wisdom—you will find no sign of luxury, no expenses, no borrowing, no panting over orgies and sleazy clubs. Vices of the belly

and guts not only don't grow smaller over time but even grow bigger. Love affairs and so-called friendship with privileges, things that aren't a problem for long for people with a harder core—they lose their fizz early and fast—have never distracted or bothered Caelius. **[45]** You heard him speaking in his own defense, you heard him previously as a prosecutor—I'm saying this as part of his defense, not boastfully—and, given your wisdom, you recognized his oratorical style, his ease, the abundance of his thoughts and words. And in him you saw not just his blazing talent, which often is propelled by its own strength even if it isn't supported by hard work, but unless he perhaps deceived me because of my favorable feelings toward him, he also displayed an understanding nourished by a good education and worked at through the effort of wakeful nights. And yet, members of the jury, you must know that the urges imputed to Caelius and the learning about which I'm speaking don't easily coexist in the same person. It's impossible for a spirit that has surrendered to lust and is bound by love, desire, greed, often by excess, occasionally by starvation, to have the strength for this, whatever it is, that we do as speakers, however we do it, not just in delivering speeches but also in preparing them. **[46]** Do you think there's any other reason for the small number of people, present and past, who have toiled in this area despite the huge rewards for eloquence, the pleasures of public speaking, the glory, the influence, and the distinction? Every pleasure must be ground beneath our feet. The pursuit of pleasure must be given up, sport, jokes, parties, even everyday conversation must almost be abandoned. For that reason the effort involved in this field troubles men and frightens them off, not any shortage of wits and basic education. **[47]** If Caelius had abandoned himself to that kind of life, would he as such a young man have brought charges against an ex-consul? If he shunned hard work, if he was bound hand and foot by pleasure, would he take part in this daily battle, incurring enemies, laying charges, enduring the risk of capital penalties, under the gaze of the Roman people would he fight for so many months about his own well-being or glory?[55] "But isn't there a whiff of something from the neighborhood? Doesn't rumor mean anything? Doesn't Baiae itself say something?" Yes, indeed: it not only speaks but shouts that

---

55. As before, Cicero is referring to two prosecutions by Caelius, the first of Gaius Antonius in 59, the second of Bestia in 56, which led to the present trial.

the sexual desires of that one woman have sunk so far that she not only doesn't look for solitude and shadows and a covering for her disgraceful behavior but even rejoices in performing obscene acts with a large audience under bright lights.

[48] If there's anyone who thinks hookers should be forbidden to young men, he's really severe—there's no denying it—but he's completely at odds not only with the lax standards of the present generation but even with the customary allowances made by our ancestors. When was this not common, when was it criticized, when was it forbidden? When, in short, was it true that what is now permitted wasn't permitted? Here I'm only defining the issue, and I'm not naming any particular woman. That much, I will leave unsaid. **[49]** If an unmarried woman opens her house to everyone's desire and openly sets herself up as a whore and decides to enjoy parties with men with whom she has absolutely no connection, if she does this in Rome, in her gardens, in the crowds at Baiae, if in short she behaves loosely not just in the way she walks but in what she wears and who her friends are, it's not just her flashing eyes and loose language but her hugs, her kisses, her beach parties, her boat trips, her carousals that make her seem not only a whore but a whore who solicits men shamelessly. If some young man perhaps hooked up with her, does he seem to you, Herennius, an adulterer or a lover; does he seem to you to have wanted to assault her modesty or just to relieve an itch? **[50]** I forget now, Clodia, the injuries you inflicted on me; I set aside the memory of my own suffering. I pay no attention to your cruel treatment of my family in my absence; I unsay everything I've said against you. But I have a question for you, since the prosecutors say you're both the source of the charge and a witness to it. If there were a woman of the kind I just described, one totally unlike you, living and acting like a slut, does it seem to you particularly shameful or dishonorable for a young man to make it with her? If you aren't that woman, as I prefer to believe, what do they have to throw at Caelius? If they want you to be that woman, then why should we have any fear of that charge if you don't care about it? So give us a logical approach to the defense: either your modesty will argue that Caelius did nothing improper, or your immodesty will give him—and others—a great opportunity for defending themselves.[56]

---

56. Again, the formal dilemma (above, n. 47), signaled this time by Cicero's use of *ratio*, translated here as "logical approach."

[51] But now that my speech seems to have gotten out of the shallows and gone past the reefs, the rest of my course is very easy. There are two charges of high crimes, involving one woman, concerning the gold that is said to have been borrowed from Clodia, and concerning the poison they accuse Caelius of having acquired in order to kill the aforesaid Clodia.[57] He borrowed the gold, according to you, to give to the slaves of Lucius Lucceius, who were to assassinate Dio the Alexandrian, then living in Lucceius' house.[58] That's a very serious charge, either in terms of plotting against an ambassador or in terms of suborning slaves to kill a guest of their master: a plan full of crime, full of boldness! [52] But with respect to that charge, my first question is whether Caelius did or did not tell Clodia why he was borrowing gold. If he didn't tell her, then why did she give it? If he did tell her, she has incriminated herself as a conspirator in the same crime. Did you dare to take gold from your strong box, to strip that notorious Venus of yours of her jewelry, the Venus who has stripped others, when you knew how great a crime it was being sought for, for the murder of an ambassador, for the eternal disgrace of Lucius Lucceius, a man of supreme morality and integrity? A free spirit like yours shouldn't be complicit in such a crime; an open house like yours shouldn't support it; your famous Venus, so welcoming to friends, shouldn't assist it. [53] Balbus[59] recognized this: he said it was concealed from Clodia and that Caelius represented himself to her as seeking gold to make his games grander.[60] But if Clodia was as familiar with him as you want while you're talking so much about his sexual activities, then he obviously said why he wanted the gold; if he wasn't so familiar, then she didn't give it to him. So since your behavior knows no bounds, if Caelius told you the truth then you knowingly gave money for a crime; and if he didn't have the courage to tell you, then you didn't give it.

---

57. After the long and central digression slandering Clodia, Cicero returns to the two charges mentioned in sec. 30.

58. Lucceius had been an ally of Cicero against Catiline, and in 55 Cicero asked him (*ad Fam.* 5.12) to write a history of Cicero's glorious achievements in 63.

59. The prosecutor Herennius Balbus.

60. Otherwise unknown; Caelius was not in office and had no responsibility to put on games, and we know of no other reason for him to do so at this time.

Is there any reason for me to deploy the countless arguments against this charge? I can say that Caelius' character is far, far removed from the viciousness of such a crime: it's impossible to believe it wouldn't have occurred to a man of such talent and brains that a crime like this shouldn't be put in the hands of someone else's slaves whom he didn't know. I can ask the time-honored[61] questions of the prosecutor as other advocates besides me generally do, where Caelius met Lucceius' slaves, how he approached them. If he did it on his own, that shows incredible gall; if he used an intermediary, who was it? I can root through all the nooks and crannies of suspicions in my speech: no reason, no place, no opportunity, no witness, no hope of carrying out or concealing the crime, no plan, no trace of a major crime will be found. **[54]** But all this is part of the orator's toolkit; it could give me good results not from my own talent but because my experience as a speaker would make it seem to be my own creation. But I'll move quickly and leave it all aside. What I have, members of the jury, is a witness whom you will easily allow to share the sanctity of your oath, Lucius Lucceius, a man of great honor and an extremely weighty witness. He would certainly have heard that a crime of such magnitude had been directed against his reputation and his fortune by Marcus Caelius; he would not have ignored it nor would he have tolerated it. Could such a humane man, with such interests and skill and learning, possibly have neglected danger to the very man who inspired his love for these studies? He would have moved strongly against such a crime aimed at a stranger; wouldn't he have been concerned in the case of a friend in his house? He would have been pained if he'd learned it had been done by men he didn't know; would he ignore an attempt made by his own slaves? He would have censured such an action in open territory or a public place; would he react mildly to its being undertaken in the city and in his own home? He wouldn't have let it pass if danger to some rustic were involved; would a man of his learning think to conceal it in a plot against a great scholar? **[55]** But why, members of the jury, do I waste your time? Observe the sanctity and authority of his oath and pay close attention to every word of his evidence. Recite.

---

61. Reading *illa* rather than *alia*. See Austin (1960) on this passage.

[EVIDENCE OF LUCIUS LUCCEIUS]

What else are you waiting for? Do you expect the case or truth itself to be able to speak for themselves? Here is the defense of innocence; here is what the case itself says; here is the unique voice of truth. In the charge there resides no suspicion, in the case there is no logical argument, in the action that's supposed to have taken place there isn't a trace of the conversation, of the place, of the time; no witness is named, no accomplice; the whole charge is brought forth from a hostile, disgraced, cruel, criminal, sex-crazed home. The house that is said to have been assaulted in this wicked crime is filled with honesty, dignity, duty, and conscience; that's the house from which the testimony under oath that was recited to you comes, leaving to be decided something about which there is no doubt, whether it seems more likely that a rash, pushy, angry woman invented the charge or a serious, wise, and balanced man gave his evidence scrupulously.

[56] What remains, then, is the charge about poison, a charge of which I can neither discover the beginning nor unravel the end. Why on earth would Caelius want to poison that woman? To avoid returning the gold? But did he ever ask for it? To avoid having the charge stick? But was anyone making it? Would anyone have so much as mentioned it, if Caelius hadn't made an accusation himself? What's more, you've heard Herennius say he wouldn't have troubled Caelius with a single word if, after his friend had been acquitted, Caelius hadn't brought the same charges again. Can you believe that such a huge misdeed was committed for no reason at all? Don't you see that this accusation of having committed a terrible crime was invented so there would seem to be some reason for his having attempted the other crime?[62] [57] To whom, then, did he consign it? Whose help did he use, what friend, what partner? To whom did he entrust so great a crime, himself, and his own safety? To the woman's slaves? That's the accusation. In your speech attacking Caelius you deny him all good qualities except brains; was he then so crazy that he entrusted his entire fortune to someone else's slaves? And what kind of slaves are they? In fact, that makes a lot of difference. The ones whom he knew to enjoy not the normal conditions of slavery but a

---

62. The terrible crime is poisoning Clodia; the other crime is the murder of Dio. If Clodia could give evidence in the latter case, there would be a motive for murdering her.

life of license, liberty, and great intimacy with their mistress? Who doesn't see, members of the jury, or who doesn't know, that where the lady of the house lives like a whore, where nothing happens that can be mentioned in public, where unusual passions, luxury, and every unmentionable vice and perversion hold sway, that in such a house slaves are not slaves, where everything is entrusted to them, where everything takes place with their assistance, where they take part in the same pleasures, to whom secrets are entrusted, who receive a cut of the daily extravagance and luxury? Didn't Caelius know that? [58] If he was as close to that woman as you say, then he knew those slaves were equally close to their mistress. If, on the other hand, there was no such close relationship as you suggest, then how could he have been so close to her slaves? And what's the story they invent about the poison? Where was it sought, how was it prepared, how, to whom, and where was it handed over? They say he had it at home and tested its strength on a slave bought for the purpose; the suddenness of his death was the seal of approval for the poison. [59] Why is it that the everlasting gods, when people commit truly awful crimes, either wink at them or postpone the punishment for present misdeeds to some vague future date? I have seen, I have seen for myself, and suffered what may have been the greatest anguish in my life, when Quintus Metellus was snatched from the embrace of his country, when a man who thought he had been born for the sake of this empire, two days after he had appeared in fine form in the senate house, on the speaker's platform, in the public eye, a man at the prime of life, a fine figure of a man at the peak of his strength, was stolen in a way he did not deserve from all men of worth and indeed from the nation as a whole.[63] At that time, when he was on the point of death, when his mind was otherwise overwhelmed, he kept his final moment of consciousness to remember his country. He looked at me as I wept and indicated by the halting speech of a dying man what a storm was hanging over me, what a tempest was hanging over the state, and striking the common wall between his house and Catulus', he often named Catulus, frequently me, most frequently the country; in this way he showed that his pain was not so much at

---

63. Cicero makes the amiable suggestion that Clodia had gotten away with poisoning her husband Metellus Celer, who died suddenly in 59. The clear implication is that poisoning her husband gave Clodia the idea of accusing Caelius of trying to poison her.

his own death as at the fact that both the country and I were being stripped of his protection.[64] **[60]** If the violence of a sudden crime had not removed him, how would Metellus, as a former consul, have resisted his lunatic cousin?[65] As consul, when Clodius was beginning his mad actions and thundering away, he said in the presence of the senate that he would kill him with his own hands. And this is the house from which that woman emerges and dares to speak about the speed of a poison? Isn't she afraid the house itself will speak, doesn't she thrill with horror before the walls that witnessed this, before the memory of that dire and mournful night?[66] But let me return to the accusation: indeed, to have mentioned that brave and glorious man stops my voice with weeping and slows my mind with pain.

[61] Back to the poison. Nothing has been said about its source or the means of acquiring it. They say it was given to Publius Licinius here,[67] a modest and good young man and a friend of Caelius; that it was agreed with the slaves that they would come to the Senian baths; that Licinius was to come there and hand over the jar of poison to them. First question: what was the point of having it brought to a meeting at a particular location rather than having the slaves come to Caelius' house? If such a close connection and such familiarity between Caelius and Clodia still existed, then why would it have been suspicious for a slave belonging to that woman to be seen at Caelius' house? But if there was already a quarrel, if the familiarity had been terminated and a division created, then that's the source of all those tears,[68] that's the cause of all these crimes and charges. **[62]** "In fact," he says, "when the slaves had reported the whole thing and Caelius' evil plans to their mistress, that clever woman instructed them to promise everything to Caelius; but so that when the poison

---

64. Quintus Lutatius Catulus, Metellus' next-door neighbor, was a staunch reactionary (his opposition to Pompey's commands against the pirates and Mithridates is discussed in *In Support of Manilius' Law*) who had died in 60. Given the fact that Metellus and Cicero were not particularly close, one may doubt the veracity of Cicero's account of his dying words—which are remarkably similar to Cicero's own descriptions of his exile.

65. Clodius.

66. The speaking house presumably refers to the Watchman's speech in Aeschylus' *Agamemnon*—yet another dramatic reference.

67. Otherwise unknown, as are the Senian baths.

68. Quoted from Terence, *Andria* 126.

was being handed over by Licinius it could be grabbed in plain sight, she ordered the Senian baths to be set as the place, so she could send friends to loiter there, and when Licinius had arrived and handed over the poison, to jump out and grab him." Now all this, members of the jury, can easily be refuted. Why did she pick the public baths in particular? There's no place there I can find for fully dressed men to hide. If they were in the changing room, they wouldn't be hidden; if they wanted to go inside, that's not easy wearing shoes and clothes, and they might not be allowed in, unless by chance that powerful woman had cozied up to the bath-keeper with her usual two-bit transaction.[69]

[63] Myself, I've been waiting on tenterhooks to find out what upright citizens would be named as witnesses to this poison's seizure in plain sight; nobody has been identified so far. But I'm sure they're very serious men. In the first place, they're close friends of a woman like this; second, they've taken on the task of being shoved into the baths—and no matter how powerful she is, they would never have done her such a favor if they weren't the most honorable men, men of great distinction. But why talk about the distinction of her witnesses? You have clear evidence of their virtue and responsibility. "They lurked in the baths." Great witnesses! "Then they jumped out too fast." Such restrained men! The story you're making up goes like this: when Licinius arrived and was holding the jar in his hand and was trying to hand it over but hadn't yet done so, at that moment these wonderful nameless witnesses of hers suddenly flew out, but Licinius, even though he'd already stretched forth his hand to pass on the jar, pulled it back and sped in flight from these men's sudden onslaught. Great indeed is the power of truth! It can defend itself easily and on its own against the wits and cleverness and wiles of men, against everyone's invented ambushes! [64] This whole tale, for instance, belongs to an aging lady poet who has written a lot of comedies—but it has no plot and no ending.[70] For instance, all those many men of hers—since there must have been quite a few in order to

---

69. Clodia as a cheap whore. In his speech, Caelius had called Clodia *quadrantaria Clytaemestra*, "a two-bit Clytemnestra"—both adultery and murder of her husband for one small price. The same two bits was the price of admission to the baths.

70. Clodia's life has consisted of lots of dirty little farces; hence, she must be a poet.

grab Licinius easily and to have the whole thing witnessed by many people—why did they let Licinius out of their hands? How was it that Licinius was less catchable when he pulled back so as not to hand over the jar than if he had handed it over? They were poised to grab Licinius, so that Licinius would openly be caught either holding the poison or when he handed it over. That was the woman's whole plan, that was the job of the men she asked, and why you say they jumped out rashly ahead of time I do not understand. They had been asked to do this, they had been placed to do this, so that the poison, the plot, and the crime itself would be caught in the open. **[65]** Could they have leaped out at any better moment than when Licinius had arrived and was holding the jar of poison in his hand? Once it was handed over to the slaves, if the woman's friends had suddenly left the baths and grabbed Licinius, he would have shouted for help and denied he was the one who handed over the jar. And how were they to refute him? Should they have said they saw it all? First, they would have laid themselves open to a criminal charge, and second, they would have said they saw something they could not have seen from where they were hidden. So they revealed themselves at the exact moment when Licinius had come, was getting out the jar, stretching out his hand, handing over the poison. That's the end of a mime, not a play: when there's no ending, somebody gets away, the clapper claps, the curtain falls.[71] **[66]** I want to know why, when Licinius was stumbling and hesitating, retreating and trying to run away, why this lady's crew let him slip out of their hands, why they didn't grab him, why they didn't give a shape to the charge of so great a crime using his own confession, the witness of many, the voice, finally, of the crime itself. Were they afraid that so many men couldn't overcome one man, that strong men couldn't overcome a weakling, that determined men couldn't overcome a man in terror?

There's no plot here, no reason for suspicion, no point to the charge.[72] As a result, this case has been completely given over to

---

71. In fact, the curtain in Rome rose from the ground to indicate the end of a performance. The clapper was attached to the feet and apparently gave a signal to end the play. The dramatic form of the Clodia drama has gone drastically downhill, from tragedy to comedy to mime, a much more popular and less formal variety of farce.

72. "No plot" applies both to the bath mime just described (or perhaps reenacted by Cicero) and to the story of the poison itself.

witnesses rather than to the arguments, inferences, and evidence
from which truth is usually illuminated. And for my part, members of
the jury, I await those witnesses not only without fear but with a certain pleasurable anticipation. **[67]** My mind yearns to see first these
clean young men who are friends of this rich and noble woman, then
the brave men placed by their commandress in an ambush guarding
the baths. I will ask them how they hid and where: was it a bathtub,
or some Trojan Horse to hold and protect so many invincible heroes
waging a woman's war? I'll make them explain why so many men of
such quality could not either grab one single weakling (as you see) as
he stood there or catch him when he fled; if they get to that point,
they'll never get themselves out of this mess. No matter how clever
and witty they are at parties or eloquent sometimes even when drunk,
the courtroom is one thing and the banquet room is something else;
reasoning in the jury box is one thing, on dinner couches another;
jurors and drunken revelers look different; and the light of the sun is
one thing, that of torches very different. For that reason we'll give a
good shaking to all their luxuries and follies, if they come forward.
Let them listen to me: they should take up some other line of work,
they should find some other source of influence, they should expose
themselves in other areas, they should flash their charms in the presence of that woman, they should be lords of luxury, they should cling
to her, lie at her feet, enslave themselves to her—but they should stay
away from the life and fortunes of an innocent man.

    [68] "But those slaves were set free by the decision of her rela-
tives, men of great nobility and fame." At long last we've found something that woman is supposed to have done based on the opinions
and authority of her relatives, those big, strong men. But I want to
know the meaning of that manumission: either a charge was cooked
up against Caelius or the possibility of torturing them for evidence
was eliminated or a reward was given for good reason to slaves who
knew too much about too many things. "But it was the wish of the
family," she says. Why shouldn't they want it, since you said that
you yourself brought the whole thing to their attention as your own
discovery, not as something reported to you by others?[73] **[69]** And
are we supposed to be surprised if the sequel to that imaginary jar

---

73. Obscure, and deliberately so. The only plausible interpretation is that
Clodia told her relatives about the plot against her and her slaves' part in
helping her, for which they deserved manumission.

was a pornographic play?[74] There's nothing here that doesn't suit a woman like this. It's all been passed around in conversation: we've all heard it. You've known for a long time, members of the jury, what I wish—or rather what I don't wish—to say. If this was done, it was certainly not done by Caelius—what good would it do him—but by some teenager who may not have lacked wit so much as he lacked shame. If it was invented, then it was not a modest lie, but perhaps it was not unclever; in any case, people's gossip and opinions would never have given it credence if it were not that everything being said involved a certain amount of disgraceful behavior—and that seemed to fit her perfectly.

[70] Members of the jury, my case is said and done. And now you understand how important the judgment is for which you're responsible, what a serious matter has been entrusted to you. You're sitting as a court dealing with crimes of violence. That law applies to the empire, to its dignity, to the condition of our country, to the well-being of us all. The law was passed on the proposal of Quintus Catulus during an armed revolt of citizens, when the commonwealth seemed on its deathbed;[75] it is the law that, after the fire during my consulship had been brought under control, put out the last smoking remains of the conspiracy.[76] This is the law under which this young man Caelius is being prosecuted not to exact punishment on behalf of the commonwealth but on behalf of the sexual perversions of this woman.

[71] At this point, I hear mention of the condemnation of Marcus Camurtius and Gaius Caesernius.[77] How stupid can you be! Or should I call it incredible gall rather than stupidity? Coming as you

---

74. Just as obscure as the last section. Apparently Clodia had been the subject of a popular dirty joke involving a jar, but the punch line is left to our imagination.

75. The Lutatian law on violence was proposed by the consul Quintus Lutatius Catulus in 78 to deal with the anti-Sullan revolt of his consular colleague Marcus Aemilius Lepidus.

76. It was the law under which Catiline's surviving colleagues in revolution were tried (in fact, the trials were under a revision of that law, the Plautian law of 70 BCE).

77. Camurtius, Caesernius, and Vettius are all otherwise unknown. Presumably the first two did something unpleasant to the last, and did so on Clodia's behalf; presumably they were also tried under the same statute on violence as Caelius.

do from that woman, do you dare bring up the names of those men?
Do you dare arouse the memory of such disgrace, a memory not
destroyed but simply suppressed over time? What was the criminal
vice that did them in? Surely it was because they avenged this same
woman's anger and insult by a perverted assault on Vettius. So was
it to bring up the name of Vettius in the trial, to bring back that old
cheap play, that you revived the case of Camurtius and Caesernius?
They were certainly not in breach of the law on violence, but they
were so bound up in that crime that they appeared undeserving
of being released from the toils of any law at all. **[72]** But why is
Caelius being summoned before this court? No charge proper to
this court is brought against him, nor indeed anything, even if not
appropriate to this law, that's appropriate to your severity. When he
was young, he devoted himself to education in those skills that arm
us for actions in the courts, for taking part in public life, for office,
glory, and honor. The older men he was friends with were those
whose hard work and discipline he particularly wanted to emulate;
his associations with his contemporaries were such that he seemed
to take part in the same contest for glory that the best and noblest
men admired. **[73]** When he got a little more mature, he set out to
Africa on the staff of Quintus Pompeius, a man of high morals and
extremely assiduous in every obligation;[78] not only in that province
was there landed property belonging to his father, but provincial
service itself is justifiably assigned to men of this age by our ancestors. He left the province having gained the enthusiastic support of
Pompeius, as his own evidence will demonstrate to you. By long-
standing custom and the example of young men who subsequently
became leaders of the state and citizens of distinction, he wanted his
hard work to become known to the Roman people through some
very visible prosecution. **[74]** I wish his desire for glory had taken
him in another direction—but the time to complain about that is
past. He brought a charge against my colleague Antonius, and the
memory of the outstanding good Antonius had provided the commonwealth didn't help him, while the belief that he had thought of
doing evil harmed him.[79] After that Caelius never allowed any of

---

78. Quintus Pompeius Rufus governed the province of Africa after his
praetorship in 63.
79. Gaius Antonius, Cicero's colleague in the consulship of 63, was believed
to have been a supporter of Catiline. Caelius prosecuted him for provincial

his contemporaries to be more active in the forum and in the business and lawsuits of his friends or to have greater influence among his own people. All the things men can't accomplish without being alert, sober, and industrious Caelius accomplished through effort and attention.

[75] At this turning point in his life—and I will conceal nothing, relying on your humaneness and wisdom—the young man's reputation stuck briefly on the turning pole because of his new acquaintance with this woman; he was in the wrong neighborhood and was not used to such pleasures.[80] When these urges are held in for too long and squeezed down in one's youth, they frequently pour forth and shoot out all at once. From this life or perhaps I should say from this rumor—for it was never so much as men said—but from whatever it was, he picked himself up, he escaped entirely and got himself out; he is now so distant from the bad reputation that goes with being close to her that he now has to fight off the enmity and hatred of this same woman. [76] And so that these spreading rumors of lust and laziness would die—he did this, to be sure, against my wishes and over my active objections, but he did it—he brought charges against my friend for electoral corruption. And after Bestia was acquitted, Caelius kept after him and brought charges again. He paid no attention to any of us, he's more of a hothead than I like. But I'm not speaking about philosophic wisdom, which is not to be found at Caelius' age; I'm talking about his mental energy, his love of winning, his burning desire for glory. All these things, as we grow older, ought to become less aggressive, but in a young man, as in a crop of grain, they give advance notice of the maturity of his excellence and the products of his toil. It's always been necessary to rein in high-spirited young men from glory rather than spur them on; more needs to be pruned at that age, if it blossoms with the praise of its talent, than grafted on. [77] For that reason, if anyone thinks he's boiled over too much—his force, ferocity, stubbornness in undertaking and conducting hostile actions—if even the least of these offends someone, if the shade of purple he wears, his crowd of friends, his gleam and glow, they will soon subside; age, experience, and time will cool them down.

---

extortion in 59 and won, despite Cicero's speaking for Antonius.

80. Cicero deliberately makes Caelius' relationship with Clodia seem to be casual and of short duration.

In sum: preserve for our country, members of the jury, a citizen of good education, of good principles, of good standing. I promise to you and I guarantee it to the country: just as I have done good service to the country, so will he never be separate from my beliefs. I make this promise not only relying on our friendship but because he has bound himself by the most stringent conditions. **[78]** It's not possible for someone who has prosecuted a former consul, who has claimed that the nation was dishonored by him, himself to be a disorderly member of the nation. It isn't possible for a man who doesn't permit someone who has been acquitted of electoral corruption to remain acquitted, to give bribes himself without being punished. The country, members of the jury, holds these two accusations either as hostages for Caelius' good behavior or as pledges for his goodwill. For that reason I make this prayer and request of you, members of the jury: in this city in the past few days Sextus Cloelius has been acquitted, a man whom you have seen over the past two years as either a participant in revolution or its leader,[81] a man without property, without honor, without hope, without home, without fortune. His mouth, his tongue, his hand, his entire life is polluted; he has burned with his own hands sacred buildings, he has burned with his own hands the census records of the Roman people and its memories; he has attacked the monument of Catulus; he has plundered my home, he has burned my brother's home; on the Palatine Hill and in the full sight of the city he has incited slaves to murder and to burn the city. In such a city do not permit Cloelius to be acquitted through the influence of this woman and Caelius to be a sacrifice to her lust; let that woman with her husband-brother[82] not be seen both to have rescued a bandit and crushed a young man of honor. **[79]** When you consider Caelius' youth, set before your eyes as well the old age of this unhappy man who relies on this, his only son, who finds serenity in his hopes for him, whose only fear is of his downfall. This suppliant of your mercy, the slave of your power, cast down not so much before your feet as before your character and sentiments—either in recollection of your own parents or in the joy of your own children

---

81. Cloelius was Clodius' head street-fighter. Census records were kept in the temple of the Nymphs, which was burned down by Cloelius acting for Clodius. The other offenses are all part of the agitation against Cicero in 58.
82. Incest with Clodius again.

raise him up, so that in the pain of another you may serve your own sense of duty or of generosity. He is already failing because of nature itself; you must not wish to hasten his demise by a wound from you rather than by his own fate. You must not wish to uproot, as if by a whirlwind or a sudden storm, this young man now in flower for the first time with the stem of his virtue now firm. **[80]** Preserve the son for the father, the father for the son; do not appear either to have contempt for an old age now almost past hope, or to have starved and even to have smitten and struck down a youth filled with the greatest of promise. If you preserve him for me, for his family, for the country, you will have him bound, dedicated, and attached to you and to your children, and it is you, members of the jury, who will particularly benefit from the rich and long-lasting rewards of his strength and toil.

.7

Against Lucius Calpurnius Piso

Lucius Calpurnius Piso Caesoninus, consul in 58 BCE, governor of Macedonia from 57 to 55, and father-in-law of Julius Caesar, was a man of high standing and considerable substance, a man of elegance and culture, a successful general and governor, at the center of the ruling class of Rome. In this speech, however, he emerges as something else: a monster of incompetence, cruelty, vice, and hypocrisy, a coward and a fool. There can be few speeches ever composed that reveal such animosity or that develop to such a high degree the arts of insult and invective. Certainly, it is not a speech that one reads for accurate historical detail; it is the vitriol that makes it memorable.

The immediate context for the speech is clear both from internal evidence and from the surviving ancient commentary on it by the first-century CE scholar Asconius Pedianus. On his return from Macedonia in 55, Piso, at a meeting of the senate, responded to previous attacks on him by Cicero and contrasted their two careers. Cicero's response was the present speech, probably delivered in the late summer of 55 but perhaps revised and elaborated before being made public, possibly early in 54.[1] Piso had good cause to complain about Cicero's treatment of him—this speech is by no means the first time Cicero expressed his hatred and loathing of Piso—but at least in his own mind, Cicero was justified in his hatred of Piso; the history (which will only be sketched briefly here) goes back to Cicero's consulship and, in particular, to the execution of the Catilinarian conspirators in December of 63.

Was the execution of the conspirators legal? That question clearly arose at the time, and the answer was by no means clear. On the last day of Cicero's consulship, one of the new tribunes, Metellus Nepos, refused to allow Cicero to give the customary speech on leaving office, on the grounds that, as consul, he had executed Roman citizens without trial. At that point, no further significant action took place, but when the question was raised again by Clodius in 58, it led directly to Cicero's ignominious departure from Rome into exile. That he was recalled in the next year did not diminish Cicero's anger at what had happened to him; Piso was one of

---

1. On the composition and date of the extant speech, see Lintott (2008) 210–11.

the consuls in the year Cicero went into exile, and Cicero blamed him, at least in part, for what had happened. Hence the animus.

A simple account like that just given, however, does not remotely do justice to the complexity of events. In the first place, there is Clodius. Publius Clodius Pulcher was a member of the Claudian family, traditionally the haughtiest of all patrician families;[2] Clodius, however, chose to spell his family name to emphasize the plebeian pronunciation and cultivated various antisocial attitudes (at least from traditionalist points of view). Although he seems to have been allied with Cicero during the Catilinarian crisis, the two later had a violent falling-out. Clodius was tried for sacrilege in 61 after being caught in drag at the all-female ritual of the Good Goddess, and Cicero gave evidence breaking Clodius' alibi (to no effect: Clodius was acquitted after bribing the jury). From that point on, Clodius aligned himself with those who thought Cicero guilty of murder in 63. He had himself adopted by a plebeian in 59 so that he could be elected tribune of the plebs for 58; once elected, he immediately promulgated the bills that led to Cicero's exile.

But the circumstances that led to Clodius' transfer to the plebs themselves contributed to Cicero's downfall as well. In 60 Julius Caesar, Pompey, and Marcus Licinius Crassus came to the informal agreement on power-sharing now referred to as the First Triumvirate; as part of that Caesar, as consul in 59, proposed and forced through a number of laws in their various interests. Caesar's colleague Calpurnius Bibulus formally protested Caesar's actions by regularly announcing that he was observing the skies for omens—meaning that no official civic action could take place. There was also a great deal of violent agitation. Hence the legality of all Caesar's acts was at best questionable, and from the point of view of the triumvirs, the risk of their annulment was real. Although Caesar courted Cicero's support, Cicero made comments clearly hostile to Caesar's actions; Caesar, as both pontifex maximus *and consul, thereupon supported Clodius' transfer to the plebs in 59, and in 58 did not oppose Clodius' actions against Cicero.*

Much of the maneuvering of the first months of 58 is described, albeit tendentiously, three years later in the speech against Piso.[3] In 58 neither Piso (Caesar's supporter) nor his fellow consul Aulus Gabinius (Pompey's ex-legate) stood in the way of Clodius, and to a certain extent they seemed to support him. Cicero claims that they were bribed by the offer of lucrative and important provincial commands to follow their consulship, but it is also perfectly clear that neither Pompey nor Caesar did anything

---

2. On the Claudian reputation for arrogance, see Wiseman (1979) 77–103.

3. For a careful account of the events surrounding Cicero's exile—and of Cicero's manipulation of the story—see Kaster (2006) 1–14.

at all to help Cicero in 58; indeed, they found it convenient to have
Clodius as an ally and to have Cicero unable to derail their plans. In the
speech against Piso, Cicero goes out of his way to emphasize his cordial
relationships with both leaders, but Piso was not at all unreasonable in
suggesting that it was Caesar and Pompey, not Piso and Gabinius, who
should have been the objects of Cicero's anger. Clodius in 58 proposed
two simultaneous measures: one granting extraordinary commands to
Piso and Gabinius, the other punishing with exile anyone who executed
a Roman citizen without trial. All the efforts of Cicero and his supporters
made no difference, and Cicero left Rome in March of 58 before the bills
were formally passed. After Cicero left, Clodius produced a bill specifically
aimed at Cicero, ordering the confiscation of his property as well as his
exile.

   The detailed political maneuvering of the next year need not be
described here; the outcome, in early August of 57, was a law recalling
Cicero, who was welcomed back to Rome in early September. The set of
speeches he gave after his return survives as a group: speeches of thanks
to both senate and people on the day of his return; speeches concerning
the restoration of his house on the Palatine Hill—which Clodius had turned
into a shrine to Liberty—and two speeches delivered in 56 at the trial of
Publius Sestius, accused of violence because of his agitation in Cicero's
favor. But in 56 Cicero's strong advocacy of senatorial dominance and
his openly expressed doubts about Caesar and Pompey led the triumvirs
to demand his silence or compliance; one result was the speech On the
Consular Provinces *later in 56, in which, despite earlier threats to try to
end Caesar's Gallic command, he instead urged the replacement of Piso in
Macedonia.*

   By the time of the speech against Piso in 55, then, Cicero's rage about
the circumstances of his exile had not diminished, but he was forced by
current circumstances to focus his rage not on Caesar and Pompey (who
deserved it) but on Clodius (who also deserved it) together with Piso
and Gabinius (who almost certainly did not). The result is an astonishing
display of eloquent vitriol. Though rarely truthful, the speech gave Cicero
the occasion for brilliant descriptions of Piso's alleged cowardice, military
incompetence, rapacity, philosophical slovenliness, disgusting personal
habits, and disreputable family—a repertory of the ways in which Romans
traditionally insulted their enemies.[4]

----

4. On the reality of Piso's character and actions, the appendices of Nisbet's
(1961) edition are invaluable; of more recent scholarship, see in particular
Griffin (2001). On the conventions of Ciceronian invective, see Corbeill
(2002); there is further useful discussion in Corbeill (1996) and Dugan
(2005).

As far as one can tell, there is not a single element of Cicero's attack that is even close to veracity. Piso's political career was very successful, and Cicero's claims that he was elected only because of his name are obviously tendentious. Piso seems to have governed Macedonia well: it was never a peaceful province, and Piso conducted important campaigns on the northern frontier, for which his acclamation as imperator was probably deserved. His command may have been defined more generously than was normal for governorships, but it is not at all clear that the unstable Macedonian frontier was not a legitimate target for intensive military activity. As a philosopher, Piso may not have been as original as Cicero himself, but his Epicureanism was serious, and Philodemus (his Greek philosophical adviser, unnamed in the speech) has become recognized in recent years as a genuinely interesting thinker, as the epigrams Cicero ridicules have become more respected as serious poetry. Piso was himself a man of intelligence and learning; at his villa in Herculaneum are preserved (in carbonized and fragmentary form) most of what remains of Philodemus' works. A decade after this speech, in 44, when Piso stood for the Republic against Mark Antony, even Cicero had to acknowledge his seriousness, courage, and political integrity. But then, of course, they were on the same side.

In L. Calpurnium Pisonem Oratio

[Approximately 10 percent of the speech is missing at the beginning and is represented only by the nineteen quotations given here.[5] The order and numbering of these fragments are those of Nisbet's (1961) edition.]

1. By the everlasting gods! Today's dawn, my fellow senators, I have yearned for: to see before me this mutant of the senate house, this monstrosity of the city, this freak of Rome!

2. I wanted nothing more;[6] perhaps you would rather hear he had been tortured to death or drowned at sea.

---

5. Two others sometimes included are not genuine and are omitted here; see Nisbet's commentary. As quotations, they lack context and are sometimes not even complete sentences. Reconstruction of their meaning is often uncertain.

6. More than has already happened to Piso. Throughout the speech, Cicero redescribes a great many unexceptionable (and sometimes laudable) actions as disasters and then further classifies them as a form of punishment of Piso.

3. Look at the wretch: although he couldn't speak, he couldn't shut up.[7]

4. His mind is shaken, a fog of crime mists his eyes, the burning torches of the Furies have stirred him up.

5. Is there a reef he didn't strike, is there a spear he didn't skewer himself with?

6. What did he dare deny—or rather, what didn't he admit?

7. Name anything more sluggish than he is, more filthy, more evil, more limp, more stupid, more furtive.

8. Is there even a tiny amount of genius in you? Genius? Is there any sign of a genuinely free man? Your complexion rejects your country, your speech your family, your character your name.[8]

9. There was once a certain Insubrian Gaul who was both a peddler and an auctioneer. When he had come to Rome with his daughter, he was so bold that he addressed a young man of the nobility, the son of Caesoninus the master thief. . . . He had his daughter engaged to this frivolous and unreliable man. . . . They say he was called Calventius.[9]

10. I'm not expressing scorn for Placentia, the town from which Piso usually boasts he was sprung: that's not my way, and a citizen town doesn't deserve it, especially one that has done a lot for me.

11. When he . . . happened to settle at Placentia, and a few years later—since he was then . . . —he rose to become a citizen there. First he was a Gaul, then he was Gaulish, and finally . . . held to be a citizen of Placentia.[10]

---

7. This and the following three fragments refer to the speech Piso had given criticizing Cicero—which Cicero chooses to describe as damning Piso himself.

8. His inherited cognomen Frugi means "thrifty."

9. Calventius was Piso's maternal grandfather, from the Latin colony of Placentia on the Po River; he was certainly not an Insubrian (the region of modern Milan) or, as Cicero suggests elsewhere, from Transalpine Gaul. His occupation as described here is a fiction of the invective. On the other hand, Piso's paternal grandfather Caesoninus may have been tried for extortion.

10. "Gaul" meaning someone not living in Roman territory; "Gaulish" (*Gallicanus*), a noncitizen inhabitant of one of the Roman provinces of Gaul

12. Of someone turbulent, seditious, conspiratorial, dangerous.

13. Did your father have a father-in-law who was more respectable than Gaius Piso . . . in that grief . . . I did not engage my daughter; he would, if I had had completely free choice, have been the one I would have chosen.[11]

14. Your mother, imported from god knows where, heaved out a sheep from her belly, not a man.

15. His Insubrian grandfather adopted the elder.[12]

16. When your whole family turned up in a farm wagon.

17. All that is faked and false and painted over.[13]

18. I thought he was a strict man, I thought he was stern, I thought he was serious; but I see an adulterer, I see a glutton, I see a man who hides his depravities behind walls, under the dirty rags of his friends, in the dark.

19. . . . is near me.

[1] Now do you see, you freak, what men object to in your face? Nobody minds having some Syrian from a gang of recent slaves made a consul. It's not your slavish, dark skin that deceived us, not your shaggy cheeks, not your rotting teeth: your eyes, your brows, your forehead, your whole face, which is a kind of silent speaking of your mind—that's what deceived men, that's what fooled, tricked, suckered men who didn't know you. A few of us knew your filthy vices, a few knew how sluggish your brain is, the numb feebleness of your tongue. Your voice was never heard in the forum, you never tried to offer any opinion, nothing you did on military service or at home was even known about, far from being famous. You crept into office through men's mistake, through support from the smoky masks of your ancestors—but you're like them only in your

---

(Cisalpine or Narbonensis). The first sentence is corrupt and something is missing.

11. Gaius Licinius Piso Frugi was Cicero's own son-in-law; he died while Cicero was in exile.

12. The elder child in this case is Piso himself; whatever the relationship between grandfather and grandson, there was no adoption and Cicero is inventing.

13. This and the next fragment describe Piso's deceptive appearance.

complexion.[14] **[2]** And is he even going to boast to me of being elected to every office without ever being defeated? I can claim that for myself with real glory: every time, the Roman people elected me, not my name.[15] When you were elected quaestor, even people who had never seen you put your name in office. You were made aedile: a Piso was elected by the Roman people, not this specific Piso. So, too, the praetorship was given to your ancestors: they were famous, if dead; you were alive, but nobody knew you yet. When the Roman people elected me quaestor at the top of the list, as the first of the two aediles, as the first praetor elected by the unanimous agreement of all the centuries who voted,[16] they were electing the person, not the family; my morals, not my ancestors; virtue they had seen, not nobility they had heard of. **[3]** Why should I say anything about the consulship, either winning it or conducting it? What a pathetic creature I am, comparing myself with this monstrous disaster! But I'm not trying to make a comparison, just pulling together things that are worlds apart. Your election as consul was declared—and I won't say anything worse than what everyone says—at a time when our country was in trouble, the two consuls were feuding, when you let the men who named you consul think you wouldn't deserve to live if you didn't turn out to be a nastier piece of work than Gabinius. I was the first to be declared consul by all Italy, by every rank of society, by the entire state, by voice even earlier than by ballot. But let's not talk about how each of us took office; let's admit that luck rules the polls. There's finer stuff to say about how we acted as consuls than how we got there.

[4] On January 1 I freed the senate and all respectable citizens from fear of the agrarian law and of indiscriminate distributions of public funds. If the Campanian territory should not have been distributed, then I preserved it; if it should, then I kept it for better

---

14. The masks are darkened from smoke; Piso is naturally swarthy.

15. The contrast between the noble who relies on his ancestors and the new man who relies on himself is an important part of the ideology of the new man, elaborated by Cicero in his description of Cato the Elder at the end of the Verrines.

16. The voting groups (centuries) voted sequentially, and once a majority was achieved, the voting stopped. For Cicero's election as praetor, see the opening of *In Support of Manilius' Law*.

people to propose.[17] In the case of Gaius Rabirius, a defendant on the charge of treason, I supported and defended against its enemies the senate resolution passed forty years before my consulship.[18] Those young men who, despite their character and courage, because of their misfortunes seemed likely to disturb public order if they became magistrates,[19] I banned from elections. They hated me, but felt no ill will toward the senate. **[5]** My colleague Antonius was greedy for a provincial command and was stirring up political trouble; by being patient, I kept him quiet. After the senate authorized money, provisions, and an army for the province of Gaul, I exchanged it with Antonius; but because I thought it was in the public interest, I resigned it in a public meeting over the loud objections of the Roman people.[20] When Catiline was planning, not in secret but openly, the slaughter of the senate and the destruction of the city, I ordered him to leave the city so that our walls could protect us even if our laws couldn't.[21] In the last month of my consulship I twisted from

---

17. Cicero refers to his speeches *On the Agrarian Law* opposing the proposal of the tribune Servilius Rullus to distribute publicly held Campanian land. The land was distributed by Caesar in 59. On Cicero's consular speeches, see the introduction to *Second Speech against Catiline*.

18. Gaius Rabirius Postumus took part in the riots resulting in the death of Saturninus in 100 BCE; he was prosecuted in 63 before the people under an archaic and obsolete statute against treason, but the trial was never completed. Cicero is here speaking of the so-called *senatus consultum ultimum* ("final resolution of the senate") instructing the consuls to make sure that no harm came to the state. It was used against the Gracchi and in the riots of 100 BCE (the occasion that Cicero is alluding to here); it was, not coincidentally, the instrument used by Cicero against Catiline in 63 and the object of vigorous legal and constitutional debate thereafter.

19. The children of men disenfranchised by Sulla were barred from electoral office; the attempt to change that was successfully resisted by Cicero.

20. Normal procedure required that the senate identify consular provinces for the subsequent year, but that they be assigned to the two consuls by lot. Cicero had won Macedonia, Antonius Cisalpine Gaul. The switch (Macedonia was more profitable) was part of the deal to keep Antonius, who sympathized with Catiline, quiet. Cicero then decided not to take any province—he never liked leaving Rome—and presents that decision as both unpopular and altruistic. The speech he refers to was part of the collection of consular speeches he made in 60 but does not survive.

21. The extant first speech against Catiline.

the criminal hands of the conspirators weapons that were aimed at
the throat of the state; the torches that were already lit to burn the
city I grasped, brought out in public, and put out.²² **[6]** In the presence of a crowded senate, Quintus Catulus, the leading member of
this order and a man of great influence in public affairs, named me
"father of my country." Lucius Gellius, a distinguished man who is
sitting near you, said in the presence of this body that I was owed a
civic crown by the nation.²³ I am the only civilian in whose honor
the senate opened the temples of the everlasting gods in a unique
form of thanksgiving. Before that, many generals had been honored
for military success, but I was honored for saving our country. At
a public meeting at the end of my term of office, when a tribune
forbade me to say what I had meant to and permitted me only to
swear my oath, I didn't hesitate to swear that the nation and the city
were preserved by my efforts alone.²⁴ **[7]** At that meeting the entire
Roman people presented me not with one day of congratulations but
with real immortality in voicing its unanimous approval of my oath,
when they took the same oath themselves. At that time my return
home from the forum was such that no one who didn't accompany
me was thought to be a citizen. In my entire consulship I did nothing without the advice of the senate, nothing without the approval
of the Roman people. I constantly supported the senate when I was

22. Cicero is referring to the arrest of five of the conspirators with incrimi-
nating evidence on December 3, 63. This and the following section are
concerned exclusively with the events of the last month of Cicero's consulship: the capture and execution of the conspirators, the honors offered to
Cicero, and the refusal of the new tribune Metellus Nepos to allow Cicero
to give a speech to the people on his last day in office. It is worth noting that
in this account of his consulship (and particularly of his consular speeches),
Cicero echoes the list of consular speeches that he was drawing together
into a single collection in 60 (see *ad Att.* 2.1.3). Understandably, he here
omits the speech in support of Roscius' law reserving the front rows in the
theater for Roman *equites*.

23. The *corona civica*, made of oak leaves, was awarded for saving the lives
of citizens in battle.

24. The tribune was Quintus Caecilius Metellus Nepos, consul in 57. In
63, as tribune, he hoped to have Pompey recalled to deal with Catiline and
hence encouraged action against Cicero. The consul's normal oath was that
he had not done anything contrary to the laws; Cicero expanded on the oath
in lieu of the speech he had hoped to give.

speaking from the public platform, and the people when I was in the senate. My goal was to join together the crowd and the leaders, the equestrian order and the senate.

[8] That, in brief, is the story of my consulship. Are you crazy enough to dare now to talk about yours? It started with the Compitalician Games, celebrated for the first time since the consulship of Lucius Julius and Gaius Marcius, against the advice and consent of this body.[25] When the late Quintus Metellus—and I do an injustice to that great man in comparing him, a man who has had very few equals in our history, with this misguided freak—was consul-designate, a certain tribune of the people used the power of his office to make the magistrates hold the games against the decree of the senate; as a private citizen, Metellus forbade their being held, and what he could not yet do by the power of office he did with his own authority.[26] But you, since the day of the Compitalia fell on January 1, permitted Sextus Cloelius, a man who had never worn a bordered toga, to hold the games and go flitting about in that new bordered toga, a filthy man who is as worthy of being kissed by you as he is of looking like you.[27] [9] Once this foundation for your consulship had been set, three days later, while you watched and said nothing, that monstrous mutant, an omen of doom to our country, overturned the Aelian and Fufian laws, laws that were the bulwark and protection of civic order and peace.[28] The fraternal societies

---

25. The Compitalia, a festival in honor of the Lares and celebrated at crossroads, took place during the winter on a date set annually by the praetor; in 58 it was January 1. It was a cult celebrated above all by slaves and freedmen, and the associated games had been banned in 64 BCE (the year given by consular date in the text) in the interest of public order. Clodius revived the games in 58.

26. At the end of 61, Quintus Caecilius Metellus Celer as consul-designate blocked an attempt by an unknown tribune to hold the games.

27. The purple-bordered *toga praetexta* was an indicator of high office but was also worn by those in charge of celebrating games (and by children). Sextus Cloelius (not Clodius, as in many manuscripts) was an active supporter of Clodius.

28. The mutant in question is Cicero's nemesis, Publius Clodius Pulcher. The Aelian and Fufian laws (two distinct laws, although often referred to as a single law) gave magistrates the right (used by Bibulus in 59) to stop elections by announcing that they were watching for omens. Cicero exaggerates

were restored, not just the ones the senate had eliminated, but new
ones beyond counting stirred up from every sewer and slave gang
of Rome. This same man, such an expert in inventive and wicked
forms of sex, was responsible for getting rid of our ancient teacher
of decency and modesty, the censorship;[29] and meanwhile you, the
funeral pyre of the nation, despite saying you were then a consul at
Rome, never uttered a word about your views while the ship of state
was going down.

[10] So far, I've only talked about what you let happen, not what
you did yourself. And yet there isn't a whole lot of difference, particularly when we're talking about a consul, whether he savages the
commonwealth by destructive laws and evil speeches himself or lets
others do it. We don't need to talk about disloyal consuls; but can
there be any excuse for a consul who just sits and stalls and sleeps
while the country is in complete chaos? For nearly a hundred years
we held on to the Aelian and Fufian laws, for four hundred years to
the judgments and scrutiny of the censors. A lot of bad men tried
to uproot these laws, but none succeeded, and nobody was so indis-
criminately violent that he tried to stop the censors from making
judgments about our character every fifth year. [11] But this, you
cutthroat, is what was buried as the preface to your consulship. Now
follow the calendar right after this funeral. Before the Aurelian tribunal, while you weren't even drifting off (which would have been a
crime itself), you watched with an unusually bright twinkle in your
eyes while slaves were drafted by the man who never thought there
was something wrong with anything he did—or with anything done
to him.[30] You betrayed all our temples. Under your eyes an armory
was organized in the temple of Castor by that highwayman who used
the temple while you were consul as a stronghold for citizens beyond
redemption, a safe house for Catiline's old soldiers, a fort for robbery
in the forum, a funeral pyre for all the laws and for all religion.[31]

---

whatever Clodius in fact did; the laws were not abolished, although they
may have been amended.

29. Overstated: Clodius' law required that formal trial was necessary before
the censors could expel anyone from the senate.

30. Clodius is the unnamed villain of this section; Piso is just looking on
and giving tacit permission.

31. Clodius used the temple of Castor in the forum as his base of operations;
he removed the steps to secure it for his own uses.

Not only my house but the entire Palatine Hill was jammed with members of the senate, with Roman knights, with the entire state and all Italy,[32] but you not only never tried to help a man you had asked to look after the tally of the first century when you were elected, whom you had called upon in third place in the senate[33] (and I set aside private matters that you would deny and mention only what is in the public record): not only did you not try to help, but you were implicated in all the plans for my destruction and with great cruelty even led the whole attack.

[12] And what was it you dared say to me in front of my son-in-law, your relative? That Gabinius was needy and out in the cold[34] and would be bankrupt without a province; that there was a tribune of the plebs[35] who gave him hope, if they coordinated their plans, but that he had given up on the senate; that you were going along with his greed just as I had done for my own colleague; that there was no point in seeking help from the consuls: it was every man for himself. I hardly dare say this; I'm afraid that there's still somebody who doesn't yet see the incredible depravity wrapped up in the furrows of his brow; but I will speak anyway. He will certainly find it familiar and will experience a certain amount of pain in recalling his crimes. [13] Do you remember, you slime, when I came to see you with Gaius Piso[36] just before noon? You crept out of some fleabag with your head hidden and wearing sandals, and from your rotting mouth you breathed over us the disgusting stench of a greasy kitchen. You used the excuse of your health; you said your regular cure involved alcohol-based medicine. We accepted your explanation—what choice did we have?—and stood for a while in the smoky fumes of your dirty saloon; you drove us away not just with your perverted replies, but by your revolting belches. [14] The same thing two days later. You were introduced in a public assembly by the man you had

---

32. To defend Cicero against the possibility of exile.

33. The presiding consul chose the order of the roll call among senators of equal rank. We do not know who was first or second, although Pompey was probably one of them.

34. Retaining *egere* and following Shackleton Bailey (1965–70) 2:221–22 in the interpretation of *foris esse*.

35. Still Clodius.

36. Cicero's son-in-law.

handed your consulship to on a platter,[37] and when asked your opinion of my consulship, you answered like some voice of weighty responsibility, some Calatinus or Africanus or Maximus[38] and not Caesoninus Half-Breed Baldhead. With one eyebrow raised up to your forehead and the other pushed down to your chin, you answered that you did not approve of cruel and unusual punishment. At that, you received praise from the man who most deserved your praise.[39] You jailbird, as consul in a public meeting you condemn the senate for cruel and unusual punishment? It's not me: I was obeying the senate; the motion was thoughtful and in the public interest; it was introduced by the consul, but the punishment and the judgment were the senate's.[40] When you criticize this, you show what kind of consul you would have been at that moment, if things had fallen out that way: I bet you would have thought Catiline deserved pay and rations to help him. **[15]** How much difference was there between Catiline and the man you sold—at the price of a province—the authority of the senate, the well-being of the state, the whole country? What I stopped Catiline from trying to do when I was consul, you two consuls helped Clodius do. He wanted to kill the senate; you eliminated it. He wanted to smash the laws; you suspended them. He wanted to terrify his country by his violence; what happened while you were consuls that didn't involve weapons? That gang of conspirators wanted to burn the city; you burned the house of the man who kept the city from being burned.[41] If they had had a consul like you two, even they wouldn't have thought about burning the city: they had no desire to make themselves homeless, but they thought that if Rome were still standing there would be no home for their crimes. They wanted to slaughter the citizens; you wanted to enslave them. In this you're even more cruel than they were: before the two of you were consuls, liberty was so ingrained in our people that death was preferable to slavery. **[16]** And this is where your plans and those of

---

37. The text is corrupt, but the sense is fairly clear.

38. Great generals of the Punic Wars.

39. Gabinius. Cicero's account of this assembly carefully omits the fact that Caesar also spoke.

40. Cicero is speaking of the debate on the punishment of the conspirators in December of 63.

41. Cicero's own house, burned after he went into exile.

Catiline and Lentulus are twins: you drove me out of my home and drove Pompey into his;[42] they believed that, as long as I was still standing and watching over the city, and as long as Pompey, the conqueror of the world, opposed them, they could never destroy the commonwealth. Of course you were also trying to punish me so as to appease the spirits of the dead conspirators; you poured out on me all the hatred those wicked men's evil minds had held in. If I had not given way to their madness, then you would have led the way to my being sacrificed on the tomb of Catiline.[43] What stronger evidence are you waiting for that there was no difference at all between you and Catiline than that you roused up the same old gang from the half-dead survivors of Catiline; that you gathered together all the dregs from every side; that you drained the jail and armed conspirators against me; that you wanted to throw my body and the lives of all respectable citizens in the path of their insane violence? **[17]** But let me get back to that grand public speech of yours. You're the man who dislikes cruel and unusual punishment? When the senate decided to declare their grief and pain through putting on mourning, when you, a man of such compassion, saw the nation grieving along with the senate's laments, what did you do? Something no tyrant in barbarian lands ever did. Let's not talk about a consul decreeing that a decision of the senate should not be obeyed, a thing that's so disgusting that nothing worse can happen or even be imagined, but I return to the compassion of a man who thinks the senate was too cruel when it saved our country. **[18]** Together with his matching colleague (although he wanted to outstrip him in every vice), he dared to order the senate, against its own decision, to return to its normal clothing. What tyrant in some Scythia ever did this, not to permit people to grieve when he caused the grief? You leave the sorrow, you eliminate the signs of sorrow; you take away their tears not by consolation but by threats. If the members of the senate had put on mourning because of private obligation or pity rather than through public decision, to forbid that by imposing your power would have been a cruel and unendurable punishment. But when a

---

42. Pompey was afraid of being assassinated and stayed indoors from August until December of 58. Clodius, not Piso, was responsible for the disturbances.

43. After his return, Cicero consistently portrays his departure as a decision made in the interests of the country rather than for his personal safety.

crowded senate had voted it and all the other orders had already done so, you, the consul dragged out of your murky dive, together with your well-trimmed dancing girl,[44] forbade the senate of the Roman people to mourn the decline and death of the commonwealth. And yet he used to ask me, not long before this, why I needed his help; why I had not fought off my enemies with my own resources. As if not only I, who had often given help to many people—could anyone ever have been so helpless as to think he would either be safer with a defender like Piso or better prepared with him as a supporter in court or as an associate in business? [19] Did I want to rely on the advice or protection of this dumb sheep, this rotting carcass? Did I seek some backing or support from this discarded corpse? Then I was looking for a consul, a consul, I repeat, not the kind I certainly couldn't find in this boar without balls, one who would support this great cause of our nation with his stature and wisdom, but at least one who, as if he were a tree trunk or a post in the ground, could hold up a sign saying "consul" so long as he stayed upright. Since my entire cause was that of the consulship and the senate, I needed the help of the consulship and the senate. But one of that pair had been twisted by you consuls to be a source of my destruction, while the other had been snatched clean out of the country. And if you're asking about my thinking, I would not have left, our country would have held me in its embrace, if my fight had been only with that graveyard gladiator[45] and with you and your colleague. [20] The case of Quintus Metellus, a truly great man and a citizen whose praise in my judgment should be linked with that of the everlasting gods, was different. He decided to give way to the great Gaius Marius, a warrior who was then consul and consul for the sixth time, and to his undefeated army, to avoid a pitched battle.[46] What similar contest faced me? Was it with a Marius or someone like him, or was it with a barbarian second Epicurus[47] with his fellow consul who used to carry a torch for Catiline? I didn't run away from your eyebrow or

---

44. Gabinius again. As he is being accused of effeminacy and had curls, "trimmed" probably refers to portions of his body other than his head.

45. Clodius.

46. Metellus Numidicus went into exile in 100 rather than swear an oath to support Saturninus' agrarian law, which was supported by Marius.

47. On Piso's Epicureanism, see below, particularly secs. 68–72.

from your colleague's castanets; given that I had steered the ship of state in a huge storm and waves and brought it safe to port, I was not so timid as to fear your overcast forehead or the polluted breath of your colleague. **[21]** There were other winds I saw, other squalls that I foresaw in my mind; I did not give way to the looming storms but offered myself to them as the sole sacrifice for the safety of all.[48] And so, as a result of my departure at that time, all the weapons of evil fell from those savage hands; and at that time you, in your complete madness, when all responsible citizens shut themselves in their houses in grief, the temples were sighing, the very houses of the city were mourning—that was when you hugged that poisonous creature compounded of illicit sex, civil war, the cruelty of every crime and the immorality of every vice; and in the same temple, the same place and time, you carried off the fee not just for my funeral but for our country's as well.[49]

[22] Why should I describe the banquets of those days, your happiness and self-satisfaction, the extremely drunken binges with your utterly revolting crew? In those days who saw you sober, who saw you doing anything worthy of a free man, who even saw you in public at all? When the house of your colleague echoed with song and cymbals, when he himself danced naked at the banquet, and even when he did his famous acrobatic tricks with a hoop,[50] even then he had no fear of the wheel of fortune. But Piso isn't such a pretty glutton and he can't carry a tune; he just wallowed in the stench and wine of his beloved Greeks. In that time of grief for the commonwealth his feast was talked about as if it were some banquet of the Centaurs or Lapiths; and nobody can say whether he drank more than he puked.[51] **[23]** Do you even mention your consulship, or do you dare say that you were consul at Rome? Do you think being consul is just having lictors and a fancy toga? While you were consul

---

48. Cicero describes his action in terms of the ancient practice of *devotio*, a general accepting death in return for the victory of his army.

49. Clodius' law exiling those who had put citizens to death without trial and his law conferring the command of Macedonia on Piso were passed simultaneously to avoid any double-crossing.

50. The precise nature of Gabinius' performance is unclear, but it probably involved a hoop usually used by dancing girls.

51. A famous mythological brawl resulted from the Centaurs getting drunk at the Lapiths' banquet.

you wanted even Sextus Cloelius to have that: do you identify the consulship with the decorations worn by Clodius' lapdog? It's the spirit that makes a consul—wisdom, integrity, seriousness, alertness, diligence—in short, watching over every function of the consulship with your entire sense of duty, and particularly (as the meaning of the title shows) in taking counsel for your country. Should I think someone is a consul who doesn't think there's a senate in the commonwealth, should I count him a consul without the council that even kings required at Rome? But let that pass. When slaves were being drafted in the forum, weapons were being carried into the temple of Castor in broad daylight, the temple was closed off, its steps were torn up, and it was being held by force of arms by what was left of the conspiracy and by Catiline's former phony prosecutor and later avenger;[52] when Roman knights were being sent into exile,[53] responsible citizens were being driven from the forum by stoning, the senate barred not only from helping the country but even from mourning for it; when the citizen the senate, with the agreement of Italy and all the Italian peoples, had judged to be the savior of his country—when this man without trial, without law, without precedent was driven out by slaves under arms with what I won't call your help, although that's what it was, but certainly with your silence: will anyone claim that at that point in time there were consuls in Rome? **[24]** If you're called consuls, then what will we call bandits, pirates, enemies, traitors, and tyrants? The title of consul is great; its appearance is great; its worth is great; its solemnity is great: your puny chest can't contain it, you're too lightweight to hold it; your lack of spirit, your weakness of mind, your arrogance at good fortune can't sustain so important a role, so serious and so stern. When the street of the perfumers[54] in Capua, as I have heard, saw you for the first time, they rejected their

---

52. Clodius had prosecuted Catiline for extortion in 65, and Catiline was acquitted. Cicero claims that it was a collusive prosecution, designed to get Catiline off. Throughout the narrative of the events of 58, Cicero tries to link his enemies in 58 with his enemy Catiline in 63; the links are not always as clear as he would wish.

53. One knight, Lucius Aelius Lamia, was banished two hundred miles from Rome by Gabinius for fomenting disturbances in Cicero's favor.

54. The street Seplasia in Capua was famous for its unguents and perfumes.

Campanian consul.[55] They had heard of men like Decius Magius and they knew something about the famous Vibellius Taurea;[56] and even if they did not exhibit the modesty normal in Roman consuls, there was still ceremony and pomp and a gait worthy of the perfumers and of Capua. **[25]** In fact, if your perfumers had seen Gabinius as their magistrate, they would have recognized him sooner. His hair was combed and the tips of his curls were oozing perfume; his cheeks were flabby and rouged, worthy of Capua, at least of old Capua: the present city is overflowing with grand people, with men of great courage, with highly responsible citizens who are friendly to me. At Capua not one of these men looked on you in your striped toga without sighing with desire for me; they remembered that it was my foresight that had saved both the nation as a whole and Capua, too. They had given me a gilded statue, they had recognized me as their one and only patron, they believed they owed their lives, their fortunes, and their children to me; when I was present they had defended me against your banditry by their decrees and embassies, and when I had gone they recalled me on the motion of their magistrate Gnaeus Pompeius,[57] who was pulling the weapons of your crimes from the body of the nation. **[26]** Were you consul when my house was burning on the Palatine, not by accident but because you urged on the arsonists? Has there ever been any bigger fire in this city when the consul did not bring help? At that moment you were at your mother-in-law's house not far from my home; you had opened up her house to empty my house, you were sitting there not to put out the fire but as the person who set the fire, and as consul you were all but handing burning torches to Clodius' Furies. For the rest of your time in office, was there anyone who thought you were consul? Did anyone follow your orders? When you came into the senate house did anyone stand up? Did anyone think that motions presented by you deserved a response? Must we count that a year in the history of this commonwealth when the senate had been struck dumb, the courts had fallen silent, the respectable citizens were in mourning,

---

55. There was a new Roman colony at Capua, ruled by a pair of magistrates (*duumviri*) modeled on the consuls at Rome. Piso was a *duumvir* at Capua at the same time he was consul in Rome.

56. Decius Magius was a Capuan supporter of Rome, and Vibellius Taurea a supporter of Carthage, during the Second Punic War.

57. Pompey succeeded Piso as *duumvir* at Capua.

the violence of your robbers flitted over the whole city? It was not a single citizen of this nation but the nation itself that retreated in the face of your and Gabinius' criminal insanity.

[27] You mud-plastered eunuch,[58] you didn't drag yourself out of the wretched filth of your own character even when at last the great man's virtue woke up[59] and quickly looked for his true friend—a citizen of sterling merit—and for the character he used to have; and he didn't permit the plague of your crimes to linger any longer in the nation he had himself enhanced and enlarged. Meanwhile, that [expletive deleted][60] who is more evil than anyone but you, could hardly pull himself together, but succeeded; and first in a fake way, then reluctantly, and finally with real energy he fought against his beloved Clodius on behalf of Pompey. As they watched that contest, the Roman people were amazingly evenhanded: whichever one died, they thought that, like the trainer of such a pair of gladiators, they would win something, and if both fell, the profit would last forever. [28] But at least Gabinius was getting somewhere: he was supporting the authority of an outstanding man. He was himself a criminal and a gladiator, but he was fighting against another criminal and his equal as a gladiator. But you, devout and holy man that you are, refused to break a treaty you had sealed with my blood in your deal over the provinces: that man who loved his sisters[61] had made a deal for himself that, if he gave you a province, an army, and money ripped from the guts of the commonwealth, then you would be his henchman and back him up in all his crimes. And so in that riot the *fasces* were broken, Gabinius was beaten; every day there were weapons, stones, flight, and finally a man was caught with a sword near the senate, and it was clear he'd been hired to kill

---

58. The text is uncertain; this translation represents one of several possible interpretations.

59. Pompey became more favorably inclined toward Cicero almost immediately after the latter went into exile, in part because he rapidly became disenchanted with Clodius.

60. *Qualiscumque est,* literally, "whatever kind he is." Gabinius followed Pompey's lead; the riot described here took place in late spring or early summer of 58.

61. Clodius. For his incest with his sister(s), see the introduction to *In Defense of Marcus Caelius.*

Pompey.[62] **[29]** Did anyone at all hear, not of your doing anything
or making a proposal to the senate, but even a word or a whine? Do
you think that you were then consul, when during the time you held
power the man who had preserved the nation with the backing of the
senate decided he could not be safe in Italy; and when the man who
had won the support of all parts of all nations in his three triumphs
decided that he could not appear in public safely? Or were you then
consuls when, whatever subject you began to talk about or bring
before the senate, the whole order shouted its opposition and showed
you would get nothing done unless you brought a motion about me
before the senate first? When you, even though you were held tight
by your bargain, still said that you wanted to, but were blocked by
the law? **[30]** Plain citizens didn't think it was a law: it was branded
on us by slaves, inscribed by violence, forced on us by robbers, when
the senate had been eliminated, all responsible people driven from
the forum, the commonwealth held captive, a law written against all
the laws, in accordance with no tradition—can men who claim to
fear this law be accepted as consuls, I won't say by men's minds, but
even by the calendars of Rome? If you didn't think that a law that
was a totally illegal tribunician proscription of a citizen who had not
been condemned and who had full civic status and property, and yet
you still were held fast by your deal, who could think of you as free
men, not to speak of consuls, men whose minds were overpowered
by a reward, whose tongue was tied by money? But if you were the
only people to view this as a law, then who would think you were
then consuls or are now ex-consuls, men who don't know the laws,
the institutions, the customs, the rights of the state of which you
claim to be leading citizens? **[31]** When you set out in uniform to
provinces that you had bought or stolen, did anyone think of you
as consuls? I suppose that even if there was no crowd to honor and
distinguish your departure, at least they followed you with good
omens as consuls, not with dire ones as enemies and traitors.

And did you, foul and disgusting mutant that you are, even dare
to turn my departure, which bore witness to your criminal cruelty,
into an occasion to smear and insult me? My fellow senators, that was
a moment when I received the immortal reward of your love for me
and your judgment of me; it wasn't by murmurs but with loud voice

---

62. The last incident took place on August 11, 58, and led to Pompey's
withdrawal to his house (above, sec. 16).

and shouting that you shattered the shameless lunacy of this broken and half-dead man. **[32]** The grief of the senate, the longing felt by the equestrian order, the desolation of Italy, the year-long muteness of the senate, the continuous silence of the permanent courts and the forum—you will use these and all the rest of the wounds that my departure inflicted on the commonwealth as grounds to smear me? Even if it had been the most damaging event possible, it still should be thought to deserve sympathy more than insult and to be accompanied by glory rather than disgrace; and of this the pain was mine alone, but the crime and dishonor is all yours. And although what I'm going to say may sound strange, I will still say what I think: since I have received such great signs of your favor, fellow senators, and such great honors, not only do I not consider it to be a disaster, but if anything of me can be separated from the commonwealth (not really possible) then I believe that privately, for the sake of my personal reputation, I should have wished for it and sought it out. **[33]** Let me compare your best day and my worst: do you think it more desirable for a reputable and wise man to leave his country with all his fellow citizens praying for his well-being, his safety, and his return, as happened to me, or what happened to you when you set out, that everybody cursed you, prayed for evil for you, wanted your path to be a dead-end one-way street? So help me, if I received so much hatred from every human being, particularly when it is right and deserved, then I would prefer exile of any sort to any province at all.

But keep going. If that moment of greatest upheaval in my life is better than your calmest day, why should I compare the rest? In your case it was full of disgrace, in mine of dignity. **[34]** January 1 brought the first light of day to our country after its death and destruction. With a crowd gathered from all Italy, on the motion of Publius Lentulus—a man of great distinction and courage—the heavily attended senate summoned me back with one concordant voice.[63] It was the senate, too, that by its resolution commended me to foreign nations, to our legates, and to our magistrates. I was not, as you the Insubrian had the gall to say, a man without a country, but as the senate at that point in time described me, a citizen and savior of the commonwealth. For my safety, the safety of one man, the senate, speaking through the voice and letter of the consul,

---

63. Lentulus became consul on January 1, 57, and strongly supported Cicero's recall.

appealed for the help of all citizens throughout Italy who wanted the commonwealth to be safe. To preserve my life, all Italy converged on Rome at the same moment, as if a signal had been given. Concerning my safety, public meetings with huge crowds and great popularity were held by Lentulus (a great man and an outstanding consul), Pompey (our most illustrious and victorious citizen), and other leaders of the state. **[35]** About me the senate made a decree (written and proposed by Pompey) that anyone who obstructed my return would be considered an enemy of the state; that resolution of the senate about me is written in such language that nobody has had a triumph decreed in more congratulatory language than were my safety and reinstatement. All the magistrates proposed a law about me—all except one praetor who couldn't be expected to join because he's the brother of my enemy, and except for two tribunes who had been bought from the auction block[64]—and Lentulus the consul carried it by vote of the centuriate assembly with the concurrence of his colleague Quintus Metellus:[65] we differed when he was tribune in our sense of the public interest, but he is a wise and virtuous man of great justice, and in his consulship the same sense of the public good brought us together. **[36]** Is there any point in my reporting the reception of that law? You tell me that no citizen had a sufficient excuse to explain his absence, and that at no election had there ever been such a large and glorious multitude of men. I see for myself what the public records show, that you supervised the voting yourselves, you did the tallying yourselves, you guarded the ballots yourselves; in a matter concerning my well-being without being asked, of your own will you did what you don't do in the elections of your relatives either because of your age or because of your rank.

---

64. The praetor was Appius Claudius (Clodius' brother); the tribunes were Sextus Atilius Serranus and Quintus Numerius Rufus.

65. The tribunes first proposed a bill for Cicero's recall in early January, but it was delayed because of rioting fomented by Clodius and by political maneuvering; ultimately, the bill was brought by all the magistrates (with the three exceptions mentioned by Cicero) at the instructions of the senate in July and passed by the centuriate assembly (the assembly that elected consuls and praetors; an unusual venue for voting on laws) on August 4, 57. Quintus Caecilius Metellus Nepos, the other consul of 57, had been the tribune who stopped Cicero from giving his speech at the end of his consulship in 63.

[37] Now, if you dare, you Epicurean from the pigpen, not the schoolroom, compare your absence from Rome with mine. You received a consular province with limits defined by the law of your own greed rather than the ones set by the law of your son-in-law.[66] According to Caesar's law—a very just and excellent law—free peoples were well and truly free, but according to the law that nobody thought to be a law except for you and your colleague, all of Achaea, Thessaly, Athens, and all Greece was assigned to you; you had an army not the size that the senate or the Roman people had given you, but the size your own desires enrolled: you drained the treasury.[67] [38] And what did you accomplish with your command, your army, your consular province? Do I ask what he accomplished? As soon as he arrived—but let's not talk about his plundering, his extortion, his thefts and demands for money; not his murders of our allies, his slaughter of his guests. I'm not saying anything about his deceit, his brutality, his crimes. Later, if it seems useful, I will speak as one should to a thief, a desecrator, a highwayman, but now I'll compare my ravaged fortunes with the flourishing fortune of a commander. Did anyone ever control a province with an army without sending a single dispatch to the senate? Such a large province with such a large army! Especially Macedonia, which has so many barbarian tribes on its frontiers that for commanders in Macedonia the border of the province has always been marked by the points of their swords and spears. Aside from a few ex-praetors, nobody with consular authority—at least if he wasn't convicted—has come back without a triumph. That's one new thing about Piso; but wait, there's more. This vulture feeding on his province was acclaimed (gods forgive me) as "commander";[68] [39] even then, you modern Aemilius Paullus,[69]

66. The Julian law on extortion of 59 limited the power of governors in making war and in interfering in the affairs of free cities within their provinces.

67. Clodius' law giving Piso the province of Macedonia gave him the right to enroll an army (normally given by the senate) and unclear but extended powers over the free cities of Greece. It is not clear whether the stipend of 18 million sesterces was unduly large for a military province.

68. *Imperator*—not an official title but one conferred by acclamation of the troops. Translated as "commander" here; there is no precise English equivalent.

69. Lucius Aemilius Paullus accomplished the final defeat of Macedon at Pydna in 168.

didn't you dare send a dispatch with laurel to Rome? "I sent one," he says. Who ever recited it, who ever demanded its recital? It doesn't matter to me if the weight of guilt on your mind kept you from daring to write to the order you had despised, assaulted, destroyed, or if your friends hid the dispatch and by their silence also condemned your rashness and folly. I don't know if I would prefer you to seem to have had no shame in sending dispatches and your friends greater shame and wisdom, or for you to seem more capable of shame than usual, or for your action not to have been condemned by the judgment of your friends. **[40]** And if you hadn't shut the senate house door to yourself forever by your wicked attacks on this order, what achievement or battle in your province was there that you should have written about with satisfaction? The pillaging of Macedonia, or the disgraceful loss of towns, the plundering of our allies, the depopulation of the countryside, the fortification of Thessalonica, the cutting of a military highway, our army's succumbing to war, starvation, cold, and disease?[70] Just as in the city you turned out to be more vile than Gabinius, so, in that you wrote nothing at all to the senate, in the province you seem a little more humble than he. **[41]** Born for his belly and not for praise or glory, he sucked up food and money; when he had stripped of their fortunes the Roman knights in his province and all the tax-farmers, men linked with the senate by shared standing and interest, when he had stripped many of their reputations and their lives, when he had done nothing else with his army except to decimate cities, destroy farms, empty houses—after all this he dared (what wouldn't he dare?) to send a dispatch to the senate asking for a thanksgiving.[71] By the everlasting gods! You, in fact both of you, whirlpools that suck the commonwealth down and reefs that break it up,[72] have you really sunk my fortune and raised yours up when there have been such resolutions of the senate about me in my absence, such public meetings, such an upheaval in all the towns and colonies, such decrees by the tax collectors, of the business associations, of every sort and rank as I would never dare wish for and couldn't even have imagined, while you have been branded for all time because of

---

70. Cicero's account of Piso's career in Macedonia (here and secs. 83–91 below) is obviously tendentious. Nisbet (1961) 172–80 provides a careful and detailed discussion.

71. For the award of a thanksgiving (*supplicatio*), see sec. 45 and notes.

72. That is, Scylla and Charybdis.

your revolting baseness? **[42]** If I saw you and Gabinius nailed to crosses,[73] would I experience greater happiness from the mutilation of your bodies than I feel from the mutilation of your reputation? We shouldn't think of anything as a punishment if it can happen to good and brave men by chance. Even those pleasure-loving Greeks of yours say this—and I wish you had listened to them the way they should be listened to; then you would never have sunk yourself in such crimes. But you hear them while you wallow in the mud, you hear while you roll in the hay, you hear while you stuff yourselves with food and wine. But those same people who equate evil with pain and good with pleasure say that the wise man, even if he were shut in Phalaris' bull and roasted by the fire underneath, will say how nice it is and that he isn't the tiniest bit upset. So much power they claim virtue has that the good man can never not be happy.[74]

[43] What, then, is a punishment, what is torture? In my opinion it's something that can happen to no one except the guilty: the embrace of criminality, a mind that is entangled and weighed down, the hatred of respectable citizens, being branded with disgrace by the senate, the loss of worthy standing. I don't believe the famous Regulus was truly tortured, even though the Carthaginians cut off his eyelids, stuck him in a cage, and killed him by making him stay awake.[75] Neither was Marius, although the Italy he had saved witnessed him sunk in the swamps of Minturnae, and the Africa he had defeated witnessed him exiled and shipwrecked.[76] Those are the weapons of fortune, not of faults, but torture is the punishment for doing something wrong. For my own part, if I ever prayed for your harm, which I often did—and the gods heard my prayers—I never prayed for disease

---

73. A punishment for slaves.

74. Piso's Epicureanism is turned against him: even though Epicurus equates virtue with pleasure, he still believes that even his sort of virtue can create happiness out of pain. A much fuller assault on Piso's philosophical pretensions and misunderstandings begins at sec. 56.

75. Marcus Atilius Regulus is the paradigm of Roman courage and honor: captured by the Carthaginians in the First Punic War then sent by them to Rome to urge an exchange of prisoners, he argued against the exchange and returned to his death at Carthage. Cicero used him as an extended example at *Off.* 3.99–115.

76. Marius was in hiding from Sulla after the latter's first march on Rome in 88.

or death or torture. This is the curse of a Thyestes, of a poet moving the hearts of the crowd, not of wise men: "May you be cast off
in a shipwreck somewhere, impaled on sharp rocks, gutted, hanging
from your side," as the poet says, "sprinkling the rocks with pus and
gore and dark blood."[77] **[44]** Of course I wouldn't mind it if things
turned out that way; but that would simply be a function of being
human. Marcus Marcellus, three times consul, a man of the highest
virtue and sense of duty and military glory, drowned at sea; even so,
because of his virtue he lives on in praise and glory.[78] That death must
be considered a matter of bad luck, not a punishment. Then what is a
punishment? What is torture, or reefs, or crosses? That there are two
generals in provinces of the Roman people who hold armies, who are
addressed as commanders; that one of them was held back so much by
consciousness of his crimes and corruption that he didn't dare send a
single report to the senate from the province that produces the most
triumphs. That's the province from which Lucius Torquatus, a man
of the highest worth, just now received the title of commander from
the senate on my motion for his great military accomplishments;[79] the
province from which in recent years we have seen the highly deserved
triumphs of Gnaeus Dolabella, Gaius Curio, and Marcus Lucullus,
but from which when you were commander not a single message
was brought to the senate. The other one sent dispatches; they were
read aloud and the senate was consulted.[80] **[45]** By the gods, could
I ever have wished my enemy to be branded with an unprecedented
form of disgrace, that the senate not believe the dispatches of one
particular man and deny honors to those who demand them, despite
having been so habitually generous that it gives new honors, new in
the length of the celebration and the language used, to those who
have served their country well?[81] I am nourished by events like this,

---

77. The exact beginning of the quotation from Ennius' tragedy *Thyestes* is
unclear; a longer version (from "impaled") is found at *Tusc.* 1.107.

78. Marcus Claudius Marcellus, consul in 166, 155, and 152, drowned while
on an embassy to Africa.

79. Lucius Manlius Torquatus, consul in 65 then proconsul in Macedonia.
Cicero was consul when he proposed the honor.

80. After a successful campaign in Judaea, Gabinius asked the senate for a
supplicatio (thanksgiving); it was rejected in May of 56.

81. The claim that no application for a *supplicatio* had ever been turned down
before Gabinius' is wrong, but it was not common. Long thanksgivings had

I'm delighted by them, I enjoy them, because the senate has the same opinion of you that it does of its fiercest enemies, because the Roman knights, the other orders, the entire state hates you, because no responsible person, indeed, no citizen who remembers that he is a citizen, does not avert his gaze from you, block you from his ears, and shudder at the very memory of your consulship. **[46]** This is what I have always sought for you, what I have wanted, what I have prayed for; it's beyond what I had hoped for. By god, I never hoped you would lose an army. That happened beyond my expectations, but I certainly don't object. I would never have thought of wishing you the deranged madness that afflicted you. But of course I should have: I'd forgotten that these are the surest punishments from the everlasting gods for impious and criminal men. You shouldn't believe, my fellow senators, that it's like what you see on the stage, criminals being terrified by burning torches carried by Furies by the will of the gods. His own dishonesty, his own evil deeds, his own crimes, his own rashness drives him from mental health; these are the Furies of the wicked, these are their flames and torches.[82] **[47]** Shouldn't I believe you're out of your mind, a lunatic, deranged, more insane than Orestes or Athamas in tragedies? First you dared to do (that's the starting point) and then, a little while ago, to admit when pushed by Torquatus, a man greatly revered and respected, that after bringing a huge army into Macedonia, you left the whole province without a single soldier? Let's not talk about the loss of most of your army—that could be just your bad luck—but what excuse can you claim for dismissing the army? What power did you have, what law, what resolution of the senate, what right, what precedent?[83] How else does one define madness? Not to recognize men? Not to recognize the laws or the senate or the state? To cover yourself with your own blood? What you did is

---

been voted to Pompey in 63 and 62 (ten and twelve days) and to Caesar in 57 (fifteen days). The award of a twenty-day *supplicatio* to Caesar for his campaign in Britain in 55 came after this speech was delivered, but probably before the text was circulated.

82. Cicero here tones down his description of the Furies as guilt found in his *Defense of Roscius of Ameria* 67—itself an adaptation of Aeschines, *Against Timarchus* 190–91.

83. Piso demobilized his army at the end of his proconsulship, presumably because the campaign was over. It is not clear that any authorization was needed, even if senatorial approval was normal.

a greater wound—to your life and reputation and well-being. **[48]** If you got rid of all your slaves, which would be nobody's business but yours, your friends would think you should be locked up.[84] Would you have gotten rid of the protection of your country, the garrison of a province, without the orders of the Roman people and senate if you had been of sound mind?

And then there's the other one. He's wasted the huge plunder he drained from the fortunes of the tax collectors and from the farms and cities of our allies; his bottomless desires have gobbled up part of the spoils, part an original and previously unknown level of luxury, part purchases made in the same places where he had plundered everything, part through money transfers to build Mount Gabinius at Tusculum.[85] And when he was broke, when that insufferable construction was first suspended and then came to a complete stop, he sold himself, his command, an army of the Roman people, the prohibition and the will of the everlasting gods, the interpretations of the priests, a resolution of the senate, the instructions of the people, the name and the dignity of the empire to the king of Egypt.[86] **[49]** Even though he had as large a province as he had wanted and hoped for, as large as he had bought at the price and peril of my life, he was incapable of holding himself in, and he led his army out of Syria. What right did he have to leave his province? He offered himself as a mercenary in the entourage of the Alexandrian king: what could be more disgraceful than that? He came to Egypt, he fought the Alexandrians. When did the senate or the people authorize this war? He captured Alexandria; what else would we expect from such lunacy than that he send a report to the senate about his great accomplishments? **[50]** If he had been in his right mind, if his madness and lunacy were not already the greatest possible penalty paid to his country and to the everlasting gods, would he have dared—and here I set aside his departure from the province, his leading the army out, his waging war on his own authority, his entry into the kingdom without the orders of

84. Being either a spendthrift or a lunatic in Roman law led to one's being placed under the control of a guardian.
85. Gabinius' excessively large villa at Tusculum was decorated with works of art taken from Cicero's villa at Tusculum.
86. Although an oracle forbade the use of an army to restore Ptolemy Auletes to the throne of Egypt, Gabinius did so in 55; he had the tacit support of Pompey and was probably encouraged by a huge bribe from Ptolemy.

the Roman people and senate, things that are very clearly forbidden both by many previous laws and in particular by the Cornelian law on treason and the Julian law on provincial extortion—I set all that aside: if he were not profoundly insane, would he have dared to take for himself the province that Publius Lentulus, a good friend to this body, had been given by vote of the senate and by the choice of the lot, and had unhesitatingly resigned for religious reasons—to take that for himself, when even if there were no religious objections it was forbidden by tradition and precedent and the most severe penalties of the law?

[51] And since we're contrasting our fortunes, let's leave out Gabinius' return. Even if he's made it impossible for himself to come back, I'm still looking forward to seeing that face of his.[87] But if it's all right with you, let's compare your return with mine. Mine was like this: from Brundisium to Rome the procession of all Italy never stopped; there was no region or town or district or colony that didn't send a public embassy to congratulate me. I don't need to say anything about my arrivals, of the way men poured out of the towns, of the throngs from the countryside of men with their wives and children, of the days that everyone celebrated like the ritual festivals of the everlasting gods when I arrived and departed. [52] That single day on which I returned to my homeland was the equivalent of immortality for me, when I saw the senate and the entire people come out, when Rome itself seemed to pull itself from its foundations to come to greet the man who saved it. The way Rome received me made it seem that not only every man and woman of every sort and age and rank, of every fortune and place, but even the walls themselves and the houses and temples of the city rejoiced. In the following days the priests, the consuls, and the senate returned me to the very house from which you had driven me, which you had plundered, which you had burned; and for me, as for nobody before me, they decided that my house should be built at public expense.[88]

---

87. Gabinius returned in September of 54. He was accused of extortion, Cicero was compelled by the triumvirs to defend him, and he was convicted and went into exile. His governorship, needless to say, was much more successful than Cicero says in this speech.

88. Cicero's house on the Palatine had been burned then replaced by a shrine to Libertas. On his return, the senate authorized payment for its rebuilding.

[53] That's my return: now contrast yours, when—since you had lost your army—you brought nothing home safely except that familiar face of yours. First, who knows the route you took with those lictors carrying laurel branches? What wanderings you took, while you were seeking out every possible deserted spot![89] What byways and twists you looked for! What town saw you, what friend entertained you, what host looked on you? You treated night like day, didn't you, solitude like crowds, roadhouses like towns: it seemed more like a criminal's funeral than the return of a noble commander from Macedonia. But Rome itself, you disgrace not only to the Calpurnian family but even to the Calventian one, not only to this city but to the town of Placentia, not only to your father's family but to your relatives in trousers[90]—how did you enter Rome itself? Who came to greet you—not just of the senate or of the citizen body, but even of your own legates? **[54]** Lucius Flaccus is a man who truly didn't deserve to be made your legate; because of his close association with me during my consulship in my efforts to save the commonwealth, he is all the worthier.[91] He was with me at the moment someone reported that you had been seen wandering around with your lictors not far from the gate. And I know that my good friend Quintus Marcius, a brave man who's exceptionally knowledgeable about war and military affairs, was relaxing at home at the time of your return.[92] It was through the efforts of these legates that you were acclaimed as commander in battle when you were far away. **[55]** But it's pointless to count the people who didn't come to greet you, since I can state that almost nobody came, not even from the most scrupulously observant tribe of candidates for office, even though they had been notified and invited on the day and for many days in advance. There were sweet little togas ready for the lictors at the gate; they put them on and took off their military cloaks and supplied a brand new crowd for their

---

89. Piso obviously did not take a direct route back to Rome, but Cicero's account is invective rather than truth.

90. The stereotypical dress of Gauls.

91. Lucius Valerius Flaccus had been praetor in 63 and had arrested the ambassadors of the Allobroges. After his governorship of Asia in 62, he was prosecuted for extortion and defended by Cicero in 59.

92. Identity uncertain; probably Quintus Marcius Crispus, later governor of Bithynia in 45.

commander.[93] That's how this commander from Macedon returned to the city from so great an army, so great a province, three years after he left—no lowly merchant ever had a more solitary return. But he's so ready to defend himself that he objects to my account. After I said that he entered the city by the gate at the Caelian Hill, this alert man threatened to sue me for slander because he entered by the Esquiline gate.[94] As if I was supposed to know it or any of you had heard it or as if it were remotely relevant which gate you entered by, so long as it was not the triumphal gate, which has always been open to previous consuls coming from Macedon. But you're something new, someone with consular powers returning from Macedon with no triumph.

[56] But, my fellow senators, you've heard the voice of the philosopher: he says that he never wanted a triumph.[95] What a criminal, what a disaster, what a disgrace you are! When you were obliterating the senate, when you were selling out the authority of this order, when you were auctioning off your consulship to a bid from the tribune of the people, overturning the commonwealth, betraying my standing and safety in exchange for a province, if you did not yearn for a triumph, what desire was it that set you on fire? In fact, I've often seen men who seemed to me and others too greedy for a province conceal and hide that greed under the label "triumph." That's what Decimus Silanus the consul said in this body, and that's what my colleague also said.[96] Nobody can desire and openly seek an army without giving "triumph" as a pretext for that desire. [57] And if the senate and the Roman people had forced you to undertake a war when you weren't seeking it or were actively avoiding it, it would still be the sign of a small and low mind to have scorn for

---

93. Lictors would in any case have to switch to civilian dress to enter the city on returning from military service.

94. The Porta Capena (near the Caelian Hill) would have been the direct route for someone coming from Brundisium, the usual port for the eastern Mediterranean. Cicero presumably had made the error in an earlier comment in the senate.

95. At this point "philosopher" is fairly unspecific: most philosophers rejected glory in favor of virtue. Epicurus enters the picture at sec. 59, and Piso's relationship with Philodemus not until sec. 68.

96. Decimus Junius Silanus, consul in 62, and Cicero's colleague as consul in 63, Gaius Antonius.

the honor and glory of a well-deserved triumph. Just as it's a sign of frivolity to grasp after empty rumors and to chase down every shadow of even false glory, so too it's a sign of a mind that shirks light and splendor to reject proper glory, which is the most honorable reward of true virtue.[97] But the senate didn't demand or force you to take a province; in fact, it was against the idea and was forced into agreeing. Not only were the Roman people unenthusiastic, but not a single free citizen took part in the vote;[98] the province was the reward for your overthrow and destruction of the state, since this was the deal governing all your crimes, that if you handed over the entire commonwealth to these unspeakable bandits, then Macedonia would be handed over to you in exchange, with whatever boundaries you determined. But your draining the treasury, stripping Italy of its young men, crossing a truly savage ocean by winter—if that was a show of scorn for a triumph, then what was it, lunatic pirate that you are, except this blind greed for plunder and spoils that drew you on? **[58]** It's too late for Pompey to use your advice. He was wrong; he hadn't had a taste of your philosophy, and that stupid man has already triumphed three times. Crassus, I'm ashamed of you. Why on earth, after your completion of a terrifying war, did you want so much to have the senate decree that laurel crown for you? Servilius, Metellus, Curio, Afranius:[99] why didn't you listen to so learned a man, so well educated, before you were drawn into this error? My close friend Gaius Pomptinus no longer has the option: he's blocked from a triumph for religious reasons.[100] Stupid men, these people like Camillus and Curius and Fabricius and Calatinus and Scipio and Marcellus and Maximus! What a madman Paullus was, what a boor

---

97. The last phrase is a close translation of Aristotle, *Nicomachean Ethics* 1123b35. Cicero implies (as in *Defense of Lucius Murena*) that the butt of his humor (Cato there, Piso here) has chosen the wrong philosophy.

98. Cicero claims throughout that the voting assemblies called by Clodius consisted only of his gangs composed of slaves.

99. Publius Servilius Vatia Isauricus, consul in 79, triumphed in 88 and 74; Quintus Caecilius Metellus Creticus, consul in 69, triumphed in 62; Gaius Scribonius Curio, consul in 76, triumphed in 72; Lucius Afranius, consul in 60, probably triumphed c. 70.

100. Gaius Pomptinus, praetor in 63, was denied a triumph, apparently with some religious justification.

Marius! How little wisdom the fathers of these two consuls had in holding triumphs![101]

[59] We can't change the past, but why does this mud-and-clay munchkin not impart his wonderful philosophic advice to his son-in-law, the great and glorious commander?[102] It's glory, believe me, that keeps that man on the move; he burns and yearns with longing for a great and justified triumph. He hasn't learned the same things as you. Send a pamphlet to him, and if you can meet him face to face, think about the words you can use to knock down and extinguish the fire of his longings. As a moderate and consistent man, you'll have influence on someone who takes wing on the desire for glory; as a scholar, on someone uneducated; as a father-in-law, on a son-in-law. Since you're a man made to persuade people, neat and perfect and burnished from the lecture room, you'll say something like this: "Why is it, Caesar, that the thanksgivings that have been so often decreed for so many days give you so much pleasure? Men are deluded about such things, and the gods pay no attention to such things. As our immortal Epicurus said, they don't favor anyone and they don't get angry at them."[103] You won't convince him, of course, in making a speech like this: he'll see that the gods both are now and have been angry at you. [60] You'll turn to your second lecture and give a discourse on triumphs: "What's the point of that chariot, the leaders in chains in front of the chariot, the images of towns, the gold, the silver, the legates and military tribunes on horseback, the shouting of the soldiers, the whole parade? Those things are hollow, I tell you, almost children's toys—to snatch at applause, to be carried through the city, to want to be seen. In all this there's nothing solid to hold on to, nothing that contributes to pleasures of the body. [61] Don't you see me? Coming from a province from which Flamininus, Paullus, Metellus, Didius, and god knows how many others held triumphs, roused by their frivolous desires, my manner of return was to trample down the Macedonian laurel at the Esquiline gate, to return myself with twelve men in

---

101. The list of great heroes of the Republic is followed by mention of the two consuls, Pompey and Crassus. Gnaeus Pompeius Strabo triumphed in the Social War in 89, Publius Licinius Crassus in 93.

102. Julius Caesar.

103. The first of Epicurus' *Principal Doctrines.*

rags,[104] thirsty, to the gate at the Caelian Hill. That was where my freedman had rented a house for me, the glorious commander, two days earlier; if it hadn't been empty, I would have pitched my tent in the Field of Mars. But the cash, dear Caesar, since I did without triumphal floats, is at home and will stay there. I took my accounts to the treasury right away, as your law commanded, and I followed your law in absolutely nothing else. And if you study the accounts you will understand that education has been profitable to nobody more than me. They are so cleverly and elegantly written that the treasury scribe who entered them, after he had copied the entire set of accounts, scratched his head with his left hand and muttered: 'The accounts are there, all right, it's the cash that's gone.'"[105] With a speech like this, I'm sure you can call him back even when he's mounting the triumphal chariot.

[62] What a creature of darkness, mud, and filth! You've forgotten your father's family and can scarcely remember your mother's. Your indescribable character—broken, humble, low, dirty—is lower even than your grandfather the auctioneer from Milan deserves. Lucius Crassus, the wisest man in our country, practically used probes to poke the Alps looking for a reason to triumph where there was no enemy;[106] Gaius Cotta, too, a man of great intelligence, had no defined enemy but was inflamed with the same yearning.[107] Neither of them triumphed, because one was kept from that honor by his colleague, the other by death. Not long ago you laughed at Marcus Piso's desire for a triumph and said you were completely different in that respect.[108] But even if he waged a relatively small war, as you said, he still didn't think the honor deserved contempt. Are you more learned than Piso, wiser than Cotta, better endowed with prudence, genius, and wisdom than Crassus? Do you scorn what those

---

104. His lictors in changed clothes.

105. Plautus, *Trinummus* 419.

106. As consul in 95, Lucius Licinius Crassus wanted a triumph for fighting bandits in Cisalpine Gaul; his colleague Quintus Mucius Scaevola the pontifex vetoed it.

107. Gaius Aurelius Cotta, consul in 75, was awarded a triumph for fighting Gauls, but he died before the ceremony.

108. Marcus Pupius Piso, consul in 61, triumphed after fighting in Spain in 69. He was a serious student of Greek philosophy.

men, "amateurs," as you call them, thought glorious?[109] **[63]** If you criticize them for wanting a laurel wreath when the wars they fought were small or nonexistent, then after subduing such great nations and fighting such great wars you shouldn't be at all scornful of the reward for your toils, the prize for your dangers, the badges of your courage. And even if you're wiser than Themista,[110] it wasn't scorn you felt but reluctance to have your brazen face smacked by the abuse of the senate.

And now you see (since I've been so hostile to myself that I compared myself to you) that my departure, my absence from Rome, and my return were all so much better than yours that the whole sequence brought me immortal glory and brought you eternal disgrace. **[64]** Even in the daily round of urban life, surely you wouldn't exalt your splendor, influence, crowds of well-wishers, courtroom responsibilities, advice, assistance, authority, or senatorial opinions over mine or, to tell the truth, over the lowest and most despised person in Rome? Consider this. The senate hates you (and you admit it's right to do so) as the man who attacked and destroyed not only its sense of worth and its authority but the entire order along with its reputation. The Roman knights can't bear to look at you, because the leading man of that order, the most distinguished of them, Lucius Aelius, was exiled when you were consul.[111] The Roman people want your ruin, because in everything you did concerning me using bandits and slaves, you brought disgrace on them. All Italy curses you, because you treated their decrees and prayers with great scorn. **[65]** Go on, if you dare, and make a test of this huge and universal hatred. The most elaborate and magnificent games of all time are about to take place, like none that ever were, and I can't imagine at all how they can be equaled in the future.[112] Expose yourself to the people, go to the games. Are you afraid of being hissed? Where are those lectures of yours? Afraid of the shouts? Philosophers don't care about that, either. Somebody might raise a hand to you? Well, pain is a bad thing in your beliefs, while reputation, dishonor, infamy, and disgrace are

---

109. "Amateurs" (*idiotae*) is the word Verres uses (*Verr.* 4:4) for people ignorant of Greek art.

110. A pupil of Epicurus.

111. Lucius Aelius Lamia; see sec. 23 above.

112. Pompey's games held for the dedication of his theater.

just words and nonsense. But I have no doubts about this: he won't dare go to the games. He'll go to a state banquet not for the sake of his standing—unless perhaps he wants to dine with the senate, that is to say, with all those admirers of his—but for the sake of his appetites. He'll leave the games to us "amateurs": **[66]** his lectures always put the pleasures of the belly over the delights of eye and ear. And in case he seems to you merely wicked and cruel, once a minor thief and now a true plunderer, low, stubborn, haughty, treacherous, deceitful, rude, and shameless, you should realize that there's nothing more decadent, nothing more lecherous, nothing more immoral, nothing more evil than he. **[67]** And you shouldn't think that his luxury is like this: there is a sort of luxury, even though it's always vicious and low, but still one that's more worthy of a freeborn man. But in his case there's nothing respectable, nothing elegant, nothing refined; to offer praise to my enemy, there's nothing at all that costs very much—except his lechery. No fancy silver plate, huge cups—and so as not to seem to scorn his own people, from Placentia;[113] the table piled up not with fish or shellfish but with a lot of rotting meat. Slaves in dirty clothes serve at table, and some of them are old men; the same one is cook and butler at once; he has no baker at home, no wine cellar: the bread is from the shop, the wine from the barrel. There are five Greeks jammed together on every couch, and sometimes more; he's alone on his, and drinking goes on until they serve the dregs.[114] When he hears the cock crow,[115] he thinks his grandfather has come back to life; he has the table taken away.

[68] I hear somebody ask: "How do you know that?" I certainly wouldn't caricature anybody in order to insult him, especially somebody so clever and learned, the kind of man I couldn't be angry at if I wanted to. There's a certain Greek who lives with him, a man, to tell the truth (and I know him) who is humane, but only so long as he's with other people or by himself.[116] When he had seen Piso as a

---

113. Earthenware rather than silver.

114. The text here is corrupt, and "dregs" is an approximation.

115. A bad pun on *Gallus* = Gaul and *gallus* = rooster, whose crow is likened to the auctioneer's call.

116. Philodemus of Gadara was both a poet and an Epicurean philosopher; some of his epigrams are preserved in the Greek Anthology, and a great deal of his philosophical writing is preserved (badly) among the remains of the Villa of the Papyri in Herculaneum. He came to Italy in about 75, and Piso

young man, already with his impressive brow, he didn't look down on his friendship, especially since he was sought after; he became such a regular that he actually lived with Piso and hardly ever left his side. I'm talking not among ignorant men but, I believe, in a gathering of men of the greatest learning and humanity:[117] I'm sure you've heard it said that Epicurean philosophers judge all things that are desirable for men by the standard of pleasure; whether that's right or wrong doesn't matter for us; and if it does, it's not relevant to this occasion. But still, it's a tricky argument and often dangerous for a young man who isn't exactly brilliant. **[69]** So our stallion here, the minute he heard that pleasure was so greatly praised by the philosopher, looked no further. All his voluptuary sensations were triggered, he whinnied at this speech of his: he thought he'd found not a teacher of virtue but someone to give a green light to his lust. The Greek first began to quibble and split hairs about the way these things were said, but Piso was just like a cripple playing catch, as they say: he held onto what he'd been given, he swore allegiance, he wanted to have it notarized, he pronounced Epicurus a man of taste. And I believe Epicurus does say that he can understand nothing to be good if one eliminates physical pleasure.[118] **[70]** To cut the story short, the Greek, an easygoing and really charming man, didn't want to fight too hard against a senator of the Roman people. And this Greek I'm talking about is highly sophisticated not just in philosophy but also in other areas they say most Epicureans neglect: he writes poems that are so cheery, so neat, so elegant that nothing more witty can be imagined.[119] You can criticize him if you want to, but mildly; not as someone wicked or reckless or tainted, but as a Greekling, a flatterer, a poet. A Greek and an immigrant, he came to Piso, or rather fell in with him, tricked by that same eyebrow as so many wise men and so great a nation;

(to whom he dedicated the treatise *On the Good King According to Homer*) became his patron very soon.

117. There is similar flattery of the jury's cultural aspirations in the Verrines, *In Defense of Lucius Murena,* and *In Defense of the Poet Archias.* Cicero's technique in this passage is similar to his deflation of Cato in *In Defense of Lucius Murena;* by suggesting that his victim does not understand even his chosen philosophy, he reveals their lack of perception.

118. Epicurus, fr. 67 Usener (1887), used several times by Cicero. See esp. *Tusc.* 3.41.

119. Epicurus notoriously did not have much use for poetry or the arts.

once he was sucked in, he couldn't get out of the relationship, and he was also afraid of getting a reputation for being fickle. By request, by invitation, on demand he wrote so much to Piso about Piso that every time the man got aroused, every hookup, all the varieties of dinners and parties, and even Piso's adulteries were described in his most refined poems, **[71]** and anyone who wants to can see his life in them as if in a mirror. I would recite a lot of them that have been read and heard by a lot of people, if I weren't afraid that my present style of speech is inconsistent with the customs of this place—and at the same time, I didn't want to discredit the man who wrote them. If he had had better luck in getting a pupil, then maybe he could have been more stern and serious, but chance brought him to this kind of writing, one that's truly unworthy of a philosopher, to the extent that philosophy, as they say, concerns the practice of virtue and duty and living well; someone who professes that seems to me to display a very serious character indeed. **[72]** But as he didn't know the meaning of saying he was a philosopher, that same bad luck smeared him with the filth and droppings of that most disgusting and uncontrolled animal.

Now Piso, after praising the actions of my consulship—praise that, coming from such a disgraceful man, seemed almost to disgrace me—said, "It wasn't hatred arising from those actions that harmed you, but your poetry." That was a really harsh punishment under your consulship for a poet who was bad or bold. "You wrote: 'Let arms give way to the toga.'"[120] So? "That's what stirred up such a storm against you." But as far as I know, nowhere in the inscription that under your consulship was carved on the tombstone of the commonwealth[121] is it written: "Is it your wish and command that because Marcus Cicero wrote a verse . . ." but "because he punished . . ." **[73]** But as a grammarian you aren't an Aristarchus but a Phalaris; you don't put a black mark against a bad line of verse but go after the poet with weapons.[122] So I want to know what it is you

---

120. A quotation from Cicero's poem *De Consulatu Suo* ("On His Own Consulship"), a work of inspired egotism if not poetic genius.

121. Clodius had the text of his law exiling Cicero inscribed on the temple of Liberty built on the site of Cicero's house.

122. The Alexandrian critic Aristarchus and the Sicilian tyrant Phalaris used their distinctive methods of assault against Homer and Stesichorus, respectively.

object to in the line "Let arms give way to the toga." "You say," he says, "that our greatest commander will yield to your toga." Idiot, why should I have to teach you to read? You need a beating more than a lesson. I wasn't talking about the toga I'm wearing now, or about the weapons, the shield and sword, of one particular commander, but because the toga is the sign of peace and order while weapons are the sign of discord and war, in speaking in the manner of poets I wanted this to be understood, that war and discord would give way to peace and order. [74] Ask your friend the Greek poet: he'll recognize and acknowledge the type of expression, and he won't be surprised by your ignorance. "But you're in trouble," he says, "with the second half, 'Let the victor's laurel yield to civic praise.'" Now, indeed, I'm very grateful to you: I would have been stuck if you hadn't gotten me out. For when you were timid and cowering at the Esquiline gate and with your own thieving hands threw away the laurels pulled from your bloody insignia of power, you displayed your own judgment that the laurel gave way not only to elaborate praise but to even my tiny amount of praise. And by this speech, you criminal, you want it to be understood that Pompey was made my enemy by that verse, so that if the verse is what harmed me, then the harm to me was desired by the man whom the verse offended. [75] Forget about the fact that the verse had nothing to do with him: I had repeatedly celebrated him as much as possible in many speeches and writings; I could not have insulted him with just one line of poetry. But assume that he was, at first, offended; didn't he weigh against this one little verse the many volumes of mine in praise of him? If he was upset, would he have been so cruel as to harm, I won't say a close friend, or someone who had done such service in praising him, such service to the commonwealth, or a consular, or a senator, or a citizen, or a free man—but to harm a human being on account of a line of poetry? Do you understand what you're saying, to whom, about whom? You want to implicate men of high standing in your and Gabinius' crime, and you make no secret of it; just a little while ago you said I picked a fight with men I despised but didn't touch people of more power at whom I ought to be angry. Of these men—and who doesn't understand whom you mean?—even though all their interests are not identical, even so the interests of all have my approval. [76] Even though a lot of people have stood in the way of his support and love for me, Pompey has always had affection for me, has always considered me completely worthy of association with him, and has always wanted me not only to be secure but even to have respect and high distinction. It's your deceit, your crime, your evil and invented accusations that I was treacherous and he was in danger, together with the accusations of those who, at your urging, used the license that comes with friendship to make a home in Pompey's ears for their utterly malicious gossip, and it's your greed for provinces that had me shut out and caused everyone who wanted me, Pompey's glorious reputation, and the commonwealth itself to be safe to be kept from seeing or talking to Pompey. **[77]** The effect of all this was that he was clearly not allowed to rely on his own judgment; even though certain people didn't estrange him from me, they did slow his aid. Didn't Lucius Lentulus, then the praetor, come to you, didn't Quintus Sanga, the elder Lucius Torquatus, Marcus Lucullus? They had all gone to him at his Alban villa, together with a large number of other men, to beg and beseech that he not desert my fortunes, linked as they were to the safety of the nation. Pompey sent them back to you and your colleague, so that you could take up the public cause and bring it before the senate. He was himself unwilling to fight against an armed tribune of the plebs without a public mandate, but if the consuls were defending the commonwealth in accordance with a resolution of the senate, then he would take up arms. **[78]** Do you have any memory, you creature of ill omen, of what you answered? All of them, Torquatus in particular, were enraged by the stubbornness of your answer: that you were not as brave as Torquatus had been as consul, or as I had been; that there was no need for armed conflict; that I could save the commonwealth for a second time if I gave way, but that there would be unbounded slaughter if I resisted. And finally, he said that neither he nor his son-in-law nor his colleague would fail to support a tribune of the people. And now can you, an enemy and a traitor, say I should be more hostile toward others than toward you? **[79]** I know that Caesar doesn't have the same political beliefs I do; but still, as I have often said about him before this body, he wanted my collaboration in all aspects of his consulship and in the positions he shared with those closest to him. He offered me positions, he invited me, he asked me. It was because of what may be an excessive desire for consistency that I was not drawn to his side; I didn't ask to be very close to someone to whom I wouldn't have surrendered my own judgment because of favors. People thought that, during your consulship, the whole matter would culminate in a struggle over whether his actions in the previous year would be maintained or rescinded.[123] There's nothing more to say. If he believed that I as an individual had so much strength and courage that his actions would collapse if I resisted them, why shouldn't I forgive him for putting his own well-being ahead of mine? **[80]** But let's set aside the past. When Pompey embraced me with all his energy and effort and danger to his life, when he approached the towns on my behalf, when he pled for Italy's protection, when he sat frequently as an adviser to Publius Lentulus the consul, the man responsible for my well-being, when he supported the resolution of the senate, when he declared in public assemblies that he was not only defending my well-being but even being a suppliant on my behalf—in all this goodwill he associated Caesar with himself as an ally and a supporter, because he knew him to have great power and to be no enemy to me. So you see that I shouldn't be merely unfriendly but a real enemy to you, while I should not only not be angry but even friendly to those men you describe. One of them, as I will always remember, has always been as friendly to me as to himself; the other, as I intend to forget, has sometimes been more friendly to himself than to me. **[81]** Life's like that: brave men, even if they fight one another in close combat, lay down the hatred that comes with struggle along with their weapons at the end of the fight. He could never hate me, not even when we disagreed. That's characteristic of virtue—something you don't even recognize—that the beauty of its appearance pleases brave men even when it's found in an enemy.

For my part, my fellow senators, I'll say with all sincerity what I feel and what I've often said in your hearing. If Caesar had never been friendly to me, if he had always been angry, if he always scorned my friendship and showed himself to be implacable and unappeasable toward me, even so, I wouldn't be able not to be a friend to him, since he has accomplished and continues to accomplish such great deeds. It isn't the wall of the Alps I set against the Gauls' crossing into Italy; it isn't the channel of the Rhine, overflowing with its torrents, I set against the vast tribes of Germans: it's Caesar's command. **[82]** The result of his efforts is that if the mountains sank down and the rivers dried up, we would still have Italy fortified not by nature's defenses but by Caesar's victory and military accomplishments. But since he

---

123. All Caesar's legislation was passed despite the fact that his colleague's constant observation of omens made it technically illegal for public action to take place, and the validity of the legislation was disputed.

seeks me out, shows affection for me, thinks me worthy of all kinds of praise, are you going to bring me back to an old quarrel through your hostility, will you pick at the scabs of past public troubles through your crimes? Even though you knew perfectly well how close I am to Caesar, you scoffed at me—although your lips were trembling—in asking why I didn't prosecute you. As far as I'm concerned, "I will never reduce your worries by denying them to you,"[124] but I must take into account the worry and burden I will be placing on a good friend who is occupied by such important public business and by so great a war.[125] But no matter how limp our young men may be in not being as concerned as they should be with the desire for praise and glory, I still have hopes that there will be some men willing to strip this exposed corpse of the spoils taken from a former consul, especially with you as the defendant, a man so beaten down, so resourceless, so weak, and so impotent, who act as if you were afraid of seeming not to deserve kindness if you didn't stand forth as almost identical to the man who sent you out.

[83] But do you really think I haven't looked closely enough at the disgraces of your command and the devastation of your province? I've followed your steps not by sniffing at mere tracks but by following through your mud holes and dens. I marked down your first crimes when you arrived; after taking money from the people of Dyrrachium to kill your host Plator, you stayed in the house of the very man whose blood you had sold.[126] After accepting gifts from him, including some

---

124. From Accius' *Thyestes* (fr. 234).

125. In other words, Cicero would prosecute Piso for provincial extortion except that he does not want to distract Piso's son-in-law, Caesar; but that does not mean that he would mind if someone less close to Caesar did so. This is a singularly disingenuous argument, raised largely to lead into the summary of Piso's Macedonian career that follows. The following sentence is somewhat contorted. In general, prosecutions were undertaken by ambitious young men (as Caelius had prosecuted Gaius Antonius); Piso, the prospective defendant, is described as if he were the corpse of a soldier wearing the armor he had taken in battle from someone else and at the same time a loyal follower of Clodius, who had sent him into battle against Cicero, not to Macedon.

126. Plator was from central Macedonia and (according to Cicero's other discussion of the incident in *On the Answer of the Haruspices* 35) Piso had him killed for refusing to give him money.

musical slaves, you encouraged him, a man in fear and great trepida-
tion, and ordered him to come to Thessalonica under your guarantee
of safety. You didn't even execute him in the traditional way, although
the wretched man yearned to put his neck under the axe of his friend,
but you commanded your personal physician (whom you had brought
with you) to open the man's veins. [84] His companion Pleuratus
was a kind of bonus to you for the murder of Plator: even though he
was in the weakened condition of extreme old age, you beat him to
death. Similarly, you beheaded Rabocentus, a leading citizen of the
tribe of the Bessi, when you had sold your services for 300 talents to
King Cottus,[127] even though Rabocentus had come into your camp
as an envoy and promised you massive support and assistance from
the Bessi of both infantry and cavalry. He wasn't the only one, either;
you killed all the other envoys who came with him, as you had sold
all their lives to King Cottus. You waged a cruel and immoral war
against the Denseletae, a tribe that had always obeyed our orders
and protected Macedonia when all the barbarians revolted during
Gaius Sentius' praetorship.[128] Even though you could have had them
as the most loyal of allies, you preferred to have them as the fiercest of enemies. That's how you turned people who had consistently
defended Macedonia into bandits and marauders: they disrupted
our revenues, they captured cities and laid waste to the countryside,
they enslaved our allies, they kidnapped their slaves, they drove away
their livestock, they compelled the people of Thessalonica to give up
hope for their city and fortify their citadel. [85] You're the one who
sacked the ancient shrine of Jupiter Zbelsurdus,[129] a place extremely
holy to the barbarians. It was for your crimes that the everlasting
gods took their revenge on our soldiers; they were attacked by a
new sort of disease from which no one, once infected, could recover.
Nobody had any doubt that it was the violation of the laws of friendship, the murder of ambassadors, the provocation of peaceful tribes
and allies in a wicked war, the plundering of shrines that brought
about so great a disaster.

---

127. The Bessi were a Thracian tribe, in fact hostile to Rome; Cottus was
king of the Astae, a neighboring Thracian tribe.

128. Sentius governed Macedonia from 93 to 87 BCE. Cicero is wrong
about the loyalty of the Denseletae, yet another Thracian tribe.

129. A Thracian god of uncertain orthography, and a correction of the
text.

From this small sample you can recognize the whole range of your crimes and cruelty. **[86]** Why should I now unfold the extent of your greed, which is tied to your unlimited criminality? I will speak under broad rubrics of the most notorious. Isn't it true that you left at Rome in interest-bearing accounts the 18 million sesterces assigned to you from the treasury that you had budgeted as "money for equipment" in the sale of my life?[130] Isn't it true that when the people of Apollonia had given you 100 talents at Rome to avoid repaying money they had been lent, you sold out Fufidius, the lender (a Roman knight and a man of outstanding qualities), to his debtors? Isn't it true that when you handed over your winter quarters to the control of your legate and prefect, you completely ruined those wretched cities, not only draining their assets but also forcing them to endure wicked and vile sexual assaults? Did you set any limit in your assessment of the value of grain requisitioned for the troops or of grain given to you in your official capacity?[131] Of course, it's hard to call something a gift when it's been extorted by force and terror. Everyone alike suffered this, but it was particularly hard on the Boeotians[132] and Byzantines, the Chersonese and Thessalonica. You were master, you were assessor, you were the sole seller of all grain throughout the province for three entire years. **[87]** I won't bother bringing up the trials on capital charges, the deals made with defendants, the purchasing of verdicts, the most savage condemnations, the acquittals based entirely on your whims. Once you realize I know about a topic, you can remember on your own how many crimes and of what magnitude fall into that category. Item: that arms factory. Do you recollect the time when through the forced requisition of all the livestock in the province, with the excuse of needing hides, you revived the lucrative practices of your family and your father? You were already a pretty big kid at the time of the Social War, when you saw your house filled with profits from your father's being in charge of making weapons. Item:

---

130. "Life" = *caput*, which can mean either "life" or "civic status." According to Cicero, Piso was being given public funds under the false budget line of "equipment," when in fact it was payment for allowing Cicero to be eliminated from Rome.

131. Extraction of profit from compulsory requisitions of grain had been one of Verres' techniques and was presumably standard extortionate practice.

132. The name may be wrong: Boeotia is far away from the other places mentioned.

the provincial taxes. Do you remember that by imposing a duty on every single thing for sale you made a Roman province the property of your slaves?[133] **[88]** Item: the positions of centurion that you sold in public. Item: ranks being assigned by your lackey. Item: soldiers' wages being paid out every year by the cities with banking tables set up in public. Item: your expedition to the Black Sea and your undertakings there. Item: your mental feebleness and dejection when Macedonia's status as a praetorian province was reported.[134] You fell down in a dead faint because not only was a successor being appointed for you but also one was not being appointed for Gabinius. Item: your appointment of an ex-quaestor as acting governor, ignoring the ex-aediles and insulting every one of your outstanding legates,[135] the refusal to see your military tribunes, the murder of that brave man Marcus Baebius at your orders. **[89]** Item: that you so often despaired of and mistrusted your own actions so much that you lay in mourning with wailing and lamentation; that you sent six hundred of our friends and allies for "the people's priest"[136] to throw to the beasts; that when you could scarcely endure your sorrow and grief at your own departure, you went first to Samothrace, then to Thasos with your delicate dancers and with the beautiful brothers Autobulus, Athamas, and Timocles; that on your return from there you lay for some days grieving in the villa of Euhadia, the wife of Execestus, and from there in shabby clothes you came to Thessalonica at night and in secret;[137] that because you could not endure the throng of people weeping and the storm of complaints, you fled to Beroea, a town off the beaten track. While you were there, when a rumor puffed up your spirits with a false hope because you thought that Quintus Ancharius

---

133. The text here is corrupt, and the translation of the last phrase is conjectural.

134. In 56 the senate assigned Macedonia to one of the prospective praetors for 55, as Cicero proposed, but he was not followed in wanting Syria similarly assigned.

135. Piso's legates had held higher office (praetor or aedile) than his quaestor, but it was customary to turn a province over to one's quaestor on departing.

136. Clodius. The title is ironic, referring to his radical politics and his sacrilegious behavior in profaning the rites of the Bona Dea.

137. None of these people is otherwise known: Cicero emphasizes his detailed knowledge of Piso's lurid life.

would not succeed you,[138] how much, you criminal, did you revive your shameless behavior! **[90]** I set aside the crown-gold[139] that kept you twisting for so long, when sometimes you wanted it, sometimes you didn't; your son-in-law's legislation forbade it to be decreed and prohibited your acceptance of it unless a triumph had been decreed. In that case, as in that of the Achaeans' hundred talents, you couldn't bring yourself to spit up the money you had accepted and swallowed up, so you just changed the descriptions and the categories of the money. Let's leave aside all the coupons and certificates you scattered over the whole province; let's leave aside the number of ships levied and the total amount of plunder misappropriated; let's leave aside the accounting of the grain that you extorted and demanded; let's leave aside the liberty you snatched away from peoples and from individuals who had received it as a personal reward. Nothing of this was not carefully forbidden by the Julian law. **[91]** Aetolia, which is separated by a great distance from the barbarian tribes, lying in the lap of peace, almost centrally located in the embrace of Greece—Aetolia, you avenging fury of our allies, you destroyed in its wretchedness at your departure from your province. Arsinoe, Stratus, Naupactus, as you just now indicated, were noble and prosperous cities, but you admit they were captured by our enemies. And by what enemies? Why, those you compelled to move away from the towns of the Agraei and Dolopians and to abandon their altars and their hearths while you were settling down at Ambracia on your arrival. And in the course of this departure, wonderful commander that you are, since the sudden death of Aetolia was a bonus added to the earlier disasters, you dismissed your army, preferring whatever penalty you owed for such a crime rather than have the number of your remaining soldiers be known.

[92] I want you now to compare two Epicureans as military commanders: Albucius, after holding his triumph in Sardinia,[140] was condemned at Rome; Piso, since he was anticipating a similar

---

138. Quintus Ancharius, praetor in 56, did in fact succeed Piso in Macedonia.

139. *Aurum coronarium* was money given by (grateful?) provincials to pay for the gold wreath worn in a triumph; a law of Caesar's limited the possibilities of extortion under this rubric.

140. In about 104 BCE. His triumph was unauthorized and celebrated in Sardinia rather than in Rome; he was convicted of extortion.

result, put up trophies in Macedonia. The things all peoples want
as visible memorials of military glory and success, our ridiculous
commander set up as mournful pointers to towns lost, legions slaughtered, a province stripped of all its military protection to the eternal disgrace of his family and his name. He wanted something that
would be inscribed on the base of his monuments; when he came to
Dyrrachium to depart from the province, he was besieged by the
same soldiers whom, as he said a little while ago to Torquatus, he
had dismissed as an act of kindness. After swearing to them under
oath that on the following day he would pay them what they were
owed, he hid himself in his house and then by dark of night, wearing sandals and a slave's clothes, he boarded his ship; he avoided
Brundisium and instead went to the furthest reaches of the Adriatic
Sea. **[93]** Meanwhile, back in Dyrrachium, the soldiers besieged the
house where they thought he was, and since they thought he was
hiding there, they torched it. Afraid and distressed, the people of
Dyrrachium reported that their commander had fled in sandals the
night before. The soldiers, however, found a statue that looked a great
deal like him, one he had wanted to stand in a conspicuous location
so that the memory of such a kind and gentle man wouldn't perish.
They knocked it down, hammered at it, broke it up, and scattered it.
In this way they poured out against a statue made in his likeness the
hatred they felt toward Piso himself. **[94]** This being the case—and
I'm sure that when you see I know the major items you won't think I
haven't heard about the middling and lower levels of your crimes—
you don't need to urge or cheer me on; a reminder is quite enough.
But the only reminder I need is the opportunity the commonwealth
will offer, an opportunity I think is getting much closer than you
ever thought. Can't you see, can't you understand the kind of judges
we'll have once the judiciary law is passed?[141] People who want to
be called won't be; people who don't, won't avoid it. Nobody will be
hurled into the pool of judges, nobody will be exempted; ambition
won't be able to exert influence, and bias won't arise from envy.[142]
The judges whom the law chooses will judge, not the ones chosen

---

141. Pompey in 55 proposed a tighter judiciary law, limiting eligibility for
service on juries to the more wealthy members of the panels and eliminating
exemptions from service.

142. This passage is extremely corrupt; the translation is very much an
approximation.

by human caprice. And that being so, believe me, no one will refuse your invitation; the case itself and the public interest will summon or dissuade either me (although I hope not) or someone else.

[95] For my own part, as I said a little while ago, I don't believe that punishments are the same as most people probably think—condemnation, exile, execution. What is more, I believe that anything that can happen to an innocent, brave, wise man or a good citizen can't be considered a punishment. The condemnation people want for you happened to Publius Rutilius, who was our country's exemplar of innocence,[143] but that seemed to me a much worse punishment for the judges and the country than for Rutilius. Lucius Opimius was expelled from the country, a man who as praetor and consul had freed the nation from the greatest of dangers;[144] the punishment for crime and guilt had no effect on the man who received the injury but on those who inflicted it. By contrast, Catiline was twice acquitted,[145] and even the man responsible for getting you your province was let off after he had brought sexual misconduct to the sacred couch of the Good Goddess. In this huge city, who was there who thought him innocent, who didn't think the men who had given such a verdict were coconspirators?[146] [96] Am I supposed to wait for seventy-five votes to be tallied[147] when every single human being of every sort, age, and class has already reached a verdict about you? Who thinks you should be let into his house? Who thinks you worthy of any honor? Who thinks you worthy even of a common greeting? Every person prays that the memory of your consulship, your deeds, your character, and your very face and name may be expunged from the commonwealth. The legates who were with you are hostile, the military tribunes are your enemies, the centurions and whatever soldiers survive from

---

143. Publius Rutilius Rufus, consul in 105 and a serious Stoic, refused to defend himself vigorously when accused of extortion from Asia, where he had been as a legate. Cicero frequently cites him as a moral example but also as a rhetorical failure: cf. *de Or.* 1.227–31.

144. Lucius Opimius, consul in 121 and leader of the mob that killed Gaius Gracchus; he was condemned to exile for taking bribes from Jugurtha in 109.

145. Of extortion in 65, of murder (during the proscriptions) in 64.

146. Clodius was acquitted of sacrilege in 61 for his profanation of the rites of the Bona Dea.

147. The size of the jury in a trial for extortion.

your army—who were not dismissed by you but scattered—they hate you, they desire a disaster to fall on you, they curse you. Achaea is drained, Thessaly is ravaged, Athens has been shredded, Dyrrachium and Apollonia emptied, Ambracia plundered, the Parthini and the Bullienses have been made a mockery, Epirus has been laid waste, the Locrians, the Phocians, and the Boeotians have been scorched, Acarnania, Amphilochia, Perraebia, and the tribe of the Athamanes have been sold out, Macedonia has been given over to the barbarians, Aetolia has been lost, the Dolopians and their neighbors in the mountains have been driven from their towns and fields; the Roman citizens doing business in these places know that you appeared as their one and only defrauder, ravager, bandit, and enemy. **[97]** In addition to the many serious judgments on you of all these people, there is the judgment made right here. The sentence of your condemnation is your concealed arrival, your furtive trip through Italy, your entry into the city abandoned by your friends, the absence of any dispatches to the senate from your province, no statement of congratulation after three summers of campaigning, not a single mention of a triumph. You don't dare say what you did and not even where you were. When you had brought back from that source and seedbed of triumphs the dried leaves of laurel, in tossing them away at the gate you pronounced your verdict on yourself: "Guilty." If you had done nothing worthy of honor, then what was the point of your army, your expense, your command? What's the point of a province rich in thanksgivings and triumphs? But if you had hopes, if you thought that the name of commander, the *fasces* bound in laurel, the trophies filled with disgrace and laughter proclaim what you had in mind, then who is more wretched than you, who has suffered a worse condemnation than you, a man who neither dared write to the senate nor say in their presence that you had performed well on behalf of the commonwealth? **[98]** I've always believed that a person's fortune should be weighed not by outcomes but by actions; that our fame and fortune are judged not in the voting tablets of a few judges but in the opinions of all citizens. Do you think you can seem uncondemned to me? You, a man whom our friends and allies, free people and subjects, businessmen and tax collectors, the nation as a whole, your own legates and military tribunes, the soldiers who remain after surviving war, starvation, and disease—all these people think you eminently worthy of any and all punishment? A man to whom neither by the senate nor by any other order of society, neither in the city nor in

Italy, any pardon can possibly be given for your enormous crimes? A man who hates himself, who fears everyone, who does not have the audacity to entrust his own case to anyone, who has voted for his own condemnation? **[99]** I have never thirsted for your blood; I have never wanted for you that ultimate penalty of the laws and the courts that can be inflicted on guilty and innocent alike. But to see you cast away and an object of contempt, despised by everyone, abandoned without hope by yourself, looking over your shoulder at everything, fearing every noise, having no trust in your own capacities, without a voice, without freedom, without authority, without any appearance of having been consul, quivering and trembling, fawning on all: that is what I wanted to see, and that is what I have seen. For that reason if what you fear happens to come about, I won't be sorry; but if it takes a while, then I'll still enjoy your worthlessness and your fears, and I'll see you frightened of being prosecuted with no less pleasure than when I see you actually prosecuted, and I will take no less joy in seeing you degraded for all time than if I see you for a short time wearing the degraded clothes of a defendant.

8

On Behalf of Marcus Marcellus

The divergences of opinion that have marked modern interpretations of On Behalf of Marcus Marcellus *would surely have pleased Cicero himself: it is a speech delivered in precarious circumstances, designed at once to flatter Caesar the Dictator and to move him toward a more republican attitude; to express Cicero's loyalty to Caesar and to alert the audience (the senate first, then readers) to his loyalty to the values of republicanism; to remain within the confines of normal senatorial language and behavior and to deliver what is in fact the first Latin example of a speech of advice to a prince, the later genre of the* speculum principis. *The opening of the speech is addressed to the senate, but before the middle of the speech the senate disappears, and the only person addressed is the dictator, Julius Caesar. It is not surprising that in an age not unfamiliar with the duplicitous language encouraged by autocracy,* On Behalf of Marcus Marcellus *has been seen as covertly critical of Caesar;[1] that is unlikely, but one would not be altogether surprised if Cicero hoped that some of his fellow senators might at least remain uncertain. It is not easy to remain a republican under a dictatorship.*

In the opening words of the speech, Cicero remarks on the length of time in which he had not spoken in public; indeed, it was a long silence. In 51 BCE Cicero had reluctantly left Rome to become governor of Cilicia for a year. He did not return until January of 49, and as a result he took no part in the senatorial debates of late 50 BCE in which Caesar's demands were rebuffed and the senatorial (and Pompeian) position hardened. After war began early in 49, Cicero vacillated for some time before eventually joining Pompey, his troops, and part of the senate at Dyrrachium on the Adriatic coast; in the end Cicero did not take part in the battle of Pharsalus in 48, and after the defeat of Pompey, he was one of the first to abandon the cause and return to Italy. Others, too, made rapid peace with the victor, including Servius Sulpicius Rufus (who became governor of Greece) and the future assassin Gaius Cassius Longinus. Not, however, Marcus Claudius Marcellus. Marcellus had been consul in 51 (together with Sulpicius Rufus), followed in successive years by his cousin Gaius (in 50) and his brother Gaius (in 49); he and his brother were among Caesar's

---

1. See Dyer (1990); for a recent assessment of the speech, see Gotoff (2002) 226–35.

most active opponents, and while Gaius the cousin was pardoned by
Caesar, Gaius the brother died, and Marcus himself chose after Pharsalus
to go into exile, self-imposed but certainly not countermanded by Caesar,
at Mytilene on the island of Lesbos.

Cicero, although he returned to Italy, was not allowed to leave
Brundisium and return to Rome for some time; it was not until Caesar
himself emerged from the Alexandrian War and returned to Italy in 47 that
he was given permission to return to Rome and resume civil life. And while
he reluctantly accepted the reality of Caesar's control (although he hoped
it would be temporary), he was not ready to voice active support for
the new regime. The period of Caesar's dictatorship is the time in which
Cicero was most prolific in writing treatises and dialogues about rhetoric
and philosophy. In 46 he wrote Brutus and Orator, the latter a technical
treatise on rhetorical style and the former a dialogue on the history of
Roman oratory that in distinctly republican tones laments the fact that the
younger generation will no longer have the free political life that alone
makes great oratory possible.

Brutus is one of Cicero's masterpieces, not to mention being one of
our most important sources for the chronology of early Roman literature;
it is also directly relevant to the speech for Marcellus. Cicero presents his
dialogue as in part a response to a "letter" from Marcus Brutus (the later
assassin), almost certainly his treatise On Virtue.[2] That work is lost, but we
know (from Cicero and from later citations) that Brutus had introduced
the figure of the exiled Marcellus as an example of the sufficiency of virtue
for happiness. So, too, and probably at the same time, the polymath
Marcus Terentius Varro entitled one of his Logistorici (works of popular
philosophy) Marcellus: On Exile. Other than the martyred Cato, Marcus
Marcellus was the outstanding exemplar of principled and philosophical
republicanism, choosing exile over compliance with the dictator. That, as
well as long-standing friendship, may well be the reason that during the
summer of 46 Cicero wrote several letters to Marcellus (ad Fam. 4.7–9)
urging him to make peace with Caesar and return: for obvious reasons, it
was not entirely comfortable to be the most eminent ex-consul who had
capitulated, and capitulated early. And even though Cicero refused to
speak in the senate, his presence in Rome was itself a legitimation of the
new regime.

In September, however, there was a new development that Cicero
reported in a letter to Sulpicius Rufus (ad Fam. 4.4.3–4). Marcellus'
name was mentioned in senatorial debate by Lucius Calpurnius Piso,
Caesar's father-in-law (and the object of Cicero's hatred in Against Lucius

---

2. Cicero discusses Marcellus on Lesbos at *Brutus* 250; on Brutus' treatise,
see, most recently, Sedley (1997).

Calpurnius Piso), and Marcellus' cousin Gaius threw himself at Caesar's feet urging mercy. The whole senate supported him, and Caesar, despite inveighing against Marcellus' hostility (acerbitas), said that he would be willing to comply with the senate's wishes. All spoke in praise of Caesar and his clemency; Cicero's speech in that context—an elegant, formal, and at times ornate expression of thanks—is what is translated here.

Cicero's gratitude toward Caesar seems genuine. It was indeed, as he says both in the speech itself and in the letter to Sulpicius, the first time he had spoken publicly since his return to Rome, and he did see in the pardon of Marcellus a hint that the old Republic might be restored. But at the same time that On Behalf of Marcus Marcellus is a speech of thanks, it is also an attempt to move the dictator ever so slightly toward a restoration of republican government. Cicero's approach to the subject was necessarily oblique, particularly in the circulated written version (it should not be forgotten that the oral version was extemporized and that only later was it written down). After expressions of thanks and gratitude to Caesar, he argues that political actions such as this pardon are more deserving of lasting glory than the military victories for which Caesar was renowned. He goes on to present a version of recent history that emphasizes the role of fate and fortune rather than of individuals, and thus he suggests that Caesar's victory was less worthy of glory precisely because it was the product of forces larger than Caesar himself. In the final third of the speech, he turns to the rumor that Caesar has said that his life had been long enough; here again, Cicero uses the insufficiency of Caesar's military glory for his eternal reputation as an argument for the importance of political rather than military action. In this case, he is urging not the restoration of a single man but the restoration of republican government as a whole, implicitly characterizing Caesar in terms reminiscent of the ideal statesman of Cicero's own On the Commonwealth, completed shortly before the Civil War.

The second part of the speech (section 23 in particular) has sometimes been taken as the presentation of a precise program for political renewal, but it is far too vague and rhetorical for that. The speech is less a political program than an exercise in redescription: by showing Caesar a portrait of himself as a statesman and the re-founder of the Republic, he hopes to make that vision attractive and thus to help make it true.

Cicero's attempt to make Caesar a republican did not work, and over the next year and a half Cicero grew increasingly bitter and disillusioned,[3] as did others, notably Brutus and Cassius, who led the group of conspirators who assassinated Caesar in March of 44. Of that conspiracy,

---

3. In Cicero's case, not just for political reasons. His daughter died suddenly early in 45.

however, Marcellus was not a member, having been assassinated himself.
Although pleased to be invited to return, and clearly grateful to Cicero
for his speech (Marcellus' letter to Cicero is preserved as ad Fam. 4.11),
Marcellus moved slowly and reluctantly toward Rome. He never got
there. A letter to Cicero from Sulpicius Rufus (ad Fam. 4.12) records that
in May of 45, Marcellus arrived in Piraeus and was stabbed to death by his
(apparent) friend Magius Cilo, who then committed suicide himself. The
motive is still unknown.

Pro M. Marcello Oratio

My fellow senators:

[1] The long silence I have maintained of late, not from fear but
in part from sorrow, in part from a sense of shame, comes to an end
this day, and at the same time I start to voice my desires and opinions
as once I did. Such gentility, such unexampled and unfamiliar mercy,
such moderation from someone holding universal power, and finally
such incredible and almost superhuman wisdom I can in no way let
pass in silence. [2] I believe, my fellow senators, that the return of
Marcus Marcellus to you and to the commonwealth preserves and
restores not just his voice and influence but mine, for you and for the
commonwealth. It caused me sorrow and sharp pain, my fellow senators, to see such a man, who had been on the same side as I, not to
have the same conditions as I. I could not convince myself, I did not
think it right for me to take up my old way of life while he, who both
rivaled and followed my hard work and studies as a companion and,
one might say, an ally, was torn away from me. My old way of life had
been closed off; you, Gaius Caesar, opened it for me, and for all of us
you have raised up a signal of hope for the commonwealth. [3] In
granting Marcellus to the senate and the commonwealth, particularly
after recalling his injuries to you,[4] you showed everyone what I had
already learned in connection with many people (not least myself),
that you place the authority of the senatorial order and the dignity
of the commonwealth ahead of injuries to you or to suspicions you
feel.[5] On this day, he has received the greatest return on his previous

---

4. The "bitterness" mentioned in Cicero's account of the senate meeting to
Sulpicius; see the introduction to this speech.

5. As throughout the speech, Cicero tries to make Caesar a constitutionalist
by redescribing him as one.

life,[6] through both the strong support of the senate and your solemn and deliberate judgment. From this, in fact, you can understand how much praise arises from the giving of a favor, when there is so much glory in accepting it. **[4]** That man is indeed fortunate whose rescue brings scarcely less happiness to everyone else than he receives himself—something he richly and rightly deserves. Who is there more outstanding in nobility or honesty or literary cultivation or integrity or in any quality deserving praise?

No one has a vein of talent so great, no one has such force or capacity in speech or in writing as to be able to recount your accomplishments, Caesar, much less to embellish them.[7] But if you permit me, I will assert this much, that your previous actions can receive no praise higher than what you have earned this day. **[5]** I frequently imagine, and frequently say so with pleasure, that no comparison can be made between all the deeds of our generals, all the deeds of foreign tribes and powerful peoples, all the deeds of famous kings, and your deeds—not in the size of the conflicts nor the number of the battles nor the geographical range nor the speed of action nor the diversity of the wars. Nor could anyone's feet traverse lands so far apart more swiftly than they have been covered not by your travels but by your victories.[8] **[6]** I would be out of my mind not to admit that such accomplishments are so great that the mind can scarcely grasp them—but there is more than that. Some people dilute the praise of success in war by what they say; they take it from the leaders and share it with the pack to avoid its belonging to the generals. To be sure, in military affairs the courage of the troops, the terrain, the assistance of allies, naval support, and provisions help a great deal, but Lady Luck claims ownership, as if by law, of the greatest portion of it;[9] she believes that whatever has been done successfully is rightly hers. **[7]** But in the glory you have just now received, Caesar, you have no partner. Such as it is—and it is worth a lot—it is entirely

---

6. "Return": *fructus* is the standard term for profit or the payment of interest. The language of this and the next sentence is financial.

7. Caesar had done so himself in his *Commentaries* on both the Gallic and Civil Wars.

8. The hyperbole is strikingly similar to that used about Pompey in *In Support of Manilius' Law*, sec. 28.

9. "Claims ownership": *vindicat*, a legal term for asserting ownership of disputed property.

yours; I repeat, entirely yours. No centurion snips off any of it for himself, no prefect, no cohort, no squadron. Lady Luck herself, the ruler of human affairs, does not make herself your partner in this glory; she yields to you, she admits that it is yours and yours alone.[10] There is nothing random about wisdom, no chance in the exercise of judgment. **[8]** You have conquered tribes of barbarian savagery and countless numbers in uncounted places with overflowing resources; but what you conquered was by nature and condition capable of being conquered. There is no force so great that it cannot be weakened and broken by the strength of arms. But to conquer one's spirit, to check one's anger, to be moderate to the conquered, to raise up an adversary outstanding in nobility, talent, and courage, and not only to raise him up when he is fallen but even to enhance his previous standing—the person who does this I do not compare to the greatest humans but judge him to be like a god. **[9]** Thus, Caesar, the praises of your military accomplishments will be celebrated not just in our language and literature but in those of virtually all peoples; no age will keep silent about your praises. Actions of that sort, however, somehow seem, even when we read about them, to be drowned out by the shouts of soldiers and the sound of trumpets. But when we hear or read of an action that displays mercy, gentility, justice, moderation, and wisdom,[11] particularly in the presence of anger, which is always hostile to deliberation, and in the context of victory, which is naturally proud and haughty, then how we are set on fire with enthusiasm, not only for actions that have actually taken place but even for imagined ones, with the result that we often cherish men whom we have never seen.[12] **[10]** But we look upon you right here;[13] we perceive your thoughts and feelings as well as your countenance; we see that you desire the well-being of whatever of the commonwealth has survived the fortunes of war—with what praise shall we extol you, with what zeal shall we attend you, with what goodwill shall we embrace you? By my faith, it seems to me that the very walls

---

10. Again, legal language: *societas* is the formal term for a business partnership.

11. The absence of courage (the fourth Platonic virtue) is notable: this is praise of a statesman, not a general.

12. An echo of the praise of the effects of poetry in *In Defense of the Poet Archias*.

13. The language is religious: one addresses a "present god" in prayer.

of this senate house yearn to offer thanks to you because in a short time such authority will dwell in this place that belongs to him and to his ancestors. When along with all of you I beheld just now the tears of Gaius Marcellus, a great man whose sense of family obligation deserves credit, my heart was flooded with memory of all the Marcelli; by preserving Marcus Marcellus you have returned their honor even to the Marcelli who are dead, and you have rescued from near extinction a family of great nobility that had been diminished to just a few men. **[11]** This day, then, you rightly place ahead of the countless great thanksgivings offered on your behalf.[14] This action belongs to Gaius Caesar alone; all the other things accomplished under your leadership were great, but they came with a large and extensive body of supporters. Of this action you are both leader and army; it is so great that, while the passage of time will make an end to your trophies and monuments—there is nothing made by human effort that age does not destroy and consume—still your justice and moderation will grow daily ever more fresh. **[12]** What the passage of time takes away from your deeds it will add to your praises. Before this you had already outdone all other victors in civil wars by your fairness and mercy; but this day you have outdone yourself. I am afraid that what I say will not be understood by my hearers in the same way that I feel it in my thoughts. In returning to the defeated what they had lost, you seem to have conquered victory itself. All of us who were conquered would have fallen by the terms that attend victory; but by the judgment of your mercy we have been preserved. It is right, then, for you alone to be unconquered by whom the very nature of victory itself has been conquered.

[13] My fellow senators, observe the broad extent of this decision of Caesar's. All of us who were driven to take up arms on that side were driven by some wretched and destructive fate of the commonwealth; even though we were guilty of human error, we were certainly free from criminal intent.[15] When at your plea he preserved Marcellus for the commonwealth, he returned me both to myself and to the commonwealth, without anyone making an appeal for

---

14. The lengthy thanksgivings (*supplicationes*) amounting to some fifty-five days in all, declared by the senate at the end of campaigns in Gaul and Britain, with another forty for his victory in the Civil War.

15. Legal language again: there is a distinction between criminality (*scelus*) and wrongfulness (*culpa*). See below, on sec. 18.

me, and he gave back other distinguished men to themselves and the country, men whose numbers and whose standing you see in this very gathering. He did not lead his enemies into the senate house but judged that the war was undertaken by most of us through ignorance and through a false and empty fear rather than through greed or cruelty. **[14]** During the war, in fact, I always thought that overtures of peace should be listened to, and I continually felt sorry that not only peace but the words of citizens demanding peace were rejected. I never followed the weapons of this civil war or any other, and my plans were always bound to peace and the toga, not to war and weapons. I followed a man from a sense of private obligation, not public;[16] and the loyal memory of a grateful mind had such influence over me that it was not only without greed but not even with any hope that knowingly and with forethought I rushed as if to a voluntary death. **[15]** My plans in this respect were scarcely hidden; before things fell apart, I said a great deal in this body about peace, and during the war itself I expressed the same sentiments with some danger to my life. As a result no one can be so prejudiced a judge as to doubt Caesar's wishes about the war, since he immediately determined to save men who urged peace but appeared rather angrier to the rest. Perhaps while the outcome was uncertain and the chances of war were balanced, that was not so remarkable; but the man who as victor shows concern for those who urged peace declares that he would have preferred not to fight rather than to win. **[16]** In this I can be a witness as far as Marcus Marcellus is concerned.[17] Our opinions were the same in war just as much as they always were in peace. How often I saw him, and with what sorrow, dreading both the arrogance of some individuals and the savagery of victory itself. To those of us who saw such things, your generosity, Caesar, deserves all the more gratitude. Not the motives but the victories of the two sides should be compared to one another. **[17]** We saw that your victory came to an end with the end of fighting; we did not see a sword unsheathed in the city. The citizens we lost were destroyed by the violence of war, not the anger of victory; as a result, no one ought to doubt that Caesar, if he could, would summon many of them up from the dead, given

---

16. Cicero turns his political decision into a personal obligation to Pompey, just as he redescribes the war itself as somehow accidental.

17. In fact, Cicero's letters to Marcellus show that he is being truthful at least here.

that he preserves whoever he can who was part of the same army. Of the other side I will say no more than what we all feared, that victory would have been marked by too much anger. **[18]** There were some who made threats not just against armed soldiers but sometimes against noncombatants; they said that one needed to consider not what anyone felt but where he was.[18] As a result, it seems to me that even if in stirring up so great and so grievous a civil war the gods claimed compensation from the Roman people because of some wrongful negligence,[19] they have been either appeased or satisfied, and they have transferred all our hopes for well-being to the clemency and wisdom of the victor.

[19] For that reason, you should take pleasure in the wonderful thing you have done, and reap the rewards not only of your good fortune and glory but of your natural character as well; for a man of wisdom, that is the source of the greatest and most enjoyable reward. When you look back on your entire life, you will congratulate yourself often on your character, but more often on your good fortune; whenever you think about us whom you wanted to take part with you in public life, you will think of the extraordinary favors you conferred, your unbelievable generosity, your unique wisdom. These are not only the highest goods but in my view the only ones. There is so much distinction in praise that is truthful, so much worthiness in greatness of mind and thought, that these things seem to be the gifts of virtue while everything else is merely on loan from luck.[20] **[20]** So do not become weary of preserving good men, particularly those who fell not from some greed or corruption but from an opinion of their duty that may have been dumb but was certainly not wicked, and from a particular vision of the commonwealth. It is not your fault if

---

18. The Pompeian side denounced as traitors all those senators who did not follow them out of Italy.

19. Cicero is using the language of law, specifically the Aquilian law that assessed damages for "loss wrongfully inflicted."

20. Cicero's language reflects the preoccupation of Hellenistic philosophy (both Stoic and Epicurean) with finding an indestructible source of happiness, viewing worldly goods as at best helpful and more often indifferent. The idea that prosperity and good fortune are (again in legal language) borrowed rather than an outright gift is parallel to Lucretius' Epicurean view of life itself: "Nobody owns life; everyone has the use of it" (*On Nature* 3.971).

some people were afraid of you; rather, it is the highest praise that they realized you were not to be feared at all.

[21] I come now to your most serious complaint and most horrible suspicion,[21] which you must provide against, but no more you than all citizens, and particularly those of us who have been preserved by you. Even though I expect it is false, I will never make light of it: to look out for you is to look out for ourselves. If one must err in one direction or the other, I would prefer to seem excessively timid than not sufficiently prudent. But who could be so insane? Someone close to you? But who is closer to you than people who received from you the safety for which they had no hope? Or one of your followers? I can't believe anyone could be so crazy that he wouldn't put before his own life the life of the man who led him to the summit of his wishes. Or if your supporters have no thought of this crime, are precautions necessary against the plans of your enemies? But who? All your former enemies either lost their lives through their own stubbornness or kept them through your mercy; either your enemies have perished or the survivors are your most devoted friends. [22] But since men's minds hold such dark hiding places, we should increase your suspicions; at the same time we will increase your watchfulness. Who in the world is so ignorant of the circumstances, so inexperienced in public life, so empty of thoughts about both his own and our common safety as not to understand that his own safety is a part of yours, and that the lives of all depend on your life alone? Night and day you are in my thoughts, as you ought to be; I fear the mischances that affect all humans, the uncertain outcome of health, and the fragility of our common nature. It gives me pain, when the commonwealth ought to be immortal,[22] that it rests on the soul of one mortal man. [23] If one adds to human misfortunes and the unpredictable instability of health a conspiracy of crime and treachery, then what god, even if he should wish, do we believe able to bring aid to the commonwealth?

You alone, Caesar, have the responsibility of raising up all those things you see fallen, crushed, and flattened as was inevitable by the onslaught of war itself. The courts must be established, credit

---

21. A fear of assassination; whether real at this time or exaggerated by Cicero for the sake of his argument is unclear.

22. In *On the Commonwealth* 3.41 (written before the Civil War) one of the speakers had argued that the commonwealth "ought to be immortal" because of its justice; the grounds for immortality have shifted.

must be restored, improper desires must be checked, childbirth must be encouraged, everything that collapsed and melted away must be bound together by strict laws. [24] In such a great civil war, with so much heat both of spirits and of arms, it would have been impossible for the commonwealth not to have been shaken. Whatever the outcome of the war, the country would have lost a lot—the trappings that give it a sense of worth and the protection that keeps it steady. Either general would have done many things when in arms that he would have forbidden in peace. All these wounds of war must now be healed by you—other than you, there is no one to treat them. [25] And so I was unhappy to hear a statement of yours that is both a noble thought and the mark of a serious philosopher: "I have lived long enough for nature or for glory." Perhaps enough, if you wish, for nature, and if you want I'll add "for glory": but—and this is, in fact, the most important thing—certainly not enough for your country. For that reason, please give up that wisdom of learned men in showing scorn for death; do not philosophize at our expense. It has often reached my ears that you say this much too frequently, that you have lived enough for yourself. I believe it, but I would listen only if you were living for yourself alone or if you had been born for yourself alone.[23] Your accomplishments have encompassed the well-being of all citizens and the whole commonwealth, but you are so far from completing your greatest deeds that you have not yet set the foundations you have in mind. At this point are you going to define the measure of your life not by the well-being of your country but by your own peace of mind? Consider the possibility that what you've done isn't even enough for glory—and you won't deny that, no matter how much a philosopher you are, you still want a lot of glory. [26] "Is my legacy," you will say, "not great enough?" Of course it is. It's enough for however many other people; you're the only one for whom it's not enough. Whatever there is, no matter how great it is, is not enough when there is something greater. And if this, Caesar, is to be the conclusion of your actions, actions that are immortal, that after conquering your opponents you leave the commonwealth in the condition in which it now is, then take care, I urge you, that your superhuman virtue not appear more astounding than glorious, at least if we define glory as the conspicuous and

---

23. Cicero is echoing Plato, *Ninth Letter* 358a; cf. *In Defense of Lucius Murena*, sec. 83.

widespread reputation for great services either to one's fellow citizens or one's country or the entire human race. **[27]** This, then, is the part that is unfinished. This is the action that remains; in this you must toil to reconstitute the commonwealth, and you must then take delight in its great calm and order. Then, if you want, when you have returned to your country what you owe it and have satisfied nature itself through length of life, then say that you have lived long enough. And in any case, what is this "long" if it has some outer limit? When it arrives, all past pleasure is as nothing, because there will be none in the future. But your spirit has never been satisfied with the narrow bounds that nature has given us for life; it has always burned with a love of immortality. **[28]** You should not define your life in terms of body and breath: that is your life, I say, that is your life that will remain vivid in the memory of every generation; posterity will nourish it, eternity itself will always protect it. To this life you must enslave yourself; to this you should show yourself. You have long given posterity much to wonder at; now it awaits something to praise. Later generations will certainly be struck with awe at your commands and provinces, the Rhine, the Ocean, and the Nile, innumerable battles and unbelievable victories, monuments and spectacles, triumphs of which they will hear and read.[24] **[29]** But unless this city is made firm by your foresight and organization, your name will wander far and wide but will have no fixed and certain home.[25] As has been the case among us, so too our descendants will have great discord. Some will raise your accomplishments to the heavens with their praise, others will think something very important is missing if you don't put out the fire of civil war by making the country sound; the first will seem to have been fated, the last the product of wisdom. So devote yourself to the judges who will give their verdict on you many generations in the future, and perhaps less corruptly than we do; for they will give their judgments without affection and greed as also without hatred or enmity.[26] **[30]** And even if, as some people wrongly believe,[27] it will make no difference to you then, it certainly

---

24. A very cursory list of Caesar's military achievements.

25. As the souls of those who do not contribute to the public good wander through the universe at the end of *On the Commonwealth* (6.29).

26. Cicero echoes the stock claim of objectivity made by historians.

27. Epicureans (of whom Caesar was one).

makes a difference for you now to act in such a way that no oblivion will ever cast a shadow over your glory.

Our citizens had different desires and divergent opinions; we were split not just in our plans and parties but in weapons and fortifications. There was a murkiness, there was a contest between leaders of great distinction; many people had doubts about what was best, many about what was in their interest, many about what was right, and quite a few about what they could get away with. **[31]** Our country made it through that wretched and destructive war. The victor was one who did not fan the flames of his hatred because of his good fortune but lessened them by his goodness; nor did he judge all those at whom he was angry worthy of exile or death. Some people laid down their weapons, from others they were snatched away. Any citizen is ungrateful and unfair who has been freed from the danger of war but still keeps his spirit under arms; it makes those who fell in battle look better, men who gave up their lives for their beliefs. What seems like stubbornness to some people looks like steadfastness to others. **[32]** But now all discord has been broken by warfare and extinguished by the fairness of the victor. It remains for everyone to have the same wishes—at least everyone who has not just any wisdom but even any sanity. If you are not safe, Caesar, and if you do not remain of the same opinion that you expressed both previously and especially today, then we cannot be safe. For that reason, everyone who wants all that we have to be safe urges and beseeches you to look after your life and your safety; and since you think you must be wary of something hidden, we all—to say on behalf of others what I feel myself—promise not only to watch and guard but even to interpose our strength and our bodies.

[33] But let me end this speech where it began: we all, Caesar, express the greatest gratitude to you, but we feel even more. All have the same opinion, as you can see from the prayers and tears of all. But as there is no need for everyone to rise and speak, they certainly want it to be said by me, who have an obligation to do so. I recognize that what is being done is what ought to be done, since Marcus Marcellus has been given back by you to the senate and the Roman people and the commonwealth. I recognize that everyone is rejoicing not as for the well-being of one man but for the well-being of all. **[34]** Everyone knows how devoted I have always been to Marcellus; in this I scarcely yield to Gaius Marcellus, his most loving and best of cousins,[28] and to no one else at all. I have exhibited that devotion through my worry, care, and toil for as long as there was any doubt about his well-being; and now that I have been freed from these great cares, worries, and sorrows, I have a distinct obligation to put it into practice. And so, Gaius Caesar, I offer you my thanks: after having been in every way preserved and even honored by you, still, by your present action I have received a great increase to your infinite generosity to me, to which I had not thought that anything more could be added.

---

28. "Brother" in Latin, but often used for cousin. Marcellus' brother Gaius was dead.

9

Fourth Philippic Oration against Antony

*Between September of 44 BCE and April of the next year, Cicero
delivered fourteen speeches to which he himself gave the title of
"Philippics."[1] Almost all were attacks on Mark Antony; they represent
Cicero as the champion of a return to the Republic and Antony as its
most significant opponent. They are filled with invective, half-truths, and
oversimplifications, and while the Second Philippic—never delivered,
and in fact a massive pamphlet rather than a speech—has been admired
since antiquity for the eloquence of its venom,[2] as a whole the speeches
are not the finest examples of Ciceronian oratory. They are speeches of
the moment—designed, for the most part, to move senatorial opinion
concerning particular policies and actions—and they are much blunter
instruments than many of Cicero's earlier political speeches. But these
speeches are more than historical evidence: the Fourth Philippic, in
particular, is an important example of Cicero's very deliberate methods
in shaping his audience and its views. It is one of only two speeches in
the set that was addressed to the people rather than the senate; its goal,
very clearly, is to influence popular perception of the senatorial debate
(represented by the Third Philippic) that had taken place on the same day.
Without having the parallel speech from the senate meeting, we might well
be at a loss to understand this speech; even worse, we might believe it.
The Third and Fourth Philippics were delivered on December 20,
44 BCE. The senate meeting on that day had been called to establish
precautions and policies for the change in administration that was (under
normal constitutional rules) to take place less than two weeks later, when
Antony and Dolabella, the incumbent consuls, were to be replaced by
the consuls-designate Hirtius and Pansa. But neither the political nor the
military situation was clear or stable. As the debate was taking place,
Antony was attempting to take control of Cisalpine and Transalpine Gaul,*

---

1. Not for the first time; he referred to his consular orations in the same way,
and he was generally aware of Demosthenes as a model to be emulated and
surpassed. More of the collection (at least another three speeches) existed in
antiquity, but they do not seem to be later than April of 43.

2. See, for instance, Juvenal 10.124–26.

*the provinces he had been given at his own wish by popular vote; he
was opposed by the previously designated proconsul then in possession
of Cisalpine Gaul, Decimus Junius Brutus, one of the assassins of Caesar
(not to be confused with the more famous Marcus Junius Brutus). Cicero,
as a supporter of the assassins and of restoring normality to republican
government, viewed Decimus Brutus as the legitimate representative of
the government (i.e., the senate) and Antony as a would-be successor to
Caesar. His unsuccessful hope on December 20 was to have the senate
declare Antony a public enemy (*hostis*) and to praise and reconcile with
one another Antony's opponents—not only Decimus Brutus (and the other
assassins, who had already left Italy for the East) but, far more precariously,
the young Octavian, the future Augustus.[3]*

*Cicero's policy after March 15, 44 (the Ides of March), is hard to
understand and even harder to justify.[4] He was a committed supporter of
the assassins (whom he thought of rather as "liberators" or "tyrannicides"),
and in the days after the assassination he did what he could to establish
a compromise, albeit an uneasy one, between the assassins and the
supporters of Caesar, including Caesar's fellow consul and devoted military
aide, Antony. The situation, however, became ever more complex over
the following weeks. Not only did popular affection for Caesar (and
perhaps the effects of Antony's funeral oration) make Rome unsafe for
Brutus, Cassius, and the rest, but the arrival in Italy of Caesar's heir added
an unknown—and, as it turned out, both intelligent and ruthless—figure
on the Caesarian side. Antony, to maintain his position as representative
of Julius Caesar, was forced into rivalry with Octavian as claimant to the
dictator's (moral and financial) heritage, and hence was compelled to
adopt a more belligerent stance toward the assassins and thus toward
the republican sentiments of the senate as well. Octavian, through wide
distribution of money and the use of his inherited name, gained much
support among the soldiers and came to Rome to claim his inheritance.
And Cicero, in order to support the position of the assassins, chose to try
to weaken Antony by enlisting the young Octavian—whom he hoped he
would be able to control.*

---

3. By modern convention, this person is called Octavian at this period, a
name he never used in real life. Born Gaius Octavius, when adopted by
the will of his great-uncle Julius Caesar he became, formally, Gaius Julius
Caesar Octavianus, but he referred to himself (and was referred to by others) simply as Caesar. After achieving sole power, he accepted the name
"Augustus" from the senate in 27 BCE. From that point on his name (not
his title) was "Imperator Caesar Augustus."

4. For a brilliant account of the events of this period, sympathetic to Antony
and decidedly unsympathetic to Cicero, see Syme (1939) 97–175.

During the first chaotic months after the Ides, however, Cicero took little active role in public life; indeed, in July he set out for Greece to visit his son. He never got past Sicily, however. When he received word of possible compromise between Antony and the assassins, he turned back, reaching Rome at the end of August. Hope for a peaceful solution had already faded by the time he got there. Although Cicero did not attend the senate meeting on September 1 when Antony gave a threatening speech, on the following day he delivered his first attack on Antony (the First Philippic), followed shortly by the undelivered but memorable invective of the Second Philippic.

All the remaining Philippics constitute (with some minor variations) Cicero's attempts to interpret events and direct policy in the period from Antony's march north to take over Cisalpine Gaul and remove Decimus Brutus, through the complex siege of Mutina and the series of battles (among a large number of armies and generals of various sympathies) that culminated in the defeat of Antony in April of 43 and his subsequent designation as a public enemy. The last Philippic, delivered on April 21, is in fact Cicero's last extant speech. Antony escaped from Mutina, reestablished his army, came to terms with Octavian and others, and, with Octavian and Marcus Aemilius Lepidus, formed the Second Triumvirate in November. Cicero was one of the first victims of the ensuing proscriptions.

Although the audience for contio speeches was a tiny and not necessarily representative part of the Roman people, the reaction of the crowd was, in Roman politics, a crucial indication of popular support (or lack of support), and the successful orator was one who was able to create and direct public sentiment while speaking.[5] The Fourth Philippic, though very brief, is in this regard a brilliantly effective rhetorical construction. Cicero assumes the interpretation of Antony (villainous) and Octavian (patriotic) that he wants the audience to express. The entire argument is based on the dilemma set out at the beginning (4.2): the consul Antony and the people fighting against him cannot simultaneously be considered patriotic Romans; since we support Octavian against Antony, then it follows that Antony is not really a consul but a public enemy. The argument, of course, depends on the interpretations of Antony and Octavian; it is the goal of the speech to show the people that they agree with those interpretations and that they are therefore true. To that end, Cicero draws the audience in by addressing them directly (Quirites, "my fellow citizens") more frequently than in any other speech; he also repeatedly draws attention to the audience reaction that he has (or claims

---

5. The significance of the *contio* and the technique of eliciting audience response ("claptrap") have been superbly explained by Morstein-Marx (2004); on the Fourth Philippic, see 139–43.

to have) aroused. *The cheers of the audience described by Cicero are themselves an affirmation both to himself and to the audience of the rightness of his position. By appearing to share the views of the people, he makes himself more authoritative in shaping their opinions and thereby the policies of the senate as well.*

In M. Antonium Oratio Philippica Quarta

My fellow citizens:

[1] The astonishing size of this crowd, a public assembly larger than I remember ever seeing before, gives me great energy for defending the commonwealth and hope for restoring it. I have always wanted that; the times were against it. But as soon as the first signs of light appeared, I was the first person to defend your liberty;[6] if I had tried to act earlier, I would not be able to act now. Do not minimize, my fellow citizens, what has been accomplished this day; the foundation has been laid for everything else we will do. Through its actions, if not yet in its words, the senate has judged Mark Antony to be a public enemy.[7] [2] And right now, I can hold my head up much higher, since your great shout of approval shows that you agree he is a public enemy.[8] My fellow citizens, there is no way not to believe one or the other: either the men who raised armies against a consul are disloyal, or arms were properly taken up against someone who is a public enemy.[9] There was no real doubt about this, but today the senate has removed any possibility of doubt. Gaius Caesar, who has protected and continues to protect the commonwealth and your

---

6. Not exactly; Cicero's former enemy Piso (see *Against Lucius Calpurnius Piso*) spoke in favor of a compromise to restore republican government in August, while Cicero was still making his way back to Rome from the south.

7. The key to the speech: the senate had not voted Antony a public enemy, and much of this speech is intended to obscure that fact.

8. Here, as frequently below, Cicero's words imply active participation and response on the part of the audience. It is not clear whether there were real shouts, or if Cicero's written recreation of the speech also creates the active responses of the audience.

9. Antony is the consul of the first clause, the public enemy of the second. Those raising armies against him are above all Octavian, but also Decimus Brutus and other supporters of the assassins.

liberty with his energy, his wisdom, and not least his inheritance, has received the greatest official praise from the senate.[10] **[3]** I praise you, my fellow citizens, I praise you because you show such enthusiastic gratitude when I name this glorious young man—or rather, boy: his deeds are timeless, but the name for his chronological age is "boy."[11] I remember a lot, my fellow citizens: I have heard a lot and I have read a lot. But I know nothing like this to be recollected in all of history: when we were being crushed into slavery; when things were getting worse every day; when we had no protection; when we feared the fatal and destructive return of Antony from Brundisium—just then he embraced a plan that was beyond the hopes of all of us and was certainly unprecedented, to put together an invincible army from his father's veterans and fend off Antony, whose madness is intensified by the wickedness of his goals, from the destruction of the commonwealth. **[4]** Does anyone not understand that if Caesar had not raised an army,[12] Antony's return would have demanded our destruction? He was on his way back, seething with hatred of you, dripping with the blood of the Roman citizens he had killed at Suessa and Brundisium,[13] with no thought except to destroy the Roman people. And what protection was there for your well-being and your freedom, if Caesar's army had not been composed of his father's bravest soldiers? Just now the senate agreed with my motion. At the earliest possible moment we should decide on the immortal honors that correspond to his immortal merits.[14] **[5]** By that decree it is completely obvious that Antony has been adjudged a public enemy,

---

10. It should be pointed out (as Syme [1939] does, emphatically) that the actions of Gaius Caesar (Octavian) were thoroughly illegal (raising a private army and attempting a coup) while Antony was the (more or less) legally elected consul. Octavian's most important method of raising armies was the promise of huge donatives to the troops.

11. At the time of this speech, Octavian was nineteen. He did not altogether appreciate references to his youth.

12. From Julius Caesar's veterans.

13. Presumably the execution of soldiers (for what cause is unclear) at Suessa Aurunca in Campania, on his route to Brundisium, and at Brundisium itself. His trip to Brundisium was to collect the four legions he had summoned back from Macedonia, two of which rapidly went over to Octavian.

14. Again, Cicero smoothes over the fact that the senate had not voted suitable honors to Octavian at the meeting on December 20.

for if the people who lead armies against him are judged by the senate to deserve new and unique honors, then what else can we call him? The Martian legion—and there is something miraculous in its taking its name from the god from whom we believe the Roman people are descended—didn't it, by its own decrees, judge Antony a public enemy even before the senate did?[15] Because if Antony isn't a public enemy, then the troops who abandoned a consul must necessarily be public enemies themselves. Your resounding response at the right moment shows that you approve the glorious action of the soldiers of the Martian legion. In supporting the senate's authority,[16] your liberty, the entire commonwealth, they abandoned him as a public enemy, a brigand, and the butcher of his fatherland. [6] In doing so, they acted not only with spirit and courage but also with careful thought; they took their station at Alba, a strategic and fortified nearby city whose citizens are outstanding men of great courage and loyalty. The fourth legion copied the bravery of these men under the leadership of Lucius Egnatuleius, whom the senate has recently rightly praised, and followed the army of Gaius Caesar. Well, Antony, what more damaging judgments are you waiting for? Caesar, who raised an army against you, is exalted to the skies; the legions that abandoned you are praised in the choicest terms—legions that you summoned and that would have been yours, if you had chosen to be a consul rather than a public enemy. The senate supports the extraordinarily brave and correct judgment of these legions; the entire people approves—unless, of course, my fellow citizens, you consider Antony to be a consul rather than a public enemy! [7] As you show, my fellow citizens, your judgment is what I thought it would be. And what about the towns, the colonies, the communities of Italy? Do you think they judge any differently? All humankind is unanimous: those men who want our way of life kept safe should take up every weapon against that monster. What about Decimus Brutus, my fellow citizens?[17] You can see his opinion from the edict we received

---

15. The Martian legion was one of those Antony collected at Brundisium. With the fourth legion, it took a position at Alba Fucens in central Italy and declared for Octavian. The god Mars was Romulus' father.

16. Again, misleading: the legions chose Octavian, not the senate, over Antony.

17. Decimus Brutus, one of the assassins, had been appointed by Caesar to the governorship of Cisalpine Gaul and designated consul for 42. He

today; nobody makes light of that, do they? "No!" you say, my fellow citizens, and you're absolutely right. It's as if the everlasting gods bestowed as a gift of goodwill to our commonwealth the family and the name of Brutus both to establish and to restore the liberty of the Roman people.[18] **[8]** And what is Decimus Brutus' judgment about Antony? He bars him from his province; he blocks him with his army; he urges on to war all Gaul, which had already risen spontaneously by its own decision. If Antony is a consul, Brutus is a public enemy; if Brutus is a savior of the commonwealth, then Antony is a public enemy. We can't have any doubt, can we, which of these is true? And just as you with one mind and one voice deny that you have any doubts, so, too, the senate just decreed that Decimus Brutus has deserved well of the commonwealth in defending the authority of the senate and the liberty and power of the Roman people.[19] From whom? From a public enemy, of course. What other defense is deserving of praise? **[9]** Next is the province of Gaul.[20] The senate praises it, as it deserves, with eloquent language because of its resistance to Antony. If that province had thought of him as consul and refused to receive him, it would be involving itself in a major crime; all provinces are obliged to respect the jurisdiction and power of a consul. Decimus Brutus, the general, the consul-designate,[21] a citizen born for public service, denies this; Gaul denies this, all Italy denies it, the senate denies it, you deny it. So other than bandits, who thinks of him as consul? And not even they actually believe what they say; and no matter how wicked and evil they may be (as they are), they can't disagree with the judgment of all humankind. The hope of plunder and spoils blinds their hearts. They are men who haven't been satisfied with gifts of money, assignment of land, and unending confiscations and sales; they have marked out for their spoils the city

---

was killed by Gallic tribesmen as he fled from the Caesarian armies after Mutina.

18. Decimus restored it; his ancestor Lucius Junius Brutus was credited with the expulsion of Tarquin the Proud and the establishment of republican government in 509 BCE. Marcus Brutus is the one whose connection to Lucius Junius Brutus is more commonly noted; it is recorded on his coins.

19. The formal wording of a senatorial resolution.

20. Cisalpine Gaul.

21. Decimus Brutus was designated consul for 42 but was killed in 43.

itself, the goods and fortunes of its citizens.[22] These men think they will lack nothing so long as there's something here for them to snatch and carry off; Antony has promised these men that he will give out shares of the city—I pray to the everlasting gods to turn aside and reject this omen! **[10]** And so, my fellow citizens, may your prayers come true and may the penalty for his madness fall on himself and his household! I'm sure it will. Not only men but even the everlasting gods, I believe, have reached agreement on the preservation of the commonwealth. If the gods announce the future to us through prodigies and omens, they have been so clearly expressed that his punishment is getting closer to him as liberty is getting closer to us. And if so significant an accord of all people could not have come to pass without a push from the gods, then how can we have any doubts about the will of heaven?

[11] What remains, my fellow citizens, is for you to stick firmly to the opinion you have proclaimed. So I will do as generals do when the battle line has been drawn up; even though they see their soldiers completely ready to fight, they cheer them on, and so too I urge you, hot and eager as you are, to regain your freedom. You are not fighting, my fellow citizens, against an enemy with whom peace of any kind is possible. Enslaving you has ceased to be his goal; now he is angry and wants your blood. To him, no sport gives more pleasure than blood, slaughter, and the butchery of citizens before his very eyes. **[12]** My fellow citizens, you have to deal not with a wicked criminal who is human but with a hideous and slavering beast, and since it has fallen into a trap, it should be crushed. If it gets out of there, it will know no limits in cruelty. But now the beast is caught, pressed, squeezed by the forces we already control and soon also by those that the new consuls will gather in a few days. Stay firm for the cause, my fellow citizens: stay the course. You have never had such complete agreement for any cause; you have never been so tightly allied to the senate.[23] No surprise in that: the issue is not the way in which we will live but whether we will continue to live or will die in torture and disgrace. **[13]** Nature has set death itself before us

---

22. Cicero's language about Antony and his troops deliberately echoes some of his language about Catiline.

23. Cicero attempts to recreate (at least in words) the *consensus omnium bonorum* ("concord of all men of property") that he claimed to have created for the fight against Catiline in 63.

all; but virtue, the property of the Roman stock and race, rejects a death that is marked by cruelty and dishonor. Keep this in mind, I urge you, my fellow citizens. It is as an inheritance left you by your ancestors. Everything else is deceitful and uncertain, fleeting and fickle. Virtue alone is anchored by the deepest roots and can never be shaken or moved by any force. That is the weapon with which your ancestors first defeated all Italy, then destroyed Carthage, overturned Numantia, and compelled the most powerful kings and the most warlike tribes to submit to our rule.[24] **[14]** Your ancestors, my fellow citizens, had to deal with an enemy who had a government, a senate house, a treasury, citizens bound by consent and concord, some kind of understanding, should that have been appropriate, of peace and of treaties; your enemy is laying siege to your commonwealth but has none of his own. He yearns to destroy the senate, the common council of the entire world, while he himself has no public council at all. He has drained your treasure but has none of his own. And who can have the consent of his citizens who has no city? What rational basis for peace can there be with someone who displays unbelievable cruelty but no trustworthiness at all? **[15]** My fellow citizens, the Roman people, the conqueror of all nations, now has its entire struggle with an assassin, a brigand, a Spartacus.[25] He has a habit of boasting that he is like Catiline. He is like him in crime but his inferior in effort: Catiline rapidly created an army because he had none, while Antony has lost the army he was given. And so just as you broke Catiline by employing my diligence, the authority of the senate, and your own enthusiasm and courage, so in a short time you will hear that the wicked brigandage of Antony has been crushed through your unprecedented harmony with the senate, through the good fortune and the courage of the armies and of your leaders. **[16]** For my own part, as much as I can strive for and accomplish with attention, toil, wakefulness, authority, and planning, I will leave nothing undone that I believe useful for your freedom; nor could I do so without criminality, given your vast kindnesses to me. On this day first, with

---

24. A triumphalist history of Rome. Carthage was destroyed in 146 and Numantia in 133, both under the generalship of Scipio Aemilianus. There are some minor textual problems in sec. 13 that make little difference to translation; I follow the text of Clark (1918).

25. The leader of the slave revolt in the late 70s.

the motion of Marcus Servilius here,[26] a man of the highest courage and goodwill toward you, and with his colleagues, men of great standing and patriotism, under my sponsorship and leadership after a long interval we have been set ablaze with the hope of freedom.

---

26. One of the tribunes who called the senate meeting on December 20.

10

Ninth Philippic Oration against Antony

On January 1, 43, under the direction of the new consuls Hirtius and Pansa, the senate began to debate its policy. Cicero was, as before, in favor of supporting both Octavian and the assassins (with Brutus and Cassius now organizing their own finances and armies in the East) and eager to pursue war against Antony with all possible speed. Support for this policy was weak. Although Octavian was recognized as a pro-praetor and his command of troops thus legitimized, the senate voted to send an embassy to Antony (now vigorously besieging Decimus Brutus in Mutina) to propose terms. Antony was to abandon his siege of Decimus Brutus, withdraw from Cisalpine Gaul, and submit to the senate and people. The Fifth and Sixth Philippics, delivered in the senate and to the people on January 1, set out Cicero's views. The embassy consisted of three distinguished ex-consuls: Lucius Calpurnius Piso (Cicero's former enemy and Caesar's father-in-law; consul in 58 and censor in 50), Lucius Marcius Philippus (consul in 56 and Octavian's father-in-law), and Servius Sulpicius Rufus (consul in 51, eminent jurist, and Cicero's opponent in the trial of Murena in 63). Sulpicius, however, was in ill health and died before he could meet with Antony.

The Ninth Philippic, delivered in the senate in early February, concerns the honors to be paid to Sulpicius: was a statue of him to be placed on the speaker's platform, as had been done for other ambassadors who died in the service of the state, or should he merely be given a public funeral? Cicero was the third speaker in the debate: the presiding consul, Gaius Vibius Pansa, appeared to have suggested a statue and probably public burial as well; the second speaker, Publius Servilius Isauricus, had rejected the statue on an apparent technicality. The question is not merely one of excessive honors or crowding the already crowded rostra.[1] From Cicero's point of view, the issue is whether Sulpicius died while on an embassy to a hostile power (as was true of his other examples) or merely while serving the state. In other words, if Sulpicius is given a statue, then Antony is a public enemy. Cicero's argument assumes Antony's status as enemy in order to prove it; the actual argument is about the question raised by

---

1. On statues and monuments on the rostra, see Morstein-Marx (2004) 48–50, 92–101.

*Servilius, whether it was enough to die while on an embassy or whether
it was necessary to be killed by the enemy—something that seems merely
of antiquarian interest now but for Cicero is an element of a much more
important question.*

In M. Antonium Oratio Philippica Nona

Members of the senate:

[1] I wish the everlasting gods had made it possible for us to give thanks to Servius Sulpicius while he was alive instead of discussing honors for him after his death. If such a man had been able to report back from his embassy, I have no doubt that his return would have received your gratitude and advanced the interests of the commonwealth. I say this not because Lucius Philippus and Lucius Piso lacked the will or effort for such an important task, but since Sulpicius was older than they and wiser than all of us, his sudden removal left the entire embassy bereft and crippled. [2] If ever honors were appropriate to an ambassador who died in office, they will never seem more so than in the case of Sulpicius. Others who met their death while on an embassy set out with no specific risk to their lives, without fear of death. Sulpicius set out with some hope of reaching Antony but no hope of returning. Even though his condition was such that the addition of physical effort to his already poor health made him fear for his life, he did not refuse to bring whatever aid he could to the commonwealth, even if it was with his last breath. The stormy winter, the snow, the length of the route and the rough roads, his worsening illness—not one of these held him back, and when he had reached the point of meeting and talking to the man who was the target of his mission, at the very moment he was planning how to approach his task, he departed from this life.

[3] As often, Gaius Pansa, you have done an outstanding job in urging us to honor Sulpicius and in your eloquent and substantial speech in praise of him. I would add nothing to what you have said except my agreement, if I did not think it necessary to reply to my distinguished colleague Publius Servilius, who stated his opinion that honorific statues should be awarded only to those who met a violent death while on an embassy. But my own view, members of the senate, is that our ancestors thought that they should pay attention to why someone died, not how it happened. That is to say, they wanted

memorials to exist of those for whom an embassy was fatal, so that in the dangers of war men would be more courageous in accepting ambassadorial duties. We should not, then, be looking to our ancestors for specific precedents: we should understand the intentions of those from whom those precedents derive. **[4]** Lars Tolumnius, the king of Veii, killed four ambassadors of the Roman people at Fidenae, and their statues stood on the rostra within my memory.[2] The honor was justified; our ancestors gave those who died in the service of the commonwealth enduring remembrance in exchange for the brevity of their lives. Gnaeus Octavius was a great and illustrious man, the first to bring the consulship into a family that was filled thereafter with men of great courage. We see his statue on the rostra. Nobody begrudged it because he was a new man; nobody failed to give honor to courage. But Octavius' embassy was one in which there was no hint of danger; he was sent by the senate to examine the attitudes of both kings and free peoples, and in particular to forbid the grandson of the Antiochus who had waged war against our ancestors to have a fleet or keep elephants. He was killed in a gymnasium in Laodicea by a man named Leptines.[3] **[5]** Our ancestors gave him a statue in return for his life. It gave honor to his descendants for many years and is now the only remaining memorial of so great a family.[4] Indeed, the reason for honoring Octavius and Tullus Cluvius[5] and Lucius Roscius and Spurius Antius and Gaius Fulcinius, the men killed by the king of Veii, is not that they died in bloodshed but that they died for the commonwealth.

---

2. In 438 BCE; the ambassadors (named below, sec. 5) were objecting to the decision of Fidenae to support Veii against Rome. The statues were apparently no longer there in 43.

3. Gnaeus Octavius, consul in 165 BCE, was sent in 163–162 with two other legates to survey conditions in the East and to convey Roman demands to various nations, including Antiochus V of Syria, whose grandfather Antiochus III had been defeated in 189. Octavius was killed at Laodicea in Syria for unknown reasons.

4. A slightly odd statement in light of the activity of Octavian, who was not, however, part of the same family.

5. The name transmitted by the manuscripts of Cicero (and printed by Clark [1918]); other sources give Cloelius. The emendation Cluilius printed by recent editors is a false archaism attempting to improve on Cicero. Antius is elsewhere given the more likely name Nautius.

Members of the senate, if ill fortune had brought death to Servius Sulpicius, then I would certainly grieve for such a wound to the commonwealth, but I would think his death should be honored by public mourning rather than by a statue. But as it is, there is no doubt that the embassy itself took his life. He carried with him a death that, if he had remained with us here, his own attention and the care of his beloved son and wife could have avoided. **[6]** Sulpicius saw that, if he did not respect your authority, then he would be unlike himself, but if he accepted it, the task he undertook for the commonwealth would end his life. He decided that it was better to die at this great crisis of the commonwealth than to seem to have given his country less than he could have. Many cities along his route offered the possibility of rest and recovery; his high standing and reputation led to invitations from friends, and his fellow ambassadors urged him to rest and look after his life. But he hurried on, rushing, eager to accomplish your instructions, and he steadfastly persevered despite being hampered by illness. **[7]** His arrival disturbed Antony greatly. The orders you gave him had been composed in accordance with Sulpicius' authoritative opinion, and in reacting with disgraceful delight to the death of this leader of the senate he displayed how much he hated the senate. Indeed, Antony killed Sulpicius no less than Leptines killed Octavius or the king of Veii killed the men I named before; the person who was the occasion of his death is the one who brought death to him.[6] For that reason, I think posterity should have a memorial that records the senate's judgment about this war. The statue itself will testify that the war was so serious that the death of an ambassador received the honor of a memorial.

[8] If you should wish, members of the senate, to recall Sulpicius' reason for excusing himself from going on the embassy, no doubt will remain that in honoring him after death we are repairing the injury we did him in life. It is you, members of the senate—and although it's a harsh thing to say, it must still be said—it is you, I repeat, who deprived Servius Sulpicius of his life. As you saw, his reason for declining, his illness, was more apparent in his person than in his words. You were not being cruel (something completely unlike this body), but since you hoped there was nothing that his authority and wisdom could not do, you objected forcefully and made him

---

6. Cicero alludes to the distinction between "slaying" and "furnishing the cause of death" discussed by the jurists.

change his opinion—a man who had always had the deepest respect for your decisions. **[9]** And when the consul Pansa added his urgings, expressed more strongly than Sulpicius was used to hearing, then finally he drew his son and me apart and spoke to this effect, that he gave precedence to your authority over his own life. And as we marveled at his courage we did not dare oppose his wishes. His son was moved by extraordinary devotion, and my own grief was not much less than his distress, but each of us was forced to yield to his greatness of mind and the weight of his words when he promised to do what you wanted (receiving great praise and thanks from all of you) and would not avoid the risks arising from a decree he had proposed himself. On the very next day we saw him off, as he rushed to carry out your instructions. As he left, his words to me seemed like an omen of his fate.

[10] For that reason, members of the senate, give him back the life you took away. The life of the dead resides in the memory of the living; let a man whom you unwittingly sent to his death receive immortal life from you. If you decree the placement of a statue on the rostra, the forgetfulness of posterity will never dim the memory of his embassy. Everything else about Sulpicius' life will be committed to eternal memory by many glorious memorials. The words of all men will celebrate his seriousness, his steadfastness, his integrity, his outstanding concern for the protection of the commonwealth, his foresight. No silence will cover his exceptional, unbelievable— almost superhuman—knowledge of the interpretation of laws and the application of the principles of equity.[7] If all those from every generation in this state who have had some knowledge of jurisprudence were gathered into a single spot, they would not stand comparison to Sulpicius. He was not so much an expert in law as in justice; **[11]** the effect was that he always judged issues deriving from statute and private law with an eye to moderation and equity, and he preferred to resolve disputes rather than go to trial. For that,[8] no memorial statue is needed; it has something better. This statue will be witness to an honorable death, but the other is the remembrance of a noble

---

7. Here and in sec. 11 below, Cicero alludes to the fundamental distinction in Roman law between strict statutory law (*ius civile*) and the equitable remedies and procedures created by the praetor (*ius honorarium*). References to equity in legal contexts generally refer to the praetor's edict.

8. Sulpicius' expertise in the law.

life; the statue will record the gratitude of the senate more than the greatness of the man. **[12]** His son's devotion will have provided a noteworthy impetus for honoring his father, and even though he is not present because he is stricken with grief, you ought to be in the same state of mind as you would have been in his presence. He is, in fact, so stricken that no one ever mourned the death of an only son more than he mourns that of his father. It is also relevant to the son's reputation, I believe, that he be seen to have provided to his father the honor that is owed him. But Sulpicius could leave behind no memorial more glorious than the image of his character, his courage, his steadfastness, his devotion, and his talent that is his son, whose grief can be lightened, if it can be lightened, by no consolation except the honor you confer.

[13] As I call to mind the many conversations with Sulpicius over the course of our friendship, it seems to me that—if there is any sensation after death—a bronze statue of him on foot would please him more than a gilded statue on horseback of the type first set up for Lucius Sulla.[9] Servius used to have a wonderful affection for the moderation of our ancestors and had nothing but scorn for the excesses of the present age. As if, then, I were seeking his legal advice about his wishes, I make a decision based on his own authority and wishes in favor of a statue on foot made of bronze; by the honor of a memorial, it will diminish and assuage the great pain and sense of loss of our citizens. **[14]** And this opinion of mine, members of the senate, certainly receives support from the opinion of Publius Servilius. He offered the resolution that a tomb, not a statue, at public expense should be voted for Sulpicius. But if the death without violence of an ambassador requires no honors, then why does he decide in favor of public burial, the greatest honor that can be offered to someone who has died? If he gives that to Sulpicius, something that was not given to Gnaeus Octavius, then why does he think Sulpicius should not be offered what was given to Octavius? Our ancestors, in fact, voted statues for many people, public burial for few. But statues pass away from weather, force, and time, but the sanctity of a tomb resides in the ground itself; it cannot be moved by force nor can it be destroyed, and while all other things are destroyed by the passage of time, burial sites become ever more holy. **[15]** Therefore let him be

---

9. Voted by the senate in 81 BCE. Not the first equestrian statue, but the first to be gilded.

exalted by this honor, too, a man to whom no honor can be given that is not owed. Let us show gratitude in ennobling the death of a man to whom we can no longer display any other form of gratitude. By offering such honors to Sulpicius, we will establish an eternal witness of the embassy that was scorned and rejected by Antony.

For these reasons, I offer the following resolution:

> WHEREAS Servius Sulpicius Rufus, the son of Quintus, of the Lemonian tribe, at a most difficult and critical moment for the commonwealth, although his health was endangered by a grave illness, placed the authority of the senate and the safety of the commonwealth before his own life and struggled against the force of his illness to reach the camp of Antony to which the senate had dispatched him; and

> WHEREAS, when he had come near to that camp, he was overcome by the force of his illness and lost his life at the greatest crisis of the commonwealth; and

> WHEREAS the death of Servius Sulpicius was consonant with a life lived in the most honorable and noble fashion doing great service to the commonwealth both as a private citizen and as an officer of state: [16]

> WHEREAS a man of such qualities met his death while on an embassy in the service of the commonwealth,

> BE IT RESOLVED by the senate that a bronze statue of Servius Sulpicius on foot be placed on the rostra by the decision of this body; that around that statue for five feet in every direction a space be left free for his children and descendants at festivals and gladiatorial displays because he died in the service of his country; and that the inscription on the base display that cause. The consuls Gaius Pansa and Aulus Hirtius, one or both of them at their discretion, are to instruct the urban quaestors to let a contract for the making and setting up of said base and statue and to ensure that the cost of the contract be allocated and paid to the successful bidder. And

> WHEREAS the senate has previously shown its desire for honoring the death of men of courage,

> BE IT FURTHER RESOLVED that his funeral be conducted in as magnificent a manner as possible. [17] And

WHEREAS Servius Sulpicius Rufus the son of Quintus of the Lemonian tribe has so well served the commonwealth that he ought to be honored in such a fashion, the senate resolves and considers it to be in the public interest that the curule aediles suspend the edict concerning funerals for the funeral of Servius Sulpicius Rufus the son of Quintus of the Lemonian tribe; that Gaius Pansa the consul assign in the Esquiline field or another suitable location a site measuring thirty feet in all directions for the tomb in which Servius Sulpicius is to be interred; and that his tomb belong to his children and descendants with the full legal rights accorded to tombs publicly granted.

Works Cited

Adamietz, J. (1989). *Marcus Tullius Cicero: Pro Murena*. Darmstadt: Wissenschaftliche Buchgesellschaft.

Adams, J. Q. (1962). *Lectures on Rhetoric and Oratory*. 2nd ed. New York: Russell & Russell. Originally published Cambridge, MA: Hilliard and Metcalf, 1810.

Alexander, M. C. (2002). *The Case for the Prosecution in the Ciceronian Era*. Ann Arbor: University of Michigan Press.

Astin, A. E. (1967). *Scipio Aemilianus*. Oxford: Oxford University Press.

Austin, R. G. (1960). *M. Tulli Ciceronis Pro M. Caelio Oratio*. 3rd ed. Oxford: Oxford University Press.

Badian, E. (1964). *Studies in Greek and Roman History*. Oxford: Blackwell.

—— (1970). *Lucius Sulla: The Deadly Reformer*. Sydney: Sydney University Press.

Baldo, G. (2004). *M. Tulli Ciceronis In C. Verrem actionis secundae liber quartus (de signis)*. Florence: Le Monnier.

Batstone, W. W. (1994). "Cicero's Construction of Consular Ethos in the *First Catilinarian*." *Transactions of the American Philological Association* 124: 211–66.

Berry, D. H. (2004). "Literature and Persuasion in Cicero's *Pro Archia*." In Powell and Patterson (2004) 291–311.

Braund, D., and C. Gill, eds. (2003). *Myth, History, and Culture in Republican Rome: Studies in Honour of T. P. Wiseman*. Exeter: University of Exeter Press.

Broughton, T. R. S. (1950–1986). *Magistrates of the Roman Republic*. New York: American Philological Association.

Butler, S. (2002). *The Hand of Cicero*. London: Routledge.

Cape, R. W. (2002). "Cicero's Consular Speeches." In May (2002) 113–58.

Clark, A. C., ed. (1905). *M. Tulli Ciceronis Orationes*, Vol. 1. Oxford: Oxford University Press.

—— (1911). *M. Tulli Ciceronis Orationes*, Vol. 6. Oxford: Oxford University Press.

—— (1918). *M. Tulli Ciceronis Orationes*, Vol. 2. 2nd ed. Oxford: Oxford University Press.

Corbeill, A. (1996). *Controlling Laughter: Political Humor in the Late Roman Republic*. Princeton, NJ: Princeton University Press.

—— (2002). "Ciceronian Invective." In May (2002) 197–217.

Craig, C. P. (1993). *Form as Argument in Cicero's Speeches: A Study of Dilemma.* Atlanta: Scholars Press.

—— (2002). "A Survey of Selected Recent Work on Cicero's Rhetorica and Speeches" and "Bibliography." In May (2002) 503–99.

Crawford, J. W. (1984). *M. Tullius Cicero: The Lost and Unpublished Orations.* Göttingen: Vandenhoeck and Rupprecht.

—— (1994). *M. Tullius Cicero, the Fragmentary Speeches: An Edition with Commentary.* Atlanta: Scholars Press.

Crawford, M., et al. (1996). *Roman Statutes.* London: Institute of Classical Studies.

Crook, J. A., A. Lintott, and E. Rawson, eds. (1994). *Cambridge Ancient History IX: The Last Age of the Roman Republic, 146–43 B.C.* 2nd ed. Cambridge: Cambridge University Press.

Damon, C. (1997). *The Mask of the Parasite: A Pathology of Roman Patronage.* Ann Arbor: University of Michigan Press.

Dorey, T. A., ed. (1964). *Cicero.* London: Routledge and Kegan Paul.

Dugan, J. (2005). *Making a New Man: Ciceronian Self-Fashioning in the Rhetorical Works.* Oxford: Oxford University Press.

Dyer, R. R. (1990). "Rhetoric and Intention in Cicero's *Pro Marcello.*" *Journal of Roman Studies* 80: 17–36.

Geffcken, K. (1973). *Comedy in the Pro Caelio.* Leiden: E. J. Brill.

Gold, B. K., ed. (1982). *Literary and Artistic Patronage in Ancient Rome.* Austin: University of Texas Press.

Gotoff, H. C. (1979). *Cicero's Elegant Style: An Analysis of the Pro Archia.* Urbana: University of Illinois Press.

—— (1986). "Cicero's Analysis of the Prosecution Speeches in the *Pro Caelio:* An Exercise in Practical Criticism." *Classical Philology* 81: 122–32.

—— (2002). "Cicero's Caesarian Orations." In May (2002) 219–71.

Gowers, E., and W. Fitzgerald, eds. (2007). *Ennius Perennis.* Cambridge Philological Society, Supplement 31. Cambridge: Cambridge University Press.

Greenidge, A. H. C. (1901). *The Legal Procedure of Cicero's Time.* Oxford: Oxford University Press.

Griffin, M. (1994). "The Intellectual Developments of the Ciceronian Age." In Crook et al. (1994) 689–728.

—— (2001). "Piso, Cicero, and Their Audience." In *Cicéron et Philodème,* ed. C. Auvray-Assayas and D. Delattre, 85–99. Paris: Rue d'Ulm.

Gruen, E. (1974). *The Last Generation of the Roman Republic.* Berkeley: University of California Press.

Hardy, E. G. (1924). *The Catilinarian Conspiracy: A Re-Study of the Evidence.* Oxford: Oxford University Press.

Heyworth, S. J., ed. (2007). *Classical Constructions: Papers in Memory of Don Fowler, Classicist and Epicurean.* Oxford: Oxford University Press.

Kaster, R. A. (2006). *Cicero: Speech on Behalf of Publius Sestius.* Oxford: Oxford University Press.

Keaveney, A. (1982). *Sulla: The Last Republican.* London: Croom Helm.

Kennedy, G. A. (1968). "The Rhetoric of Advocacy in Greece and Rome." *American Journal of Philology* 89: 419–36.

Leigh, M. (2004). "The 'Pro Caelio' and Comedy." *Classical Philology* 99: 300–35.

Lintott, A. (1999). *The Constitution of the Roman Republic.* Oxford: Oxford University Press.

——— (2004). "Legal Procedure in Cicero's Time." In Powell and Patterson (2004) 61–78.

——— (2008). *Cicero as Evidence: A Historian's Companion.* Oxford: Oxford University Press.

Malcovati, E., ed. (1976). *Oratorum Romanorum Fragmenta.* 4th ed. Turin: Paravia.

Manuwald, G. (2007). *Cicero, Philippics 3–9.* Berlin: W. De Gruyter.

Maslowski, T., ed. (2003). *M. Tulli Ciceronis Orationes in L. Catilinam quattuor.* Munich: Saur.

May, J. M. (1981)."The Rhetoric of Advocacy and Patron-Client Identification." *American Journal of Philology* 102: 308–15.

——— (1988). *Trials of Character: The Eloquence of Ciceronian Ethos.* Chapel Hill: University of North Carolina Press.

——— ed. (2002). *Brill's Companion to Cicero: Oratory and Rhetoric.* Leiden: E. J. Brill.

Mitchell, T. N. (1979). *Cicero: The Ascending Years.* New Haven, CT: Yale University Press.

——— (1986). *Cicero: The Senior Statesman.* New Haven, CT: Yale University Press.

——— (1991). *Cicero: Verrines II.1.* Warminster: Aris and Phillips.

Morstein-Marx [as Kallet-Marx], R. (1995). *From Hegemony to Empire: The Development of the Roman Imperium in the East from 148 to 62 B.C.* Berkeley: University of California Press.

——— (2004). *Mass Oratory and Political Power in the Late Roman Republic.* Cambridge: Cambridge University Press.

Nisbet, R. G. M. (1961). *M. Tulli Ciceronis in L. Calpurnium Pisonem Oratio.* Oxford: Oxford University Press.

—— (1964). "The Speeches." In Dorey (1964) 47–79.

Peterson, W., ed. (1917). *M. Tulli Ciceronis Orationes*, Vol. 3. 2nd ed. Oxford: Oxford University Press.

Powell, J., and J. Patterson, eds. (2004). *Cicero the Advocate*. Oxford: Oxford University Press.

Rawson, E. (1975). *Cicero: A Portrait*. London: Allen Lane.

—— (1985). *Intellectual Life in the Late Roman Republic*. Baltimore: Johns Hopkins University Press.

Riggsby, A. (1999). *Crime and Community in Ciceronian Rome*. Austin: University of Texas Press.

Roberts, D. H. (2007). "Translating Antiquity: Intertextuality, Anachronism, and Archaism." In Heyworth (2007) 258–80.

Seager, R. (1964). "The First Catilinarian Conspiracy." *Historia* 13: 338–47.

Sedley, D. (1997). "The Ethics of Brutus and Cassius." *Journal of Roman Studies* 87: 41–53.

Shackleton Bailey, D. R. (1965–70). *Cicero's Letters to Atticus*. Cambridge: Cambridge University Press.

Skinner, M. (1983). "Clodia Metelli." *Transactions of the American Philological Association* 113: 273–87.

Skutsch, O. (1985). *The Annals of Quintus Ennius*. Oxford: Oxford University Press.

Steel, C. E. W. (2001). *Cicero, Rhetoric, and Empire*. Oxford: Oxford University Press.

Syme, R. (1939). *The Roman Revolution*. Oxford: Oxford University Press.

—— (1964). *Sallust*. Berkeley: University of California Press.

Tatum, W. J. (1999). *The Patrician Tribune: Publius Clodius Pulcher*. Chapel Hill: University of North Carolina Press.

Thompson, D. C. (1994). "Egypt." In Crook et al. (1994) 310–26.

Usener, H. (1887). *Epicurea*. Leipzig: Teubner.

Vasaly, A. (1993). *Representations: Images of the World in Ciceronian Oratory*. Berkeley: University of California Press.

—— (2002). "Cicero's Early Speeches." In May (2002) 71–111.

White, P. (1993). *Promised Verse: Poets in the Society of Augustan Rome*. Cambridge, MA: Harvard University Press.

Wiseman, T. P. (1969). *Catullan Questions*. Leicester: Leicester University Press.

—— (1971). *New Men in the Roman Senate, 139 B.C.–14 A.D.* Oxford: Oxford University Press.

Wiseman, T. P. (1979). *Clio's Cosmetics.* Leicester: Leicester University Press.

—— (1982). *"Pete Nobiles Amicos:* Poets and Patrons in Late Republican Rome." In Gold (1982) 28–49.

—— (1985a). *Catullus and His World: A Reappraisal.* Cambridge: Cambridge University Press.

—— (1985b). *Roman Political Life, 90 B.C.–A.D. 69.* Exeter: University of Exeter Press.

—— (1994a). "The Senate and the *populares,* 69–60 B.C." In Crook et al. (1994) 327–67.

—— (1994b). "Caesar, Pompey, and Rome." In Crook et al. (1994) 368–423.

Zetzel, J. E. G. (1994). Review of Crawford (1994). *Bryn Mawr Classical Review,* June 11.

—— (2003). "Plato with Pillows: Cicero on the Uses of Greek Culture." In Braund and Gill (2003) 119–38.

—— (2007). "The Influence of Cicero on Ennius." In Gowers and Fitzgerald (2007) 1–16.

Biographical Index

Accius, Lucius.   Second-century BCE dramatist and scholar. *Arch.* 27

Achilles.   *Arch.* 24

Acilius Glabrio, Manius.   Consul in 67; proconsul in Bithynia-Pontus, 66. *Man.* 26

Aelius Lamia, Lucius.   Roman knight expelled from Rome for his support of Cicero in 58. *Pis.* 64

Aelius Tubero, Quintus.   Scipio Aemilianus' nephew; failed to be elected praetor because of his austere brand of Stoicism. *Mur.* 75

Aemilius Paullus, Lucius.   As consul for the second time in 168, defeated Perseus of Macedon at Pydna, ending Third Macedonian War. Publius Cornelius Scipio Aemilianus and Quintus Fabius Maximus Aemilianus were his biological sons. *Verr.* 4.22; *Mur.* 31, 76; *Pis.* 39, 58, 61

Aemilius Scaurus, Marcus.   Consul in 115, censor in 109, and the leading conservative senator in the late second/early first century BCE; a patrician who restored his family from obscurity. Cicero admired him; Sallust thought him corrupt. *Mur.* 16, 36; *Arch.* 6

Aeneas.   Trojan ancestor of Rome. *Verr.* 4.72

Aeschrion of Syracuse.   Collaborator with Verres. *Verr.* 4.59

Aeschylus of Tyndaris.   Otherwise unknown. *Verr.* 4.48

Afranius, Lucius.   Consul in 60. *Pis.* 58

Africanus.   See *Cornelius*

Agathocles.   Tyrant of Syracuse and king of Sicily, d. 289. *Verr.* 4.122

Albucius, Titus.   Praetor before 104; celebrated unauthorized triumph in Sardinia. Convicted of extortion and retired to Athens. *Pis.* 92

Alexander the Great.   *Arch.* 24

Ancharius, Quintus.   Praetor in 56; succeeded Piso in Macedonia. *Pis.* 89

Antiochus III Magnus.   King of Syria, d. 187. *Man.* 14, 55; *Mur.* 31; *Phil.* 9.4

Antiochus V Eupator.   King of Syria, assassinated in 162. *Phil.* 9.4

Antiochus X Eusebes Philopator.   King of Syria, d. c. 90. *Verr.* 4.61

Antiochus XIII Asiaticus.   King of Syria, recognized by Lucullus in 69, killed by Pompey in 65. *Verr.* 4.61, 62, 65–67, 70

Antius, Spurius.   Envoy to Fidenae in 438, killed by order of Lars Tolumnius. *Phil.* 9.5

Antonius Hybrida, Gaius.   Consul with Cicero in 63, sympathetic to Catiline. Given the rich province of Macedonia to ensure his cooperation;

prosecuted by Caelius for extortion in 59, convicted, and sent into exile. *Mur.* 40; *Cael.* 74; *Pis.* 5

Antonius, Marcus.   Consul in 44; member of Second Triumvirate with Octavian and Lepidus. *Phil.* 4.1, 3–6, 8–9, 15; *Phil.* 9.7, 15

Antony.   See *Antonius*

Apollodorus of Agyrium.   *Verr.* 4.50

Apollonius.   See *Clodius*

Archagathus of Haluntium.   *Verr.* 4.51, 53

Archias.   See *Licinius*

Archimedes.   Mathematician and engineer, killed in siege of Syracuse in 212. *Verr.* 4.131

Archonidas of Helorus.   *Verr.* 4.59

Ariobarzanes I.   King of Cappadocia. *Man.* 5, 12

Aristarchus.   Second-century librarian of Alexandria and editor of Homer. *Pis.* 73

Aristotle.   *Mur.* 63

Aristus of Panhormus.   *Verr.* 4.29

Arrius, Quintus.   Praetor in 73; supposed to succeed Verres as governor of Sicily but instead employed in the war against Spartacus. *Verr.* 4.42

Asicius, Publius.   Acquitted of murder of Dio the Alexandrian. *Cael.* 23–24

Athamas.   (Mythological) king of Thebes. *Pis.* 47

Athamas.   One of group of beautiful brothers. *Pis.* 89

Atilius Calatinus, A.   Consul in 258 and 254, dictator and censor; general in First Punic War. *Pis.* 14, 58

Atilius Regulus, Marcus.   Consul in 267, 256. Commander in First Punic War. Captured and sent to negotiate a prisoner exchange, argued against it, and returned to Carthage to be tortured to death. *Pis.* 43

Atratinus.   See *Sempronius*

Attalus, from Netum.   *Verr.* 4.59

Aurelius Cotta, Gaius.   Consul in 75; supported restoration of tribunician powers. *Pis.* 62

Aurelius Cotta, Lucius.   Consul in 144; prosecuted by Scipio Aemilianus, probably in 138. *Mur.* 58

Autobulus.   One of group of beautiful brothers. *Pis.* 89

Baebius, Marcus.   Murdered on Piso's orders. *Pis.* 88

Balbus.   See *Herennius*

Bestia.   See *Calpurnius*

Boethus of Chalcedon.   Artist in silver from third/second centuries BCE. *Verr.* 4.32

Cacurius, Gaius.   Otherwise unknown. *Verr.* 4.37

Caecilius Metellus, Lucius.   Verres' successor as governor of Sicily; died while consul in 68. *Verr.* 4.147–48

Caecilius Metellus, Quintus.   Tribune and legate in successive years. Probably the same man as one of those listed below. *Man.* 58

Caecilius Metellus Celer, Quintus.   Praetor in 63, consul in 60. Brother of Metellus Nepos and husband of the Clodia attacked in *In Defense of Marcus Caelius*. Died suddenly in 59. *Cat.* 2.5, 26; *Cael.* 34, 59–60; *Pis.* 8

Caecilius Metellus Creticus, Quintus.   Consul in 69; fought pirates in Crete as proconsul, 68–65. *Pis.* 58

Caecilius Metellus Macedonicus.   Consul in 143, censor in 131; triumphed over Macedon in 146. *Verr.* 4.126; *Mur.* 31; *Pis.* 61

Caecilius Metellus Nepos, Quintus.   Tribune in 62, consul in 57. Became tribune three weeks before the end of Cicero's term; used his power to veto the customary speech given by a retiring consul on the last day of the year. In 57 supported (or at least did not obstruct) Cicero's recall. *Pis.* 35

Caecilius Metellus Numidicus, Quintus.   Governor of Sicily in 111, consul in 109, commander in the Jugurthine War for two years. Went into exile in 100 rather than swear an oath to support Saturninus' agrarian law but was recalled not long after. *Verr.* 4.146; *Pis.* 20; *Arch.* 6

Caecilius Metellus Pius, Quintus.   Consul in 80. Son of Numidicus; the praetor who accepted Archias' registration in 89. With Sulla in second march on Rome. *Arch.* 6–7, 9, 26, 31

Caecilius Metellus Pius Scipio, Quintus.   Consul in 52, one of Verres' advocates. Born Publius Cornelius Scipio Nasica, adopted by the consul of 80. *Verr.* 4.79–80

Caecilius Statius.   Comic poet, d. 168. *Cael.* 37

Caelius Rufus, Marcus.   Cicero's client in 56. Tribune in 52; supported Caesar; killed while praetor in 48 while trying to start a rebellion. *Cael.* 3, 5–6, 9–10, 12, 14–26, 29, 31–35, 37–38, 44–45, 47, 50–54, 56–57, 61–62, 68–70, 72, 74, 76, 78–79

Caelius.   Father of Cicero's client. *Cael.* 3, 79

Caelius [or Coelius] Latiniensis, Quintus.   Tribune and legate in successive years; otherwise unknown. *Man.* 58

Caesar.   See *Julius*

Caesernius, Gaius.   Condemned, possibly under the same law under which Caelius was being tried. *Cael.* 71

Caesetius, Publius. Verres' quaestor in 72. *Verr.* 4.146

Caesoninus. See *Calpurnius*

Calatinus. See *Atilius*

Calidius, Gnaeus. Roman knight. *Verr.* 4.42–46

Calpurnius Bestia, Lucius. Prosecuted by Caelius; prosecuted Caelius with his son Sempronius Atratinus. *Cael.* 26, 76

Calpurnius Piso, Gnaeus. Quaestor 65; killed in Spain. *Mur.* 81

Calpurnius Piso Caesoninus, Lucius. Grandfather of the consul of 58. Consul in 112, possibly tried for extortion, but not certain. *Pis.* fr. 9

Calpurnius Piso Caesoninus, Lucius. Consul in 58, attacked by Cicero in *Against Lucius Calpurnius Piso*. Father-in-law of Caesar. Ambassador to Antony with Sulpicius Rufus in 43. *Pis.* fr. 10, secs. 2, 18, 22, 38, 68–70, 72, 92–93; *Phil.* 9.1

Calpurnius Piso Frugi, Gaius. First husband of Cicero's daughter Tullia. Quaestor in 58, died before Cicero's return from exile. *Pis.* fr. 13, sec. 13

Calpurnius Piso Frugi, Lucius. Consul in 133; as tribune in 149 sponsored the law establishing a permanent court to try cases of provincial extortion. *Verr.* 4.56, 108

Calpurnius Piso Frugi, Lucius. Praetor in 113(?) in Spain; killed in battle. *Verr.* 4.56–57

Calpurnius Piso Frugi, Lucius. Son of the above. Verres' colleague as praetor in 74. *Verr.* 4.56

Calventius. Piso's maternal grandfather. *Pis.* fr. 9

Camillus. See *Furius*

Camurtius, Gaius. Condemned, possibly under the same law under which Caelius was being tried. *Cael.* 71

Carbo. See *Papirius*

Carpinatius, Lucius. Representative of tax collectors in Sicily. *Verr.* 4.137

Cassius Longinus, Gaius. Consul in 73; supporter of Manilian law. *Man.* 68

Catiline. See *Sergius*

Cato. See *Porcius*

Catulus. See *Lutatius*

Cicero. See *Tullius*

Claudia. See *Clodia*

Claudia. Vestal Virgin; helped her relative Appius Claudius Pulcher triumph in 143. *Cael.* 34

Claudia Quinta. In 204 freed barge carrying Magna Mater from sandbar. *Cael.* 34

Claudius. See *Clodius*

Claudius Caecus, Appius. Censor in 312. *Cael.* 33

Claudius Marcellus, Gaius. Praetor in 80, governor of Sicily in 79; a member of the jury in the trial of Verres. It was his statue to which Sopater of Tyndaris was tied. *Verr.* 4.37, 86–87, 89–90

Claudius Marcellus, Gaius. Consul 50, cousin of Marcus Marcellus. *Marc.* 10, 34

Claudius Marcellus, Marcus. Consul five times; captured Syracuse in 212. *Verr.* 4.115–16, 120–23, 130–31, 151; *Man.* 47; *Arch.* 22; *Pis.* 58

Claudius Marcellus, Marcus. Consul in 166, 155, 152; grandson of previous. Drowned in 148 on embassy to Masinissa in Numidia. *Pis.* 44

Claudius Marcellus, Marcus. Consul in 51; supporter of Pompey. Subject of *On Behalf of Marcus Marcellus. Marc.* 2–3, 10, 13, 16, 33–34

Claudius Marcellus Aeserninus, Marcus. Otherwise unknown. *Verr.* 4.91

Claudius Pulcher, Appius. Praetor in 89; consul in 79. Apparently kept poor records. *Arch.* 9

Claudius Pulcher, Appius. Consul in 54; Clodius' brother. Only praetor to oppose Cicero's return from exile in 57. *Pis.* 35 (not named)

Claudius Pulcher, Gaius. Aedile in 99, consul in 92; the first person to exhibit elephants in Rome. *Verr.* 4.6–7, 133

Cleomenes of Syracuse. *Verr.* 4.59

Clodia. Wife of Metellus Celer, sister of Clodius. *Cael.* 30–31, 50–53, 61

Clodius, Publius. One of the prosecutors of Caelius. Not Clodius Pulcher. *Cael.* 27

Clodius (or Claudius) Apollonius, Aulus. *Verr.* 4.37

Clodius Pulcher, Publius. Cicero's archenemy. Violated rites of Bona Dea, tried and acquitted for sacrilege in 61. Transferred by adoption from patrician to plebeian in 59, as tribune responsible for Cicero's exile in 58. A brilliant street politician, he was killed in riots on January 18, 52; his public cremation burned down the senate house. *Cael.* 17, 36, 60; *Pis.* 15, 23, 26–27

Cloelius, Sextus. One of Clodius' most active supporters; celebrated the Compitalia in 58 and cremated Clodius' body in 52 (among other services). *Cael.* 78; *Pis.* 8, 23

Cluvius [Cluilius], Tullus. Envoy to Fidenae in 438, killed by order of Lars Tolumnius. *Phil.* 9.5

Coelius, Marcus (possibly an error for Cloelius). Roman knight. *Verr.* 4.37

Cottus. King of the Thracian Astae. *Pis.* 84

Crassus. See *Licinius*

Cratippus of Tyndaris. *Verr.* 4.29

Critolaus of Aetna. *Verr.* 4.59

Curidius, Lucius. *Verr.* 4.44

Curio. See *Scribonius*

Curius Dentatus, Manius. Consul in 290 and twice more, censor in 272; military leader renowned for his austerity. *Mur.* 17, 31; *Cael.* 39; *Pis.* 58

Demetrius. Gymnasiarch of Tyndaris. *Verr.* 4.92

Didius, Titus. Proconsul in Macedonia in 100, consul in 98; a new man. *Mur.* 17; *Pis.* 61

Dio. Alexandrian philosopher and ambassador; murdered. *Cael.* 23–24, 51

Diocles of Lilybaeum, "called Popilius." *Verr.* 4.35

Diodorus of Malta. *Verr.* 4.38–41

Diodorus son of Timarchides. Senior Syracusan senator. *Verr.* 4.138

Diogenes of Sinope. Fourth-century Cynic. *Mur.* 75

Dionysiarchus of Catina. Magistrate. *Verr.* 4.50

Dolabella. See *Cornelius*

Domitius, Gnaeus. Presided over Caelius' trial. Precise identity uncertain; probably praetor in 54. *Cael.* 32

Egnatuleius, Lucius. Quaestor in 44; brought fourth legion from Macedonia to Italy, then went over from Antony to Octavian. *Phil.* 4.6

Ennius, Quintus. The early poet Cicero most admired; author of *Annals* (epic on Roman history), many tragedies, and a variety of recondite and learned poems. *Arch.* 18, 22, 27; quoted *Pis.* 43 without name

Epicurus. Fourth/third century BCE founder of philosophical school emphasizing ascetic pleasure as the goal of life. In Cicero's Rome, his most notable followers were Lucretius and Philodemus. *Pis.* 20, 59, 69

Euhadia. Wife of Execestus. *Pis.* 89

Eupolemus of Calacte. *Verr.* 4.49

Execestus. Husband of Euhadia. *Pis.* 89

Fabius Maximus, Quintus. *Verr.* 4.42 (unclear which one)

Fabius Maximus Allobrogicus, Quintus. Consul in 121, nephew of Scipio Aemilianus. *Mur.* 75

Fabius Maximus Eburnus, Quintus.　Defeated Marcus Aemilius Scaurus for consulship of 116. *Mur.* 36

Fabius Maximus Verrucosus, Quintus.　Consul five times, dictator in 217. His epithet *Cunctator* ("Delayer") came from the strategy of attrition used against Hannibal in the Second Punic War. *Man.* 47; *Arch.* 22; *Pis.* 14, 58

Fabius Sanga, Quintus.　Senator in 63; possibly the same as Quintus Fabius Maximus, suffect consul in 45. *Pis.* 77

Fabricius Luscinus, Gaius.　Consul in 282 and 278, censor in 275; commander in war against Pyrrhus. *Cael.* 39; *Pis.* 58

Falcidius, Gaius.　Uncertain date and identity; legate in the year after he was tribune. *Man.* 58

Flaccus.　See *Valerius*

Flamininus.　See *Quinctius*

Flavius, Gnaeus.　Son of a freedman, scribe and eventually aedile in 304. Made public the forms of legal procedure and the official calendar. *Mur.* 25

Fufidius.　Roman knight, sold out by Piso. *Pis.* 86

Fufius Calenus, Quintus.　Witness in prosecution of Caelius; consul in 47. *Cael.* 19

Fulcinius, Gaius.　Envoy to Fidenae in 438, killed on orders of Lars Tolumnius. *Phil.* 9.5

Fulvius Nobilior, Marcus.　Victor over Aetolia. *Mur.* 31; *Arch.* 22, 27

Furius Camillus, Marcus.　Military tribune with consular power six times, dictator 396 and after. Conquered Veii; exiled for embezzling plunder; recalled to save Rome from the Gauls in 387. *Cael.* 39; *Pis.* 58

Furius Philus, Lucius.　Consul in 136; close associate of Scipio Aemilianus. *Mur.* 66; *Arch.* 16

Gabinius, Aulus.　Consul in 58; blamed by Cicero for his exile. As governor of Syria disobeyed both the senate and an oracle and invaded Egypt to put Ptolemy XIII back on the throne. *Man.* 52, 57–58; *Pis.* 3, 12, 25–26, 28, 40, 42, 48, 51, 75, 88

Gabinius, Publius.　Praetor in 89; subsequently convicted of extortion. *Arch.* 9

Galba.　See *Sulpicius*

Gallus.　See *Plotius*

Galus.　See *Sulpicius*

Gellius Poplicola, Lucius.　Consul in 72, censor in 70; Pompey's legate in pirate war. Supported Cicero against Catiline. *Pis.* 6

Glabrio.   See *Acilius*

Gracchus.   See *Sempronius*

Grattius.   Prosecutor of Archias; otherwise unknown. *Arch.* 8, 12

Hannibal.   Carthaginian leader in Second Punic War; victor at Trasimene and Cannae, defeated at Zama in 202 by Scipio Africanus. *Mur.* 32

Heius.   An orphan. *Verr.* 4.37

Heius, Gaius.   Mamertine. *Verr.* 4.3–7, 10–19, 27, 150

Heraclius.   A rich Syracusan. *Verr.* 4.136, 139

Heraclius.   A Syracusan magistrate. *Verr.* 4.137

Herennius, Marcus.   Consul in 93; a new man. *Mur.* 36

Herennius Balbus, Lucius.   One of the prosecutors of Caelius. *Cael.* 25, 27, 30, 49, 53, 56

Hiero.   One of Verres' "hunting dogs." *Verr.* 4.30–31, 96

Hiero II.   Third-century king of Syracuse. *Verr.* 4.29, 118

Hirtius, Aulus.   Caesar's legate in Gaul (and author of *Gallic Wars* Book 8); consul in 43. Killed at Mutina. *Phil.* 9.16

Homer.   *Arch.* 19, 24

Hortensius Hortalus, Quintus.   Consul in 69; defended Verres in 70 and was one of Murena's advocates in 63. The leading orator in Rome until overtaken by Cicero. *Man.* 51–52, 56, 66; *Mur.* 10, 48; *Arch.* 6

Ismenias of Tyndaris.   *Verr.* 4.92

Jugurtha.   King of Numidia by violence and trickery; conducted war on Rome by bribery, then force. Defeated by Marius (and Sulla); executed in 104. *Man.* 60

Julius Caesar, Gaius.   Consul in 59, participant in First Triumvirate with Pompey and Crassus; victor in Civil War (49–48) against Pompey; dictator. Assassinated March 15, 44. Son-in-law (for a time) of Lucius Calpurnius Piso (consul in 58). *Pis.* 37, 59, 61, 79–82; *Marc.* 2, 4, 7, 9, 11, 13, 15–17, 23, 26, 32–34; *Phil.* 4.4

Julius Caesar, Lucius.   Consul in 90, censor in 89. *Arch.* 11

Julius Caesar, Lucius.   Consul in 64; supporter of Julius Caesar. *Mur.* 71; *Pis.* 8

Julius Caesar Octavianus, Gaius (Augustus).   Great-nephew and heir of Julius Caesar; joined Antony and Marcus Aemilius Lepidus in Second Triumvirate (43); Cicero was one of the first to be killed in the ensuing proscriptions. *Phil.* 4.2, 4, 6

Junius Brutus, Decimus.   Consul in 138; friend/patron of the poet Accius. *Arch.* 27

Junius Brutus Albinus, Decimus.   Praetor in 45, consul designate for 42, but was dead by then. Assassin of Caesar (not to be confused with Marcus Junius Brutus); killed 43. *Phil.* 4.7–9

Junius Silanus, Decimus.   Consul in 62. As consul-designate, proposed putting the Catilinarian conspirators to death but then changed his mind. *Mur.* 82; *Pis.* 56

Laelius, Gaius.   Consul in 140. Close friend and associate of Scipio Aemilianus. *Mur.* 66; *Arch.* 16

Lamia.   A wealthy woman from Segesta. *Verr.* 4.59

Lentulus.   See *Cornelius*

Leptines.   Killed Gnaeus Octavius in Laodicea. *Phil.* 9.4, 7

Licinius, Publius.   Allegedly involved in poisoning plot; otherwise unknown. *Cael.* 61–66

Licinius Archias, Aulus.   Poet from Antioch; defended by Cicero. *Arch.* 1, 2, 4–5, 7, 9–11, 18–19, 21, 25–26, 28, 32

Licinius Crassus, Lucius.   Consul in 95, censor in 92. Cicero studied with him briefly (before Crassus' sudden death in 91); he was the orator of the previous generation whom Cicero most admired. His sudden death in September of 91 is described by Cicero in the preface to *de Or.* 3. *Verr.* 4.133; *Arch.* 6; *Pis.* 62

Licinius Crassus, Publius.   Consul in 97, censor in 89; committed suicide after victory of Cinna and Marius in 87. Father of Marcus Crassus (below). *Arch.* 11

Licinius Crassus Dives, Marcus.   Follower of Sulla who defeated the revolt of Spartacus. Consul with Pompey in 70 and again in 55; part of First Triumvirate with Caesar and Pompey; one of Murena's advocates. *Mur.* 10, 48; *Cael.* 9, 18, 23; *Pis.* 58

Licinius Lucullus, Lucius.   Praetor in 104, governor of Sicily. *Verr.* 4.147

Licinius Lucullus, Lucius.   Quaestor under Sulla (and his most loyal supporter); consul in 74; commander in Third Mithridatic War, 73–67. Retired to his villas and fishponds until his death in 56. *Verr.* 4.49; *Man.* 5, 10, 20–21, 23, 26; *Mur.* 20, 33–34, 37–38, 69; *Arch.* 11, 21

Licinius Murena, Gaius.   Brother of the consul of 62. *Mur.* 89

Licinius Murena, Lucius.   Praetor probably in 88; father of Cicero's client; fought disastrously in Second Mithridatic War (83–81) until ordered by Sulla to stop. *Man.* 8; *Mur.* 32

Licinius Murena, Lucius.   Cicero's client; consul in 62. *Mur.* 1–3, 7–8, 11–15, 18, 20–21, 32, 34–35, 37, 41–43, 49, 52–56, 58, 68–69, 72–73, 78, 82–84, 86–87, 89

Livius Drusus, Marcus.   A close associate of Lucius Licinius Crassus; his murder when tribune in 91 was a proximate cause of the Social War. *Arch.* 6

Lucceius, Lucius.   Host of Dio the Alexandrian; senator and historian. *Cael.* 51–55

Lucullus.   See *Licinius;* see also *Terentius*

Lutatius Catulus, Quintus.   Consul in 102; victor (with Marius) over the Cimbri in 101. Devoted Sullan who committed suicide in 87. Archias came to Rome during his consulship. *Verr.* 4.126; *Mur.* 36; *Arch.* 5–6; *Cael.* 78

Lutatius Catulus, Quintus.   Son of consul of 102, himself supporter of Sulla and (later) of Sulla's legislation. Consul in 78, censor in 75, and a member of the jury in the trial of Verres in 70; the senior living ex-consul and *princeps senatus* ("first senator") in the sixties. *Verr.* 4.37, 69, 82; *Man.* 51, 59–60, 63, 66; *Pis.* 6; *Arch.* 6; *Cael.* 59, 70

Lutatius Diodorus, Quintus.   *Verr.* 4.37

Lyson of Lilybaeum.   *Verr.* 4.37, 59

Magius, Decius.   Capuan supporter of Rome in Second Punic War. *Pis.* 24

Mallius, Gnaeus.   Unexpectedly defeated Catulus in the consular elections for 105; went on to be disastrously defeated by the Gauls. Exiled in 103. *Mur.* 36

Manilius, Gaius.   Tribune in 66; proposed law giving Pompey command against Mithridates; convicted of treason in 65. *Man.* 69

Manlius, Gaius.   Ex-centurion, supporter of Catiline; started military action at Faesulae. *Cat.* 2.14, 16, 20

Manlius Torquatus, Lucius.   Consul in 65, proconsul of Macedonia 64–63; ally of Cicero at the time of his exile and against Piso in 55. *Pis.* 44, 47, 77–78, 92

Marcellus.   See *Claudius*

Marcius Crispus, Quintus.   One of Piso's legates in Macedonia 57–54; later governor of Bithynia-Pontus in 45. *Pis.* 54

Marcius Figulus, Gaius.   Consul in 64; mentioned for dating only. *Pis.* 8

Marcius Philippus, Lucius.   Consul in 91, censor in 86; opposed Livius Drusus and Lucius Crassus; active supporter of Sulla. *Man.* 62; *Mur.* 36

Octavius, Gnaeus. Consul in 87, when he expelled Cinna from Rome and was in turn murdered by him. Cicero's reference to the family presumably includes him as well as his son, consul in 75. *Arch.* 6

Opimius, Lucius. Consul in 121; violently anti-Gracchan. Exiled in 109 for having been bribed by Jugurtha. *Pis.* 95

Orestes. *Pis.* 47

Otho. See *Roscius*

Palla. Identity uncertain; possibly connected by marriage to the family of Sempronius Atratinus, one of the prosecutors of Caelius. *Cael.* 23

Pamphilus of Lilybaeum. *Verr.* 4.32, 35

Panaetius of Rhodes. Second-century BCE stoic philosopher, relatively flexible and accommodating to Roman beliefs; friend of Scipio Aemilianus. *Mur.* 66

Papinius, Lucius. *Verr.* 4.46

Papirius Carbo, Gaius. Tribune 89, coauthor with Marcius Plautius Silvanus of law under which Archias claimed citizenship. *Arch.* 7

Papirius Potamo, Lucius. *Verr.* 4.44

Peducaeus, Sextus. Praetor in 77, governor of Sicily 76–75. *Verr.* 4.142–43

Perseus. King of Macedon; defeated in Third Macedonian War by Lucius Aemilius Paullus at Pydna in 168. *Man.* 55; *Mur.* 31

Phalaris. Sixth-century BCE tyrant of Agrigentum; invented torture by roasting victims in a hollow bronze bull. *Verr.* 4.73; *Pis.* 42, 73

Philip V of Macedon. Defeated in Second Macedonian War by Flamininus at Cynoscephalae in 197. *Man.* 14; *Mur.* 31

Philip, counterfeit (Andriscus, Pseudophilippus). Pretender to rule of Macedonia; defeated by Metellus Macedonicus in 148. *Mur.* 31

Philippus. See *Marcius*

Philodemus of Gadara. Poet and philosopher, many of whose prose works survive in carbonized form in the Villa of the Papyri at Herculaneum; about thirty of his epigrams survive in the Greek Anthology. *Pis.* 68–72 (not named)

Philus. See *Furius*

Phylarchus of Centuripae. *Verr.* 4.29, 50

Pinarius Natta, Lucius. Murena's stepson and Clodius' brother-in-law. As pontifex consecrated Cicero's house as a shrine of liberty on behalf of Clodius. *Mur.* 73

Piso. See *Calpurnius* and *Pupius*

Plato. *Mur.* 63

Plator.   Piso's host and victim. *Pis.* 83–84

Plautius Silvanus, M.   Tribune in 89; coauthor with Gaius Papirius Carbo of law under which Archias claimed citizenship. *Arch.* 7

Pleuratus.   One of Piso's victims. *Pis.* 84

Plotius Gallus, Lucius.   First rhetorician to teach in Latin; had some relationship with Marius; assisted Sempronius Atratinus in prosecution of Caelius in 56. *Arch.* 20

Poleas.   Took the statue of Mercury from Tyndaris to Messana. *Verr.* 4.92

Polyclitus.   Fifth-century BCE sculptor. *Verr.* 4.5, 12

Pompeius, Quintus.   Consul in 141; a new man; badly defeated in Numantine War. *Mur.* 16–17

Pompeius Basiliscus, Gnaeus.   *Verr.* 4.25

Pompeius Magnus, Gnaeus.   Great military leader with a career of astonishing irregularity: consul in 70 with Crassus after holding no lesser office; partner in First Triumvirate with Caesar and Crassus; consul again in 55 and sole consul in 52. Defeated Mithridates (66–63), among others; defeated by Caesar in Second Civil War; killed in Egypt in 48. *Man.* 3, 10, 27–29, 34–36, 41, 44–46, 48, 50–52, 57, 59–60, 63–64, 67; *Mur.* 34; *Arch.* 24; *Pis.* 16, 25, 27–28, 34–35, 58, 74, 76, 80

Pompeius Percennius (at least two of them).   *Verr.* 4.25

Pompeius Philo, Gnaeus.   *Verr.* 4.48

Pompeius Rufus, Quintus.   Praetor in 63. *Cael.* 73

Pompeius Theophanes, Quintus.   From Mytilene; historian given citizenship by Pompey. *Arch.* 24

Pompey.   See *Pompeius Magnus, Gnaeus*

Pomptinus, Gaius.   Praetor in 63; later Cicero's legate in Cilicia. *Pis.* 58

Popilius Laenas, Publius.   Consul in 132; opponent of Tiberius Gracchus. His consular colleague Rupilius finally ended the slave revolt in Sicily. *Verr.* 4.112

Porcius Cato, Gaius.   Consul in 114. Defeated in Macedonia and convicted of extortion. *Verr.* 4.22

Porcius Cato, Lucius.   Consul in 89; friend of Archias. *Arch.* 6

Porcius Cato, Marcus (Cato the Elder; Cato the Censor).   Consul in 196, censor in 184; model of rectitude and stern morality; the greatest orator before Cicero and the first historian to write in Latin. *Verr.* 4.22; *Mur.* 17, 32, 59, 66; *Arch.* 16, 22

Porcius Cato, Marcus (Cato the Younger; Cato of Utica).   Great-grandson of censor. A rigid Stoic who prosecuted Murena and argued for execution of Catilinarian conspirators. Praetor in 54 but failed to be elected consul for 51; he committed suicide in 46 at Utica as a grand but futile republican gesture after being defeated by Caesar. *Mur.* 3, 6–7, 13, 31, 34, 54, 56, 58, 60–64, 67, 71, 74–75, 78, 81–83; *Arch.* 22

Porcius Laeca, Marcus.   The host of Catiline's secret meeting on November 5, 63 BCE. *Cat.* 2.13

Postumius, Gaius.   One of the prosecution speakers against Murena. *Mur.* 54, 56, 57, 69

Potamo.   See *Papirius*

Praxiteles.   Fourth-century BCE Athenian sculptor. *Verr.* 4.4, 12

Ptolemy XII Auletes.   King of Egypt; deposed 58, restored by Gabinius in 55 for a fee of 10,000 talents. *Cael.* 18

Publicius.   Henchman of Catiline, otherwise unknown. *Cat.* 2.4

Pupius Piso, Marcus.   Consul in 61; triumphed from Spain in 69. *Pis.* 62

Pyrrhus.   King of Epirus 297–272; invaded Italy in support of Tarentum, eventually defeated at Beneventum in 275. *Mur.* 31; *Cael.* 34

Quinctius Flamininus, Titus.   Consul 198; defeated Philip V at Cynoscephalae. *Verr.* 4.129; *Mur.* 31; *Pis.* 61

Rabirius Postumus, Gaius.   Prosecuted in 63 for treason for participation in the death of Saturninus in 100; defended by Cicero. The trial was never completed. *Pis.* 4

Rabocentus.   One of the Bessi. *Pis.* 84

Roscius, Lucius.   Envoy to Fidenae in 438, killed by order of Lars Tolumnius. *Phil.* 9.5

Roscius Gallus, Q.   Actor; much admired (and imitated) by Cicero. *Arch.* 17

Roscius Otho, Lucius.   Tribune in 67; carried law reserving front rows in the theater for knights. *Mur.* 40

Rupilius, Publius.   Consul in 132; ended Sicilian slave revolt. *Verr.* 4.112

Rutilius Rufus, Publius.   Consul in 105; a serious Stoic exiled in 92 (wrongly, in Cicero's view) for extortion from the province of Asia. *Pis.* 95

Sappho.   *Verr.* 4.126–27

Scaevola.   See *Mucius*

Scipio.   See *Cornelius;* see also *Caecilius*

Scribonius Curio, Gaius.   Officer under Sulla in First Mithridatic War, consul in 76, proconsul of Macedonia 76–73, censor in 61. *Man.* 68; *Pis.* 44, 58

Selene (Cleopatra Selene).   Mother of Antiochus XI. *Verr.* 4.61

Sempronius Atratinus, Gaius.   Prosecutor of Caelius. *Cael.* 1–2, 7

Sempronius Gracchus, Tiberius.   Reforming tribune of 133; murdered by senatorial mob. Cicero only speaks well of him in addressing the people. *Verr.* 4.108

Sentius, Gaius.   Praetor in 94(?). *Pis.* 84

Sergius Catilina, Lucius.   Unsuccessful patrician candidate for consul in 64 and 63; leader of the conspiracy uncovered and defeated by Cicero. *Cat.* 2.1, 3, 6, 7, 9, 12–18, 20, 22–24, 26–27; *Mur.* 6, 17, 48–49, 51–52, 78–79, 81, 83–85, 87; *Cael.* 10–12, 14–15; *Pis.* 5, 11, 14–16, 20, 23, 95; *Phil.* 4.15

Sertorius, Quintus.   Praetor in 83, then led Marian resistance in Spain for ten years until assassinated. *Man.* 10, 21; *Mur.* 32

Servilius, Marcus.   Tribune in 43. *Phil.* 4.16

Servilius Vatia Isauricus, Publius.   Consul in 79; governed Cilicia 78–75. Member of the jury in the trial of Verres. *Verr.* 4.21, 82; *Man.* 68; *Pis.* 58, *Phil.* 9.3, 14

Silanion.   Fourth-century BCE sculptor. *Verr.* 4.126

Silanus.   See *Junius*

Silvanus.   See *Plautius*

Sopater.   Magistrate of Tyndaris. *Verr.* 4.85–87, 92

Spartacus.   Gladiator, led major slave revolt against Rome in southern Italy, 73–71. *Phil.* 4.15

Sthenius of Thermae.   *Verr.* 4.41

Sulla.   See *Cornelius*

Sulpicius Galba, Publius.   Unsuccessful candidate for consulship of 63. *Mur.* 17

Sulpicius Galba, Servius.   Consul in 144; attacked by Cato the Elder for his treatment of the Lusitanians in 150. *Mur.* 59

Sulpicius Galus, Gaius.   Consul in 166; served under Lucius Aemilius Paullus in Macedonian War. *Mur.* 66

Sulpicius Rufus, Servius.   Consul in 51; leading jurist of his time. Prosecuted Murena in 63; died on embassy to Antony in 43. *Mur.* 7, 9–10, 15–16, 19, 21, 24, 28, 30, 35, 43, 48–49, 52, 56, 72; *Phil.* 9.1–3, 5–10, 12–17

Sulpicius Rufus, Servius.   One of Murena's prosecutors; presumably a relative of the consul of 51. *Mur.* 54, 56

Tadius, Quintus.   Paid money to Verres' agents. *Verr.* 4.31

Terentius Varro Lucullus, Marcus.   Born Marcus Licinius Lucullus, adopted by Terentius Varro. Consul in 73, triumphed for Macedonian victories. *Arch.* 6, 8, 31; *Pis.* 44, 77

Themista.   Pupil of Epicurus. *Pis.* 63

Themistocles.   Fifth-century BCE Athenian general, architect of victory over Persia at Salamis. *Arch.* 20

Theodorus of Henna.   *Verr.* 4.113

Theomnastus of Syracuse.   *Verr.* 4.59, 148

Theophanes.   See *Pompeius*

Thrason of Tyndaris.   *Verr.* 4.48

Thyestes.   Ate his own children served him by his brother Atreus. *Pis.* 43

Tigranes II.   King of Armenia, son-in-law of Mithridates, briefly Rome's most powerful eastern neighbor. *Man.* 4, 23, 45

Timarchides.   Verres' freedman. *Verr.* 4.22, 35, 94

Timocles.   One of group of beautiful brothers. *Pis.* 89

Titius, Lucius.   *Verr.* 4.58

Tlepolemus.   One of Verres' "hunting dogs." *Verr.* 4.30–31, 96

Tolumnius, Lars.   Fifth-century BCE king of Veii. *Phil.* 9.4, 7

Tongilius.   Henchman of Catiline; otherwise unknown. *Cat.* 2.4

Torquatus.   See *Manlius*

Tubero.   See *Aelius*

Tullius Cicero, Lucius.   Cicero's first cousin. *Verr.* 4.25, 145

Tullius Cicero, Marcus.   Cicero. *Verr.* 4.79

Valentius, Aulus.   Verres' interpreter. *Verr.* 4.58

Valerius Flaccus, Lucius.   Praetor in 63 and an active supporter of Cicero against Catiline. Prosecuted for extortion as governor of Asia and defended by Cicero in 59; presumably acquitted. Legate of Piso in Macedonia, 57–55. *Pis.* 54

Verres, Gaius.   Praetor in 74, governor of Sicily 73–71; went into exile in anticipation of being convicted of extortion in 70. *Verr.* 4.1, 3–4, 7, 10, 12–13, 15–18, 22, 24, 26–27, 30–33, 35–36, 38–51, 53–55, 57–63, 65–68, 70–73, 75–76, 78–87, 89–97, 99–104, 109–11, 113–16, 118–19, 121–24, 126, 129–31, 133, 136, 138–46, 148–51

Verrucius.   False name for Verres. *Verr.* 4.137

Vettius.   Did something adulterous connected to trial of Caelius. *Cael.* 71

Vibellius Taurea.   Pro-Carthaginian Capuan leader in Second Punic War. *Pis.* 24

Vibius Pansa, Gaius.   Consul in 43; died of wounds in battle, April of 43. *Phil.* 9.3, 16–17